D0208162

REPRESENTED

The Black Imagemakers Who Reimagined
African American Citizenship

Brenna Wynn Greer

PENN

University of Pennsylvania Press
Philadelphia

ART HISTORY
PUBLICATION INITIATIVE

This book is made possible by a collaborative grant from the
Andrew W. Mellon Foundation.

Published by
University of Pennsylvania Press
Philadelphia, Pennsylvania 19104-4112
www.upenn.edu/pennpress

Printed in the United States of America on acid-free paper
10 9 8 7 6 5 4 3 2 1

A catalogue record for this book is available from the Library of Congress.
ISBN 978-0-8122-5143-2

To my students,
of course

Contents

Preface

I never set out to write a book about the image-management and image-making work of black capitalists and entrepreneurs. This project grew out of an extended battle I waged with a single photograph of the civil rights activist Rosa Louise McCauley Parks taken the morning of December 21, 1956, the day that African Americans in Montgomery, Alabama, ended their 381-day boycott of the city's buses, following the United States Supreme Court's decree that segregated buses were unconstitutional. That morning, reporters tracked Parks down at her home in the Cleveland Court projects and cajoled her to come downtown, where she "got on and off buses so they could take pictures."[1] One of the resulting photographs depicts Parks seated in front of a sullen white man in a suit, quietly gazing out of the bus window (Figure 1). The following week, *Time* magazine ran this photograph with a caption identifying Parks as "the one who started it all."[2] The image has since circulated many times over, in newspapers, textbooks, encyclopedias, exhibits, and advertisements, which led Parks to dub it her "symbol shot."[3] The symbol shot photograph works symbiotically with popular histories of Parks as "the mother of the civil rights movement," in which she figures as a respectable, saintly elderly woman who single-handedly launched the modern black freedom movement. Her symbol shot representation obscures her activities as a lifelong radical activist who devoted her energies to combatting racism, civil rights violations, and sexual abuse of black women. The photograph also overshadows, if not completely obscures from view, the extensive organizing by countless others that culminated in and sustained the Montgomery bus boycott of 1955–56, the protest event many associate with the beginning of the modern civil rights movement.

Like many, I grew up with the ideal of Parks as a courageous but accidental activist, and I held it—discouraged by no one—into adulthood and through more than a few history courses. Only when I began researching

Figure 1. Rosa Parks seated on bus in Montgomery, Alabama, December 21, 1956. Getty Images.

black women's activism in Montgomery did the myth crumble. I came to view Parks's symbolic nature as particularly problematic in its falsehood and its power to exclude. This exclusionary power became most apparent (and frustrating) in the classroom, where the mythic Parks spawned further myths about the Montgomery bus boycott and the larger civil rights movement.

In her iconic form, Parks has value as an inspiring and commemorative figure based in certain truths. She is also, however, a flat, simplistic representation that encourages similarly simplistic narratives of black protest and the black freedom struggle. The symbolic Rosa Parks belongs to a set of mythologized historical black figures, including Harriet Tubman, Booker T. Washington, Martin Luther King Jr., and Malcolm X, whose stories obstinately form the entirety of too many of my students' knowledge, regardless of race, concerning African American history and the black freedom struggle. From where did these black figures derive their defining power? The answer to this question varies across time and context, but media representations of black civil rights activists operating after World War II, such as Parks's symbol shot, remain a primary engine fueling the longevity and potency of these activists' symbolic power.

Many of the images of post–World War II civil rights activism or activists that we now consider iconic circulated through "white" media channels. It is tempting, therefore, to assume that images such as Parks's symbol shot, which have thwarted complex histories that might be useful for negotiating subsequent struggles, were the creation or the imposition of white journalists, photographers, and editors. To the contrary: these images were very much the product of African Americans carefully cultivating (or performing) media representations of blackness that they deemed politically expedient given immediate civil rights concerns. Why did the civil rights activists we associate with the "classic" period of the civil rights struggle (approximately from the 1954 *Brown v. Board of Education* decision through the 1968 assassination of Martin Luther King Jr.) produce, perform, or promote the images of blackness they did, particularly since many of these images now prop up faulty narratives of them and their struggle? What cultural and economic resources, social circumstances, and political objectives shaped their politics of image? What theories and tactics determined how they elected to represent blackness? These questions transformed what I had originally imagined as an analysis of the image strategies of civil rights activists into a study of black professional imagemakers and their image products. This shift in direction occurred because my efforts to identify the sources for, or the products of, representation politics (by which I mean theories and tactics of image or imaging) central to African Americans' campaigns for first-class citizenship and national belonging consistently led to the imagemaking enterprises of black market-based cultural producers. Attached as I was to my activist subjects, initially I interpreted these findings as detours, distractions—the ever-threatening rabbit holes common to historical research. Only when I accepted the oft-recurring pattern that emerged did I understand that mine is a story of how primarily *non*activist

African Americans produced media representations of black people and black life that activists enacted during the drama that was the postwar civil rights movement.

The preponderance of civil rights literature focuses on grassroots activism and highlights resistance; consequently, nonactivists and, especially, unabashed capitalists have been neglected and even unwelcome in the story. If these figures do appear, it is generally as individuals who used their money to fund or protect other African Americans in their activism. Their exclusion reflects three distinct but related interpretive boundaries that have long hindered understanding of the various ways African Americans have combatted racism and pursued first-class citizenship: the assignation of activist motivations to black actors despite more convincing explanations; the notion (and fear) that to highlight African Americans' capitalism is to impugn their character and negate the heroism historians spent so much time and energy unearthing; and discomfort with or outright rejection of the inherent relationship of capitalism to modern civil rights politics.[4] To exile capitalists and capitalism, however, prevents an understanding of how, in addition to marching in the streets, blacks pursued their freedom by participating in political, corporate, and even racist or sexist agendas. In the past half century, scholars have unearthed multitudes of "everyday" participants who advanced the struggle through all manner of activities, across various sites. Yet the reigning civil rights story remains one of how blacks "opted out": the struggle, we are to believe, has always been activist inspired, oppositional, and uncompromising. The trend reflects a larger cultural investment in the ideal of a "pure civil rights movement," clearly understood as a moral campaign of progressive "good" against past "evil" that occurred outside or in direct opposition to institutions of corruptive power, such as capitalism or white power. It is as if accepting that African Americans used the market and principles of profit to realize their full citizenship somehow taints the cause. Desire for civil rights stories that either redeem or vilify the figures at the center of those stories precludes messier but more useful narratives about how African Americans existed in relation to the state and the market.

When in the classroom (and, truth be told, at more than a few conferences), I have witnessed time and again a somewhat compulsive need—again, regardless of race—for black historical actors to be of particular minds and behave in limited ways. If they are to be legible to my students, the black subjects under study must be engaged in struggle and operating from a stance of opposition. Walter Johnson lays partial blame for this phenomenon at the feet of social historians of U.S. slavery who, in their well-meaning efforts to attribute agency to blacks, and particularly enslaved blacks, had a tendency to conflate agency, humanity, and resistance. Johnson laments that the project of "restoring agency"—which held finding evidence of agency (in the form of resistance) as the end goal—impeded questions about the complex political and cultural contexts in which blacks have operated, which certainly resulted in varied and conflicting theories, experiences, and practices.[5] The restoration project was not without its triumphs, however. Whereas once blacks were background characters who were only legible as victims in historical narratives, New Social History scholarship placed them at the center of histories to which they were indeed central. The ironic legacy of this work (broadly speaking), however, is a widespread failure to present, understand, or accept blacks in historical narratives who are not fighting the system. It seems we traded one flat representation for another one-dimensional, albeit more inspiring, or heroic representation. A scholarly project intended to assert their humanity, to some extent, robbed blacks of their personhood. Little wonder my students find it difficult to conceive of anyone but members of the dominant class as complex, confusing, and inconsistent—recognition of which is certainly the basis for identifying, if not empathizing, with others.

The American civil rights movement remains one of the most important anticolonial movements in world history—meaning activists and their protest *should* necessarily figure centrally in the story. Moreover, civil rights protest actions were often sensational and dramatic, meaning they were most visible and therefore more scrutinized, which accounts for why images of protest dominate within our public memory of the struggle. It is folly, however, to think that African Americans could or would have chosen to pursue their civil rights through activism alone in the consumer capitalist culture of the mid-twentieth-century United States. My purpose with this study is not to claim all black Americans as civil rights actors. Rather, I mean to challenge the notion that all civil rights actors were activists and all civil rights activities took the form of activism. We must seriously consider what lies behind our continued investment in civil rights narratives of grassroots protest. More important, what might this investment be costing us?

Figure 2. "Watermelons to Market," cover of *Life* magazine, August 9, 1936. © 1937 Time Inc. All rights reserved.

Introduction

The history of the black liberation movements in the
United States could be characterized as a struggle over
images.

—bell hooks, "In Our Glory"

In August 1937, less than one year into its publication, *Life* magazine ran a photograph of a black man on its cover for the first time. In the black-and-white photograph, a shirtless black man dressed in dungarees sits atop a wagonload of watermelons, which, the caption explains, are headed "to market" (Figure 2). Upon first glance, it appears the man is driving the wagon, because the photograph's perspective causes the road pictured to triangle upward, such that it seems the wagon is heading in the direction of the horizon near the top of the page. Also, because the man faces directly away from the viewer, it seems he might hold reins in front of his body that are not visible to the viewer. Closer inspection reveals, however, no horse or team before him. The man actually is seated at the rear of the wagon bed, where he is being carried along with the fruit "to market." The cover is a study in obscurity. The caption fails to acknowledge, let alone name, the black man pictured; the photograph itself also renders him unidentifiable. In the image, his position makes it impossible to see his face. Only the back of his bald head and his naked back, crisscrossed by suspenders, are visible to the viewer. The man's nakedness highlights his physicality, rather than his personhood—an effect further facilitated by the absence of a face or name.

The "Watermelon Man" reflects tensions unique to that moment in the history of how African Americans have been depicted through the media. The first time an African American man appeared on *Life* was significant by sheer virtue of the magazine's import as a visual cultural product. In the span of a year, the photo-magazine had already achieved a readership numbering several million: one would be hard pressed to find a more influential media space than the publication's cover.[1] For precisely this reason, however, African Americans likely did not celebrate the cover as a "breakthrough" representational event. For one, as a portrait of anonymity—which none-too-subtly tapped prevailing stereotypes linking blacks and watermelons—the photograph stymies recognition of black subjectivity. The image also did little to define black America away from its enslaved past. From his perch atop the melons, the man pictured looks to the road unfurling behind the wagon: he is quite literally looking backward. Finally, the photograph of the wooden wagon traveling along on a rural, dirt road offers not one sign of twentieth-century modernity—no pavement, motorized vehicles, or utility poles. At best, the cover photograph reflected the position of many African Americans at the time as laborers in the nonindustrial South; at worst, it connoted a lack of civilization commonly attributed to blacks. As a representational event, *Life*'s first depiction of a black man symbolized the struggle African Americans at the time faced when it came to their appearance in media.

During the World War II era, many African Americans, including prominent black political thinkers, tied their social position to their representation in popular and media culture. Walter White, executive secretary of the National Association for the Advancement of Colored People (NAACP), the largest, and therefore most powerful, civil rights organization of the period, voiced a common desire among blacks for mainstream images that depicted blacks as "an integral part of the life of America and the world."[2] In White's mind, media representations affected how people thought about and thus treated black people. Consequently, during the war, he lobbied advertisers and Hollywood executives to produce media images that affirmed African Americans as equal, entitled, and modernized members of the body politic. "Watermelon Man" failed thoroughly as a response to this call. African Americans like White credited such images with popularizing conceptions of blackness that underwrote African Americans' second-class citizenship and all the injustices, indignities, denials, and dangers of that position.

The "Watermelon Man" photograph captured the subordinate status of African Americans living in the 1930s United States. More troubling, it combined with a bevy of other media images to construct African Americans as inferior. That same issue of *Life*, for instance, included three photographs arranged in a vertical column under the headline, "All southerners like watermelon." In the top photograph, white "Georgia girls" enjoy "a watermelon picnic" while sunbathing by a creek. The middle photograph shows a black woman—identified as a "colored mammy"—eating a large slice of watermelon while nursing a black infant. The bottom photograph pictures pigs in a pen feasting on watermelon rinds. Taken as a series, these photographs constitute a visual hierarchy in which blacks rank below whites and above farm animals. Notably, the magazine's editors apparently believed that the line separating the bottom two positions was so blurry as to possibly create confusion among viewers. The caption shared by the photograph of the black woman and the photograph of swine reads, "What melons the Negroes do not consume will find favor with the pigs *(below)*" (emphasis in original).[3]

Media representations that implied black inferiority, even black inhumanity, emerged from historical circumstances in which the popular representation of blackness, whether visual or discursive, remained primarily a white project. African Americans possessed little access to, or control over, mainstream media or processes of image production. (In addition to the absence of any black involvement in *Life*'s production at the time, it is safe to assume the black man photographed with the watermelons had little, if any, say in whether he would be photographed, how he would be photographed, or how the resulting images would circulate.) Developments in media and marketing that occurred during the New Deal and World War II eras bore directly on the ability of African Americans to self-define. The commercial success of *Life* signaled a moment when images were becoming a choice means for making and conveying meaning. This dynamic intersected with, and was very much mutually constitutive of, several concomitant developments, including advances in visual media and the rise of photojournalism, the increased political and commercial uses of public relations, and the considerable expansion of U.S. consumer culture and the corresponding growth of the marketing industry and all of its technologies. These developments presented African Americans with new challenges, as "Watermelon Man" demonstrates; however, they also offered African Americans new resources to define themselves anew to national audiences through media representations that reinforced their citizenship demands.

Represented is the story of just that: African Americans representing themselves as American citizens. More specifically, this is a history of the visual politics of black citizenship as enacted through the market. I trace how black entrepreneurs and cultural producers participated in trends that characterized mid-twentieth-century U.S. media and consumer culture on their way to popularizing media representations of African Americans that claimed their legal and cultural national belonging. These "black image professionals" made the representation and promotion of black citizenship central to their cultural production and entrepreneurialism because national, international, and race politics of the time created demand for such images. The definitions of blackness that their image work introduced into political discourse and popular culture of the time set terms for how African Americans asserted and framed their citizenship rights.

Chief among this group of professional imagemakers were public relations guru Moss Hyles Kendrix, photographer Gordon Parks, and publishing magnate John H. Johnson, publisher of *Ebony* and *Jet* magazines; these men are the historical actors at the center of this study. The Great Depression and World War II inspired federal initiatives that provided a small cadre of African Americans opportunities to learn image-making and image-management skills associated with modern marketing. Kendrix and Parks trained in the practices of public relations, propaganda, and mediamaking while crafting conceptual and visual representations of black America for New Deal and wartime government programs. Johnson spent the war years developing media appeals to, media products for, or media representations of African Americans through his fledging publishing enterprise. Following the war, all three made the representation of blackness the cornerstone of their professional lives, encouraged by several factors to do so. For one, their talents were well suited to the consumerist postwar moment, and their wartime work opened for them doors to commercial marketing and media spaces previously closed to African Americans. In addition, African Americans came out of the war with higher incomes thanks to their participation in war industries, and their desires and demands as consumers carried more weight. One of those demands was for media images that portrayed them as something other than, as Walter White described, "scared of ghosts, addicted to tap dancing, banjo plucking and the purloining of Massa's gin."[4] This desire reflected the general awareness among African Americans of the increased ability of the visual to construct the political field, particularly within an expanding consumer culture organized by and saturated with marketing messages. Collectively, these dynamics created markets for new mainstream images that claimed to define black America. Kendrix, Parks, and Johnson leveraged these markets with advertisers to build bridges to mainstream media for new images of blackness.

The commercial nature of their work allowed these black marketers, mediamakers, and cultural producers access to government, corporate, and popular means of communication, which granted them considerable power, relatively speaking, to affect the representation of African Americans in mass media. Through their reimaging of black citizenship, they performed important "civil rights work"—work essential to how African Americans at the time pursued and acquired their civil rights. I use the term *civil rights* to refer to the protected class of rights, granted by virtue of one's citizenship, that prohibits infringement on one's individual freedom by other individuals, organizations, or the state. Going into World War II, African Americans suffered keenly for their government's failure to observe their civil rights—including their rights to vote, to a fair trial, and to education, and their right to equal access to public accommodations. In reference to the twentieth-century black American experience, however, *civil rights* has a broader meaning that entails "incorporation into the U.S. polity, as well as American society." Therefore, in this study, *civil rights struggle* refers to a broad quest in which campaigns for that protected class of rights necessarily intersected with and included battles for political and social equality, economic freedom, and belonging and recognition as integral members of U.S. society.[5] By comparison, *civil rights movement* refers to the classically defined period of nonviolent, direct-action activism from 1955 through 1968.

The concept of "civil rights work" distinguishes the entrepreneurial activities of black image professionals that furthered civil rights agendas from explicitly political social change efforts—that is, from activism. This concept both calls attention to and challenges the historiographical focus on grassroots organizing and protest. Within the civil rights historiography, the image of the "activist" has determined—*over*determined—how we understand the "civil rights movement." On the road to securing their civil rights, African Americans engaged in activities that were not oppositional, explicitly political, or even progressive. The black marketers studied here, for example, invoked essentialist conceptions of race and discourses of traditional womanhood to construct African Americans as valued citizens by way of their consumer role in the Cold War United States. Their image work circulated through the marketplace, re-presenting African Americans in keeping with prevailing notions of Americanness and challenging denials of their belonging and their equality. This provided African Americans necessary conceptual grounds and key cultural resources for making claims on the state. In other words, through their cultural production and their capitalism, these imagemakers performed work prerequisite to African Americans' securing their civil rights. That these representations of black citizenship were generated through black entrepreneurialism with the objective of financial profit does not negate the political and cultural work they performed. Indeed, the entrepreneurs who generated black media images understood their compound functions, which they recognized as part of their value.[6]

This study of black mediamakers and marketers contributes to the growing field of scholarship that considers the relationship between capitalism and African American history. Historians upset the story of capitalism in the United States when they took it out of northern factories and financial institutions to consider slavery. Logically, this scholarship largely focuses on the capitalism of whites, the slaveholders and the landowning class within the slave system; as property-in-person, blacks were capital goods, labor, and consumer products.[7] Other historians of capitalism have put African Americans at the center of works that examine black experiences of capitalism and consumerism. These works have redefined the marketplace as a site of black intellectualism, cultural production, political development, and identity making. A number of these works draw connections between black capitalism and consumerism and the civil rights struggle. In *Cutting Along the Color Line*, Quincy Mills argues that, through their black-owned business, black barbers from the nineteenth century into the twentieth century participated in, but also forged, a "black commercial public sphere," through which they became community leaders and provided space—the barbershop—for the discussion, development, and enactment of black politics.[8] In their studies of black culture in Chicago from the beginning of the Great Migration through World War II, Adam Green and Davarian Baldwin suggest that African Americans forged modern identities in the marketplace and through their relationship to consumerism.[9] These works identify black commercial industries and black cultural production as giving birth to the national consciousness among African Americans that fueled the post–World War II civil rights movement. *Represented* builds on these scholars' insights but traces the development of African Americans' national consciousness to the representations of citizenship that black marketers and mediamakers conceived or promoted. These image professionals often juggled the wants of black consumers with those of state officials or white advertisers. Because their image work served federal and large corporate agendas, black imagemakers like Kendrix, Johnson, and Parks walked the line between encouraging African Americans to conceive of themselves as a nation within a nation, united by race and experience, and urging them to consider themselves members of the larger nation. Their attempts to negotiate antiblack racism, national politics, and market dynamics determined their definitions of blackness and fundamentally altered institutions of postwar U.S. capitalism—including, most especially, marketing, visual media, and consumerism.

Central to this history of black capitalism is the examination of black participation in the development of modern public relations, a history in which African Americans are strikingly absent. Historians of black business have certainly drawn attention to black market representatives—the "Brown Hucksters"—who helped identify and serve African American consumer markets. There has yet to be, however, consideration of the relationship of this marketing activity to the broader history of how public relations developed in response to national crises and cultural trends. *Represented* traces that history through Kendrix, who, after World War II, founded the highly successful Moss H. Kendrix Organization, a Washington, DC–based public relations firm, the flagship client of which was the Coca-Cola Company. Kendrix's public relations career provides this book's primary through-line. The first black pitchman for Coca-Cola, Kendrix found his way into the rarefied white spaces of corporate boardrooms, executive offices, private clubs, film studios, fancy restaurants and hotels, and first-class compartments, where he rubbed elbows with the elite of white corporate America. His personal address book also included the names of numerous black celebrities, such as bandleader Duke Ellington, singer-actress Pearl Bailey, boxer Joe "the Brown Bomber" Louis, and baseball player Ernie Banks, with whom he had built relationships in the course of developing public relations campaigns and marketing tie-ins for his various federal and corporate clients. In his heyday, Kendrix numbered among the most visible black businessmen in the United States—literally. The bulk of his public relations work entailed his participating in public, community, or organizational events, such as conventions, golf tournaments, beauty contests, and parades. It is safe to say that, outside of famous black movie stars, musicians, and athletes, Kendrix was one of the most photographed African American men in the postwar period. Because of his association with Coca-Cola, he was also one of the most prominent African Americans in mainstream marketing, and his fingerprints are everywhere when it comes to the postwar marketplace representation of blacks. Yet few students of business or marketing history have heard of him.

Why is Kendrix absent from histories to which he is so central, especially given his visibility at the time?[10] For one, the historiography of marketing and public relations privileges corporate, rather than nonprofit or noncommercial, uses of public relations.[11] This concentration has resulted in a relatively "white" history, because African Americans have generally lacked the capital to own their own marketing firms and the power necessary for leading roles in mainstream corporations. Consideration of black uses of public relations tends to focus on the activities of civil rights organizations, most notably the NAACP and the Student Nonviolent Coordinating Committee.[12] In the history of commercial marketing, African Americans have figured primarily as the targets of theories or strategies developed by white marketers. Kendrix's history reveals black marketers to be innovators in public relations who shaped post–World War II marketing and consumer culture.

This history of black marketers and imagemakers making business out of representing black citizenship brings into conversation areas of study that, as of yet, have existed in isolation from one another: black cultural production and capitalism and the visual politics of citizenship. Visual studies scholars have increasingly considered the relationship between visuality and citizenship. Collectively, their scholarship acknowledges visual culture as "a contested public sphere of hegemonic and counterhegemonic practices that produce historical knowledge" about people's subjectivities.[13] Photography scholars, in particular, have demonstrated how images have enabled the citizenship claims of marginalized, and even stateless, peoples.[14] These works illuminate how people have negotiated regimes of representation produced by the state and through mass media that construct their otherness or exclusion. Missing, however, is an examination of how their relationship to the market—in addition to the state—determined how and why they visually constructed their citizenship. The capacity of images for layered, simultaneous signification offered African Americans a means for representing blackness in complex manners that addressed their legal status, rights, and political participation, in addition to their cultural identity or belonging.[15] It was the value of visual images that claimed, highlighted, and celebrated black citizenship that determined, as much as facilitated, the enterprise of visually re-presenting black citizenship.

World War II–era black image professionals belong to a long history of blacks trying to shift their social position through strategic media redefinitions of blackness. Noted black literary critic and intellectual Henry Louis Gates Jr. dates blacks' impulse to "'reconstruct' their image" back to when slave traders forcibly brought the first Africans to Virginia in the seventeenth century. In the eighteenth and nineteenth centuries, enslaved blacks, including, most famously, Linda Brent and Frederick Douglass, attempted this reconstruction with explications of their humanness in slave narratives. W. E. B. Du Bois curated a photographic exhibition of middle-class black Georgians for the 1900 Paris Exposition as a counterarchive to images of black inferiority propagated through scientific racism.[16] During the same period, other black intellectuals propagated the trope of the civilized "New Negro" as an antidote to the plantation-rooted "Old Negro." This project gained both national and international recognition during the 1920s and 1930s, when artists associated with black renaissance movements in Harlem and Chicago created innovative visual representations that alternately, and often concurrently, emphasized black beauty, pride, and militancy.[17] During the 1950s and 1960s, civil rights activists deftly harnessed the white media for their performances of nonviolent, deserving righteousness (as well as performances of disturbing whiteness). These many attempts by African Americans to shift their social position through their strategic representation supports feminist scholar bell hooks's assessment: "The history of the black liberation movements in the United States could be characterized as a struggle over images as much as it has been a struggle for rights, for equal access."[18]

In their struggles for first-class citizenship rights and cultural belonging, African Americans have deployed both conceptual and visual images. The field of visual representation, however, became an arena of increased potential for waging war against injurious definitions of blackness because "America was giving birth to a full-blown image culture."[19] The interwar period saw a surge in reliance on the visual—in public relations, photojournalism, movies, newsreels, billboards, window displays, print advertising, consumer packaging, and so on—to attract attention, deliver news, and shape public opinion. Visual propaganda had become a choice technology of the federal government and big business to direct how Americans imagined themselves in relation to the state and one another. When he defined "imagined communities" in the 1980s, Benedict Anderson rooted their creation in "print capitalism." The invention of the printing press in fifteenth-century Europe, he explained, facilitated the commodification of print language such that books and newspapers circulated in volumes and vernaculars capable of creating abstract communities of readers physically and culturally separate from one another.[20] By the 1930s, images had risen to parallel, if not surpass, text as the unifying language for, as Anderson put it, "re-presenting the kind of imagined community that is the nation."[21] The visual increasingly set the frame of intelligibility that determined how people "[took] on meaning as citizens and as Americans."[22]

Failure to consider the visual component to how African Americans marketed themselves as American citizens obscures the central role of mass media to their efforts and robs us of important information about the context in which they operated. Today, we take for granted the significant, even overriding, role of visual representations (as circulated through mass media) in politics. The people studied here, however, acted in the moment when this "given" was a thing becoming, when visual media was emerging—due in part to their actions—as a powerful force for determining the political field. The commercial nature of mass media means that representations circulating through mainstream media provide insights into the concerns, demands, and visions of the (consuming) public. Therefore, black media representations generated through black entrepreneurialism provide the historian useful evidence about the theories of representation—or the representation politics—of, especially, the black (consuming) public. Considering the relationship of media and marketing to black citizenship and civil rights politics contextualizes the "struggle" within significant dynamics that shaped broader U.S. culture during and after the World War II era. These dynamics include the increased prominence of marketing theory, practice, and media in U.S. culture and politics and the correspondent reorientation of both around mass consumerism. *Represented* counters narratives in which African Americans appear as background characters or bystanders to these developments, trapped inside or distracted by their civil rights struggle, rather than participants who contributed to these trends while in struggle. Through their enterprise, black image professionals made the market work for racial progress on their way to making money; they did so because they understood these projects—advancing the race through media representations and making money—to be indivisible. Their activities reveal how and why, steeped in a culture of consumer capitalism, blacks necessarily advanced their cause through media and marketing techniques.

This history begins during the Great Depression with Kendrix's experience as a New Deal public relations officer. An unprecedented relief program, the New Deal reflected, but also greatly facilitated, the explosion in public relations that characterized the 1930s. During the Depression, both the government and business leaders tried to sway the public to their generally conflicting agendas. The Roosevelt administration relied extensively on public relations, more than any previous administration, to sell New Deal programs and policies to the constituencies they targeted. Chapter 1 outlines how these circumstances offered African Americans entry into the public relations profession by reconstructing how Kendrix forged a path to doing public relations work for the Division of Negro Affairs of the National Youth Administration on the strength of amateur publicity work he performed as a student member of Atlanta's community of historically black colleges and universities. As a government employee, Kendrix performed public relations work that encouraged African Americans to invest in the New Deal. His address to black constituencies emphasized civic duty and tied African Americans' fate—and their freedom—to the fate of the nation. This work served the Roosevelt administration, but also black political agendas that relied on recognition of African Americans' national belonging. Working within the New Deal, Kendrix appropriated federal discourses of citizenship, national unity, and democracy to broadcast the historical, continued, and vital contributions of blacks to American democracy. His public relations work belongs to a broader effort by black New Dealers to encourage African Americans to imagine themselves as a national people—as people who are members of a nation—in terms specific to their unique contributions as African Americans, but also on the basis of their citizenship and membership to the larger body politic.

Chapter 2 follows Gordon Parks, a self-identified "activist-artist" who earned a spot in the Office of War Information, the nation's propaganda outfit, thanks to his series of photographs that explored the impoverished living conditions of urban blacks. As a federal photographer, he created images of blacks that obscured or elided the antiblack racism that contributed to African Americans' compromised experience of freedom in the democratic United States. His photographs, however, visualized blacks as industrious Americans and claimed their belonging as patriotic citizens integral to American life and Allied victory. As a point of comparison to Parks's federal imagemaking, this chapter demonstrates how the novelist Richard Wright actively strayed from the official party line in his wartime representation of black life. Unconstrained by federal representational guidelines, Wright used photography to put forth a sustained criticism of the black experience within American democracy, which clashed with state-sponsored narratives of U.S. superiority, preparedness, and unity. Discourses of freedom and democracy inspired by the war against Nazism and fascism, in addition to the practical needs of a government at war, created wide, receptive audiences for Wright's and Parks's media products. Their photographic renderings of black life in the United States literally illustrate tensions inherent to advancing national interests and black people in the mid-twentieth-century United States. The different fate each man experienced as an image professional and citizen, which varied in direct correspondence to how each one's interpretations squared with federal agendas, testifies to the heightened political significance that representations of black life within American democracy had during the war. Collectively, Chapters 1 and 2 reveal New Deal and World War II federal initiatives as incubators for black imagemakers who profoundly redrew the contours of how black citizenship could be defined in mainstream political and consumer media spaces.[23]

This history pivots on the third chapter, which marks the beginning of a sustained examination of how black marketers parlayed their New Deal and World War II experiences as image managers and makers into capitalist ventures. Chapter 3 examines Kendrix's activities as the public relations officer for the Republic of Liberia from 1945 through 1947. During this period he spearheaded a campaign to finance the Centennial and Victory Exposition in Monrovia, Liberia, in celebration of the hundredth anniversary of the former U.S. colony's independence. As a member of the Liberian Centennial Commission, Kendrix walked the line between private businessman, government representative, and political lobbyist and managed to attend to the objectives of all three by promoting black people as constituencies and consumers. He encouraged U.S. investment in Liberia's postwar development by representing black Americans and Americo-Liberians as longtime adherents to democracy and consumer capitalism. Within the context of the budding Cold War, these representations constructed blacks in the United States and West Africa as essential to U.S. economic growth and national security, thereby increasing the significance of both populations among U.S. state officials and business leaders. In selling Liberia as a good investment, Kendrix presented African Americans as representative of the civilization that Americo-Liberians desired, which constructed West Africans as modern-leaning people who presented potential new markets for U.S. corporations. The same rhetoric elevated African Americans as fully civilized on the basis of their American citizenship, and on the basis of their Americanness, which Kendrix signified by their eagerness to consume. The Liberian Centennial Commission produced public relations materials for a domestic audience that defined black citizenship in both the United States and West Africa in ways that served political and business interests on both sides of the color line.

Chapter 3 also begins to make clear the circumstances that account for why black men are at the heart of this history of the business and politics of black media representations in the postwar United States. African American women did participate in New Deal public relations and World War II propaganda efforts, albeit in scarcer numbers. They were limited, however, by constructs of gender (in addition to race) when it came to building an enterprise around imagemaking or image management: generally speaking, they did not have the capital, the economic autonomy, or the social position necessary. Chapters 4 and 5 reveal that black women participated in the redefinition of blackness that occurred within the media after World War II by acting as the black subjects featured in the media representations facilitated by black businessmen like Kendrix or John H. Johnson. That they did not profit to the same degree, however, does not negate the vital role that African American women played in opening U.S. media and visual culture to new images of blackness, many of which pushed the civil rights aims of black America. There remains an important history to tell especially about the women who were the administrative force behind commercial and noncommercial endeavors of black media representation; their fingerprints are all over the records of the organizations and businesses studied here.

Chapter 4 explores the growth of the black periodical press in relation to black representational desires and considers how this dynamic intersected with postwar civil rights politics. Coming out of the war, African Americans had high expectations that they could no longer be denied their national allegiance or the rights of full citizenship, due to their significant contributions to the war effort. Moreover, as contemporary black marketers insisted, African Americans constituted a valuable untapped consumer market in the postwar moment. In this context, representing black Americans through the media in manners that corresponded with their social and political strivings—with their sense of themselves as Americans in the postwar United States—was fertile ground for black enterprise. Black image professionals who stepped onto this ground could not sidestep the politics of race and racism that ensured a market among African Americans and advertisers for innovative media images that defined black America. This chapter explores these circumstances by detailing how Johnson built the media empire of the Johnson Publishing Company in Chicago by publishing risqué images of black women that helped generate circulation numbers attractive to major advertisers. This representational strategy offended the sensibilities of many black political thinkers (and consumers) who worried that such images provoked stereotypical ideas about black sexuality and undermined uplift campaigns rooted in demonstrations of respectability. As a marketing strategy, however, the reliance on sexualized imagery of black women also resulted in circulation numbers that made black markets visible. A conduit to black consumers, Johnson reaped advertising revenue unprecedented in black publishing, which enabled him to publish multiple publications, through which he injected numerous and varied visuals of black people and black life into the marketplace and publicized issues of cultural, social, and political importance to a wide black audience, including most notably the Emmett Till murder in 1955. The Johnson Publishing Company's *Jet* magazine covered the Till case for weeks, with photo-essays that included horrific pictures of the fourteen-year-old Till's brutalized body. African Americans often cite their viewing of these photographs in *Jet* as the beginning or maturation of their civil rights activism. Using a combination of marketing tactics, the Johnson Publishing Company publicized and sold the Till case in a manner that solidified its place in civil rights history—and the black American consciousness.

Chapter 5 continues to explore how black capitalism was a catalyst for visuals that proclaimed black citizenship after World War II through a case study of Kendrix's work for the Coca-Cola Company. After his stint as Liberia's public relations officer, Kendrix built his own DC-based public relations business by promoting his unique ability as an African American marketing specialist to help corporations court "the Negro market." Using this approach, he landed the world's top beverage company as a client. As Coca-Cola's first "special markets" representative, Kendrix directed the company to produce marketing that represented African Americans as typical Americans. The resulting ad images pictured blacks as enthusiastic consumers central to healthy and happy nuclear families and modern, middle-class households. These marketplace representations cultivated a consumerist identity for African Americans, which established their normality—their commonness as average Americans—according to the middle-class ideal that lay at the heart of (now-iconic) postwar conceptions of the "American dream."[24] Their construction as members of the American consumer class enabled African Americans' citizenship claims in the postwar U.S. society, which was organized around an ethos of mass consumption. To establish a black consumer ideal, Kendrix, along with other black marketers, established them as a special market and built an infrastructure of organizations, practice, and theory in support of their designation as such. Such marketers' business methods contributed to the market segmentation and the melding of consumerism and politics that defined the remainder of the twentieth century.

Black image professionals and their capitalism provide the analytical bridge necessary to reveal intersections among the rising political significance of consumerism, developments in commercial marketing, and the civil rights struggle of the postwar era. The image work of black marketers such as Kendrix and Johnson visually redefined African Americans as consumers at precisely the moment the civil rights struggle began to coalesce into a nationally recognized movement. These two developments—the professional, profit-driven representation of black America in the media and political, activist-fueled nonviolent direct action—were not parallel. They were overlapping, intersecting, and intertwined developments in African Americans' mid-twentieth-century civil rights campaign.

Chapter 1

A Way In: The Public Relations of New Deal Black Citizenship

We have fought America's cause of freedom, of Unity, of
Imperialism, and of Democracy!
    . . . But, Are We Americans?

                 —Moss Kendrix in the *Maroon Tiger*

The public relations counsel, then, is the agent who . . .
brings an idea to the consciousness of the public.

                 —Edward Bernays, *Propaganda*

In 1937, eight years into the Great Depression, *Life* magazine published a photograph taken by Margaret Bourke-White, a noted documentary photographer. The black-and-white photograph depicts how a great many African Americans experienced the worst economic crisis in U.S. history (Figure 3). The documentary image shows black men, women, and children lined up, waiting to collect food and clothing from a relief agency. Several among them hold empty bags, pails, and buckets to carry away the much-needed goods they hope to collect. Others brought only their "hungry stomachs." The African Americans pictured were residents of the "Negro" quarter of Louisville who narrowly survived the recent flooding of the Mississippi River: "refugees," the magazine dubbed them. In the photograph, a large billboard serves as the background: it pictures an exuberant, well-dressed, white family of four and their terrier crowded into an automobile that the smiling father figure steers through a rolling countryside. One might imagine this is a family enjoying a Sunday drive after church. The wholesome cheeriness of the billboard images gives it the appearance of being in full

Figure 3. *The American Way*, Margaret Bourke-White photograph, 1937. Getty Images.

color, despite the black-and-white medium of the photograph. Written across the billboard's top in large block letters is "WORLD'S HIGHEST STANDARD OF LIVING," and in script letters to the right of the car is written the declaration, "There's no way like the American Way."[1]

Bourke-White's photograph is a composite of key occurrences that defined the Depression era. Most apparent, the photograph is a visual representation of hardship. The juxtaposition of the billboard and the downtrodden black "refugees" lined up before it symbolized a dramatic decline in the "real world" American experience. Erected as it was in the soil of the depressed South, the billboard seemed more indicative of the prosperity and "good times" that characterized the previous decade. Behind the queue of unsmiling, beleaguered-looking, African Americans, the cheery tableau is especially mocking—a colorful and gay backdrop for a bleak and tragic play. The clashing images in Bourke-White's photograph, of white bounty and black need—each of which, the image suggests, is the "American Way"—

emphasized the separateness and severity of blacks' economic plight during the Depression.

In addition to being a record of blacks' Depression-era experience, the *Life* photograph is an artifact of the phenomenal expansion of public relations during the 1930s, in large part as a response to the nation's economic crisis. When she took the photograph of black Louisianans, Bourke-White worked on behalf of the Farm Security Administration (FSA). One of the many New Deal agencies established to spur recovery during the Depression, the FSA addressed issues of rural poverty exacerbated by the Depression. The agency employed a team of first-rate photographers to roam the country taking pictures of the nation's poor and displaced agricultural workers. The FSA photography program represented the Roosevelt administration's embrace of public relations to shape public opinion concerning its experimental economic and social programs. The New Deal allowed for government involvement in economic matters to an unprecedented degree, which threatened corporate interests. For their part, industrialists devised public relations campaigns to revive trust in the free enterprise necessary to their survival. The billboard pictured in Bourke-White's photograph belonged to a campaign implemented by the National Association of Manufacturers (NAM), an industrial trade and lobby organization. The Depression era witnessed both government and private business interests increasingly turn to public relations to advance their respective agendas. Bourke-White's photograph is a convergence of these trends. But what about the African Americans pictured?

In the *Life* image, the blacks pictured appear as black Americans were: among the most impoverished, disenfranchised, and vulnerable in the nation. They unwittingly perform the public relations work of the FSA image as the emotional center of the scene. They are public relations objects. This chapter tells the story of how the crisis in capitalism in the 1930s provided an opening for African Americans to enter the field of public relations. The training they received as New Deal imagemakers and image managers would prove essential to black campaigns to redefine blackness and, in particular, black citizenship.

In 1933, newly elected Franklin Delano Roosevelt initiated the New Deal to "stop the bleeding," save U.S. capitalism, and aid the nation's psychic healing. A series of emergency relief, public works, and financial reform programs, the New Deal constituted the largest government relief apparatus in U.S. history. It was also a public relations apparatus larger than any to that point in the nation's history. The scale of operation of this federal public relations machine required the participation of African Americans, particularly when it came to selling New Deal programs to black America.

Moss Hyles Kendrix is a central black figure in the development of public relations, particularly in relation to the New Deal. A young, southern black man, Kendrix became an official New Deal publicist when hired to represent the National Youth Administration (NYA), an agency that addressed unemployment among American youths between the ages of sixteen and twenty-five. Born on March 8, 1917, he experienced the Great Depression while coming of age in Atlanta, Georgia, a city enveloped by federal employment, education, and public works programs that permeated life across racial lines. His Depression-era experiences highlight connections between Roosevelt's New Deal, federal conceptions of "America" and American citizenship, contemporary black political concerns, and the development of modern public relations. As a New Deal publicist, Kendrix promoted New Deal programs, as well as ideas about American character, citizenship, and capitalism that legitimated the government's expansive role. The New Deal had many skeptics and outright opponents, including multiple members of Congress, due to the politics of interventionism and social democracy at its center. Roosevelt's recovery initiatives required constant selling and reselling, as did the worthiness of the constituencies these programs served—largely recognized as the first generation of modern welfare recipients.

Those who knew Kendrix best swear he was born for public relations. Remembering his father, Moss Kendrix Jr. puts it plainly: public relations was "his avocation as much as his vocation."[2] Contemporaries described the elder Kendrix as a "well-known, well-liked, handsome, intense [and] sophisticated" man who desired to "work with people" and who was indefatigable and relentless by nature.[3] He was also a handsome man with a soft face and smooth, caramel-taffy-colored skin, the agelessness of which suggested that, like Oscar Wilde's fictional character Dorian Gray, he might have an enchanted portrait stowed in his attic that bore his wrinkles for him. Large, doe-like eyes stared out from beneath his thick, dark eyebrows, which were often raised with inspiration or expectation and rarely furrowed in worry. "All I want is one new idea each day," he liked to say.[4] In personality and countenance, Kendrix possessed traits that smoothed the way for him into upper-crust circles, both white and black. One reporter summarized, "[He could] mingle with equal ease in the politic phrase-tossing of an Inaugural Ball or the hail-fellow of a national convention"—which he did.[5]

At the height of his career in the 1950s and early 1960s, Kendrix enjoyed a reputation as one of the most, if not the most, ambitious, and therefore successful, African American marketing specialists on the Eastern Seaboard. With a client list that included large advertisers such as Coca-Cola and Carnation Foods, he interacted with the elite of white corporate America and counted as friends prominent African Americans across the realms of entertainment, sports, business, and journalism. Given his disposition and inclinations, Kendrix was seemingly well suited to professions of persuasion, but, as he was an African American male born and raised in the Jim Crow South, entry into such professions was hardly inevitable. How did he enter a field that, when he reached adulthood, was still in the making and dominated by white, educated businessmen servicing white corporate clients? The answer lies in the necessity to elicit support for the New Deal, which provided African Americans of a particular cultural class the opportunity to become New Deal publicists. In this role, they received training in persuasion politics and contributed to the professionalization, standardization, and legitimization of modern public relations.

As a black New Deal publicist, Kendrix's job was to sell the national recovery program to southern blacks, which entailed convincing them to participate in New Deal initiatives and commit to the nation's economic recovery but also, more importantly, to embrace the principles and institutions of democracy. The target market for this sell was hardly primed. African Americans had come to the nation's aid not so long ago. During World War I, many heeded the instruction of the intellectual and activist W. E. B. Du Bois, who instructed African Americans to join the fight, despite their collective experience as second-class citizens. As editor of the *Crisis*, Du Bois wrote, "Let us not hesitate. Let us . . . forget our special grievances and close our ranks shoulder to shoulder with our own white fellow citizens." German victory, Du Bois reasoned, meant "death to the aspirations of Negroes . . . for equality, freedom and democracy."[6] Over three hundred thousand African Americans answered his call. But when they returned, they experienced a "red summer" of nationwide race riots, during which whites lynched dozens of African Americans.[7] "This country of ours," Du Bois wrote on the other side of the war, "is yet a shameful land."[8] How to appeal to this disenchanted, disenfranchised population?

For one, as a New Dealer, Kendrix promoted the Roosevelt administration's conceptions of American citizenship, which encouraged hard work, displays of unity, and—somewhat ironically, given the circumstances—faith in capitalism. Officials of the New Deal presented national belonging in terms of individual civic contributions. Kendrix, however, bent these "official" discourses of citizenship to contemporary black political concerns, including self-definition, community development and education, and political representation. The publicity and events he produced encouraged African Americans' sense of duty as citizens and asserted a black citizenship ethos essential to the nation's greatness. His Depression-era public relations work illuminates the growing recognition of African Americans' significance as Americans and intentional efforts on behalf of the federal government to identify their concerns and interests and target them on that basis. The nation's economic crisis provided opportunities and technologies through which Kendrix and other black New Dealers—African Americans employed to promote or administer New Deal programs—redefined and publicized the national belonging of African Americans.

The popular history of the Great Depression remains a white story, populated mainly by dusty and tired, rural white farmers, like the Joad family of John Steinbeck's Pulitzer Prize–winning 1939 novel, *The Grapes of Wrath*. When schoolchildren in the United States do encounter African Americans in the Depression story, it is often as former slaves, because a popular educational source from the period is firsthand accounts of slavery collected by the Works Progress Administration (WPA)—a New Deal agency—during the Depression. While invaluable (if also problematic) historical sources, WPA slave narratives foreground the inferior social position of blacks within U.S. history. Moreover, these Depression-generated narratives of blacks' enslaved experiences supplant stories of how African Americans actually experienced the Depression.

When African Americans appear in historical studies of the Depression or New Deal, it is generally in the form of voter-relief recipients (the "poor black masses"), artists, or bureaucrat-reformers—most notably the educated black activists that composed the Federal Council of Negro Affairs, popularly known as Roosevelt's Black Cabinet.[9] Kendrix offers an alternative and understudied example of the New Deal agent. What prompted Kendrix and other African Americans to assist the government in its promotion of American democracy and capitalism, given their collective experience as marginalized citizens? What black political agendas did black participation in the New Deal public relations machine serve? Finally, what does knowledge of black New Deal public relations work add to our understanding of the Depression, the New Deal, African Americans' Depression-era experiences, and the development of public relations as a profession? Kendrix's story provides a way to understand the historical connections among African Americans' experiences of the Depression and the New Deal, the rise of marketing technologies within federal politics, and the evolution of black citizenship in the United States.

When the stock market crashed on October 29, 1929, it did so with such speed and depth that typesetters the world over made heavy use of big block letters to spell out the words "worst" and "panic" for newspaper headlines announcing the crash. On that day, forever after known as Black Tuesday, the market lost $14 billion (roughly $200 billion in 2018 dollars) and initiated a global economic crisis.[10] Certain Wall Street insiders might have seen it coming (although many did not), but for most, the crash was a bombshell. The devastation touched the lives of nearly all Americans, cutting across class lines to strike tycoons, small-business owners, laborers, and farmers alike. The unprecedented economic depression that followed was a shocking catastrophe of capitalism—the celebration of which had characterized the previous decade. During the 1920s, corporations and industrialists profited greatly, while workers' wages rose only slightly. Yet Americans wildly embraced capitalism as responsible for new innovations in communications, transportation, and material goods that improved the collective standard of living. Then-president Herbert Hoover championed capitalism as a fundamental force of the "rugged individualism" central to the American character. When the bust following the crash did not abate, but rather solidified into the worst economic crisis in U.S. history, Americans began to question what many had assumed was the superior and natural socioeconomic system. Economists, scholars, and politicians alike called into question laissez-faire economics—defined by unregulated markets and business, speculation, and mass production—that put the roar in the 1920s. By 1933, roughly 25 percent of the U.S. labor force was out of work and $7 billion in bank deposits had evaporated.[11] So dismal was the financial state of affairs that West Africans took up collections for starving New Yorkers.[12] Multitudes of Americans sought work in Joseph Stalin's communist Soviet Union—one can hardly imagine a greater damnation of capitalism.[13]

Hoover, a Republican, rejected federal intervention as a solution and the crisis steadily worsened. Surveying the economic landscape in 1931, Hoover's predecessor Calvin Coolidge declared, "I now see nothing to give ground to hope."[14] Mired down by stubbornness and defeatism, the Republicans lost their grip on the White House. The nation's desperate citizens were in want of hope and, more pressing, relief. Presidential candidate Franklin Delano Roosevelt promised both. When he accepted the Democratic Party nomination in the summer of 1932, Roosevelt promised "a new deal for the American people" while "Happy Days Are Here Again" played in the background.[15] Upon his inauguration in 1933, Roosevelt's abstract "new deal" of the campaign almost immediately solidified into a series of agencies, including (to name a few) the National Recovery Administration, the Public Works Administration, and the National Labor Board. After these early New Deal programs came the Federal Housing Administration, the WPA, and the FSA. Substantial legislation accompanied the establishment of these various agencies. Besides the repeal of Prohibition (no small thing to a nation of woeful citizens), Roosevelt signed into law the Social Security Act of 1935, which guaranteed pensions for retired persons, provided aid to children, and established unemployment insurance, all of which was financed by payroll taxes.

Chief among those who suffered from the economy's collapse were the nation's twelve million African Americans, for whom the Great Depression piled unwelcome insult onto long-standing injuries. The unemployment rate of blacks reached nearly 50 percent (compared to the general rate of half that).[16] By 1934, nearly 18 percent of the total black population was "on relief"—receiving welfare from the federal government—twice the percentage of white Americans.[17] This relief came largely in the form of foodstuffs delivered by government trucks, which, as one resident of Chicago's South Side remembered, made a family's need shamefully visible to the entire neighborhood.[18]

While African Americans did benefit from New Deal programs, their race and class conspired to limit their relief. The poet Langston Hughes summarized the black experience of the New Deal in "Ballad of Roosevelt."[19] The 1934 poem opens,

> *The pot was empty,*
> *The cupboard was bare.*
> *I said, Papa,*
> *What's the matter here?*
> *I'm waitin' on Roosevelt, son,*
> *Roosevelt, Roosevelt,*
> *Waitin' on Roosevelt, son.*

Originally, Roosevelt's New Deal generated hope among African Americans, but disappointment and disillusionment quickly replaced that hope, a turn Hughes captured by poem's end:

> *And a lot o' other folks*
> *What's hungry and cold*
> *Done stopped believin'*
> *What they been told*
>
> . . . .
>
> *Cause the pot's still empty,*
> *And the cupboard's still bare,*
>
> . . . .
>
> *Mr. Roosevelt, listen!*
> *What's the matter here?*

For many blacks, the New Deal turned out to be (to further rely on Hughes's language) "a dream deferred," because important New Deal legislation tied eligibility to whiteness.[20] The Social Security Act, most notably, excluded agricultural and domestic workers—the majority of whom were African Americans—as eligible recipients for unemployment.[21] The act also constructed eligibility in terms of gender. It defined *employment* as "any service . . . performed . . . by an employee for *his* employer" (emphasis mine); of the eligible employer, the legislation reads, "*he* is at least sixty five years of age; and . . . wages paid to *him* . . . before he attained the age of sixty-five, was not less than $2000" (emphasis mine).[22] The act's language assumed that "breadwinners" were white American men—and constituted them as such—and defined their relief in terms of an entitlement, rather than welfare (or charity).

The publicity developed to promote the benefits of Social Security visualized the association between deserving wage earners and whiteness. Posters created by the Social Security Board feature a young white mother and her white child, an older white man, and an older white woman (Figures 4, 5, and 6). The two posters that picture women identify them as widows—that is, former dependents who can rely on Social Security to take care of their needs after the deaths of their (white) husbands, the providers for their households. The poster that features the elderly white man informs viewers that Social Security insurance protection will take care of him in retirement. Moreover, the pipe he grips between smiling lips suggests that he can be assured of a degree of leisure and comfort in his old age. All those pictured are smiling, despite their age or loss of loved ones, and above them in large block letters is the phrase, "MORE SECURITY FOR THE AMERICAN FAMILY." The implication is that Social Security not only supplied economic relief but also supplied the emotional or psychic relief necessary to keep Americans and their families strong and optimistic. Excluded from this vision were African Americans. These posters envisioned the representative American family as white and denied black men their role as "heads of the household," a protected class within the Depression-era United States. They also denied black women the womanly role of wife and mother and, more importantly, worthy dependent. Social Security publicity reflected the fact that the Social Security Act denied large numbers of black men and their dependents benefits that offset the hardships of unemployment, single parenthood, or old age.

"The Depression caused a crisis [among African Americans]," writes historian Mary Poole, "because of the history that preceded it." Poole refers here to the history of chattel slavery in the United States, but also to more immediate trends that ensured the Depression affected African Americans especially hard. Three-quarters of the nation's blacks lived in the rural South stuck in a system of peonage—one of the many unfortunate legacies of slavery.[23] When the Depression hit, severe unemployment in southern cities gave rise to white mobs and terrorist groups that marched through cities like Atlanta with signs that read, "No jobs for niggers until every white man has a job," and, "Niggers back to the cotton fields. City jobs are for white men." These whites sometimes resorted to violence and even murder

Figure 4. "More Security for the American Family," woman with baby.

Figure 5. "More Security for the American Family," elderly woman.

Figure 6. "More Security for the American Family," elderly man.

Social Security posters, 1939. National Archives.

to secure jobs for white southern men.[24] Such circumstances compelled many African Americans to leave the South for employment and their personal safety. Throughout the 1920s, scores of black men had migrated to the North for manufacturing and other industrial jobs. With the Depression, however, employers fired African Americans first when jobs became scarce, saving the available jobs for white men. Writer Richard Wright was one of many southern black migrants living on Chicago's South Side who were desperate for work. "I haunted the city for jobs," he wrote later. "But when I went into the streets in the morning I saw sights that killed my hope for the rest of the day. Unemployed [black] men loitered in doorways with blank looks in their eyes, sat dejectedly on front steps in shabby clothing, [and] congregated in sullen groups on street corners."[25]

Black women suffered greatly, too. Leading into the 1930s, they were among the poorest U.S. citizens, and their lot only worsened with the Depression.[26] A legacy of slavery was that the majority of black women found employment as domestics, which excluded them from Social Security benefits. Moreover, their already meager wages fell, such that black domestic workers in the South made less than four dollars weekly.[27] Among this group of struggling southern domestics was Kendrix's mother, Mary Hamilton Kendrix. A single black woman (according to family members, Moss's father was "out of the picture" before his birth), she was one of nearly twenty thousand black women employed as domestic workers in Atlanta.[28] Fortunately for Kendrix, kinship networks and his environment ensured that his mother's meager earnings did not doom him to a working-poor existence.

An only child, Moss Kendrix grew up in a black neighborhood on Atlanta's west side, down the street from Atlanta's historically black colleges and universities and a notorious black slum called Beaver Slide, whose residents lived crammed together in ramshackle wood shacks and walked dirt streets that turned to thick mud when it rained (Figure 7). With much of its population out of work, Beaver Slide was infamous for poverty and crime. The local police chief summarized the desperate circumstances that led many men, in particular, to turn to bootlegging or stealing: "Hard times and criminality," he said, "seem to go together."[29] Kendrix's neighborhood was one of several that solidified after the deadly 1906 Atlanta riot, in which whites motivated by the fear of "Negro domination" attacked African Americans and drove them into black ghettos, the boundaries of which they maintained through threat, reprisal, and violence. Unable to spread throughout the city, African Americans of varied incomes, occupations, and educational levels were bound up together in single neighborhoods, unlike whites, who separated along socioeconomic lines.[30] "Whether you worked as a domestic or you were a schoolteacher," a former resident remembered, "everybody lived in the same neighborhood."[31] Therefore, Kendrix spent his childhood years traversing class lines. Each day, this son of a domestic moved among un- and underemployed blacks doing, as one resident described, "anything they wanted," as well as black academics, professionals, and entrepreneurs, including his mother's brother John Russell Hamilton.[32]

Hamilton and his wife, Reacie, had migrated with their small children to Atlanta in the winter of 1909–10 from Monticello, Georgia, where cotton

Figure 7. Beaver Slide slum in Atlanta, Georgia, date unknown. Atlanta University is visible in the background. Charles Forrest Palmer Collection, Special Collections Department, Robert W. Woodruff Library, Emory University.

was king and peaches were quickly becoming queen. They fled Monticello when John's younger brother, George, provoked the anger of local whites by speaking casually to a white woman on the train.[33] Their fear was justified. Between 1900 and 1920, whites lynched an average of seventy-four African Americans per year (mostly men) in the United States, with Georgia topping the list of states in which the most lynchings occurred.[34] Shortly after the Hamiltons escaped Monticello, a mob of masked local white men kidnapped and hanged Dan Barber, an African American farmer; his son Jesse; and his two daughters, Ella and Eula. Observers deemed the Barber family lynching "fiendishly cruel" and "the worst in [Georgia's] history," based on its female victims and unique brutality—the mob hanged and shot each member of the family one at a time, saving Mr. Barber for last to ensure that he witnessed his children's violent deaths.[35]

Once in Atlanta, the Hamiltons first lived in an apartment in Beaver Slide, and John found employment as a driver for a local grocery. Within two decades of their arrival, John and Reacie, who by then had nine children, had established a cleaning and pressing business.[36] They also realized a dream unobtainable for many African Americans in the early twentieth century when they purchased a home in a housing development financed by Heman Perry, founder of the Standard Life Insurance Company of Atlanta. In the 1920s, ever the shrewd black businessman, Perry bought up the land to the west of Atlanta University, on which he built small bungalow homes. He mortgaged these homes to African American families, giving them the opportunity to own homes on par with those available to white Atlantans.[37] The Hamiltons' two-bedroom Perry home at 981 West Fair Street boasted hardwood floors, a back porch, and a large backyard.[38] When Moss Kendrix's mother, Mary, followed her brother John to Atlanta, she lived for some time in his house, as did all of his siblings who migrated to the city. Over the years, John and Reacie's modest residence housed scores of relatives, such that the extended clan called it the "home house."[39]

John was a surrogate father figure to Moss. Both a family man and entrepreneur, Uncle John modeled for his sister's son tenets of "socially responsible individualism," which included individual betterment (for the sake of the common good) through community involvement, industriousness, and education.[40] After a long week of cleaning, pressing, and delivering clothes throughout the West End, for example, Uncle John shepherded his clan to the Saint Paul African Methodist Episcopal Church, where he was a respected member and the first recipient of the house of worship's Father of the Year award.[41] So fierce was his belief in the importance of education that he refused to give his daughter Ruth away at her wedding when she opted to marry rather than go to college.[42] Hamilton understood that, for African Americans fortunate enough to obtain it, higher education offered potential (though hardly guaranteed) escape from slum life, racial discrimination, and the lynch mob; and for black women in particular, education could provide access to occupations that made them less vulnerable to sexual exploitation.

The number of black institutions of higher education in close proximity to the Hamiltons reinforced the message that education was the key to black social progress, as did prominent members of those institutions. At Kendrix's high school graduation, Atlanta University president John Hope opined that the number of top-quality black colleges in the city meant that Atlanta's black families could "send their children to college and university without getting themselves or their children into debt and without breaking the home ties."[43] Because higher education was uniquely convenient and affordable for Atlanta's young black men and women, Hope implied, it should be the goal, *even* in the midst of the Depression. As a member of the Hamilton clan, Moss Kendrix imbibed this sentiment, and it surprised no one when, in the fall of 1935, after graduating from Atlanta University Laboratory High School, he entered Morehouse College, the nation's most prestigious all-male black college (Figure 8).[44]

At the same time that Kendrix was preparing for college, the New Deal was becoming increasingly present within the lives of African Americans in Atlanta. Of the black domestics, laborers, professionals, and teachers in Atlanta who lost their jobs when the Depression hit, approximately sixteen thousand found employment in jobs subsidized through the Federal Emergency Relief Administration.[45] The New Deal became especially tangible to Atlanta's poorer classes when it physically transformed their neighborhoods. Empowered by the National Industrial Recovery Act of 1933, the president introduced federally funded slum clearance and housing projects. These projects were meant to provide employment and revitalize the construction industry as much as to provide housing.[46] Atlanta became ground zero for New Deal housing initiatives when, in the mid-1930s, construction began on the Techwood Homes and University Homes projects, the nation's first public works, low-rent housing developments. Intended for white

FRESHMAN CLASS

Figure 8. Morehouse College Freshman Class, 1936, *Maroon Tiger.* Kendrix stands third from the right in the front row. Robert W. Woodruff Library, Atlanta University Center.

families, Techwood Homes was located to the immediate northwest of Atlanta's downtown, just south of the Georgia Institute of Technology.[47] Its black counterpart, University Homes, was sandwiched between Atlanta University and Morehouse and Spelman Colleges (Figure 9). The two housing projects would house 604 white families and 675 black families, respectively.[48]

The public housing program was one of the "most inclusive" New Deal programs, if not the most, with half of the proposed housing projects in the South reserved for blacks.[49] And for black Atlantans like Moss Kendrix, Roosevelt's housing initiative literally changed the landscape. Inherent to the rise of housing projects was the demolition of previous dwellings. University Homes went up on the site of the Beaver Slide slum, much to the satisfaction of members of Atlanta's black academic and reformer communities. From the elevated perch of Atlanta University, prominent blacks like the university's president John Hope perceived the slum, which lay at the foot of the campus (Figure 7), as degrading the university—labeled by the *Atlanta Daily World* as "the finest flower of civilization"—with its supposed high

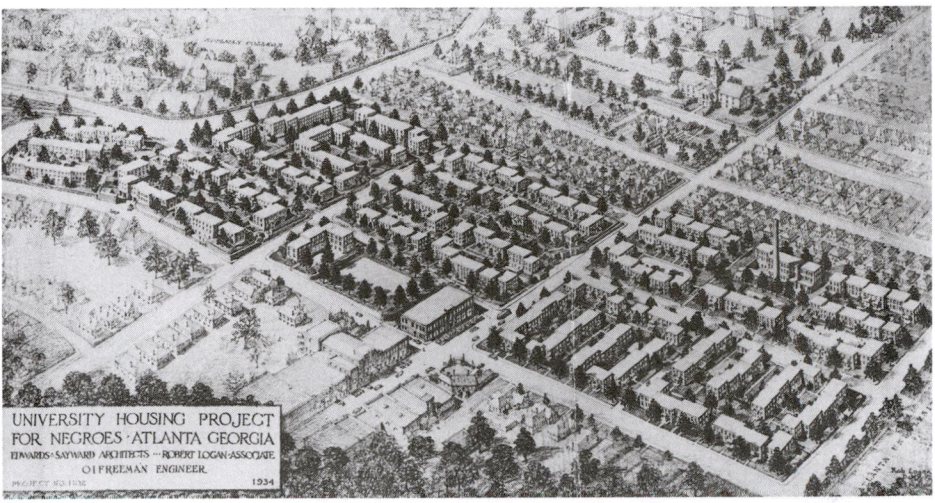

Figure 9. Architect's rendering of University Homes housing project, 1934.

level of vice and disease.[50] The residents of Beaver Slide suffered worse than the disapproval of their better-heeled neighbors. Most lived with no electricity, toilets, or running water, and all endured overcrowding, filth, and crime.[51]

The University Homes project replaced the dilapidated wooden homes and tenement dwellings of Beaver Slide with what one contemporary observer described as "modern fireproof buildings," which boasted amenities such as hot and cold running water, bathtubs, toilets, and electric stoves.[52] Additional uplift elements of the nation's first black housing project included paved roads, lawns, shrubbery beds, and playgrounds where there had been none. A scene of linear red brick buildings and engineered green spaces had risen up from an area once defined by dirt, dust, and disorder.[53] As the physical environment changed, so, too, did the demographics. By design, the subsidized rent of approximately six dollars per room for the new housing units proved too expensive for the African Americans who had lived in the demolished slums. Deemed undesirable, they were priced out of New Deal housing and pushed to the edge, if not out of Atlanta all together. Similarly, Techwood Homes displaced the poor African Americans who lived in the predominantly black slum of Techwood Flats that previously occupied the site. The segregated projects of the "inclusive" New Deal ensured that the black population of Atlanta's West Side became increasingly middle class.[54]

In addition to housing programs, black Atlantans also encountered the New Deal in the form of education initiatives, particularly through the NYA. Established by Executive Order 7086 in 1935, the NYA's mission was to "provide funds for the part-time employment of needy school, college, and graduate students . . . so as to enable them to continue their education" and to "provide funds for the part-time employment of youth from relief families on work projects designed . . . to give the young people valuable work experience."[55] African Americans made up approximately 40 percent of the youth population in Georgia, and the NYA was essential to their education and employment during the Depression.[56] Georgia's black high school students received more NYA funds than students in any other state. According to W. A. Robinson, principal of Kendrix's high school, NYA funds allowed his students "their first and only opportunities to work for wages under conditions which call for a high degree of responsibility and serious purpose."[57] During his undergraduate days, Kendrix was likely among the more than two thousand "promising" Georgia college students to receive a monthly check from the NYA for approximately fifteen dollars for work he performed for Morehouse, one of the many colleges and universities in Atlanta that received NYA aid to create jobs for their students.[58]

It was at Morehouse that Kendrix began to pursue his interest in public and media relations. He entered college intending to pursue a law career and, to that end, he majored in history and political science. But, as Kendrix put it, he primarily "majored in extra-curricular activities" that ranged from participating in the Debating Society and Peace Services to competing as a member of Morehouse's first golf team.[59] As a Morehouse Man, Kendrix also became a member of Alpha Phi Alpha, the significance of which cannot be overstated in light of his career options and decisions. Founded in 1906 at Cornell University, Alpha Phi Alpha was the nation's first black fraternity and was commonly characterized as an organization for light-skinned, middle- to upper-class, enterprising African American men from "good" families. The organization boasted a membership of prominent African Americans across academia, business, politics, and entertainment. At the time Kendrix pledged the fraternity, members included former Morehouse College president John Hope; Rayford Logan, educator and member of Roosevelt's Black Cabinet; W. E. B. Du Bois, intellectual and founding member of the National Association for the Advancement of Colored People (NAACP); Charles Johnson, Fisk University president and founder of the magazine *Opportunity*; and Norris Herndon, president of the Atlanta Life Insurance Company. Kendrix's membership in the educated black class provided him with fraternal associations that influenced and furthered his professional objectives as a business-minded young man interested in media communications. He would draw on these connections throughout his professional life.

The majority of Kendrix's extracurricular activities revealed a partiality—not to mention a talent—for communications and journalism, which aligned with trends shaping media culture beyond Morehouse. He entered college at a time characterized by the growing acceptance of media-driven public relations as a particularly effective tool of public persuasion and social control, a phenomenon driven in large part by one man, Edward Bernays. Beginning in the 1920s, Bernays—who owned and operated his own public relations firm—began promoting the social role of public relations. The purpose of public relations, he explained, was to put ideals before the public in manners such that they gained acceptance. Bernays came to this thinking while serving the Woodrow Wilson administration as a member of the Committee on Public Information, the federal propaganda agency, during World War I. Dubbed the "first press agents' war," World War I was characterized by an unprecedented use of propaganda to direct public opinion regarding U.S. military involvement.[60] As an agent of the Committee on Public Information, Bernays imagined the nonmilitaristic importance of public relations. He subscribed to what his contemporary Walter Lippmann described as the "manufacture of consent."[61] When it came to public opinion, Bernays determined that public relations should not be reactive or a tool of damage control, as traditionally had been the case. It should be a guiding force. When appealing to the public, the state, corporations, and political organizations should make use of "just the right word or image to capture the popular imagination, the way they had in rallying the nation to war."[62]

After the war, Bernays waged a campaign to legitimize public relations as a fundamental tool of good business and effective government; he was quick to find converts to whom he sold his philosophy, as well as his services. By the time the stock market crashed in 1929, Bernays and his business partner, Doris Fleischman (also his wife), amassed an enviable client list that boasted America's largest corporations, including Procter & Gamble, General Electric, Westinghouse, and the American Tobacco Company, not to mention the White House, which, in 1924, hired Bernays and Fleischman to improve the public perception of the notoriously remote president Calvin Coolidge. The demonstrable success of Bernays's methods profoundly influenced how commercial, nonprofit, and governmental institutions viewed and utilized public relations: as a modern means by which, as Bernays said, "to bring order out of chaos."[63]

Whereas Coolidge likely begrudged the use of public relations to make him likeable, Franklin Roosevelt fully embraced its promise as a persuasive technology. A massive relief and recovery program, his New Deal was also a massive public relations machine: in fact, the former necessitated the latter. The new economic order supposed what economist John Maynard Keynes described as "an elemental conflict between private enterprise and the general good" that required the government to "intercede as an agent on behalf of the social body."[64] This radical departure from the tenets of "free market" capitalism, Keynes argued, required a comprehensive publicity and public relations campaign if it were to succeed.[65] Roosevelt clearly concurred, because faith in the power of public relations defined his administration's approach to politics.[66] New Deal agencies made use of every medium imaginable to publicize various relief programs and triumphs, inform Americans about health issues, and advertise the artwork and theater productions of New Deal cultural programs.

The president himself proved to be a skilled public relations man. Within days of taking office, he initiated the practice of evening radio addresses, which gave him entry into Americans' private homes. Branded "fireside chats," these addresses made the president of the United States available and familiar to "the masses" like never before.[67] Despite their homey nature, there was nothing informal or unplanned about these chats, which were scripted by a playwright in addition to Roosevelt's advisers. Conducted nowhere near a fireplace, these radio addresses constructed a (false) intimacy between the president and the American people, as if he, too, gathered at the family hearth. Through his fireside chats, Roosevelt engendered trust essential to his administration's attempts to shape public opinion in favor of its policies.

Roosevelt routinely offered himself in manners that personalized government and encouraged in Americans feelings of familiarity and ownership concerning his administration and its programs. In November 1935, for example, he traveled to Atlanta to dedicate Techwood Homes as the first historic step in the transformation of urban living for the nation's poor. Before the crowd of fifty thousand that packed Georgia Tech's Grant Stadium, he praised the housing development as the answer to prayers of "people who never before could get a decent roof over their heads." His speech was little more than a grand advertisement for the New Deal. Techwood Homes was concrete evidence, in the most literal sense, of the "revival of material prosperity" engineered under his leadership, New Deal politics come to fruition.[68]

A fundamental element of Roosevelt's messages to the American public was the culpability of the nation's business leaders for the Depression. When the market collapsed, Americans eyed big business with growing disapproval; it did not help that the president explicitly (and frequently) laid responsibility for the economy's collapse at the feet of America's industrialists. In response, corporations beefed up their public relations operations to rehabilitate their images. To survive, American corporations that had mastered selling material goods now had to master selling themselves.[69] Corporations also turned to public relations to promote principles essential to capitalism (and their bottom line), which the radical politics of the New Deal disparaged. The billboard discussed earlier was part of the multifaceted Free Enterprise public relations campaign devised by NAM in the late 1930s to restore the public's faith in industry. Between 1934 and 1937, NAM's public relations budget rose from $36,000 to over $790,000 as the organization publicized the virtues of industry and free enterprise through film, radio, marketing, direct mail, lectures, and news items.[70] At precisely the moment that professionals such as Bernays were promoting public relations as a useful tool of social control, Depression-era circumstances prompted both the federal government and private businesses to test his theory extensively. During the 1930s, the Roosevelt administration, corporations, and business organizations all employed increasingly sophisticated public relations campaigns to achieve their respective objectives. Their efforts occasioned an explosion in public relations.

African Americans were among the intended audience of federal public relations. The proverbial canary in the coal mine, blacks suffered first and worst and composed a disproportionately large percentage of the unemployed during the Depression. Therefore, as a matter of national recovery, New Deal public relations necessarily addressed their circumstances through various programs and campaigns. Certainly, the growing relevance and reach of public relations would have been evident to Kendrix, who, as a young man, displayed a keen interest in media relations.[71] While a student at Morehouse, Kendrix worked for the college paper, the *Maroon Tiger*, every year excluding his first year—first as a contributor; then as assistant advertising manager, assistant editor, and columnist; and finally as editor in chief.[72] He used the *Tiger* to publicize his views about local and global matters, as well as issues of concern to communities with which he identified.

In addition to articles and editorials, Kendrix penned his own column for the *Tiger* called "Kendrix' Kandid Komments." A cheeky co-optation of the Ku Klux Klan's KKK brand, the title identified the column as a media space for considerations of race and politics. Kendrix's writings for the *Tiger* revealed his political development as a young, urban black man contemplating his social position as such in the United States, as well as his place and responsibilities as an American citizen of the world. He offered commentary on topics such as black progress (or the lack thereof), segregation and disenfranchisement, local and national matters, congressional and other governmental business, and foreign relations and policy. In one column, Kendrix turned rumination on an ant trail he observed into a statement on human society. "I noticed that each ant would pause as if to speak upon meeting another ant," he wrote, which was "of profound significance" because "this principle of society has lost none of its qualities." In his close scrutiny of the tiny insects, Kendrix had pulled back from his immediate world to position himself above the world (of ants) and divine order. The passage is particularly interesting in juxtaposition to the column's main section, entitled "War Marches On—America What Now?" Here, ants became countries and Kendrix warned that, because of increasing globalization, "we are not too far removed from the toils of Europe and the Far East that we should neglect deliberately all consideration of the resulting effects of a major conflict in those parts." In his reference to Japan's war on China and the rise of Nazism and fascism in Europe, Kendrix urged his readers to look beyond their immediate circumstances and beyond the "black community" to pay attention to issues that, on the surface, did not appear racial. He expressed a sense of himself as a black member of a larger nation, the United States, which had responsibilities as a member of a larger global family. At the time, he believed the cost of that membership was preparation for war.[73] Although his topic was America at war, Kendrix absolutely conceptualized the conflicts overseas and U.S. involvement through the lens of race. The consistent underlying question in his *Tiger* writings was, How does this issue interest African Americans?

Kendrix's college education clearly influenced his sense of self as a black man in an increasingly connected world. His experience differed from that of the majority of African Americans, who, if fortunate enough to continue schooling, did so at normal schools such as Booker T. Washington's Tuskegee Institute and other institutions with vocational curricula of domestic, mechanical, or agricultural sciences. By contrast, at Morehouse, Kendrix was a liberal arts student who studied history, political science, and economics. He was an especially avid student of U.S. history, which affected his view of current affairs and African Americans' relation to them. In particular, he cogitated on black citizenship and publicized his musings through the *Tiger*. In a piece entitled "Looking from the Under-side Up," Kendrix criticized a bill moving through Congress that was meant to weaken the Fourteenth Amendment. As he understood it, the purpose of this bill was to "solve the 'Negro problem'" by constraining black citizenship. Viewing the bill as a racist solution to a racist perception of African Americans, Kendrix argued the case of black America. "[African Americans'] presence has served to make the destiny of this great nation," he wrote. "[They have] suffered the ills of every American crisis and shedded [*sic*] blood in every major conflict involving the United States." "We have fought America's cause of freedom, of Unity, of Imperialism, and of Democracy!" Here, Kendrix expressed the sentiment contained in the title of Langston Hughes's 1926 poem "I, Too, Sing America." The editorial revealed, however, that he did not necessarily believe that declaring African Americans as first-rate, first-class American citizens made it so. Echoing Hughes, he concluded, "We too sing 'America.' But, Are We Americans?"[74]

While overtly political on matters of race, in his early college years, Kendrix displayed the conservatism of one who put his faith in systems, whether educational, judicial, or electoral. He found much fault with the traditional treatment of African Americans in these systems. Imperfect though they were, however, he regarded them as the best channels through which to fight racism. Concerning education, he granted that African Americans had been "harassed and retarded" in their education, but they had also been "nursed and aided" by whites and God. African Americans could not claim, in other words, their accomplishments as theirs alone.[75]

Over and over again, Kendrix articulated African Americans' place and progress in terms of their membership in the larger mechanism or organism of the United States; he did not engage in "us (blacks) versus them (whites)" thinking.

After watching antilynching reform die in Congress, Kendrix shifted his perspective. He explicitly identified white racism as the barrier to black civil rights, and thus as something to be fought actively, strenuously, and persistently. In an especially "Kandid" column, he chided his peers (black college students) for their failure to mobilize against racial injustices, especially lynching. He summarized his generation's attitude: "We met, we resolved, and . . . we dissolved!" Young black men and women, he charged, should step onto "the scene of action" with their elders, who were putting the younger generation to shame when it came to the fight for full citizenship.[76] In clear terms, he called for a movement. As he was a member of the educated black class in the black education capital of the world, however, his movement would not look like the protests we have come to associate with black civil rights. His call for militancy did not have him taking to the streets; it would not have occurred to him to do so. He had other means.

As a fledgling journalist, Kendrix trusted in the power of the press to combat social inequality.[77] He lived in the city in which the *Atlanta Daily World* was published. The first (and, at the time, the only) black daily newspaper, the *Atlanta Daily World* threw a spotlight on important black journalists and other "men of letters"; moreover, it drew this set to Atlanta. The newspaper operation provided Kendrix, who was a member of the academic world from which the newspaper drew many of its "expert" commentators, a unique view of the press and its value as an industry and a platform for social causes. It dismayed him, then, that black universities and colleges, including Morehouse, offered few journalism classes. Who would helm the institution of the black press if young black men and women were not schooled in journalism? How would African Americans compete politically and press their interests without access to or, better yet, control of the press? These concerns compelled Kendrix (along with two of his Morehouse brothers) to found the Delta Phi Delta Intercollegiate Journalistic Society in 1937 as a vehicle to attract young black men and women to the field of journalism. A national society from its founding, Delta Phi Delta formalized black students' access to influential African Americans in literary, journalism, and publishing circles. An architect of this structure, Kendrix became well connected with members of the press and black academia. The advisory board that he helped assemble for the society included prominent African Americans such as literary critic Alain Locke, publisher and poet W. S. Braithwaite, journalists George Schuyler and Carl Murphy, and educator and activist James Weldon Johnson.[78]

Kendrix headed the journalism society's promotional division, and in this position he exhibited an impressive penchant for public relations, and especially publicity. In 1938 he founded National Bigger and Better Newspaper Week—an annual, weeklong observance of the black press, its history, and its contributions. The *Chicago Defender* recognized the event as "the first of its kind ever attempted within the Race [*sic*]."[79] Notably, in name, Kendrix's press event borrowed language from the black fraternity Phi Beta Sigma, which had the national theme of "A Bigger and Better Negro Business Program." The overlap reflects Kendrix's own participation in Greek life as an Alpha and indicates that, even while wrapped up in promoting black journalism, he kept a steady eye on the world of black business.[80]

Kendrix, who had used the *Maroon Tiger* to expound on issues of black education and citizenship, as well as the fate of Morehouse's "depression babies," determined that the black press was "his scene of action."[81] Over the next five years, he performed as director of National Bigger and Better Newspaper Week, which came to be commonly called Negro Press Week. From this platform, he heralded the black press as a "special advocate" necessary to "convince America that . . . bringing the democratic ideal within reach of Negro people [served] the best interests of the nation as a whole."[82] With Negro Press Week, Kendrix enacted, on a grand scale, the model he developed as editor of the *Tiger*, in which he used the press as a tool to promote the tool itself and the publics it served.

Directing Negro Press Week resulted in Kendrix's name and photograph appearing regularly within national black newspapers, including the *Defender* and the *Atlanta Daily World*, which increased his visibility. The journalism and publicity experience Kendrix gained as a Morehouse student, combined with his growing reputation as a publicist for black institutions, made him an attractive candidate for public relations work that related, in particular, to black people and interests. New Deal officials took notice and, in 1939, Georgia's Division of Negro Affairs of the NYA employed him as its educational supervisor, making him responsible for the division's public relations and publicity efforts.

By the time the NYA came calling, Kendrix no doubt understood public relations to be an actual occupation. He spent his Morehouse years doing public relations, and especially publicity, for the Delta Phi Delta Intercollegiate Journalistic Society and Negro Press Week largely on a volunteer basis. All around him was evidence that he might be paid for similar work. By the time he graduated, the role of "public relations counselor" was widely recognized. Conceived of and promoted by Bernays, the public relations counselor was an expert who assiduously studied constituencies, markets, and media so he could advise his clients how to direct the public to behave in manners beneficial to them.[83] The designation of "counselor" distinguished modern public relations practitioners from the press agents of previous decades, whose main objective had been "getting something for nothing from publishers," and the equally crude "circus advance-man" and "semi-journalist promoter of small-time actresses."[84] Bernays intended the association with lawyering that "counselor" evoked: public relations and law professionals were both experts and advocates who advanced their clients' viewpoint or objectives. The NYA public relations position opened an alternative route of professionalism to Kendrix. He had applied and been accepted to the Howard University School of Law. But shortly after graduation, he married his college sweetheart, Dorothy Johnson, a Spelman coed, and decided he needed to, as he put it, "get some money in his pockets" sooner rather than later.[85] His personal circumstances aligned with his interests and experience to make the NYA position particularly opportune.[86]

The NYA hired Kendrix to be their expert. Early in the organization's existence, NYA leadership identified a public relations problem for the agency among African Americans. The perception in black circles was that the NYA was "totally a relief organization," rather than an agency that offered citizenship courses and programs organized around athletics, dancing, music, and arts and crafts, in addition to educational aid and job training. Financial aid the NYA offered, therefore, carried the stigma of charity, which affronted the pride and respectability of many African Americans who, like John and Reacie Hamilton, had done everything within their power to be self-reliant. Even black youths who received student aid were inclined to "keep the fact . . . a secret because it is . . . a disgrace."[87] These attitudes had an undesirable public relations effect, because when people would not speak of their experiences with the agency, they suppressed information about what the NYA had to offer black communities. In response, NYA leadership determined the need for targeted publicity that formulated NYA benefits and programs as a reputable route to black professional development, as opposed to shameful handouts.[88] The Division of Negro Affairs of the NYA made space within its structure for public relations, called educational divisions, to execute this publicity, and Kendrix began his professional public relations career directing a division of this sort.

The NYA was unique as a New Deal agency for the opportunities it provided African Americans for professional development, as well as for the authority and autonomy it afforded its black employees. NYA national leadership infused the agency with race conscious, starting at the top with executive director Aubrey Williams. A white social worker from Alabama, Williams was among a group of white liberal New Dealers (others included Labor Secretary Frances Perkins, Secretary of the Interior Harold Ickes, and FSA administrator Will Alexander) who advocated for social and racial equality and for African Americans' civil rights. These race liberals believed that the circumstances of the Depression and the political liberalism of the New Deal elevated the concept of a "mutual community" over the individualism of the previous decade, and they argued that this new climate should encourage black progress and better race relations.[89] Along these lines, Williams established the Division of Negro Affairs to ensure that the financial aid and staffing dedicated to the employment of black youths on the state level corresponded to the percentage of blacks in any given state. To head this division, Roosevelt appointed Mary McLeod Bethune, then president of the historically black Daytona Educational and Industrial Training School (later Bethune-Cookman University) and a member of Roosevelt's Black Cabinet. The decentralized structure of the NYA also contributed to the opportunities and status its black employees had. Rather than a single federal office that developed or oversaw projects throughout the nation, each state had its own "Negro division," and the directors of these state divisions enjoyed much latitude in how they opted to address the needs of the communities their office served.[90]

Kendrix came into the NYA Division of Negro Affairs in Georgia as a member of the small team of employees working under State Director William H. Shell out of offices in Atlanta's black YMCA located on Butler

Street. Georgia's Division of Negro Affairs was the most successful of all the state "Negro divisions"—providing, for instance, more educational aid to African Americans, especially graduate students, than any other state. This success lay in the division's personnel and organization. The Negro Division of Georgia had its own black staff, larger than that of any other state. Also, the Georgia state NYA office left the operations of its Negro Affairs division to that division's black employees.[91] As one of those employees, Kendrix experienced a great degree of independence, the extent of which was matched only by that of his responsibilities. In the role of educational supervisor, he oversaw the creation, implementation, coordination, and supervision of all public relations for Georgia's NYA Negro Division (Figure 10).[92]

It is no surprise that, when it came to promoting the NYA and its programs or events, Kendrix favored newspapers. He relied on the black press, in particular, as a no-cost way to publicize NYA programs and successes. His division (which consisted of him and one assistant) distributed news releases and editorial commentaries to black news agencies and newspaper syndicates and directly to local, state, and national white and black news-

Figure 10. Moss Kendrix, educational supervisor for the Negro Division, Georgia National Youth Administration, 1940, *Crisis.*

papers, as well as black colleges and high schools, churches, and other community organizations.[93] In addition, he arranged for a column entitled "Day by Day," which discussed the relevance of the NYA Division of Negro Affairs to the needs of young black Americans, to run in the venerated black weekly the *Pittsburgh Courier.*[94] Kendrix also publicized NYA programs, events, and services in person. He regularly met with or spoke before various groups, such as the African Methodist Episcopal Ministers' Union and the Congress of Colored Parents and Teachers.[95] A lack of funds for paid speakers partially explains Kendrix's hands-on approach. At no point in his public relations career, however, did he relinquish the role of getting out among the people to generate goodwill for his clients.

Beyond these basic publicity practices, Kendrix also deployed more sophisticated tactics such as tie-in and cross marketing—the promotion of one product, service, or event through the promotion of another, related product, service, or event. A primary example is his promotion of his division's Public Forums Project—an annual, four-month-long event that entailed assemblies in which African Americans from multiple rural and urban communities gathered in schools, churches, private homes, and community centers to discuss "subjects of civic, economic, political and social significance."[96] In October 1939, to publicize the project, he distributed literature about the forums at a state meeting of the NYA Division of Negro Affairs. This grand educational and promotional event featured an invocation by Rev. Martin Luther King Sr. and a closing address by Mary McLeod Bethune. Making an appearance, Kendrix further plugged the forums in his remarks before the assembly.[97] That same month, he had a display of forum materials installed at the Atlanta University Library. A publicity photograph of the exhibit (Figure 11) features a cleanly shorn young black man wearing a double-breasted suit and a smiling black woman of similar age with fashionable makeup and a hairstyle of relaxed, soft curls. They stand before a large glass display case that contains booklets entitled *Peaceful Change*, *Changing Governments*, and *Church and State*. A sign hung above the booklets identifies the "Exhibit of Free & Inexpensive Pamphlets on Public Affairs" as cosponsored by the Negro Public Forum Project and the library. An advertisement of free materials, the sponsorship sign conveys the welfare characteristics of the NYA and signifies the agency's relationship to black institutions and black education. In the photograph, the smiling young woman points directly at the *Changing Governments*

Figure 11. African American students viewing Atlanta University Library National Youth Administration exhibit, 1939.

booklet, which visually connotes a positive and active relationship between African Americans and their democratic government. The photograph publicized the forums, the NYA, and black youths. It also conveyed the loftier function of the NYA.

As demonstrated by the NYA library exhibit, NYA employment programs provided the federal government a way to manage American youths by inculcating in them the tenets of civic responsibility as a means of social control. "We have got to bring these young people into the active life of the community," Eleanor Roosevelt claimed at the time. She warned that the costs for not doing so were "vandalism and crime and expenditures on jails, asylums, and hospitals."[98] In addition to its employment and education programs, Georgia's NYA Division of Negro Affairs also relied on its Public Forums Project to combat the social death of young African Americans. Contemporary black historian Marian Thompson Wright identified a chief purpose of the forums as "the integration of youths into activities of American citizenship."[99] In light of this mission, in 1939 Kendrix's division sponsored a statewide Citizenship Day Celebration, during which forums devoted to the theme of "the Negro and citizenship in Georgia" took place at fifty-two black high schools and all of the state's black colleges and universities.

New Deal programs like the Public Forums Project provided a useful vehicle for delivering official directives at a time when the nation continued to lick its Depression-inflicted wounds and cast a wary eye toward events brewing in Europe. This function explains articulations of black citizenship that minimized its second-class nature. When Bethune delivered a speech at the 1939 Annual Conference of the National Council of Negro Women, she said, "My people, I want you to look up and have gratitude in your hearts for what is being done to give you more security in the great, beautiful land that we love and serve." In her conclusion, she emphasized the mutual reliance between the nation and black America's progress: "Stand closer together," she told her audience, "be loyal to the flag, and permit no isms to come in and destroy us."[100]

Kendrix, too, promoted an "all for one, one for all" formulation of citizenship that tied blacks' welfare to Roosevelt's New Deal and the Democratic platform. One month after Bethune's address to the National Council of Negro Women, he traveled to a forum in Cartersville, Georgia, to address the African Americans in attendance. In his talk, he invoked Adolf Hitler's invasion of Poland two months earlier and told his black audience that they ignored events in Europe at their own peril. "Where the principles of democracy are not practiced," he said, "the principles of citizenship cannot be practiced; such as plainly seen in the case of Germany."[101] Kendrix did not instruct his audience to overlook all isms, including racism—a big request of people who daily endured limitations and humiliations imposed by Jim Crow. He did, however, encourage his audience's fidelity to "the American way of life."[102] Democracy, he reasoned, was the necessary foundation for black freedom; therefore, it behooved African Americans to embrace the responsibilities of American citizenship, which he conveyed as loyalty, patriotism, and civic involvement, even if they had yet to fully enjoy the rights of citizenship.

The government relied on figures such as Bethune and Kendrix to circulate through black communities as ambassadors carrying the New Deal gospel to black Americans, many of whom had every reason to distrust their government. Black New Dealers' critics accused them of being accommodationists who gave cover to an administration that, despite hiring blacks for federal posts and giving voice to racially progressive politics, routinely shored up segregation and refused to adopt a civil rights plank.[103] African Americans who performed public relations work on behalf of Roosevelt's New Deal struck many as window dressing: they provided a black face for programs and policies targeted at blacks, the public relations value of which was significant in and of itself.[104] The administration benefited from having its messages of unity and civic duty come from black mouthpieces.

Black New Dealers suffered by comparison to black civil rights organizations and political leaders, whose commitment to civil rights and social equality appeared less compromising in its activist nature. No issue drew the line between civil rights conservatives and progressives more starkly during the 1930s than that of lynching. In 1934, after much lobbying from the NAACP, Democratic senators Edward Costigan and Robert Wagner sponsored a federal antilynching law.[105] When the bill failed, the *Chicago Defender* indicted the president for his "deathly silence" but especially condemned members of the Black Cabinet, including Bethune, who "failed to function in the interest of their Race [*sic*]."[106] By contrast, the NAACP had been uncompromising. Walter White, executive secretary of the civil rights organization, took the fight directly to the White House. In a private meeting arranged by the first lady, he pressured Roosevelt to support the bill and countered the president's reticence point for point. Despite the NAACP's best efforts, Roosevelt refused to get behind the Costigan-Wagner bill because, as he angrily explained to White, he dared not anger the southern leadership, who could derail recovery and relief legislation he deemed necessary. As head of the NAACP, White held the position of a respected and tolerated external adviser. He had been granted a seat at the table; however, his seat was often opposite the administration.

Kendrix operated from within the fold, a position that came with benefits, but certain strictures as well. As a federal employee, he promoted conceptions of black citizenship that elided African Americans' second-class citizenship status. He differed from Bethune, however; he did not instruct African Americans to consider themselves fortunate, overlook racism, or suppress their criticisms. Instead, he toed a line similar to that which Du

Bois walked when the elder black activist instructed African Americans to "close ranks" during World War I. Nevertheless, compared to activists like White, New Dealers like Bethune and Kendrix were suspect as representatives of black interests. Were they governmental lackeys? Were they patriots who, as members of a black class that had fared much better than most, believed unity and civic involvement were crucial to the health and security of a nation that they claimed, or imagined, as theirs? Were they astute tacticians who understood that their audience always extended beyond the black faces before them at any point? Did they think they could best advance black causes by appearing not to question the agendas of the white authorities to which they were ultimately beholden? Likely all of these scenarios carry some validity: negotiating racism is rarely a matter of either-or. Bethune and Kendrix sought racial uplift and equality, without a doubt. Equally true, as members of the black educated class, they had opportunities inaccessible to most African Americans. Their backgrounds certainly affected their personal objectives and their view of the American government and the "black experience." All of these factors help explain why they collaborated with the government in its approach to black America when other black political thinkers of the time joined unions that advocated for racial equality, became Communists, organized civil rights organizations, pursued civil rights through the courts, and boycotted racist employers and businesses. Whatever their motivations, Bethune and Kendrix were hampered in representing black interests by constraints inherent to their positions in a federal bureaucracy.[107] Kendrix, however, did find some wiggle room within the New Deal machine for black priorities.

During the late 1930s, the Public Forums Project provided Kendrix a sturdy platform from which to promote black citizenship. For one, as the only one of its kind, the program was the centerpiece of Georgia's NYA Division of Negro Affairs activities; therefore, it offered great public relations potential. Kendrix exploited that potential and, in the process, demonstrated his familiarity with current trends in the field of public relations that advised the combination of publicity events and heavy use of communications media. To promote the forums, Kendrix traveled throughout Georgia to meet with community groups and solicit speakers, produced and distributed the *State-wide Forum Report*, disseminated press releases to black newspapers, wrote articles on the Public Forums Project for national black periodicals, and coordinated with other state agencies to plan and publicize forums across Georgia.[108] Publicizing the Public Forums Project provided numerous opportunities to raise the public profile of the NYA. Also, because these were events in black communities, the actual forums facilitated awareness and goodwill among the public, encouraged interracial cooperation, and attracted news coverage that resulted in press items and generated word-of-mouth publicity and buzz that carried beyond the events themselves. They were a prime example of the event-driven public relations Bernays developed and popularized during the 1920s.[109]

The forums project provided Kendrix more opportunities to instruct African Americans in their citizenship and to promote that citizenship than any other aspect of NYA programming. In an article written for the *Crisis*, the official organ of the NAACP, he claimed the forums armed African Americans with an "intelligent understanding of the privileges and duties pertinent to a democratic society," which was essential to their political influence.[110] Civic education, he suggested, was the most significant step African Americans could take toward a "renewed evaluation of their relationship to their community and to their state."[111] Moreover, this route of social advancement was open to "wash women, domestics, share-croppers, turpentine workers, farmers, professional men and women, business executives, educators and people of every walk of life."[112] Kendrix offered an alternative black class organized by civic intelligence and involvement, rather than occupation, wealth, or status. He also countered prevailing racist notions of blackness that undermined black citizenship claims. The conception of responsible citizenship central to the NYA Public Forums Project promoted an educated, informed, and involved black populace, which challenged prevailing stereotypes of blacks as indifferent, ignorant, passive, and childlike. Finally, Kendrix formulated African Americans' citizenship along lines of their knowledgeable participation within democratic processes: blacks could both assert and experience national belonging through their civic engagement. The image of citizenship he publicized on his way to promoting the forums project both legitimized and encouraged African Americans' claims for recognition and treatment as first-class citizens by their government.

The Public Forums Project urged African Americans to think of themselves in terms of their membership within the body politic of the United

States. Appeals to their citizen selves implied that blacks should avail themselves of state programs. This tack also suggested that participation in New Deal initiatives geared toward national recovery constituted African Americans' tacit endorsement of the state, despite its failings on their behalf. Through the public forums, Kendrix advanced conceptions of black citizenship that emphasized the mutual dependence of Americans on each other and the government. President Roosevelt struck this chord in his first inaugural address, on March 4, 1933, when he instructed the American people that the "larger purposes" of economic recovery "bind upon us all as a sacred obligation with a unity of duty hitherto evoked only in time of armed strife."[113] Roosevelt proposed a covenant among Americans that envisioned all citizens as equally valuable and necessary to realization of "the common good." Four years later, when reelected, he further stressed that because the nation's survival depended on the contributions and commitment of all, the government was "determined to make every American citizen the subject of his country's interest and concern; and [to] never regard any faithful law-abiding group within our borders as superfluous."[114]

With the start of World War II, Kendrix echoed Roosevelt's expressions of citizenship to promote African Americans' citizenship rights by virtue of their contributions to national preparedness. Shortly after the United States entered the war, he learned that no training centers were being set up for blacks in Atlanta, though state funds had been allotted for nine such centers in the city for whites. By this time, Kendrix was the public relations officer for the NYA Division of Negro Affairs for the entire southeastern region. From this position, he threw a spotlight on the state government's "flagrant discrimination." Writing for the *Chicago Defender*, he argued that failing to train black Atlantans for work in the defense industries made little sense because a "huge Bell Bomber plant" being built in a nearby suburb required more than forty thousand workers and African Americans "constituted 42 per cent of the [city's] total population." He further publicized plans to "import" white labor to work for the plant, rather than employ local blacks, which ratcheted up his accusation of discrimination on the government's part to one of racism.[115] That Kendrix received no condemnation for his outspokenness from New Deal higher-ups speaks to the autonomy he experienced in his public addresses. During the early war years, he continually used the platform his position provided to emphasize the important role of African Americans in the war effort, as well as their investment in protecting the nation and its democratic principles.

The war thoroughly transformed the NYA. Industry generated by war production achieved what the New Deal could not and unemployment dropped from 14 to 2 percent. Finding jobs for America's youths—the NYA's bread and butter—was no longer a pressing issue, and conservative members of Congress targeted the NYA for elimination. It became necessary to strenuously promote the organization's relevance in a war context, which Kendrix achieved by repackaging the NYA as an offshoot of the War Manpower Commission. Rather than the "school beautification and construction projects" or "domestic service, sewing and arts and crafts projects" of the Depression years, Kendrix explained, the NYA now put its efforts into a War Production Training Program that turned out skilled workers for defense-related jobs in "shipbuilding, aviation, machine tools and other vital war industries."[116] In December 1940, a year before the United States went to war, Roosevelt championed the defense industries in one of his fireside chats. At the time, Americans continued to oppose entering the war, but the majority did support providing aid to the Allied powers, the necessity of which was becoming increasingly evident. Speaking to these circumstances, Roosevelt said, "Guns, planes, and ships have to be built in . . . America." "It is the purpose of the Nation," the president continued, "to build now . . . every machine and arsenal and factory that we need to manufacture our defense material." "We must be," he declared, "the great arsenal of democracy."[117] Kendrix seized on the commander in chief's mandate and endeavored to convince Congress that the fate of the country, the *world*, depended on black NYA-trained young men and women. In an essay entitled "The National Youth Administration Goes to War," he identified the preparation of America's (black) youths for "critical war occupations" as the NYA's new mission. He highlighted the number of former NYA trainees at work producing essential defense materials as machinists, assemblers, sheet metal workers, smelters, grinders, drill press and hydraulic press operators, patternmakers, chippers, and welders. He drew a direct line from NYA programs to skilled black defense workers to war readiness. The young black men and women who went through the NYA War Production Training Program, he insisted, "contribute their share to the battle of production which must be won if the enemy is to be subdued." On his way to making the case for the NYA, he made the case for the belonging of blacks as equal

American citizens based on their equal commitment and significance to national wartime objectives, including national unity, U.S. preparedness, and Allied victory.[118]

During World War II, Kendrix used Negro Press Week, in particular, to forge positive associations between black America and American democracy. Under his directorship, themes selected for the annual observance—which included "the role of the Negro press in the struggle to preserve American democracy," "the Negro press is an American institution," and "the Negro press and America's war effort"—branded the black press and, more importantly, black people as wholly American and as the guardians of democracy. In March 1942 he appeared as a guest on the Sunday Columbia Broadcasting System (now CBS) radio program *Wings Over Jordan* to publicize the fourth annual Negro Press Week. On the broadcast, he was joined by Percival Prattis, executive editor of the *Pittsburgh Courier*, who also promoted the weeklong observance, which was scheduled to run through the upcoming week and conclude the following Saturday night with a nationwide radio address by Claude Barnett, director of the Associated Negro Press. By this time, the United States was officially in the war on the side of the Allied powers, and Prattis assured listeners that black newspapers would "assail the ancient evils at home to the end that American Negroes may fully participate in all America's war effort." Kendrix assumed black participation in an Allied victory and projected beyond it: "When we have beaten the enemy to his knees . . . and America turns its attention toward the building of a great postwar society free of the ills which dominate the civilized world, the Negro press will be on hand working for those things which shall spell progress for America, working for those things which must spell progress for America's Negro population."[119]

In their remarks, Prattis and Kendrix brought together the articulations of black citizenship that Du Bois expressed in relation to World War I. In the context of World War II, African Americans must "close ranks" and join the fight for democracy, but the price for their participation was nothing less than unqualified freedom upon their return. "Make way for Democracy!" Du Bois had declared. These sentiments reflected larger, concurrent black movements. Even before the United States entered World War II, African Americans had protested barriers to their participation in the war effort; they sought desegregation of the armed forces and equal employment in the defense industries. When Roosevelt failed to respond to these demands, the president of the Brotherhood of Sleeping Car Porters, A. Philip Randolph, called for "an 'all-out' thundering march [of African Americans] on Washington" on July 1, 1941. A seasoned civil rights activist, Randolph wagered that Roosevelt would have a change of heart when he saw "masses—ten, twenty, fifty thousand Negroes on the White House lawn."[120] Writing in the *Black Worker*, the brotherhood's newspaper, he adopted the language the government had relied on during the Depression to summarize the position of African Americans in relation to the war and within the nation: "We believe in national unity which recognizes equal opportunity of black and white citizens. . . . We condemn all dictatorships, Fascist, Nazi and Communist. We are loyal, patriotic Americans all."[121]

Racial discrimination deprived African Americans of the opportunity to demonstrate their patriotism. Squeezed out of the defense industries, they also were missing out on financial gains of a war production economy, gains promised them by New Deal engineers in exchange for their support. The week before the planned march, the president did indeed blink and signed Executive Order 8802, which prohibited racial discrimination in the defense industry and established the Fair Employment Practices Committee. The United States, asserted Roosevelt, "can be defended successfully only with the help and support of all groups within its borders."[122] Randolph canceled the march but formed the March on Washington Movement to keep up the pressure on the government to honor its commitment to freedom and democracy at home, as well as abroad.

Randolph's "Americans all" claim was echoed in a letter published in the *Pittsburgh Courier* on January 31, 1942, one month before Prattis and Kendrix appeared on the *Wings Over Jordan* program. In the letter, James G. Thompson, a twenty-six-year-old black man, expressed his absolute support for the war but questioned, "Should I sacrifice my life to live half American?" "Would it be demanding too much," he asked, "to demand full citizenship rights in exchange for the sacrificing of my life?" Thompson referenced the symbolism of the "V for Victory" signs "displayed prominently in all so-called democratic countries" and suggested "we colored Americans adopt the double VV for a double victory" with the second *V* symbolizing "victory over our enemies from within." He closed his letter with a statement of remarkable patriotism: "I love America and am willing to die for the America I know will someday become a reality."[123] In response to Thompson's letter, Prattis's paper launched the Double V campaign, described as a "two-pronged attack against our enslavers at home and those abroad who will enslave us." Lest there be any confusion about the campaign's message, the paper declared, "WE ARE AMERICANS, TOO!"[124]

During the *Wings Over Jordan* radio program, Kendrix and Prattis kept up the "Americans all" campaign and made it known that black Americans meant to fight on their nation's behalf if allowed: they meant to perform as the citizens they were. Coming from Kendrix, the Double V articulation of black citizenship represented a subtle yet seismic shift. When in college, he consistently, *persistently*, laid out the case supporting African Americans' citizenship, understanding their status to be in question: "But are we Americans?" When representing the New Deal, he no longer argued their status but rather encouraged African Americans to conceive of themselves as obligated to aid in the nation's recovery by virtue of their citizenship. When the United States went to war, Kendrix joined the many African Americans who held the government to its obligations to *them*, by virtue of their citizenship.

Chapter 2

A Choice Weapon: World War II and Black Propaganda

I saw that the camera could be a weapon against poverty, against racism.

—Gordon Parks

We black folk, our history and our present being, are a mirror of all the manifold experiences of America.

—Richard Wright, *12 Million Black Voices*

The conscious and intelligent manipulation of . . . the masses is an important element in democratic society.

—Edward Bernays, *Propaganda*

During the late 1930s, Moss Hyles Kendrix steadily climbed the ladder with the National Youth Administration (NYA). Within two and a half years of coming on staff as educational supervisor of Georgia's Division of Negro Affairs, he rose to the position of public relations and personnel officer for the agency's southeastern region, which, in addition to Georgia, included Alabama, Florida, Mississippi, South Carolina, and Tennessee.[1] His experience of the New Deal, both as beneficiary and as employee, was completely southern. Gordon Parks (Figure 12) encountered it as a midwestern black man of substantially different background and circumstances. Born five years earlier than Kendrix, in 1912, Gordon Roger Alexander Buchanan Parks was the youngest of fifteen children born to tenant farmers in Kansas. Frustrated by the limits to his education imposed by segregation, at age fourteen he dropped out of school, left home, and embarked on a decade of traveling between Minneapolis, Chicago, and New York; working odd jobs; and struggling to make ends meet. While Kendrix matriculated at Morehouse, Parks was among the many African American men in the United States employed in service jobs in the railway industry. From 1936 to 1938, he worked for the Northern Pacific Railway.[2] A newly married man in his midtwenties with a newborn son, Parks and his small family lived a meager life in Saint Paul, Minnesota. These circumstances motivated him to take a job as a dining car waiter on the North Coast Limited, which, because it traveled between Chicago and Seattle, allowed him to see his family in between runs.[3] To say waiting tables was less than satisfying to him is a gross understatement. "I loathed the job," he declared later, summing it up as "serving bigoted businessmen."[4] He could not have imagined upon taking the menial and demeaning job that it would launch him on a path to becoming one of America's most famous photographers.

Figure 12. Gordon Parks reading *Yank, the Army Weekly* in the Office of War Information, 1943. Library of Congress Prints and Photographs Division.

It was on a moving passenger train that the long arm of the New Deal public relations machine caught up with Parks. When he worked long runs from the Midwest to the West Coast and back again, he was ever looking for something to occupy his mind or, better yet, stir his imagination. While his coworkers slept and gambled in their down time, he read magazines discarded by passengers. One day, he picked up an abandoned photo-magazine and began to leaf through it. The magazine included a photo-essay about migrant workers.[5] The series of grainy black-and-white photographs depicted impoverished agricultural workers who, displaced by economic disaster, dust storms, and floods, had taken to the road to find work and, along the way, sought shelter in shanties made of cardboard boxes. The photographs were products of the Farm Security Administration (FSA), which, during the latter 1930s, sent documentary photographers throughout the country to record the effects of the Depression on Americans. These images circulated through various channels, including popular magazines such as the one Parks stumbled on as a railroad worker.

This chapter follows Parks from his first encounter with FSA documentary photography to his becoming first an FSA photographer and then an Office of War Information (OWI) photographer employed by the state to produce propaganda during World War II. As a federal photographer, Parks created images of black life in the United States that obscured the federal government's role in the oppression experienced by most African Americans. Complex circumstances compelled, and allowed, him to propagate images of American democracy and freedom that belied his own observations and experience as an African American. Artifacts of a particular moment in U.S. history, Parks's FSA/OWI images hold information about the relationship between black citizenship politics and federal concerns during World War II and the significance of African Americans to both psychic and practical aspects of the war effort.

World War II marks a watershed moment in the visual representation of African Americans and black life, compelled in large part by the practical concerns of war and U.S. officials' visions of a postwar world order in which the United States reigned supreme. In the period that immediately preceded U.S. entry into the war, the concept of U.S. responsibility based in national superiority emerged and figured heavily in U.S. politics and foreign policy. Publishing magnate Henry Luce publicized these sentiments in his 1941 essay, "The American Century," which counseled Americans to accept "our duty and our opportunity as the most powerful and vital nation in the world and . . . to exert upon that world the full impact of our influence."[6] Federal administrators worried about how the truth of African Americans' second-class citizenship affected perceptions of the nation's moral standing as it claimed a leadership role in a war against tyranny. Moreover, whether Luce envisioned it so, African Americans counted among the public he called on to enact his twentieth-century vision of manifest destiny. War officials understood that African Americans' support was necessary to national preparedness, military strength abroad, and domestic stability. But they struggled with how to inspire their participation, let alone their patriotism, when, as one OWI officer noted, "the pure principles of democracy are far from fulfillment in the life of the American Negro."[7] When blacks withheld their participation, they presented the federal government with more than a manpower problem: they compromised the readiness, unity, and morale essential to the nation's ability to rise to the challenge of war.

Visual representations of black life in the United States were a tool within this context that could either facilitate or hinder state agendas. During the war, federal agencies, most notably the OWI, commissioned, produced, and disseminated propagandist images of the "black experience" to inspire black patriotism, contain black protest, and convey the strength and superiority of the "American way of life" to both domestic and international observers. The OWI conscripted documentary photographers, in particular, to depict black life in manners that corroborated official narratives of American democracy. Parks was the primary black imagemaker of the U.S. wartime propaganda machine, and his contributions were uniquely valuable to the state's image campaign for their perspective and credibility.

Black propaganda was not the purview of the government alone. In 1941 black author Richard Wright published *12 Million Black Voices*, a phototext that relied on FSA documentary photography to publicize the historically oppressed state of African Americans in the United States. Federal officials targeted Wright and his representations of black life, which interrogated American democracy and highlighted the government's failure to grant or protect the rights of its black citizens. The varied reception of these two black imagemakers' representations of the black experience reveals how government propaganda and censorship activities during World War II occasioned a visual reimaging of African Americans as adherents to and beneficiaries of U.S. democracy.

Parks's role as a federal photographer and Wright's use of federal photography prompt consideration of how blacks have redefined blackness using "the master's tools" and, sometimes, working alongside and in cooperation with "the master." While certainly political, the image work Parks performed during the war was not oppositional: it resists the common classification of black representational strategies as primarily resistance to oppressive regimes (be it the state or "the gaze").[8] His photographs disrupt notions of either-or black agency, in which African Americans are portrayed as choosing either purely oppositional or purely accommodationist tactics to advance their politics. Parks pursued his personal, professional, and political objectives with the flexibility of priority and method that African Americans have historically found necessary, or at least effective, when operating in white spaces. His propaganda contributed to hegemonic articulations of the black experience and injected innovative images of African Americans—their experiences, values, and aspirations—into the official portrait of American democracy. He used his wartime assignment as a federal imagemaker to visually assert, again and again, the national belonging of African Americans through representations of their participation, patriotism, and commonness. This was propaganda useful to black citizenship campaigns. The image campaigns of Parks and other African Americans and the state visibly converge and even reconcile in his photographs. The FSA/OWI photographs of Parks reflect a moment in U.S. history when the state objective of positioning the United States as a global authority, by virtue of its being a democratic society of free people, compelled federal representations of blackness that aligned with the objective of African Americans to *be* free people in the world's foremost democratic society.

Parks had a profound reaction to the FSA's visualization of the Depression as portrayed through the life of migrant workers. He squirreled away the magazine that contained the photo-essay in his bunk and then took it home with him for repeated study.[9] The photographs that so captivated him were the product of a moment when several dynamics merged in the 1930s to transform visual culture and politics in the United States.

For one, by the time Parks encountered the FSA photo-essay on the train, visual imagery had become a common medium by which Americans received information. The camera, which had once been reserved for private or artistic use, had become a journalistic tool.

News outfits increasingly relied on photographs to relate news, once advances in camera and printing technologies, and the advent of wire services and photo agencies, made it sensible (which primarily meant affordable) to do so. The interwar period experienced a "quantum leap in the proliferation and social dispersion of photographic images."[10] Every development in the history of photography provoked changes in U.S. culture and grand statements about those changes. What distinguished the post–World War I image culture? The difference was a changing hierarchy in which the image was overtaking the written word as the preeminent means for the exchange of ideas and information. The rise of photojournalism, especially, established seeing as the grounds for knowing. Writing on the eve of the Depression, philosopher Walter Benjamin seized on this phenomenon and projected forward. "The illiterate of the future," he forecast, "will not be the man who cannot read the alphabet, but the one who cannot take a photograph."[11] Contemporary artist and novelist John Dos Passos concurred: "From being a wordminded people we are becoming an eyeminded people."[12] Benjamin and Dos Passos realized a cultural shift far more profound than an increase in the number of pictures populating the visual landscape. The aesthetic or artistic value of an image was no longer its primary characteristic or value: visual imagery was becoming the privileged unit of American thought.

The rise of an image-based informational culture compelled—as much as it reflected—changes in governing, a phenomenon quite visible in how the Roosevelt administration publicized different programs and instructed the public during the Depression. New Deal agencies relied heavily, even primarily, on imagery and altered the appearance of American public space. In the 1930s, for example, image-based posters created by the Works Progress Administration (WPA) proliferated as publicity for work programs, sanitation and nutrition practices, natural and urban attractions, and even the WPA itself (Figure 13).

No New Deal agency relied on images more than the FSA. Launched in 1935, the FSA photography project ran through 1944, the last two years as an OWI operation drafted to the production of war propaganda. During that

Figure 13. Works Progress Administration poster, ca. 1935. Library of Congress Prints and Photographs Division.

time, the agency's team of full-time and freelance photographers produced approximately 177,000 black-and-white and color photo images of American life during the Depression and World War II.[13] Their predominantly black-and-white documentary images are largely responsible for how Americans, then and now, imagine the Great Depression and the toll it took. Most famous among these photographs is Dorothea Lange's 1936 photograph *Migrant Mother* (Figure 14), which depicts a beleaguered woman in tattered clothing and with a heavily creased and weathered face who stares beyond the camera with a look both despondent and contemplative as two young children cling to her and she cradles a baby. The woman, Florence Owens Thompson, was a migrant worker who followed crops, from cotton, to beets, to peas: the stress and strain of the migrant experience gave her the look of a woman well beyond her thirty-two years. The photograph is black and white; however, it seemed possible that Thompson might actually be gray in real life. In Lange's portrait, Thompson appears as if she could be a character in *The Grapes of Wrath*, which tells the story of one family's exodus from Oklahoma to escape the Dust Bowl. John Steinbeck confessed that the photograph had inspired him in the writing of his most famous novel.[14]

The FSA's public relations successes lay in its use of documentary photography, which was, at the time, a preferred visual medium for the representation of "truth." The defining aesthetic characteristic of documentary photographs was realism: rather than art or souvenir, their currency lay in their supposed veracity as images that mirrored a real-world referent at a particular moment. Moreover, the advent of portable cameras such as 35 mm models gave birth to "the man on the scene," or photographers who encountered scenes in the world rather than staging them in the studio.[15] Documentary photographs gave the look of a visual report captured by the camera's eye through a mechanical process, rather than a vision manufactured by the camera's human operator. The literal black-and-white composition of most Depression-era documentary photographs led to perceptions of the medium as an unambiguous and reliable representational form.

By the mid-1930s, images that appeared to show the world as it "really" was had real value as market commodities. Luce assessed America's new viewing habits and declared, "To see, and to be shown is the will and new expectancy of half mankind." Americans, he decided, wanted to be informed and transported through images of the world around them, much

Figure 14. Dorothea Lange's *Migrant Mother*, February 1936. Library of Congress Prints and Photographs Division.

of which they would never visit but could now hope to know. To capitalize on these desires, he founded *Life*, a large-format photo-magazine of heavy, glossy pages that complemented its photojournalist content.[16]

The first issue of *Life*, published in November 1936, made visible how both photography and the New Deal had become central forces within U.S. culture at the time. On the cover is a black-and-white photograph taken by Margaret Bourke-White of the Fort Peck Dam on the Missouri River (Figure 15). The hydroelectric dam, construction of which began in 1933, was a massive federal undertaking, the nation's largest public works project at the time. The dam itself would provide flood control and generate power for the surrounding areas, which were no small achievements. In the bleak times of the early Depression, however, its construction was the real boon, as it provided much-needed jobs to thousands of workers throughout the 1930s. Bourke-White's photograph captured the endeavor's grandiosity. The image features the dam's spillway, still under construction. In the picture, the spillway's huge gate piers reach for the sky, concrete pillars un-burdened by the yet-to-be fabricated concrete-lined reservoir channel. The upper left-hand perspective gives the viewer a sense of zooming in on the leftmost pier, and as the eye reads left to right, the angle makes the other piers appear to recede in size. Two bent male workers appear at the base of that first pier. Compared to the massive uprights, the men are tiny, inscru-table figures. Their small, curved forms further emphasize the spillway's height and bulk, while the mixture of flat edges, rounded surfaces, and art deco influences bespeaks its careful design. In the photograph, the piers symbolize tension and potential. Each is a mammoth study in concrete and engineering but only a very small part of the grander design to tame the Missouri, transform the landscape, and bring light—in every sense— to inhabitants in the surrounding areas. Framed by Bourke-White, the dam appears as a testament to human capacity and modernity. Featured as it was on the cover of *Life*, as the magazine's inaugural visual offering, the image reflected the intersection of government, commercial culture, and visual culture trends. Such were the circumstances that brought the FSA to Parks's attention.

Parks's first encounter with FSA photographs kept him "thinking, thinking, looking and looking."[17] The images of the nation's dispossessed and displaced agricultural workers, he said, compelled "anyone with any feeling . . . to look and notice and . . . absorb the message that they were preaching."[18] As one of the more controversial New Deal initiatives, the FSA had to preach hard, and preach often. Conservative members of Congress, business leaders, contingents of the press, and members of the American middle class criticized the agency as socialist based on its relief programs for farmers and other agricultural workers. While they largely accepted Social Security as an entitlement program, many Americans viewed the FSA as dealing in handouts for a population of lazy or backward country folk. To combat these attitudes, the FSA publicized the need among the popu-lations it served and, more important, represented those populations as

Figure 15. Margaret Bourke-White photograph of Fort Peck Dam, cover of inaugural issue of *Life* magazine. © 1937 Time Inc. All rights reserved.

resilient and hardworking—characteristically American, in other words. Photography was the agency's chief tool of publicity and persuasion.

Parks was struck by the photographs' emotional power and their aesthetic power, dynamics he understood to be entwined. The combination was intentional, manufactured to inspire comprehension, curiosity, and, most of all, empathy within viewers. Roy Stryker, head of the FSA Information Division photography unit, promoted this formulation, and he equipped his photographers with precise instructions about the particular items, actions, and even social moments they should seek out. When Stryker dispatched Arthur Rothstein for a feature on small towns, he advised, "The main theme of your pictures should be corn," in order to convey the importance of farming to the economy.[19] When he sent Marion Post Wolcott to the Great Plains, he told her to send him images that "give the sense of the loneliness experienced by the women folks who have helped settle this country."[20] He also provided her with a bibliography of books she should read or at least "take along," which included Willa Cather's *O Pioneers!*, to shape her perspective and help her grasp the narrative slant he wished her photographs to have.[21]

The subtext of FSA photographs was starkly apparent to Parks. He described the photographs he viewed as "tragic images" that told the story of "human beings caught up in the confusion of poverty."[22] One photograph from the photo-essay on migrant workers stayed in his mind's eye for years. Taken by Rothstein, the picture features a tall, lean farmer and his two sons leaning into a dust storm as they walk past a shanty or shed on their farm (Figure 16). In the image, the dust and dirt collect around and cover the low wooden structure, making it appear as though the earth is slowly swallowing it. The more compelling element, however, is the younger of the two boys, only a toddler, who holds his hands up to cover his face as he trails blindly behind his father and older brother. Of his photograph, Rothstein said it "had a very simple kind of composition, but there was something about the swirling dust and the shed behind the farmer. . . . It showed an individual in relation to his environment."[23] The photograph dramatized and also humanized the experience of farmers and their families suffering the perfect storm of the depressed economy, the drought and multiple dust storms that devastated the Plains States, and the resultant bank closures and farm foreclosures.

The FSA's propaganda convinced Parks of photography's power as a tool of social commentary. In 1937, no longer satisfied by just looking, he bought his first camera during a stopover of the North Coast Limited in Seattle and began learning photography. Through strong self-promotion and the support of Marva Louis (wife to then-celebrated black boxer Joe Louis), Parks quickly gained a reputation and some business doing studio photography. By 1940, he was able to quit the railroad, and he and his wife, Sally, moved with their two small children from Saint Paul to Chicago's South Side, where

Figure 16. *Farmer and Sons Walking in the Face of a Dust Storm*, Arthur Rothstein, April 1936. Library of Congress Prints and Photographs Division.

he quickly became the photographer of choice among the black elite and even "wealthy white sitters."[24]

Parks's early studio work reveals that he grasped photography's function as being to promote a particular "truth." One studio portrait he produced when he arrived in Chicago, which features his wife, Sally, appeared in the newspaper (Figure 17). The photograph's caption (likely written by Parks) identifies its subject as the "exotic" and "popular" "wife of one of the city's leading portrait photographers" and states that she had joined "the smart social circles of the Windy City." The photograph and accompanying text transformed Sally—and thus Parks—from a working-class outsider to a member of Chicago's black high society. In addition to the caption's

POPULAR NEWCOMER

EXOTIC MRS. GORDON ROGERS PARK
Wife of one of the city's leading portrait photographers, has joined the smart social circles of the Windy City. Formerly of Minneapolis, Minn., Mrs. Park is now an ardent supporter of the South Side Community Art Center and is working with the committee for a bigger and better Ball the theme of which will be "Pan America."   (Photo by Gordon Rogers Parks)

Figure 17. Studio portrait of Sally Parks taken by Gordon Parks, circa 1941. Wichita State University Special Collections and University Archives.

description of Parks as a successful photographer, the modern feathered turban and chunky costume jewelry his wife wears suggest that he and his craft kept his family in high style. In fact, the Parkses lived in a dingy apartment in a run-down, crime-ridden neighborhood. More broadly, Parks's studio portraits visually reaffirmed the dignified sense of self and standing that his middle-class black subjects claimed; they also countered common assertions about the difficulty blacks—a rural, southern people—faced in their attempts to thrive or even rise in the metropolis of Chicago.[25] Such difficulties, if they existed, could be pushed out of frame, allowing for images of African Americans using the resources available to them (such as a well-chosen hat, photography, and the black press) to define and express themselves.

Studio photography sustained Parks and his family, but the documentary form continued to hold and inspire his interest as a visual artist. He became a serious student of FSA photography, which he tracked through magazines and, especially, photo-texts. Photo-texts, which combined prose and documentary photographs, emerged as a popular trend in the late 1930s, a direct result of the rise of photo-magazines and New Deal agencies' flooding of mainstream media with documentary imagery. As lengthy visual narratives, these commercial products were social commentaries advanced through carefully selected photographs captioned with great intention. The photo-essay of migrant workers that Parks first viewed on the train was formulated to inform and inspire sympathy among viewers. By comparison, photo-texts of the late New Deal era editorialized the circumstances pictured and instructed viewers in their response.

The photo-text *You Have Seen Their Faces*, published in 1937, popularized the form, and Parks studied it.[26] The collaboration of photographer Margaret Bourke-White and author Erskine Caldwell, this book gave Americans a picture of life for sharecroppers and tenant farmers, both white and African American, in the rural South. And the picture was grim. The focus on agricultural workers would have resonated with Parks, much as the photo-essay of migrant workers had. Raised in Kansas, he belonged to that class of African Americans, generally forgotten in U.S. history, who neither languished in the South nor followed the drinking gourd to the "promised land" of the North but rather migrated west, with some making it just midway to the opposite coast. The son of a dirt farmer who grew beets, turnips, and potatoes, Parks grew up in the arid landscapes featured in FSA photographers' representations of the nation's rural poor. He knew the life of having one's fortune, and misfortune, tied to the land, to say nothing of the invisible markets and federal policies that determined what the fruit of that land was worth.

Bourke-White and Caldwell had an agenda, which they divulged by admitting that "the legends under the pictures are intended to express the authors' own conceptions of the sentiments of the individuals portrayed; they do not pretend to reproduce the actual sentiments of these persons."[27] In photograph after photograph, Bourke-White zeroed in on the gaunt and weather- or work-worn faces of agricultural workers and their families, all of whom—regardless of age—appear beaten down or beaten up by working land that was "plumb worn out."[28] Caldwell amplified the message of Bourke-White's photographs with captions that ascribed sentiments to the impoverished souls depicted, whom, he supposed, pined for fried chicken and suffered for their lack of birth control.[29]

You Have Seen Their Faces strived for pity among reader-viewers that inspired compassion and, more important, action as it moved toward a conclusion that called for unionization and government intervention on behalf of the sharecropping class of the South. Little wonder that contemporary reviewers labeled the text a "propagandist social survey."[30] Through its prose, pictures, and contrived captions, the book pointed to sharecroppers' dire circumstances. Yet quiet dignity characterizes a number of Bourke-White's photographs, particularly her close-ups of her subjects' faces, which adhered to the FSA formula—no surprise, given that Bourke-White freelanced for the agency regularly. The photographs combined the depiction of hardship with the representation of stoic determination, such that those in need appeared respectworthy, and therefore entitled to assistance. *You Have Seen Their Faces* conveyed sharecroppers' pathetic circumstances—with images of run-down shacks, overcrowded schoolhouses, tattered clothes, and dirt, lots and lots of dirt—without making them appear pathetic and therefore beyond help. The appearance of dignity (even when fatalistic) suggested that the right form of assistance would not go wasted in these people's hardworking hands.[31] For the amateur Parks, the particular phototext provided a primer for taking documentary photographs and using them to intervene on behalf of the underrepresented.

Before Parks moved to Chicago, he frequented the city as a railroad employee. During those stops, he photographed Lake Michigan, seagulls, and skyscrapers near the train station. He also visited the Chicago Art Institute often, which inculcated in him a rather conventional conception of "true" art. Then he began visiting the South Side Community Art Center. Established in 1940 and funded through the New Deal's Federal Arts Project, the center fostered works of primarily black, but also Jewish, writers and artists. Parks spent more and more time in this space, and when he relocated to the city, he entered an arrangement in which he photographed the center's exhibits and activities at no charge in exchange for use of its darkroom. His relationship to this generative environment shifted his thinking about art and its purpose. The artists on display at the center had, as Parks recounted, "forsaken the lovely pink ladies of Manet and Renoir, the soft bluish-green landscapes of Monet." Their works convinced Parks that, in addition to a vehicle for beauty, art could be a medium of protest.[32] With this mind-set, he trained his camera on Chicago's South Side, the worst of which he described as "bruises on the face of humanity."[33] The African American inhabitants of Chicago's Black Belt became the central focus of his documentary explorations and the basis of his portfolio of what I term "race photographs," photographs of black life that signify on the lived experience of race and racism.

Two opportunities drove Parks to photograph black life on the South Side. First, a painter friend told him of the Julius Rosenwald Fellowship, which the friend informed him was "for exceptionally able spooks and white crackers."[34] Designed especially to fund "Negro creative workers" and white southerners, the Rosenwald fellowship was a key source of support for black visual artists during the New Deal and World War II eras. The Rosenwald Foundation did not award art for art's sake: it had loftier goals for artistic production. Recipients of the fellowship had to exhibit a commitment to service through their art, which coincided perfectly with Parks's shifting perspective about his responsibilities as a photographer.[35] To enhance his candidacy for the fellowship, the center agreed to an exhibit of Parks's photographs. For over a year, Parks spent his weekends working on his South Side series, which he displayed at the center in November 1941 as part of his show entitled (not so creatively) *Creative Photography*.[36] His documentary images of Chicago's "depressed black people and the shacks and brick tenements that entombed them" drew praise from William Haygood, director of the fellowship program, and FSA photographer Jack Delano.[37] Their endorsements no doubt contributed to Parks's being named a Rosenwald Fellow. Parks lobbied to serve out his fellowship with the FSA. After some prodding by the Rosenwald Foundation (and presumably Delano), Stryker agreed to bring Parks on as the only African American in the FSA Information Division photography unit.[38]

By the time Parks reached Washington, DC, in January 1942, the United States was at war and Stryker's photography unit had been given the mandate to document what Franklin D. Roosevelt described as America's conversion from "Old Dr. New Deal" to "Dr. Win-the-War."[39] The war supplanted and also greatly ameliorated the crisis of unemployment. There was no longer the pressing need for publicity-propagandist portraits that chronicled the nation's dispossessed or landscape photographs that celebrated America's natural beauty and encouraged its preservation (what one photographer referred to as the FSA's version of a pinup girl).[40] The agency was to shift its focus from the hardships of ill-fed, ill-clothed, and ill-housed rural folk to the "bustling activity in American defense centers and a quality of life worth fighting for."[41] War officials deemed such images necessary to recruit manpower, encourage morale, and manage perceptions of the United States among both Allied and enemy nations. Visual artists of all types were called upon to produce the required propaganda.

For the majority of the time the United States was in the war, the OWI was the center of the federal government's propaganda operation. This agency brought together all the existing government information agencies for the primary purpose of producing, disseminating, and policing propaganda domestically and abroad. Congress initially resisted the creation of such an office. The opposition was a legacy of World War I propaganda, which had been very effective—too effective. Following World War I, evidence emerged that the Allied powers had fabricated "atrocity propaganda," which attributed heinous and violent acts, like rape and baby murder, to the German and Austro-Hungarian troops. After this revelation, many Americans felt they had been manipulated away from their isolationism. The power to manipulate, however, constituted propaganda's chief value as a governing tool. In his 1928 book *Propaganda*, then–public relations guru Edward Bernays implied that opposition to propaganda reflected naïve, outdated thinking. In his expert opinion, "The conscious and intelligent manipulation of . . . the masses is an important element in democratic society."[42]

To justify governing through propaganda during the New Deal era, top U.S. officials redefined manipulation as an efficient method by which to direct the masses to a better condition. They perceived propaganda as being much like advertising, and, in keeping with Committee on Public Information practice, they even called it such.[43] Use of this marketing term suggested that whatever the government had to sell was a product worth selling, and therefore of value to the American people. A change in terminology, however, did not convince Americans, the bulk of whom continued to view propaganda as a sinister, coercive, and deliberate act of deception or brainwashing. It took the attack on Pearl Harbor on December 7, 1941, to eliminate challenges to the creation of a propaganda machine: the Japanese made Americans' concerns about being manipulated out of their isolationism a moot point. In June 1942 Roosevelt created the OWI, and shortly thereafter, the agency's Bureau of Publications and Graphics subsumed Stryker's FSA Information Division photography unit.

When Parks joined Stryker's team, he numbered among a scant handful of African American photographers working for federal agencies at the time. James Stephen Wright, a black photographer who worked his way up from a position as a chauffer for a New Deal agency, ran the photographic unit of the Federal Works Agency, which oversaw public works construction, relief efforts, and legislation. Another black photographer, Randolph MacDougall, worked under Wright. Finally, Roger Smith handled "black coverage" for the Negro Press Section of the OWI's Domestic News Bureau.[44] To an extent, all federal photographic divisions had a propagandist function, but Stryker's photographers produced images for the sole purpose of propaganda, meaning Parks's propagandist role surpassed that of his black peers.

Stryker explained that the primary responsibility of his unit was to produce visual "statements of our [national] strength."[45] When it came to this mission, Parks presented a mixed bag. He found his way onto Stryker's team on the merits of his photographs of black life on Chicago's South Side. These photographs demonstrated his potential value to the government as an imagemaker. First of all, the South Side images had the right "look." After all, Parks trained himself as a documentarian using a curriculum comprising FSA image products, which were synonymous with excellence at the time.[46]

Parks offered more than technical skill, however. His race, and the perspective it allowed, was particularly valuable when it came to the government's wartime propaganda needs in relation to shaping ideas of black life in America. His representations had currency as uniquely intuitive, perceptive, and credible. Parks was "an observer who is nevertheless participant."[47] Parks's race made him a particularly reliable witness, because many assumed it granted him innate skills for conveying black subject matter through photography. "The camera passes from the anthropologist to the native."[48] *U.S. Camera*, the magazine of authority among professional and amateur photographers at the time, claimed that Parks's "instinctive talents" and "immense capacity for rich creative power" as an African American best equipped him to photograph other blacks, whose "profound expressions, excellent rhythm and naturalness" encouraged their role as the object of photographic studies.[49] The magazine fell back on the trope of African Americans as emotional, sensual folk driven by impulse rather than intellect. When the black periodical *Negro Digest* reprinted this article, it appeared to endorse these ideas. Parks also contributed to this essentialism. In one interview, he struck down the idea that his race contributed to his success as an imagemaker dealing in black life *but* for the "heightened sense of timing," which the editor confirmed was borne out by "Negro athletic records."[50] Commentators on both sides of the color line invested Parks with an authoritative vision, which enhanced the veracity—or, at least, perceptions of the veracity—of his black documentary photographs. Much as black New Dealers Moss Kendrix and Mary McLeod Bethune functioned as black endorsements for the Roosevelt administration's policies or plans, Park conferred integrity on the state's representation of black America through his participation.

War officials sought propaganda that asserted the value and belonging of African Americans as citizens, which they deemed important to efforts to recruit blacks to the war effort and to establish the nation's preeminence as the defender of freedom. They feared the effects of what one official termed "Divide and Conquer" propaganda that seized on the nation's race problem.[51] Well before it was clear the United States would be dragged into the war, federal authorities, including President Roosevelt, fixated on the "loyalty and devotion" of African Americans. Six months before Pearl Harbor, Roosevelt had barely prevented one hundred thousand African Americans from marching up to the capitol's doorstep in protest of the segregated armed forces and racial discrimination in the defense industries. How, then, to draft them to the cause at hand and present a united front to the rest of the world?

The leadership of the National Association for the Advancement of Colored People (NAACP) offered a solution. In the days immediately following Pearl Harbor, Walter White, executive secretary of the organization, contacted the Treasury Department about its depiction of blacks in its wartime materials. He explained that the NAACP's national office had received "a large number of complaints . . . regarding the omission from posters, murals, and other visual aids to the sale of Defense Bonds and

Stamps of Negro faces." As examples, he identified a mural in New York City's Grand Central Station and a poster that supposedly pictured children of the various races that "make up America." Neither included any black people. Those making the complaints, White said, did not consider this oversight a small matter. He insisted that the inclusion of blacks in the visual materials promoting the U.S. war effort was essential to "indicat[ing] that Negroes, too, are a part of America."[52] The head of the nation's largest civil rights organization inferred a correlation between the extent to which blacks could be expected to identify with the nation and its war and the state's visual representation of their position within U.S. society. The one African American on the FSA/OWI photography team, Parks had the opportunity and supposed capacity to satisfy White's demand with "true" images of black life more likely to engender goodwill and trust, and even patriotism and participation, among African Americans.

Parks's "authority" on black subjects also presented a liability, however. The South Side series, which documented black Chicagoans' experience of racial and economic oppression, visually indicted the nation's treatment of its black population. In Parks's hands, the camera became a weapon (as Parks always claimed it was), a means for documenting the adversity inherent to being black in the United States. His presumed insight concerning the subject matter only amplified the critique embedded in his photographs. His race photographs did not perform as statements of national strength; they testified to African Americans' strength in enduring their place within the nation. Discussions of Parks's membership to the FSA/OWI war-era photography team focus on his being African American, the only black photographer charged solely with producing propaganda. The greater significance lies in the seeming conflict between the objectives that he and the government held for his photography. How was he able to marry his proclaimed activist-artistic vision to the wartime mission of the FSA/OWI?

In fact, Parks's arrival at the FSA/OWI coincided with his growing conception of photography as a form of activism against "what [he] hated most about the universe: racism, intolerance, poverty."[53] He began to consider the political utility of his art in earnest while at the South Side Community Art Center, influenced by the example of artists who cycled through the space. The South Side series reflected this influence. No single source, however, compelled him more to identify and perform as an activist-artist than the photo-text *12 Million Black Voices: A Folk History of the Negro in the United States*. The collaboration of writer Richard Wright and white photographer Edwin Rosskam, picture editor for the FSA, this book provided a composite picture of African Americans' experiences—rooted as they were in slavery—as sharecroppers and tenant farmers, migrants, and urban dwellers. Like *You Have Seen Their Faces*, *Black Voices* offered a sustained commentary with its representation of the collective experience of a marginalized group. Similarly, it, too, accomplished this through narrative prose, black-and-white documentary photographs selected primarily from the FSA files, and selective captioning. Published by Viking Press in October 1941, this text became available just as Parks prepared to mount his show at the art center, the show that drew the attention of the FSA. To understand Parks's sense of himself as a photographer who used his camera as a weapon requires consideration of his relationship to Richard Wright's photo-text. For the remainder of his life, Parks identified this photo-text as a great influence on his approach to photography and, importantly, his thinking about race in America. Why this particular text?

Black Voices was not the first documentary project to represent the black experience. Many FSA photographs, in fact, featured African Americans, and in keeping with the New Deal documentary aesthetic, the poorer the better. In *You Have Seen Their Faces*, blacks figured prominently in Bourke-White's photographs of the sharecropping class: indeed, their omission would have resulted in a woefully inaccurate picture of sharecropping in the South. The combined effect of Bourke-White's photos and Caldwell's prose, however, reveals the problem of having two white artists represent black life and sentiment with the objective of spurring sympathy.

In the early pages of *You Have Seen Their Faces*, a photograph of a black woman sitting on wooden steps occupies roughly three-quarters of the 8¼″ × 11¼″ page (Figure 18). A young black girl sits to the woman's right, and a sleeping baby lies across her lap. The woman is large, and she wears a shapeless, simply patterned cotton housedress; her hair is parted and braided, as is the young girl's hair. All three are barefoot. Captured in full-body profile, with her jaw firmly set, the woman stares straight ahead, perhaps out on a field or road that stretched beyond her wood cabin; she looks neither happy nor solemn but contemplative. The young girl appears more open, as she has cracked a bit of a smile—at what, the viewer can only wonder. The baby's face is most visible due to the infant's position in the

Figure 18. *Ocelot Georgia*, Margaret Bourke-White, 1936. Photo © Estate of Margaret Bourke-White/Licensed by VAGA, New York, NY.

woman's lap, although half is darkened by the shadow cast by the woman's bosom. Dressed in a gown that appears bright white in the black-and-white photograph, the infant's dark, chubby limbs and face convey the relaxed tranquility of a child at rest in its mother's protective grasp. The photograph is cropped tight, placing the triad—their beings, thoughts, and relationships to one another—at the center of what the viewer can see, or imagine. The caption puts the following words in the woman's mouth: "I got more children now than I know what to do with, but they keep coming along like watermelons in the summertime."[54] At best, the sentiment suggests the woman is helpless to prevent herself from getting pregnant because, in her impoverished rural world, the medical interventions necessary are unavailable. Other interpretations come rushing in, however, fueled by stereotypical ideas of black women and men as oversexed and of blacks' fondness for watermelon. The subsistence nature of the scene seems obvious, but all else is open to interpretation. However, because the reader-viewer has been informed that Caldwell has imagined the thoughts for the woman pictured, the white ethnographic reading asserts itself.

When it came to the black sharecropping experience, *You Have Seen Their Faces* was the representation of "outsiders," which was true of noncommercial FSA products as well. Not a single African American numbered among Stryker's team of photographers during the New Deal era.[55] *Black Voices* was significant, therefore, as a vision of black life engineered by an African American that circulated through the popular form of the phototext. True, the book drew heavily on FSA photographs, so the literal picture it presented comprised visual units produced by nonblacks. Of the eighty-six photographs used, only one, supplied by Richard Wright, was the work of an African American. What distinguished this photo-text was that Wright had editorial control: he owned the image under construction.[56] Credited with "photo-direction," Rosskam selected photographs guided by Wright's text, to the extent that some crities objected to the "single-minded[ness]" with which he molded his selection to conform to the image Wright painted with his prose.[57] When one major newspaper tried to assign Rosskam the primary role in the book's production, he wrote a correction: "I was the pupil, he [Wright] the teacher."[58]

How was it that the black writer—rather than the white photographer and picture editor for the FSA—controlled the image presented by *Black Voices*? The answer is Wright's *Native Son*. Published in 1940, *Native Son* is the story of Bigger Thomas, a seething, twenty-year-old, black male whom readers first encounter in a cramped tenement on Chicago's South Side, where he has come to live by way of Mississippi, with his mother and two younger siblings. Besides his circumstances, readers immediately learn that Bigger is rageful, as evidenced by his beating a rat with a shoe after having killed it with a skillet. That anger performs as the lead character of Wright's novel, helping to explain how, as one review recounted, the young black man "managed within only seven days to threaten a playmate with a knife, kill the daughter of his white employer, bash in the head of his Negro girl . . . and finally earn the penalty of death."[59] White and black reviewers alike accepted the novel as a comment on the black American experience. And, rightly interpreting Bigger as signifying on U.S. race relations in a particular manner, they identified the murderously angry black man as a "symptom of the chronic malady" of American race prejudice and a warning of the psychosis lurking in a "large percentages of Negro youth" handicapped by "racial barriers and low social position."[60]

Native Son arrived on the literary scene when the "Negro problem"—a term used to reference various matters, including black oppression or black inferiority, depending on the point of view—was a choice topic of discussion within media, political, and scholarly circles. At the time, the United States was becoming steadily imbricated in the war against fascism and Nazism. President Roosevelt signaled the shift from noninterventionism with his 1941 State of the Union address, during which he declared that people all over the world had the right to the fundamental freedoms of speech and worship, and from want and fear, and committed U.S. resources—but for troops—to that cause. These circumstances compelled Americans to consider what blacks' experiences revealed about American democracy in practice, rather than in theory. For example, during the same period, Swedish sociologist Gunnar Myrdal conducted a massive study funded by the Carnegie Foundation that outlined the conflict between African Americans' social position and the "American creed," distributed publicly under the title *An American Dilemma*. These were the historical circumstances in which the publishing industry, critics, and the reading public embraced, or at least consumed, *Native Son* as a contribution to the conversation about this particular "problem," even though the novel performed as an indictment of American race relations.

Published by a major New York imprint and selected by the Book-of-the-Month Club as a main selection, *Native Son* found a wide audience, selling 215,000 copies in just three weeks.[61] Reviewers commented that Wright offered a portrait of black America that "only a Negro could have written."[62] They received Wright's image of black America as an inside perspective made possible by his cultural position and knowledge as a black man, which increased the book's power to make claims about black life and motivated its popularity. Wright's *Native Son* revealed a market for presumably "authentic" representations of black life.

After *Native Son*, Wright experienced an increased ability to traffic his interpretations of the black experience beyond literary and black circles, "dominating in op-ed columns, sociological conferences, and the literary field."[63] His presumed "second-sight" about black life and race matters placed him squarely in mainstream discourse spaces and he became a household name, a marketable name.[64] Viking Press, publisher of *You Have Seen Their Faces*, banked on that marketability and commissioned *Black Voices*. Wright came to the project most willingly. He was one of a number of writers who "scrambled" to attach their words to documentary images once Bourke-White and Caldwell demonstrated the narrative power and profits of doing so.[65] In addition, Wright had worked with photographers and photojournalists while working for the Federal Arts and Federal Writers' Projects and the leftist *Daily Worker*, which frequently featured the work of documentary photographers. Wright's experience of photojournalism impressed on him photographs' use beyond illustration: photographs had become, as a contemporary newspaper editor stated, a "*primary* means of conveying information" (emphasis in original).[66] For Wright, the camera and photography became additional tools for storytelling.

The story at the center of *Black Voices* was African American life from slavery through emancipation and sharecropping and the exodus to the North in the Great Migration. Wright applied the term *folk* to the black people at the center of his photo-book, as well as to their ways. He supplied no definition for the term, but it is implied by whom he excluded from his "folk history." He writes in the preface, "This text . . . intentionally does not include . . . those areas of Negro life which comprise the so-called 'talented-tenth,' or the isolated islands of mulatto leadership . . . or the growing and influential Negro middle class professional and businessmen."[67] Wright's folk are farmers and laborers, whom he calls the "debased feudal folk," and their culture, their way, is poverty; he chose to publicize their lives because they represented the "normality" of black life.[68]

Wright has been criticized for introducing into the marketplace a representation of black life composed of sweeping generalizations that do not account for change over time, let alone from person to person. Much of this criticism stems from his distinct use of the first person plural throughout the narrative: "Each day when you see us black folk . . . you usually take us for granted and think you know us, but . . . we are not what we seem."[69] With his use of "we," Wright took ownership of the picture he conjured, a portrait grounded in his personal experience as an African American who migrated from the rural South to the urban North and experienced poverty and racism in both places. With "we," he cast his lot with the "folk" and linked himself directly to the sentiments expressed, in contrast to Caldwell and Bourke-White. Critics, however, argue that the use of "we" reduced African Americans to the monolithic black masses, common in white treatments of black life. Some have found Wright's narrator-as-protagonist rhetorical choice as an "act of cultural suppression" in which he arrogantly substituted his voice for that of the collective.[70] Representation of a simplified, singular experience allowed for condescending interpretations of Wright's photo-text, such as that by the contemporary leftist newspaper *PM*: "This is what the Southern Negro sings when he feels blue."[71]

Wright's focus on collective experience in *Black Voices*, however, had particular significance in relation to immediate national and black political concerns. For one, the first person plural was politically in vogue and meant to signify Americans, as in "we Americans" versus them, the fascists and Nazis. This rhetorical turn in nationalist discourse blurred ethnic, racial, and economic lines in order to stress national unity. In this context, immigrants were brought into the fold, at least discursively, as evident in the radio program *Americans All . . . Immigrants All*.[72] Over the course of the narrative arc that Wright's prose formed, the conception of who "we" is shifts in manners that all emphasize the significance of how African Americans had experienced life in the United States. In reference to African Americans, "we" emphasizes a common experience of oppression, which draws attention to its systemic nature. When Wright refers to "us," "black or white," he evokes the democratic notion of "We the People" and "inserts African American experience into the midst of this seemingly inclusive core American identity."[73] By the end of *Black Voices*, Wright has flipped the script of mutual dependence popular among New Deal publicity, in which blacks' freedom was reliant on the recovery and dominance of the United States. Wright informs readers that blacks and their experiences "are a mirror of the manifold experiences of America. . . . If we black folk perish, America will perish."[74] Months after the book hit the market, this message took on new meaning when Japan's attack on Pearl Harbor catapulted the United States from its position of straddling the fence into the thick of World War II. Faced with the prospect of going to war for others' freedoms on behalf of a nation that failed to recognize theirs, African Americans held up full freedom at home as the cost for their loyalty and participation.

Like *Native Son*, and likely *because* of it, *Black Voices* was commercially successful. The book sold roughly three hundred thousand copies, which far outpaced the photo-text collaboration of writer James Agee and photographer Walker Evans, *Let Us Praise Famous Men*, published during the same period.[75] Critics, particularly white critics, fixed on the power of Wright's account, which they tied to its credibility as the account of a black man respected at that moment for his sociological grasp on black life and race in America. "I know of no other book," stated one radio personality, "that brings home as clearly to the white reader what it means to be a Negro."[76] With his photo-text, Wright carried forth his critique of race relations in the United States—which were responsible for the anger that fueled Bigger Thomas. *Black Voices* claimed to document the circumstances of systemic racism and poverty that gave birth to the "living personality" (versus the individual) of Bigger.[77] Wright explicitly indicts the "kitchenette"—broken-down, one-room tenements rented to African Americans at inflated costs—where readers first encounter Bigger in *Native Son*. "The kitchenette is our prison, our death sentence without a trial," he writes. "The kitchenette, with its filth and foul air, with its one toilet for thirty or more tenants, kills our black babies." "The kitchenette," he continues, "scatters death so widely among us that our death rate exceeds our birth rate." According to Wright, if the kitchenette did not kill its occupants, it changed them, and not for the better. "The kitchenette throws desperate and unhappy people into an unbearable closeness . . . producing warped personalities."[78] Photographs of this squalor and overcrowding accompany the text. *Native Son* had sown the market and whetted consumer appetites for the representation of black life that *Black Voices* presented, which anticipated Myrdal's finding that the "Negro problem," however defined, could be traced directly to white racism.[79]

Among African American readers, Wright's representation of a collective black experience countered the isolating, disempowering effects of racial oppression and provided a sense of a political identity to rally around. Ralph Ellison declared as much: "The book makes me feel a bitter pride; a pride which springs from the realization that after all the brutalization, starvation and suffering, we have begun to embrace the experience and master it. And we shall make of it a weapon more subtle, more effective than a fighter plane!"[80] Ellison's militaristic analogies drew attention to the two-fronted war African Americans faced at the time. The race pride and militancy *Black Voices* inspired in him reveal the text's function as a piece of propaganda engineered for a mixed audience. Writing for the *Nation*, Charles Curtis Munz declared, "The book is really . . . an appeal . . . a defiance, a demand, and a promise—and possibly even a threat . . . that Uncle Tom is finally dead and buried [and] the Negro . . . is determined to take what he regards as his proper place in the American scene."[81] Those who evaluated the book on its merits as a documentary record of black life objected strenuously to its exaggerations, emotionally loaded language, and forced pairings of text and photo. "His whole effort is to shock, touch, enrage his audience, as he was enraged," wrote one critic, "and he used any means to this end."[82] The assumption of this detractor appears to be that the provocative impulse of *Black Voices* is a failing on Wright's part, rather than evidence of his primary objective. Wright definitely wrote with an agenda: "One has to write cold and hard about black life in America," he explained, "and not allow whites to face the words with the consolation of a few tears."[83] He wrote *Native Son* under this belief. The novel about black life, however, did not engender the expectations for objective accuracy that a photographic representation of black life did. The use of documentary photographs implied the potential for the "real" picture, and some critics clearly felt he had not realized that potential. Wright went for the picture that no doubt struck him as "true."

Parks experienced *Black Voices* as propaganda: it worked on him as a provocative, "forceful" experience that moved him.[84] As he had with the photo-essay on migrant workers, he read *Black Voices* repeatedly. While the photo-essay of migrant workers had inspired him to pick up a camera, it was Wright's photo-text that awoke an activist sensibility within him.[85] In particular, the closing to *Black Voices* "flavored [Parks's] thoughts" about his place and purpose in the world: "The seasons of the plantation no longer dictate the lives of many of us. . . . We are with the new tide. . . . Men are moving! And we shall be with them."[86] The gendered interpretation and message of this passage, delivered in the book's "obviously male voice," resonated with Parks, who said it spoke directly to him and his circumstances, telling him that "black men were moving forward—and [he] should be moving with them."[87]

Interestingly, in his discussion of *Black Voices*, Parks consistently focuses on how the book reads or tells, rather than how it shows or documents. When he spoke of the photo-text, the photographer rarely discussed the photographs, and he never mentioned Rosskam. This omission is striking, given how the FSA images of migrant workers stayed with him and how FSA photographers engendered his great admiration. He saved his comments entirely for Wright and his prose. Parks viewed Wright as an activist working for black equality; he elevated the black writer to hero status based on his "daring" commentary on the hierarchies of race and class that relegated people of color to the bottom of the social ladder in the United States.[88] "Few whites who read it," Parks believed, "could escape their conscience."[89]

Although he saved his praise for Wright's words, photographs in *Black Voices* testified to black life as Parks had experienced and observed it. In contrast to previous photo-texts, Wright followed his black subjects out of the rural South and into the urban centers of the North. The photographs that accompanied Wright's narration about the effects of migration and urbanization on African Americans mirrored scenes that Parks documented with his South Side series, scenes he experienced while living in the region. The photo-text's visual representation, and recognition, of his reality no doubt contributed to his embrace of the text. The book inspired him "to keep [his] camera moving where it might do the most good."[90] And Wright's representation, and indictment, of systemic racism became the filter through which Parks saw the world around him. The influence of Wright's protest text is clearly evident in Parks's most famous photograph, *American Gothic* (Figure 19).

American Gothic features Ella Watson, a black charwoman who worked in the same DC government building as Parks.[91] In the photograph, Watson— a thin, bespectacled black woman with pressed, graying short hair and a

Figure 19. *American Gothic*, Gordon Parks, 1942. Library of Congress Prints and Photographs Division.

faded, polka-dot cotton dress—stands in front of a large American flag that hangs lengthwise on the wall behind her. The flag fills the upper half of the photograph and appears slightly out of focus. Photographed straight on, Watson stares directly into the camera, at the viewer, with a gaze that is tired but unflinching. She holds a broom, bristles up, in her right hand. A mop is propped, also head end up, just behind her left shoulder; at first glance it appears she holds the mop as well. In the visual tableau, the flag is an obvious symbol of the United States and American democracy. The mop and broom that frame Watson mark her as a member of the laboring, or service, class. The flag's distorted appearance makes it appear somewhat ethereal, as if it belongs to a world different from that of the woman standing before it, out of reach. As a whole, the image brings into focus Watson's included-excluded status in American society.

American Gothic constitutes an attempt by Parks to be intentionally propagandist with his FSA photography. Produced in August 1942, shortly after Parks joined the agency, the photograph had its roots in the jumble of disappointment and disillusionment he felt upon his arrival in the Jim Crow world of Washington, DC. Before his FSA appointment, Parks had lived and worked entirely in the North and Midwest and, as he told it, his life had been devoid of the repeated humiliations he experienced in DC. His experience of being black in the nation's capital fueled a hot anger within, which he channeled into his portrait of Watson. He modeled the photograph after the famous Grant Wood painting also titled *American Gothic*, which he had viewed on his many visits to the Chicago Art Institute.[92] With Wood's painting in mind, Parks positioned Watson in front of the vertically hung flag, placed a broom in her hand, and told her to stare directly into the camera while thinking about the racism she experienced. The resulting photograph, Parks acknowledged, was an extremely loaded and engineered representation of black life, and particularly black employment in the United States. Parks's closeness to the topic and current state of mind affected his art in such a way that his initial foray into the production of propaganda was quite heavy-handed.

In the many decades since Parks photographed Watson, scholars, critics, and curators have held up *American Gothic* as evidence of his oppositional use of photography.[93] No one furthered the notion of Parks as an activist photographer more than Parks himself, particularly in the five autobiographical works he penned during his lifetime. Reflecting on his photographic career, an elderly Parks explained that his desire to address "all sorts of social wrongs" inspired his career as a photographer: "I understood [the camera's] significance as a weapon against poverty and racism." He stated, "I had to have a camera."[94] This representation of Parks's photographic sensibilities and politics as a visual artist corresponds with knowledge of him as the man who documented segregation, photographed civil rights figures for *Life* magazine, and directed *Shaft* (1971), a seminal blaxploitation film that valorized militant black masculinity. The ready acceptance of Parks and his photography as oppositional, in the conventional or militant sense, however, has resulted in a failure to adequately incorporate or account for the propaganda he produced on behalf of the government while employed by the FSA and then the OWI during World War II. Parks's contrived photograph of Watson was more an aberration than a symbol of his wartime portfolio.

The blatant protest slant of *American Gothic* conflicted with the FSA's project to the point that Stryker deemed that it "[couldn't] be published."[95] Instead, the image was buried in the deep recesses of the FSA files and thereby prevented from tainting the official narrative of black life.[96] The image is lucky to have survived at all. In previous years, when Stryker was unsatisfied with a photograph—or frightened by it, as was supposedly the case with *American Gothic*—he "killed" it. In an act that Rosskam described as barbaric, Stryker punched holes directly through the primary subject matter of photographs, ensuring that there was no way to save the images with creative cropping for publishing.[97] Stryker ceased killing photographs in response to the strong objections of his photographers, but the practice indicates that he had particular ideas about the representations of Americans and American life that should emanate from his office, and he policed his photographers accordingly. Parks claimed to have sneaked *American Gothic* to a leftist newspaper that published it.[98] There is no evidence that the photograph was published at any point during the war. Nevertheless, Parks's assertion that he tried to get the photograph before the public illustrates his sense of himself as rebelling against the constraints of FSA visual politics and narrative boundaries.

In the context of war, however, little tolerance existed for those who pushed against the boundaries. Those who challenged the propagandist image of American democracy under construction had more to fear than a hole punch, as demonstrated by Wright's experience after the publication of *Black Voices*. With his photo-text, Wright drew attention to the healthy existence of racial and economic oppression, and its side effects.[99] In *Native Son*, he had defined blacks' position within the United States as one of acute *dis*belonging. However, the protagonist-antagonist, Bigger Thomas, was so disturbing, and thus fascinating, as a product of American society and U.S. relations that he blunted *Native Son*'s critique of both. In Wright's photo-text there was no angry black boogeyman to draw the critique. Wright clearly placed responsibility for the impoverished physical and emotional conditions the majority of blacks in the United States endured on white America and the federal government. He directly contradicted the narrative of "black-white unity in perilous times." "[African Americans] feel our hurts so deeply," he wrote, "we find it impossible to work with whites."[100]

The success of *Black Voices* troubled government authorities because Wright had a following across race lines among Americans. The photo-text offered these consumers a documentary record of "unimpeachable—because racialized—authenticity."[101] Perceptions of the book's authenticity inspired concern within government circles that *Black Voices* would inflame existing currents of black discontent. Black morale was a real problem at the outset of World War II. Antiblack racism on the domestic front, segregation within the armed forces, and discrimination in the war industries had many African Americans thinking, like Wright, that this was not their war. An OWI survey of blacks in the nation's cities revealed that the low morale among African Americans "[did] not stem from lack of patriotism, isolationist sentiment or any lack of enthusiasm for democratic values"; rather, it was the "direct result of the frustrations they experience[d] daily in their lives," including poor housing, unemployment, and Jim Crow policies.[102] In addition, African Americans felt little to no investment in the conflict abroad: they viewed it as a white man's war.[103] The government's own research corroborated the conditions and sentiments that Wright publicized. The problem, of course, was that he publicized them.

In 1942, under the direction of J. Edgar Hoover, the Federal Bureau of Investigation launched an investigation into Wright on the basis of his photo-text.[104] Reports generated by that investigation reveal that the FBI believed Wright attempted to foment ideas harmful to the "all out 'win the War' effort by America and her allies."[105] The portrait of black suffering and alienation Wright presented challenged federally approved representations of the United States and its citizenry that emphasized common ground and solidarity. Blacks were so removed from the rights and experiences of first-class American citizenship, Wright suggested, that some "ardently" rooted for the Japanese.[106] The government classified the act of highlighting anti-war or anti-America attitudes among African Americans as one of "sabotage" and investigated Wright for possible violation of sedition statutes (with no recognition of the irony that Wright had relied primarily on government propaganda [that is, FSA photographs] to formulate what the FBI deemed anti-American propaganda).[107] Notably, the FBI failed to investigate Rosskam for his contribution to *Black Voices*—further evidence that Wright was considered chief architect of this "folk history of the Negro" and that his race was of key importance regarding perceptions of the book's propaganda value.

At the very moment the FBI condemned *Black Voices*, Parks embraced it. Stryker's response to *American Gothic*, however, demonstrates that Parks could not have employed the protest element evident in that photograph and succeeded in the OWI: his skills as a documentary photographer would not have been sufficient, and they would not have excused his aberrations. Several questions arise. How did Parks reconcile his embrace of Wright's text with his responsibility as a photographer employed by the nation's top propaganda agency? How did Parks's representations of black life within American democracy, shaped as they were by Wright's subversive text, satisfy his activist-artist sensibilities and the federal government's wartime propaganda agendas? We can assume Parks did produce images that fit the federal propaganda bill, because when the FSA was abolished in 1942, Stryker chose Parks and a select handful of other FSA photographers to make the move with him to the OWI.[108]

Scholarship concerning African Americans and photography consistently frames black use of the medium as primarily oppositional, which corresponds to recognition of blacks' historical photographic objectification.[109] This analytical impulse suggests a framework in which blacks figure either as victims of the dominant class's photographic practices or as visual activists who use photography to disrupt dominant visual representations of blackness. Parks was a key contributor to the state's depiction of American democracy. He does not, then, fit neatly into conventional frameworks that construct black uses of photography primarily in terms of resistance, despite his repeated identification as an activist-minded visual artist. The photographs Parks produced as a member of the FSA/OWI photography unit prompt a both-and consideration of the black uses of photography. His photographic representations envisioned African Americans in manners that interrogated the ideas fueling their oppression precisely because they presented life within the democratic United States in accordance with official representation guidelines.

In his role as a federal photographer, Parks had to adopt his vision to FSA/OWI narrative and political objectives. Initially, Stryker allowed, even encouraged, Parks to experiment with both form and subject because, as an intern, his photographs had no assigned purpose, so he was afforded relative "free rein," which resulted in *American Gothic*.[110] But, to train the green intern, Stryker insisted that Parks pore over the FSA files. "It was my daily chore when I first went there," Parks said, "to look at all the pictures . . . study them and imprint them on my own conscious."[111] This visual orientation also impressed on Parks his role within a much larger project and clarified the hierarchal relationship between his vision and the FSA's project.[112] His retrained eye is evident in the subsequent photographs Parks produced of Watson after he startled Stryker with the rather bombastic *American Gothic*. These ensuing photographs follow Watson out of the workplace into her social and home life. They document her poverty and segregation as a black woman raising her daughter's two illegitimate children on, as Parks reported, "a salary hardly suitable for one person."[113] Compared to *American Gothic*, however, these photographs sever Watson's circumstances from her relationships with whites and her work as a government employee. They conformed to the FSA tradition of using documentary images to illuminate social problems and needs, rather than responsible parties. This series of photographs did not comment explicitly on white discrimination against blacks or the government's discriminatory employment practices, a particularly hot topic given that the recently established Fair Employment Practices Committee was, at that very moment, advocating fair employment of blacks within the defense industries. With his follow-up photographs to *American Gothic*, Parks demonstrated an understanding of FSA narrative boundaries.

Over the next year, Parks accommodated these boundaries to produce depictions of black life, which presented a challenge while he was centered in Washington, DC, which journalist Alden Stevens described as a "blight on democracy." "Negroes who have lived in many parts of the country," Stevens explained, "say that nowhere else in America is there such bitter mutual race hatred."[114] This had certainly been Parks's experience of the city. Generally, black life in DC mirrored the impoverished black experience he had observed on Chicago's South Side, but with the added challenge of Jim Crow. During his time in DC, Parks documented scenes that Wright could have used appropriately to illustrate his interpretation of the perils of urbanization for African Americans. The images he captured of black suffering in the capital of the democratic United States reflect Parks's continuing impulse to use his camera as a weapon against social injustice—or at least to gather evidence for that fight.

While he certainly witnessed and documented hardship, Parks produced photographs that satisfied expectations of him as a federal propagandist. While he toured the city's black sections, he took multiple photographs of "everyday" African Americans. Many are close-ups of blacks whom Parks clearly persuaded to halt their activities so that he could photograph them. Parks posed his subjects in manners that conferred on them a dignified air and highlighted their communal role: a firefighter shoulders a hose, a delivery driver leans out the window of his truck, a construction worker carries a coil of rope, a mechanic holds a gas nozzle, a security guard stands post, and students carry books. Although constructed as individual portraits, the collective constituted an archive of blacks' civic belonging within an American community (albeit a black community), as well as their embrace of the responsibilities they had to that community.

In DC, Parks produced a photographic series in 1942 that depicted black life in the city's then-brand-new Frederick Douglass housing project that especially asserted African Americans' belonging as normative and even quintessentially "American." This series included pictures of, as the captions state, a "mother watching her children as she prepares the evening meal," a "father of three shaving while his wife prepares dinner," a "family saying grace before the evening meal," "boys playing leapfrog," and a "dance group" of little black girls with bows in their hair who are wearing short, bright white dresses and striking various ballet poses (Figure 20).[115] These photographs signaled blacks' embrace of values and activities associated with middle-class family life, which at that very moment was solidifying as the ideal representative of life in the democratic United States.

One photograph from Parks's Frederick Douglass series appeared in a large-format OWI booklet entitled *Negroes and the War*, which purported to tell "the important contributions [of African Americans], in all fields, to

Figure 20. *Dance Group, Frederick Douglass Housing Project, D.C.*, Gordon Parks, 1942. Library of Congress Prints and Photographs Division.
Figure 21. *Mother and Daughter, Frederick Douglass Housing Project*, Gordon Parks, July 1942. Library of Congress Prints and Photographs Division.

the fighting of the war." The photograph pictures a young, light-skinned, black mother seated on the edge of a tub, holding her toddler daughter in her lap while she carefully washes the young girl's fingers with a cloth (Figure 21). Mother and daughter are both smiling gaily and each is dressed in appropriately feminine clothes from head to toe: a big floppy bow adorns the little girl's hair. Although cropped for publication, in addition to the stylishness of the subjects, the photograph clearly displays the modern elements of their bathroom, which boasts a tub, a sink with gleaming fixtures, a medicine cabinet, and a toilet complete with a fabric toilet seat cover that matches the bath mat and the curtains decorating the room's large window. In the published photograph, these symbols of middle-class living become the backdrop to the mother and daughter, who take up more space in the cropped image. The portrait of maternal care asserts black modernity and normality, in addition to the government's commitment to better living for African Americans. The photograph satisfied federal propaganda needs as intended, but it also functioned as useful propaganda for black equality campaigns.

The Frederick Douglass photographs are void of any white presence. They do not, however, construct their subjects as segregated blacks confined to federally funded housing. Because these photographs focus on domestic, familial spaces, they read as if they were framed to zoom in on life in these private spaces, rather than to crop out external forces that might paint a different picture. With his focus on nuclear black families, domestic rituals, and happy, healthy children, Parks created a picture of black life that adhered to the "official" narrative of American democracy and its promise. These photographs suggested that, despite Jim Crow and racism, African Americans thrived in the United States. Moreover, these photographs pictured African Americans conforming to traditional gender roles, which helped to counter or contain the cultural shifts, and anxieties, fueled by women's wartime recruitment into the workforce, and to combat prevalent stereotypes about black familyhood.

The Frederick Douglass housing series, in particular, demonstrates how Parks worked within FSA/OWI representational boundaries to promote definitions of blackness that challenged African Americans' inferior social position. With the series, he injected blacks into the nationalist portrait, in manners that both served federal image campaigns and advanced African Americans' "true" Americanness through their embrace of uniquely "American" values, practices, and things. OWI administrators had feared the consequences of excluding African Americans from the wartime "American story" under construction; Parks helped bring them into frame and into focus as patriotic Americans.

Parks was by no means the only federal photographer charged with portraying black life or African Americans' participation in the war effort—as discussed previously, he was not even the only black federal photographer doing so. As one of the scant few black federal photographers, however, Parks focused largely on black subject matter.[116] Stryker dispatched all of his photographers, including Parks, to community and military training centers, as well as shipyards, oil refineries, steel mills, and factories, to photograph Americans at work in the nation's defense industries.[117] He relied especially on Parks, however, to access black spaces, as Parks had when he followed Watson "into her home, her church and wherever she went" for several weeks.[118]

Photography historians have observed that the intimacy between Parks and his subjects is evident in the images he created: it distinguished his documentary photographs. His ability to gain the trust of those he photographed allowed him "close-in, low-angle shooting" that created a sense of immediacy for the viewer.[119] In this sense, Parks brought his studio experience to the job of documenting black Americans during World War II. The combined aesthetics are particularly evident in his photograph *Welder Trainee* (Figure 22), which Parks produced on assignment at the National Youth Administration (NYA) Production Training Center located at Bethune-Cookman College.[120] Pictured from midtorso up, the NYA trainee is wearing a jumpsuit of heavy denim. Her arms are crossed over her midsection, with her hands and forearms completely hidden by the huge protective gloves she is wearing. Her welder's mask is tilted back, fully exposing her face, which boasts the smoothness of youth. The woman's face, and particularly her smile, which is wide enough to provoke two dimples and reveal two rows of perfectly straight, bright white teeth, is the photograph's compositional center. Although the young woman does not look directly into the camera, at the viewer, the openness of her face, exaggerated by Parks's shooting her from below, invites a viewing relationship through which the viewer learns how to interpret the image before him or her and the world beyond it. Herein lay the value of documentary

Figure 22. *Welder Trainee*, Gordon Parks, January 1943. Library of Congress Prints and Photographs Division.

photography, which Parks's experience with portraiture amplified. In *Welder Trainee*, the young woman's work gear and the industrial setting combine with her smile to construct her as an enthusiastic participant in the war effort. The image performs as a uniquely attractive representation of the cross-cultural unity the OWI strived to promote.

The stark difference in perspective and tenor between this photograph and the grim, straight-on portrait of *American Gothic* speaks to how Parks adjusted his photographs to accommodate his employer's vision, which became decidedly more prescriptive once the FSA came under the OWI and became a war propaganda operation. John Vachon, a former FSA photographer who, like Parks, also made the transfer to the OWI, resented the new directive to photograph "always the happy American worker." The resulting pictures, he said, "began to look like those from the Soviet Union."[121]

Welder Trainee and its state-approved message transmitted louder and wider than most OWI black propaganda. In 1943 the national magazine *U.S. Camera* published Parks's photograph in its annual edition.[122] Entitled *The U.S.A. at War*, the publication features over two hundred photographs, and the picture of the NYA trainee appears opposite another Parks photograph, one featuring a white male welder whom Parks photographed while creating a documentary series of the defense industry in New Britain, Connecticut. The accompanying text unites the two photographs and incorrectly (but perhaps intentionally) identifies the female welder as employed at the same factory as her white male counterpart pictured on the opposite page. The "story" presented by the images and their captions belied the black female welding student's actual relationship to the white male or the defense industry. In reality, she operated in the segregated black space of the NYA training camp on a black college campus, and there is no evidence that she found wartime employment as a welder. Denied this perspective, the reader received the images as evidence of interracial participation and cooperation. The text and the juxtaposed photographs, in other words, manage what neither image can accomplish on its own since, individually, each actually records racial separation. Combined, Parks's welder images performed as the propaganda that they were and propped up narratives of a nation of unified citizens who enthusiastically supported the promise (if not the experience) of American democracy in its storied form. Presented as it was with Parks's white welder photograph, *Welder Trainee* also literally brought African Americans (and women) into the picture of the United States at war.[123] The image constituted a common civil rights strategy in which African Americans offered up evidence of blacks soldiering or at work in the defense industries to claim their full citizenship rights as, to use Walter White's words, "an integral part of the civilization of our country."[124]

During the war, the NAACP's national office publicized African Americans' war work through photographs in its official organ, the *Crisis.* For example, when the sheer manpower needs gave birth to the Tuskegee

Airmen in 1941, the magazine began to feature cover images and photo-essays that chronicled the activities of black air cadets, gunners, and infantry soldiers (Figure 23). The photographs themselves depicted primarily black men, generally in uniform, saluting, loading machine guns, repairing plane engines, engaging in target practice, marching in formation, riding horses, driving jeeps, staring at girlfriends' pictures in their bunks, sitting in airplane cockpits, reading letters from home, and playing baseball while stationed in locations such as Italy, France, India, and Guadalcanal. Individually, and as an archive, these images put the lie to dominant ideas that defined war service as the privilege and work of whites and soldiering, in particular, as the domain of white men. These representations of black patriotism and participation differed from those that Parks created in that the NAACP explicitly politicized them through editorials that outlined discriminatory policies and practices that frustrated African Americans trying to answer the call to serve. Nevertheless, placed in a mainstream, national magazine, Parks's *Welder Trainee* performed the same function of claiming black citizenship to an audience much larger than that of the already convinced NAACP membership who received the *Crisis*.

Welder Trainee and the *Crisis*'s depictions of blacks at war inferred that "Negroes, too, are a part of America" on the basis of their role as defenders of democracy at home and freedom the world over.[125] These images contrasted with the representations in Parks's *American Gothic* and Wright's *12 Million Black Voices*, which emphasized African Americans' separation (indeed, segregation) within U.S. society and alienation from aspirational, inclusive concepts like the "American dream." The "American way of life," as constructed by federal agencies (and increasingly characterized by freedom from want), completely lacked the kinds of photographs and imaging that Wright deployed in his "folk history."

Shortly after the war ended, Parks gave an interview in which he said that his time with the FSA/OWI taught him "to underscore tragedy and subtly emphasize the hypocrisy of the words 'free and equal.'"[126] Photographs such as *Welder Trainee*, his DC portraits, and the Frederick Douglass housing series seemingly contradict this statement. In their documentation of black life, these photographs toed the approved official narrative line as images that obscured racism, emphasized unity and patriotism, and implied blacks in America had opportunities equal to those of their white counterparts. These images are not explicit indictments of

20 Pages of Army Pictures

The CRISIS

February, 1942   •   Fifteen Cents

AIR CADET MAC ROSS

Photo by U. S. Army Signal Corps

Figure 23. Photograph of air cadet Mac Ross, cover of the *Crisis*, February 1942. Photo credit, U.S. Army Signal Corps.

systemic racism like those found in Wright's *Black Voices*, which Parks referred to as his "catechism" at the time.[127]

Parks could not escape the "national mythologies in which documentary photography was enmeshed . . . mythologies not altogether realized in the consciousness of the photographer."[128] As a result, his photographs were co-opted to institutional agendas. Ripped from their context, or considered individually, Parks's FSA/OWI photographs suggest he abandoned his activist sensibilities concerning black freedom in service of the narrative expectations imposed by his role as a federal photographer and propagandist. As creator, however, Parks had the perspective to view his oeuvre as a complete portfolio. Within his mind's eye, his South Side series, *American Gothic, Welder Trainee*, and the Frederick Douglass housing series existed alongside one another. Taken as a collection, his documentary photographs captured the diversity of experiences among African Americans, but also the commonalities of a black experience shaped by racism. His photographs that documented life in Chicago's and DC's black slums condemned the conditions, not the people suffering them; his images of African Americans striving for a middle-class lifestyle in the Frederick Douglass development challenged prevalent racist notions about the civilization and morality of blacks. The composite portrait of black life that Parks created exposes the disparity between African Americans' contributions to and their experience of democracy in the early 1940s. Parks's total body of work to that point makes visible the limited and contingent nature of the government's recognition, and representation, of African Americans as "integral"—to use Walter White's word—members of American society.[129] His wartime photographs represented black life in the United States as it should be, *if* the state delivered on the core principle of "freedom for all" and rights promised by virtue of American citizenship.

Coming after and compared to *Black Voices*, Parks's FSA/OWI work appears less radical and definitely less oppositional. His responsibilities as a federal photographer and his visionary representation politics compelled a different rendering from Parks from that of his hero. Moreover, Wright's case demonstrated the consequences of contradicting the government's representation of black life, particularly in a historical moment when the propaganda value of such representations raised the stakes. Based on his representation of black life, the FBI concluded that Wright carried a "complete disapproval of the 'American way of life.'" The FBI investigated him throughout the war and determined that he was even more "radical and militant with respect to the advancement of the Negro" than the Communist Party. In agreement with this assessment, the Selective Service Board classified Wright unfit to serve because his "interest in the problem of the Negro" was such that it constituted "severe psycho-neurosis."[130] In other words, according to the U.S. government, Wright's interpretation of the black American experience made him crazy. Threatened and censored for his interpretation of black life in America, Wright opted out of the "American way of life" that he had continually called into question, and moved to Paris, permanently.

For Parks, the vision and credibility he developed while he produced black propaganda for the government during the war became his ticket to financial success and renown as a photographer. In 1945 he followed Stryker to the Standard Oil Company to become one of eleven principal photographers on the New Jersey Standard Oil Photography Project. Revelations about the oil company's secret dealings with German enterprises during the war had tarnished its reputation among the American public. The photography project was a massive public relations effort on behalf of the corporation to rehabilitate its image through visual testimony to the importance of oil to Americans' everyday lives. To that end, Stryker instructed Parks and other photographers, many of whom had worked for the FSA, to document how "oil seeped into every joint" of America.[131] How far had Parks strayed? Drawn to photography for its social justice function as much as its storytelling function, he turned to the documentary form to record, or expose, deplorable living conditions among Chicago's poor blacks. After a short stint as an FSA/OWI photographer, he then became a propagandist for a "bastion of corporate capitalism.[132]

Parks symbolized racial progress as the only black photographer on the "largest photographic documentation project undertaken in America by anyone other than the federal government."[133] As a corporate photographer, he enjoyed a "high-paying contract" that allowed him to move his family into an interracial, middle-class neighborhood in White Plains, New York.[134] His two children, Parks said, had suffered in Chicago and DC after having experienced the green lawns of Minnesota. "A home in the suburbs seemed the only answer," he explained. Officially suburbanites, the Parkses lived in a Tudor-style home, owned two cars, and enjoyed the "well-bred congeniality" of white and Jewish neighbors.[135] Parks had both experienced and documented the effects of segregation and poverty on African Americans' ability to realize "the American dream." Then, once able, he actualized for his own family that dream, which his wartime propaganda had claimed for African Americans.

The trajectory that took Parks from Chicago's South Side to White Plains, New York, tracked his seemingly apolitical turn as a photographer on the Standard Oil photography project. His new perspective, born out of his economic stability and occupational responsibilities, worked its way into images he produced in the immediate postwar period—and it did not go unnoticed. Within black circles, critics accused Parks of "forgetting his people and his function as a reporter-critic of the larger aspects of life" and suggested that, as a Standard Oil representative, his "contribution to better race relations stems more from his good-humored, good looking presence in that office and in the field than from his . . . pictures."[136] A black photographer employed (and paid handsomely) by a for-profit organization to take photographs of nonblack subjects, Parks decreased in value as a documentarian among African Americans (but still had value as a representation of black success). He had, in today's parlance, sold out. His situation spoke to the dissonance between "the black experience" and "the American dream": in moving closer to the latter, the presumption was that he no longer represented or could accurately portray the former. To separate the man or his image products into tidy categories, or phases of purpose and performance, however, obscures a complex convergence of key dynamics that shaped the postwar period, a convergence traceable through Parks's photographs.

As part of the Standard Oil project, Parks took a photograph of a smiling black man, presumably a Standard Oil employee, who wore a railroad-type cap and a heavy, denim-like collared shirt (Figure 24). The narrowness of frame makes it difficult to determine what is behind him, but large rivets and hinges visible in the photograph suggest it is a large piece of machinery (requiring oil, of course). In form, content, and attitude, the photograph is reminiscent of the picture Parks produced as an FSA/OWI photographer of the female NYA welding trainee. In 1950 Parks's Standard Oil version of black workerhood found its way into *Ebony* magazine, the popular and commercially successful black photo-magazine published by Johnson Publishing (Parks's pictures routinely showed up in *Ebony* during the postwar decade).[137] The photograph accompanied an editorial entitled "The 15 Outstanding Events in Negro History." In this context, the picture served as an example of what *Ebony* deemed "the New Negro," who, the caption read, with his "newly-won political power" and "industrial skills," took charge and challenged the Jim Crow way of life—North and South. The caption for this visualization of the trope of black progress declared that this new class of black American "demonstrated conclusively his capacity for freedom and today stands at the threshold of new heights."[138]

This same photograph, originally taken to serve Standard Oil's public relations objectives and then used by *Ebony*, next found its way into a 1951

Figure 24. *Railroad Worker,* Gordon Parks, circa 1947. *The Negro in American Life,* circa 1951, United States Information Agency.

pamphlet produced by the United States Information Agency entitled *The Negro in American Life.* This propaganda booklet represents the U.S. government's attempt to counteract propaganda circulated by the Soviet Union regarding antiblack racism in the United States through the propagandist presentation of American democracy as the only context that "made reconciliation and redemption possible."[139] Appearing on the inside of the pamphlet's front cover, the image of the smiling black man is the first narrative note, after the title, in the booklet's story of the black American experience.[140] In the *Ebony* photo-essay, the photo furthered an ideal that tied African Americans' advancement to their own perseverance and abilities; in the government pamphlet, it affirmed a story of black progress, and the pursuit of happiness, made possible by American democracy and encouraged by enlightened Americans. The point here is that the same photographic representation of black employment served corporate, government, and black narratives of the black experience in the United States, which indicates an overlap in political and representational strategies, if not agendas.

Scholars generally gloss over the moment when Parks moved from the world of nonprofit, publicity-propaganda photography to the commercial realm. A conscious move on his part, this transition contradicts the conventional perception of Parks as a radical intervention in photography, in his person and his images. In overlooking this, scholars appear to follow cues issued by the man himself. In the postwar years, Parks mounted a campaign to reform or, more accurately, reestablish his public image as a black photographer of black people and things. In 1946, presumably to combat criticisms of his alignment with Standard Oil, he announced his plans to infiltrate a Harlem gang to produce a photo-study of African American juvenile delinquents, or, as he called them, "good, poor kids gone wrong." He publicized the project in the pages of *Ebony*. "Wait and see," he promised.[141]

Parks delivered the photo-study of gang life in Harlem in 1948. Rather than *Ebony*, however, it appeared in *Life* magazine. In fact, Parks lobbied hard to have the photo-essay appear in the large, mainstream, white magazine. The resulting ten-page photo-essay, entitled "Harlem Gang Leader," documented the drama-filled, violent existence of Leonard "Red" Jackson and his gang, the Midtowners, as they jockeyed for control of the streets. The piece ran in the November 1, 1948, issue of *Life*. In its introduction to the essay, the magazine traded on notions of the racialized vision that provided Parks's special insight into, and therefore access to, the black world of Harlem. Parks's byline described him as "a young Negro photographer who won Red Jackson's confidence." Through *Life*, his depiction of black urban masculinity reached 22.5 million consumers. The response generated by "Harlem Gang Leader" demonstrated the continued currency of black-authored portraits of black life, with one reader identifying it as "the best sociological study of [the] magazine's career."[142]

Parks had little control over his Harlem images once they moved from the creative process and became consumer products or simply pictures consumed by others. He envisioned that he would use his camera to show the "home background" of his Harlem subjects, which would, "by inference, show the way out of juvenile crime to any social agency which wants to wipe it out."[143] Here, Parks expressed an activist sensibility similar to that which had fueled him as a documentarian on Chicago's South Side. His chosen vehicle for distributing his social commentary, however, undermined representation of his black subjects as *of* America, in the manner his FSA/OWI photographs had. Framed as they were by the magazine's editors, the black subjects of his first *Life* photo-essay read as "a social problem of some complexity, but not as complex human beings."[144] In the pages of a popular magazine targeted at a wide audience, the black gang members fell too easily into stereotype as the scary, black criminals that the majority of America had been primed to believe they were. Much as did the FSA photographers Parks so admired and then joined, he strove for a particular representation of a particular black experience that commented on society in a particular manner; but de- and recontextualized as his images were in *Life*, his vision underwent significant revision. Had he produced the photo project for *Ebony* and its black reader-viewers, perhaps the commentary and instruction he intended would have transmitted clearly. That he did not speaks to his ambitions.

As he attests to in his autobiographies, Parks pitched the Harlem story to *Life* because he desired to work for that magazine in particular. After the demise of the FSA and OWI, *Life* reigned as the preeminent source for photo-journalistic and documentary photography; thus, working for the magazine was the gold standard for photographers. Parks realized his goal. The Harlem essay distinguished him as a photographer who could, as another *Life* photographer said, present portraits of black life that "no white photographer could."[145] In 1948 he became the magazine's first black staff photographer and transitioned from propagandist, public relations work to commercial photography. In this new role, he produced representations of black life—among various other subjects—for a magazine whose success lay in its ability (and promise) to satisfy consumers' voyeuristic desires, rather than its function as a tool of social reform or justice.

However.

The lead photograph in "Harlem Gang Leader" constitutes a compli-cated visual event in the history of African Americans' popular media representation (Figure 25). The photograph, approximately three-quarters the size of the large *Life*-size page, is a profile shot of Red Jackson. Cloaked half in shadow, the man-boy stares out the broken window of an abandoned building as a cigarette juts from his mouth. Through spaces where glass should be, the viewer can see the facade of a multistoried, brick apartment building across the street. The scene outside the window is out of focus, which makes that world appear further removed, less available to Jackson. The photo's caption reveals that Parks has captured Jackson hiding out from a rival gang. "Trapped," the text reads, "Red Jackson ponders his next move." The photograph appears on the left-hand page, opposite the open-ing text of the piece, which declares, "Red Jackson's life is one of fear, frus-tration and violence." This photograph is imposed on a two-page spread that pictures Harlem—"under . . . smoke and haze"—against a backdrop of the grand, sky-reaching buildings of Columbia University and "elegant apartments of some of the city's leading citizens." The juxtaposition highlights the seclusion but also, more profoundly, the isolation of the seventeen-year-old gang leader. In locale and circumstance, Jackson ap-pears stuck, static, cut off. Contrary to the caption, however, he seems any-thing but trapped. That is, he betrays no sign of fear; nor does he seem to be pondering. While he looks alert, what strikes the viewer is his sem-blance of calm despite his dangerous situation. He is waiting, and the lack of affect on his face gives him a fatalistic air that suggests he understands death is as likely as escape; moreover, the photograph suggests the synonymy of the two outcomes.[146]

As a portrait of black urban masculinity, Parks's photograph of Jack-son reflects the blending of the activist-artist vision that characterized the documentary images he produced of black life on the South Side with the character-driven propagandist portraits that defined much of his FSA/OWI work. If readers dismissed Jackson as a street tough, troubled youth, or confirmation of stereotypical blackness, they failed to see the social com-mentary that echoed in Parks's portrait of developing, urban black mascu-linity. Given the influence that Wright had on his sensibilities, it is perhaps no surprise that, with his portrait of Jackson, Parks offered a visual image of the problem-in-person that Wright had authored almost a decade ear-

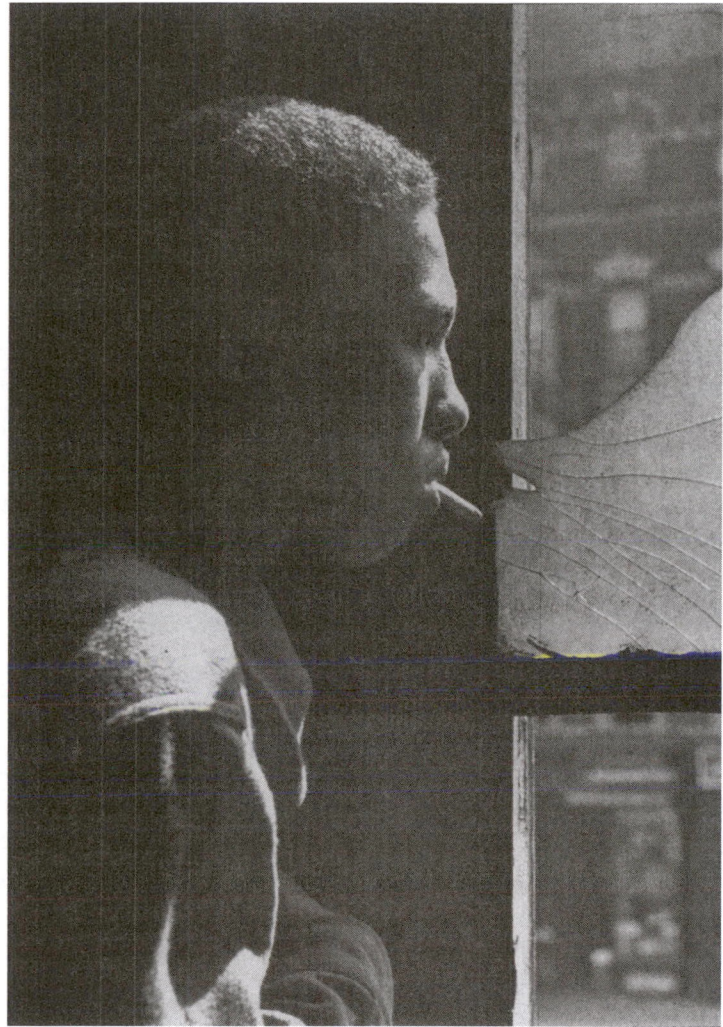

Figure 25. *Harlem Gang Leader "Red" Jackson*, Gordon Parks, 1948. © 1948 Time Inc. All rights reserved.

lier. More than a few *Life* readers must have recognized Bigger Thomas when they saw him.

The ways in which Wright and Parks portrayed black life in the World War II era reflect their different objectives and obligations as image-makers. Each produced propagandist images of black life intended to communicate or comment on the positions African Americans inhabited within U.S. society and their experiences of and contributions to American democracy. Published before U.S. entry into World War II, Wright's photo-text belonged to the New Deal—if not temporally, then at least stylistically—in which the propaganda function of documentary photography was social commentary. Federal agendas during the New Deal era required photographs that exposed aspects of American life. The purpose of the New Deal FSA was, as Stryker stated, to "introduc[e] America to Americans."[147] During the Depression, middle-class Americans, and certainly politicians comfortably ensconced in their DC offices, had little reason to encounter the rural poor, and therefore little reason to consider or care for them. FSA photographs knocked down barriers forged of ignorance, prejudice, and neglect between the classes to reveal the hardships and humanity of the nation's working poor. The propaganda needs of a war against racism and fascism were different from those of a war against poverty. The purpose of the FSA/OWI was to sell America to Americans and, at times, the rest of the world. In this context, U.S. officials squashed representations that functioned as critiques of the United States, its government, its people, or its principles, as Stryker had with *American Gothic*. War officials sought images of African Americans that belied their position as second-class citizens who endured de jure, de facto, and violent racial discrimination. Representations of black inferiority undermined efforts to recruit Americans—especially African Americans—to the war effort, encourage unity, achieve and demonstrate national preparedness, and counter accusations about the validity, let alone the supremacy, of the United States as a free nation.

The propaganda needs of World War II allowed for, and even required, representations of blackness that asserted African Americans' equality through records of their patriotism, industriousness, diversity, morality, and aspirations. As war propaganda, these images infiltrated popular visual culture as state-sponsored challenges to conceptions of black inferiority and *dis*belonging. World War II marks an unprecedented moment in U.S. history when federal and black image politics aligned such that the government compelled representations of black citizenship in accordance with the expectations of the nation's black citizens. These circumstances presented openings for an increasing number of visual images of blackness—created by blacks and nonblacks—that defined African Americans away from stereotype and drew blacks into the body politic as normal, important American citizens. These circumstances reflected and also drove the imagemaking of African Americans like Parks who gained access to mainstream media channels. When Parks did finally meet his hero Wright (shortly before the author exiled himself to Europe), the man who had so profoundly inspired and directed his photography autographed a copy of *Native Son* for him. Wright's inscription, which Parks "cherished," simultaneously highlighted the overlap of their political sensibilities as African American (men) and the difference between the politics of representation they employed on behalf of those sensibilities. Consciously echoing the closing paragraph of *Black Voices*, Wright wrote, "To one who is moving with the tide."[148]

Chapter 3

Selling Progress: Liberia and the Early Cold War Trade in Black Markets

By all ye will or whisper, by all ye leave or do,
your black Liberian Brothers will weigh your God and you.

—Rayford Logan, 1946

The ties between Negroes in the United States and the
citizens of Liberia are great.

—Moss H. Kendrix, 1946

Like Gordon Parks, Moss Hyles Kendrix came out of World War II desirous to transition from not-for-profit propagandist publicity work into commercial business. And his ability to do so depended greatly on his experience and reputation as a federal propagandist, as Parks's did. There was not, however, a clear path to his career of choice. Kendrix's ambition was to own and operate his own public relations firm, through which he would direct clients' appeals to black constituencies, in particular. Few African Americans had managed to do this. The small number of black marketers at the time worked within the few large corporations that had an eye on black consumers. Kendrix balked at this arrangement. By war's end, he had overseen large, successful public relations campaigns. These experiences gave him the taste for autonomy and the confidence to seek it. While he imagined a different model for his public relations career, he did view black consumerism as the foundation on which to build that model. His business plan was uniquely tailored for the circumstances and concerns that emerged with reconversion and the nascent Cold War.

During the Depression years and World War II, the state, business organizations, and other cultural institutions had defined Americans in terms of civic involvement, work, and service—whether in the form of volunteerism, participation in New Deal and other government initiatives or the defense industries, or active duty in the armed services. Conceptions of citizenship rooted in sacrifice and national obligations reflected the discourses of responsibility motivated by economic crisis and then war. Priorities shifted, however, when the war ended and the United States entered a period of reconversion and consuming Americans surpassed civically engaged Americans in their value to the nation's strength and security. Coming out of the war, Americans feared the economy might stumble back into depression. In fact, they were told to expect it. The assumption was that the "shock of de-stimulus" brought on by military and economic demobilization would have dire consequences for the U.S. economy.[1] In August 1945 the Office of War Mobilization and Reconversion predicted eight million would be unemployed within a year of the war's end. One day before Japan's official surrender, *Business Week* warned that the gross national product would fall to 20 percent below the 1944 levels.[2] These were rational fears shaped by the Keynesian principles that had ruled the day since the economic collapse of the previous decade. In hindsight, they were largely unwarranted, but at the time they had great purchase. Of that moment, the founder of *Kiplinger* magazine, Austin Kiplinger, remembered, "Nobody could remember what 'normal' had been. The national mood was one of great uncertainty."[3] And, immediately after the war's end, the nation did slip into a recession as government spending decreased by over $50 billion (the equivalent of approximately $644 billion in 2018 dollars).[4] In this context, consumerism took on great importance. In lieu of massive government spending, Americans themselves inherited the job of both ensuring and demonstrating capitalism's supremacy as an economic-political system after more than a decade of massive government assists fueling its viability.

Since early 1942, Americans had been required to ration basic goods, such as butter, sugar, canned milk, nylons, shoes, and gasoline, in addition to those items that made life easier or more enjoyable, including cars, refrigerators, vacuum cleaners, washing machines, sewing machines, typewriters, phonographs, and radios. With the war over, U.S. industry, which had been conscripted to the war effort (from animation studios to car manufacturers), reconverted to the production of consumer goods, and the restraints were off when it came to consumption. So, while many worried about recession, others rejoiced in a consumer market and industry freed up for the business of unfettered consumer capitalism. The U.S. consumer market of the immediate postwar moment, and its potential, was of primary interest at home and abroad, and it became a site on which postwar foreign relations were negotiated. State officials and private interests promoted democracy, capitalism, and mass consumerism as the ultimate realization of civilization and the way of the future. These circumstances provided new opportunities for aspiring capitalists and marketers in the United States, especially those who claimed access to new markets. Kendrix came out of World War II making such claims.

In the immediate postwar era, Kendrix secured a position as the public relations officer for the Centennial Commission of the Republic of Liberia, identified at the time as "one of the nation's most important public relations positions."[5] The Liberian Centennial Commission was the U.S. arm of a committee formed by Liberian officials to plan a grand exposition to showcase the small West African nation on the one hundredth anniversary of its independence in 1947. The commission provided the vehicle by which Liberia would secure investments in the exposition and, more importantly, in the nation's postwar development; it was Kendrix's job to promote Liberia domestically and to plan and publicize the commission's activities. It was not an easy task. To promote Liberia as a national interest entailed convincing the U.S. government and corporate America to invest in blacks, African and African American. But U.S. state officials and business leaders were largely (and often willfully) ignorant about the identities, aspirations, and advances of African Americans, let alone Americo-Liberians (Liberians of African American descent). To make matters more difficult, stereotypes abounded concerning blacks' backwardness and inability to self-govern, which hardly motivated U.S. corporations to hitch their wagons to black constituencies or initiatives.

Generating American interest in Liberia required that Kendrix construct the black republic in terms that made it less foreign and more appealing to U.S. government officials, as well as investors looking for new markets in a postwar economy. The official brochure produced to promote the exposition made his primary tactic clear: to present Liberia as a historically Western and forward-looking state committed to democracy and open for business. Illustrated by the internationally renowned Harlem Renaissance artist Lois Mailou Jones (Figure 26), the elaborate publicity piece assured a global audience that the centennial celebration would "present the

Figure 26. Liberian Centennial and Victory Exposition brochure, Liberian Centennial Commission, 1946. Moorland-Spingarn Research Center.

progress and development of a Democracy in Africa over this span of One Hundred Years, and a unified and comprehensive picture of LIBERIAN PLANNING designed to conform with other progressive people of the world to ACHIEVE a sustained WORLD PEACE based on cooperation, mutual understanding and progressive enterprise." This theme of progress would run through all public relations and publicity for the exposition.[6]

As public relations officer for the Liberian Centennial Commission, Kendrix devised campaigns that promoted blacks as modern subjects, receptive to the material goods and democratic values of the United States. Cast as such, African Americans and Americo-Liberians acquired a particular value as combatants against the perceived Soviet threat as a new global order took shape and the Cold War coalesced. For one, their enthusiastic participation in postwar capitalism was essential to the growth of American consumer culture and, by extension, U.S. economic stability. Similarly, their adherence to Western ideals, including democratic governance, free enterprise, commercial expansion, and globalized trade, underwrote the global dominance of the United States after World War II.

Kendrix's role as public relations officer to Liberia also provided him the vehicle through which he advanced his objectives as a public relations professional. The African American representative of a West African republic, he promoted African Americans and Americo-Liberians as untapped consumer markets, the targeting of which would benefit the United States and Liberia, both economically and politically, during the "internationally sensitive postwar era."[7] With an eye toward establishing his own marketing business, he billed himself as the marketer uniquely positioned to facilitate the relationships necessary to capitalize on these markets. His efforts intersected in complex ways with concurrent civil rights campaigns in the United States. The same black stereotypes that challenged his efforts to secure investments in Liberia and black markets, whether African American or West African, retarded racial equality in the United States. Western nations moved toward the position of universal human rights after the war, under the unifying umbrella of the United Nations; nevertheless, blacks in the United States continued to experience second-class citizenship in all its forms—discriminatory employment and housing practices, curtailed voting rights, restrictive housing covenants, unequal education opportunities, and racial violence, including lynching and other acts of murder. Many African Americans linked their continued oppression to definitions of blackness that cast them as people incapable, or undeserving, of self-determination and that defined them out of their citizenship. In his combined role of marketing entrepreneur and Liberia's pitchman, Kendrix articulated conceptions of blackness in the press and to U.S. government officials and corporate leaders that emphasized societal progress, political maturity and acuity, and modernity, which coincided with concurrent citizenship campaigns waged by African Americans.

Kendrix was not quite thirty years old as World War II came to a close, yet he had already gained quite the reputation as a talented public relations man through his work as director of Negro Press Week and as an educational adviser for the Division of Negro Affairs of the National Youth Administration (NYA). In 1943, his tenure as a New Dealer ended when Congress defunded the NYA. The New Deal agency had always had its congressional opponents, and when the war solved the issue of unemployment, these critics made the argument that the employment and education agency was obsolete. The demise of the NYA might have ended Kendrix's career as a government public relations agent. But, in 1944, the U.S. Army drafted him and put him to work doing publicity.

On the basis of his public relations past, Kendrix was stationed at Georgia's Fort Benning and assigned the position of assistant public relations officer. In that role, his primary responsibility was to manage the Fort Benning Reception Center Chorus, an all-black choir of servicemen, an assignment that kept him close to home. Rather than work from the post, Kendrix conducted much of his business as the choir's manager from the Butler Street YMCA in Atlanta, where he had formerly worked for the NYA, presumably because the choir often appeared at Atlanta venues. Operating from the familiar "headquarters," he organized appearances for the choir on college campuses and military bases and before social, civic, religious, and business groups.[8] He also wrote all copy and scripts for the choir's weekly radio broadcasts on the Georgia Network (over WRBL radio in Columbus, Georgia) and the occasional national broadcast through Columbia Broadcasting System (now CBS) and National Broadcasting Company (NBC) hookups.[9] His crowning achievement, however, was the Fourth Service Command war bond tour in 1944. Organized in correspondence with the Sixth War Loan Drive, this tour took the Fort Benning chorus to twenty-five cities throughout seven southeastern states to perform, with the vital purpose of fund-raising for the war effort. In addition to the chorus's musical talents, the tour featured guest appearances by black entertainers such as bandleaders Duke Ellington and Billy Eckstine. Kendrix had forged professional "friendships" with many celebrated black figures through his public relations duties on behalf of the black press, and he called on them personally to lend their celebrity to the cause.[10] The tour found large audiences among African Americans and, according to Kendrix, "stimulated the sale of $10,000,000 worth of bonds."[11] No evidence existed to back his claim, but repeated in the press and over radio airwaves, this was a statement of publicity, not accounting. Accuracy mattered less than generating excitement for the traveling black chorus.

The Fort Benning Reception Center Chorus war bond tour testified to the military importance of personnel like Kendrix who executed public relations on a much smaller and more local scale than the Office of War Information. Beyond the monies raised, the tour of black servicemen—or "singing soldiers," as Kendrix termed them—encouraged African American support of the war, or at least allowed for the appearance of such support, both of which had certain value. When they paid their sixty to seventy cents to attend rallies at which the Fort Benning chorus appeared, blacks invested (quite literally) in the war effort. Military officials sought financial backing by African Americans for U.S. involvement in World War II not merely as a practical matter but also as a matter of public relations or, more accurately, propaganda. The $10 million that Kendrix claimed in war bond sales among blacks provided tangible (if inflated) quantification of their support of the U.S. state, despite their maltreatment at its hands. This representation of black commitment to American democracy had high propagandist value as other nations pointed to antiblack racism in the United States to undermine its claims as leader of the free world. For African Americans not in the armed services, the tour provided the opportunity to demonstrate their patriotism, an act that asserted their membership as citizens of the United States. Whether it was their intent, blacks bought a stake in the nation, and its promise, when they paid to see the Fort Benning Reception Center Chorus and bought war bonds. Through Kendrix's war bond tour, African Americans enacted the sentiment put forth by the *Pittsburgh Courier* when it called for "double victory" for African Americans against enemies within (Jim Crow and racism) and without (the Axis powers and fascism).[12]

The Fort Benning Reception Center Chorus war bond tour was successful in both financial and public relations terms. It so impressed officials at the U.S. Treasury Department that they plucked Kendrix from his Fort Benning post for a three-month publicity assignment with the War Finance Division.[13] It was this assignment that brought Kendrix to Washington, DC. He made the move without his family. Tight finances led his wife, Dorothy, and him to make the difficult but sensible decision that she and their two young sons, Moss Jr. and Alan, would move to Columbus, Ohio, to live with her parents until Kendrix secured a stable livelihood. His relocation and independence, along with his extensive public relations experience, positioned him perfectly to assume the job of public relations officer for the DC-based U.S. division of the Liberian Centennial Commission.

The Liberian Centennial Commission had its roots in Monrovia, the capital city of Liberia. In the months leading up to the war's end, Liberian officials presented the U.S. government with a proposal for a grand celebration of Liberia's independence.[14] Central to this proposal was a two-year exposition—the "Centennial and Victory Exposition"—projected to open in 1947, the republic's centennial year. The proposed expo represented a shift in official Liberian attitudes to external investment in Liberia, heretofore viewed as a threat to the nation's sovereignty, which kept all capital out.[15] This assessment glossed over the glaring exception of the Firestone Tire and Rubber Company. In 1926 the large American company established one of the world's largest rubber plantations in Liberia in a covenant that supplied the struggling West African republic with a "sizable loan" and the rubber manufacturer with cheap land and an "indigenous and practically inexhaustible" labor source.[16] By the 1940s, consequently, Liberia's economy was largely dependent on one crop, and one company. Fraught with tensions, the relationship with Firestone had helped maintain Liberia's continued independence. It had also fortified distaste for foreign investment. The 1943 election of William V. S. Tubman as president of Liberia ushered in a new day. Tubman (an original proponent of Firestone's entry into Liberia) diagnosed Liberia's lack of infrastructure as a symptom of its independence, which, he explained, had denied Liberia the "benefits of colonization."[17] To remedy the situation, Tubman opened the door to foreign enterprise in 1944.

The Tubman administration conceived of the Victory Exposition as an apparatus through which to harness foreign interests to its immediate goals. In addition to commemorating Liberia's history as a "free, sovereign, and Independent State," the committee devised the expo to achieve a primary and pressing purpose, fulfilling the "crying need of public buildings" to accommodate the business of governing Liberia.[18] Specifically, they sought new buildings of relative "propinquity" to one another that would house the executive branch, Senate, House of Representatives, and Supreme Court, as well as the Departments of Justice, State, the Interior, the Treasury, Public Works, War, and the Post Office. A grouping of such buildings, explained one contributor, would not only house government, it would facilitate it by making communications between departments easier.[19] Citing budgetary restraints, the commission figured eight new buildings should suffice, with some serving double or triple duty.[20] The commission's executive committee estimated the cost of these "necessary buildings" at $350,000, an expense they reasoned would be "justified" if the construction resulted from a celebration of Liberia's independence. Compatibly, they also believed that the promise of these buildings ensured that "no criticism . . . of the Government's efforts to hold this celebration could plausibly be launched from any source."[21] It was a symbiotic relationship: the Victory Exposition rationalized the buildings, and the buildings rationalized the exposition.

The Liberian Centennial Commission members sought more than new buildings; they envisioned a modern, capital city that proclaimed Liberia's "progress and development."[22] The collection of new buildings was central to this vision. For one, the infrastructure necessary to establish a permanent seat of government required a water system. One committee member suggested that if the expo brought running water to Monrovia, this alone would render the centennial celebration a success. Still, the executive committee also desired macadamized (or stone-crusted) roads to protect government officials from the "welter of dust from soft laterite [soil] roads," deemed necessary to preserve the officials' dignity and engender respect for their offices.[23] Beyond government offices and basic infrastructure, as part of their centennial capital city, the commission also proposed institutions meant to show off Liberian intelligence and culture, including a national museum, amphitheater, and state university.[24] Manicured green spaces and professionally designed landscaping would beautify Liberia's new, westernized capital seat.[25]

These practical construction plans and aesthetic visions dovetailed with lofty political objectives for a post–World War II Liberia. President Tubman and his administration viewed the proposed centennial commission as an opportunity to put forth a "modern Liberia" through display of the nation's "industrial development, agriculture, transportation, communications, health education, arts, and crafts."[26] The Victory Exposition, in other words, was to put the small republic on the postwar global map.

From the onset, Liberian officials factored U.S. participation into the execution of the centennial celebration. They cited the "political consanguinity of Liberia and America" as grounds for determining an "American Committee" to be "fitting and appropriate."[27] More to the point, they sought

U.S. funding. Given the vast devastation from the war, the committee figured it could not expect much support from those nations attempting to rebuild. The United States, by comparison, came out of the war relatively unscathed and prosperous. Thus, the Tubman administration perceived and courted the United States as an essential partner to modernizing Liberia. Later in his presidency, Tubman would display support for African independence initiatives. For example, in 1958 he joined Kwame Nkrumah, revolutionary and president of the new republic of Ghana, at the First Conference of Independent African States. Historian Kevin Gaines has detailed how, as leader of Ghana, Nkrumah staked its future in Africacentric principles such as African solidarity and continental unity, which transformed the African republic into a haven for black peoples throughout the diaspora who sought freedom and were committed to self-determination. When Tubman first came to rule in 1944, however, he showed a greater commitment to alliances with the United States than demonstrations of Liberian independence or African cooperation.[28] In fact, a primary tactic of the Liberian Centennial Commission was to distinguish Liberia as more Western than African.

It is unclear precisely when and how the U.S. arm of the centennial commission came into being, but by 1945, Liberian officials had recruited several African Americans to the Liberian centennial cause. Howard University professor Hilyard Robinson appears to have been first on board. A respected African American architect, Robinson assumed the position of technical director for the centennial commission, making him responsible for designing and supervising construction of exposition and government facilities.[29] As early as the winter of 1944–45, Robinson was on the ground in Monrovia to survey the landscape, literally, and draw up plans for the facilities the Liberian officials deemed necessary. Beyond overseeing construction of exposition and government facilities, the Liberian Centennial Commission had another primary function: to mobilize U.S. political and financial support in Liberia's postwar development. In other words, it was the public relations vehicle for the exposition and Liberia, and Kendrix was responsible for its functions as such.

How Kendrix came to hold this position is not clear. Why he was selected is less a mystery. Doing public relations and publicity for the NYA and on behalf of the black press, Kendrix had developed a network of professional connections that transgressed race boundaries and spread throughout entertainment, press, political, and academic circles. What is more, as discussed in Chapter 1, as the chief promoter of Negro Press Week, he stepped out from behind the scenes. He appeared in the press often and made numerous public appearances, which increased his renown as a talented promoter. In addition, for a brief period from 1943 to 1944, before he was drafted, Kendrix held the position of managing editor for *A Monthly Summary of Events and Trends in Race Relations*, a publication commissioned by the Julius Rosenwald Fund that came out of the Institute of Race Relations at Fisk University. In this position, Kendrix worked under the supervision of Charles S. Johnson, a prominent black sociologist who contributed to Gunnar Myrdal's *American Dilemma*. In 1930 Johnson became the American representative for the League of Nations International Commission of Inquiry into the Existence of Slavery and Forced Labor in the Republic of Liberia, which investigated the relationship between presidential corruption and slave labor. The findings of the commission resulted in the resignation of the Liberian president and vice president. As a member of the commission, Johnson toured Liberia and became a recognized expert on the West African nation and defender of its indigenous people. It is probable that Johnson was the connection through which Kendrix was selected for the centennial commission. With or without Johnson's endorsement, by 1945, Kendrix was arguably the best-known and most visible African American publicity practitioner on the East Coast. That is, he was a natural, and likely coveted, choice for director of public relations for the Liberian Centennial Commission.[30]

Although the brainchild of Liberian state officials, the centennial commission and exposition served U.S. interests as well. The histories of the two nations were, after all, inextricably intertwined. Supported by the American Colonization Society, in the early 1820s, former American slaves and free blacks established the colony of Liberia on the southern end of Africa's western tip. Over the next two decades, that colony subsumed several other small American colonies and the American colonists and their descendants, Americo-Liberians, assumed power over the area's indigenous people. In 1847 the ruling Americo-Liberians declared Liberia independent—again, with the blessing of the American Colonization Society. That independence, however, rested heavily on U.S. support, which U.S. officials supplied, with varying degrees of enthusiasm, because they viewed Liberia as an extension of democracy into Africa, an ally in that region, and a source of natural resources. Over the next century, that support took different forms, including the installation of a legation in Monrovia, the shoring up of the Liberian army, and the protection of the small republic from colonization by the colonial European powers surrounding it.

During World War II, the United States received a return on its inconsistent investment in Liberia, as the coastal country became a chief source of Allied rubber and, due to its location, served as a strategic base from which, according to the press, American air forces "turn[ed] the tide of the North African campaign."[31] In the spring of 1945, able to anticipate the war's end, U.S. officials imagined a postwar world and demonstrated unprecedented interest in Liberia. In April 1945, Acting Secretary of State Dean Acheson wrote to Franklin D. Roosevelt, "The inefficiency and lack of initiative of the ruling group, the corruption in government circles, the scandalous treatment of the native inhabitants, and the lack of democratic practices in this independent republic are of particular concern to us at a time when the problem of dependent peoples is under widespread discussion."[32] These conditions, Acheson advised, threatened American interests in Liberia, and he recommended the United States intercede. Mere days before he died on April 12, Roosevelt signed off on the State Department's recommendation, writing "DA O.K. FDR" in the margin to Acheson's memo.

Acheson encouraged American investment in Liberia because of several factors of significant importance to U.S. officials. First, Tubman expressed enthusiasm for reforms the State Department deemed necessary for Liberia to be a worthy ally and trading partner after the war. The Liberian president sought support from the U.S. government because he anticipated challenges from the ruling class of Americo-Liberians, who feared a lessening of their power and the comparative wealth that went with it. Under Tubman's leadership, Liberia also sent delegates to the United Nations Conference on International Organization in San Francisco in the spring of 1945. There, along with fifty other Allied nations, Liberia signed the United Nations Charter, which established an intergovernmental organization responsible for international peace and security and universal protection of human rights. As a UN member nation, Acheson claimed, Liberia demonstrated commitment to the very principles on which the United States would stake its claims as a global leader after the war—"world-wide progress and better standards of living."[33] Even as U.S. state officials applauded Liberia as an ally in the fight to spread and protect democracy, they feared how the former American colony reflected on the United States. Surrounded by British and French colonies, Liberia suffered in comparison. The British colony of Sierra Leone, which shared a border with Liberia and was roughly the same size, had approximately four times the trade and revenue of Liberia and invested twenty times more on education, health care, and other areas significant to its native population's welfare.[34] These circumstances left the United States open to criticism as the defender of democracy just as it positioned itself as the leader of free peoples. Acheson summarized the liability Liberia posed when he advised Roosevelt to authorize relations with Liberia that simultaneously encouraged its development and tied the black republic to the United States and its postwar agendas: "Whether or not we admit it," he said, "Liberia is widely regarded as a responsibility of the United States."[35]

Beyond its symbolic value as a black democracy (or a failure of such democracy), Liberia became of great economic interest to the United States during World War II. Besides representing a supply of cheap land and labor, Liberia could also be a profitable trade partner and a key supplier of valuable raw materials, from iron ore to cocoa. Moreover, for the United States, as one Liberia expert stated at the time, Liberia might be a "springboard into the rest of Africa."[36] Well before the war's end, plans were afoot to facilitate trade between the two nations. Trade with Liberia was hampered because the country had no adequate port to receive large ships: all incoming goods had to be brought in small, oar-driven craft. This would not do. In December 1943, the governments of Liberia and the United States entered into an agreement in which the United States would fund the survey and construction of a deep-water port at Monrovia, Liberia's capital and largest city, for use by the United States, Liberia, and their allies. Construction of the port began in 1944 and signaled a significant investment in Liberia and its future. Liberian efforts to secure American support for the Victory Exposition were made easier because of expectations held by U.S. government officials and business leaders about Liberia's postwar potential.

In addition to U.S. state officials, African Americans also demonstrated an interest in postwar Liberia. Some apparently viewed the West African republic as a place they might have better luck finding employment (if not greater freedom). For example, one college-educated African American woman wrote a letter to the National Association for the Advancement of

Colored People (NAACP) in 1945 requesting information about jobs that her electrician husband and she might obtain on U.S. naval or army bases in Liberia.[37] As Liberia's pitchman, Kendrix presented Liberia as more than a place to satisfy private, individual needs, however. He formulated U.S. interest in Liberia as a route by which African Americans might elevate their political standing and secure a seat at the table of postwar U.S. foreign policy.[38] This is the opportunity he dangled before Walter White when he solicited the NAACP executive secretary's participation in promoting Liberia and the centennial celebration.

Throughout the 1930s and World War II, the NAACP expressed complex attitudes regarding Liberia. The civil rights organization disapproved of the Liberian government's systematic exploitation of indigenous peoples' labor but favored Liberian self-rule and was critical of the "corrupting" influence of American capital and investments on Liberian society. In the context of the Liberian Centennial Commission's promotion of Liberia, White expressed reservations about the West African republic and its government.[39] Kendrix met these reservations by appealing to the political possibilities that postwar relations with Liberia presented African Americans. "For the first time in the history of our nation," he explained, "the Negro population of America is afforded the opportunity to lend its influence in the shaping of our government's policies as they relate to foreign relations."[40] This slant worked. The NAACP national office directed the organization's DC office to "keep an eye on [the DC-based centennial commission and its activities]," and White insisted that it would be "wise for [him] to serve [on the commission]."[41] With wartime circumstances driving the United States and Liberia into closer economic, and, by extension, diplomatic, relationships, the centennial commission offered the NAACP an organized and officially recognized vehicle for influencing those relations.

As evidenced by the publicity materials he devised and his proposals to influential black political thinkers, Kendrix understood Liberia's significance to black political agendas. To him, however, Liberia was, above all, a new market, the selling of which provided a necessary stepping-stone to his profitable career in marketing and public relations. Heretofore, while his public relations work often involved raising funds, he had worked for government or not-for-profit outfits. With the New Deal and World War II over, however, the curtain was coming down on the "cultural apparatus" of state bureaucracies that enlisted African American artists, propagandists, and administrators to reach and reassure black publics.[42] These circumstances steadily pushed Kendrix to establish his own enterprise.

At the same time Kendrix served on the centennial commission, he embarked on his own private business venture. Together with Hilyard Robinson and another black business associate, Kendrix founded Robinson-Kendrix-Simmons (RKS), which the men described as a "Negro trade and business" development firm that offered white corporate America access to black consumer markets.[43] To found a black business and conduct public relations for a black republic simultaneously were not simply the goals of an ambitious man attempting to multitask. To Kendrix's way of thinking, the two ventures were hardly separate, and his efforts for both coincided, sometimes inadvertently, but often intentionally.

If Kendrix's personality, skills, and upbringing predisposed him to a career as a successful businessman, federal initiatives also encouraged his drift toward private enterprise. During the war, the Commerce Department's Division of Negro Affairs helped black businesses secure government contracts and business loans.[44] Under the leadership of Emmer Lancaster, a former NAACP chapter president, the division assembled a Negro business advisory council to educate and assist "all Negro businesses throughout the country."[45] Operating in the wake of Roosevelt's signing of Executive Order 8802 in the summer of 1941, Lancaster asserted the importance of black business to the "War Emergency," and he tied the growth of black wartime enterprise to equal opportunity employment in the defense industries.[46] According to Lancaster, "the integration of Negro business into the Nation's productive effort" was both rational and required.[47] Institutional racism, however, hampered the ability of African American businesses to secure prime defense contracts. Black businesses typically lacked the capital necessary to compete with white-owned manufacturers and the contracts they offered, which confined these businesses to subcontracts, if they secured any contracts at all.[48] Therefore, Lancaster also looked to the future in his approach to black enterprise.

Throughout the war, the Commerce Department's Division of Negro Affairs conducted research on black enterprises and black consumers. The primary purpose of this research was to grow black capitalism, rather than to help white businesses profit from black consumerism, which had often been the case. Beginning in 1943, the division began compiling data on black professionals across multiple U.S. cities, an effort that anticipated and prepared for the postwar economy. Well before the war's end, Lancaster's council educated African American capitalists and would-be capitalists— such as Kendrix—about how to either grow or start their enterprises after the war.[49]

Foreign markets were integral to federal conceptions of postwar black business. In a 1943 report entitled *Post-war Planning and the Negro in Business*, Lancaster insisted that foreign trade offered black capitalists plenty of opportunity, noting that "Negro officials [in Central and South America and parts of Africa] have publicly express [*sic*] their desire for business relations with American Negroes."[50] When the war ended, Lancaster convened a conference on black business, the plenary session of which was "Foreign Trade and the Negro," meant to educate African American entrepreneurs about their counterparts in the Caribbean and Africa and "stimulate 'pan-African' economic activity."[51] Among those who participated in the 1946 Conference on the Negro in Business were delegates from various U.S. states, Haiti, the U.S. Virgin Islands, and Liberia. It is unclear whether Kendrix participated directly in any of these official programs in support of black business or was tangentially aware of them (it is near impossible to believe he was not). Regardless, under Lancaster, the Commerce Department's Division of Negro Affairs cultivated a climate that encouraged him to trade on his relationship to the Liberian government and exposition to advance his private enterprise.

The entire time he represented Liberia, Kendrix drew on the contacts and relative clout that his association with the Liberian Centennial Commission provided to launch RKS. It is clear that he and his partners founded RKS, in part, as the vehicle through which to manage business relationships brokered on behalf of Liberia and its exposition. Acting as Liberia's public relations man, Kendrix contacted large U.S. corporations, including beverage companies and aircraft and automobile manufactures—all industries seeking peacetime markets for the consumer products they were again free to produce. With each company, he sought contributions for the Victory Exposition in the form of sponsorships or product, or both.[52] During the same period (but writing on different letterhead), he contacted some of the same companies (most notably Coca-Cola) to also pitch the services of RKS. Additionally, Kendrix wrote proposals on behalf of RKS to home manufacturers.[53] In all of these cases, he touted his role on the centennial commission in an attempt to convince these companies to contract his fledgling firm to market their products specifically to black markets.[54]

In a very practical sense, black markets were the linchpin that linked U.S. capitalism and corporatism, African American entrepreneurialism and economic advancement, and U.S.-Liberian postwar relations. Earl Parker Hanson, an American journalist who participated in an economic mission to Liberia in 1944, explained that the economic relations the United States and Liberia sought with each other required that Liberia's "social and economic structure [be] rebuilt to lift the living standards and purchasing power of its great masses of people." According to Hanson, this would create the markets necessary to stimulate the commercial trade the United States sought and bring about the social reform the Tubman administration deemed crucial to modernizing Liberia. Furthermore, only once Liberians were "content and prosperous," the thinking went, could the country "provide a secure foothold for [the United States] on the African continent." Hanson and other contemporary observers assumed that other African nations would seek and embrace a modern, capitalist culture organized around consumption once they were exposed to the material comforts that such a culture offered.[55]

Kendrix tapped into currents linking U.S. capitalism to the growth of Liberia's consumer culture. And, to promote Liberia's development and his own business interests, he joined these forces to African American consumption. Whether approaching U.S. corporations as a representative of the Liberian Centennial Commission or RKS, he tied the objectives of each venture to the other, and he did so by offering up black markets— African and African American. Notably, he made little effort to distinguish African American and West African consumers, beyond stressing their un- or undertapped buying power. Instead, he generally presented blacks in Liberia and the United States as belonging to a monolithic, global black market. This conception of black consumerism had a flexibility that suited the multiple agendas that intersected in the Liberia project and was therefore quite useful to Kendrix's objectives as an enterprising marketer.

In his role as representative of both RKS and Liberia, Kendrix exploited the circumstances of reconversion. His savvy in doing so is clear in the pitch he made to auto executives on behalf of the Victory Exposition. After the war, the automobile market offered boundless possibilities. In 1941 U.S.

automakers produced roughly 3.5 million cars; then, in February 1942, all civilian automobile production ceased when U.S. manufacturers went to work producing tanks, planes, and other vehicles necessary for the war effort.[56] When the war ended, Americans wanted cars; moreover, they could afford them. As then-director of the Office of Economic Stabilization Fred Vinson stated, "The American people are in the pleasant predicament of having to learn to live 50 percent better than they have ever lived before."[57] When automobile manufacturing resumed in October 1945, several new manufacturers stepped into the fray. These included the Kaiser-Frazer Corporation, the collaboration of steel magnate Henry Kaiser and automobile executive Joseph Frazer. Formed just before the war's end, Kaiser-Frazer was poised to take advantage of pent-up consumer demand.[58] In 1946, rather than approach one of the established automakers—Ford, General Motors, and Chrysler—Kendrix pitched to Kaiser-Frazer. In the competitive arena of the postwar car market, he understood that this new venture sought to establish a solid consumer base among markets the "Big Three" had yet to corner. In his pitch, he suggested that Kaiser-Frazer present Tubman with a new automobile. The gesture, Kendrix advised (and no doubt believed), would have "promotional significance as far as the African market" and "far-reaching goodwill in the American Negro Automotive Market."[59] In other words, the public relations stunt would provide Kaiser-Frazer inroads to black markets in both the United States and Liberia at the precise moment both nations were reconverting to consumption-based economies. The proposed plan highlighted commercial ties between the United States and Liberia. Moreover, putting Tubman into an American-made car allowed for an image of black advancement and modernity through black people's consumption of modern material goods.

For their part, Liberian officials believed representations of Liberia's progress as a black republic were essential to securing foreign investments in the development of the country's transportation and communication systems, as well as profitable trade agreements. The problem, however, was that the West African nation suffered from a horrible public image. A contemporary historian of Liberia stated matter-of-factly, "The almost incredible backwardness of Liberia is well known."[60] Many, including U.S. officials, viewed the small republic as a "'demigovernment' run by a race considered lacking in the requisite skills and capacities for national self-government."[61] After his visit to Liberia's capital city, Charles Johnson reported, "The view of Monrovia from the sea is perhaps its only advantageous aspect."[62] This perspective found expression beyond political and academic circles. Writing for *Harper's* magazine, Hanson described Liberia as "incredibly backward—a museum-piece among nations."[63] Likewise, in an editorial recognizing Liberia's centennial, *Time* magazine deemed Liberia a nation "bypassed by history" where "policemen go barefoot [and] telephone poles are . . . devoured by insects."[64] Mainstream commentaries such as these furthered the conception of Liberia as backward and insignificant, Africa as savage and prehistoric, and blackness as primitive and uncivilizable.

The blueprints that Hilyard Robinson drafted for the centennial commission of the Liberian government and exposition facilities all but shouted down such depictions and reflected Tubman's mission to formulate Liberia, ideologically and materially, as a "modern" republic. Entitled "A Project in Step with New World Planning and Economy," Robinson's architectural drawings featured vast compounds of low, symmetrical, and geometric buildings that simultaneously echoed Egyptian and modernist themes (Figures 27 and 28). Courtyards and roadways, similar in their contemporary design, surrounded the built structures. The angled buildings and landscaping, as drawn by Robinson, both complemented and contrasted with the curvatures of the nearby coastline, signifying Liberian harmony with, but mastery over, nature.[65]

Beyond relying on Robinson's vision to combat stereotypes of Liberia's primitiveness, Tubman's administration launched and publicized a campaign of material consumption. While it is unclear whether Tubman ever climbed into a Kaiser-Frazer automobile, in the months surrounding Liberia's centennial, he outfitted the presidential mansion with furnishings and appliances shipped from Macy's in Manhattan. Tubman was the driving force behind plans for the "development and modernization" of Liberia. According to Hanson's observations, Tubman, who was inaugurated in 1944 for an eight-year term, initiated reforms "so drastic as to amount almost to social revolution." Specifically, Tubman instituted controversial programs meant to dissolve the socioeconomic divide between the Americo-Liberian ruling class and the indigenous population. He connected his nation's economic and social health to the increased "purchasing and taxpayer power" of all its inhabitants, which he believed required "absorb[ing] the aborigines fully into national life" with equal rights and opportunity.[66]

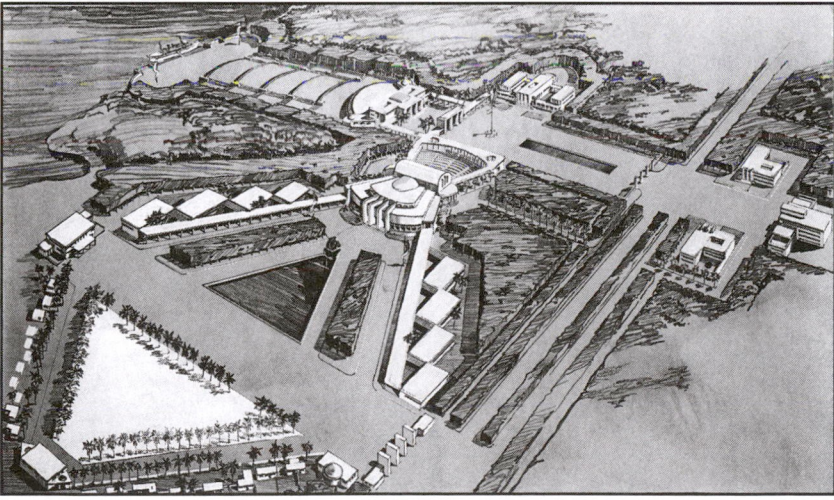

Figure 27. Hilyard Robinson's architectural rendering of government center to be built in Monrovia, Liberia, 1945. Moorland-Spingarn Research Center.
Figure 28. Hilyard Robinson's architectural rendering of exposition facilities to be built in Monrovia, Liberia, 1945. Moorland-Spingarn Research Center.

Robinson took on what one observer called the "'backward people' problem" at a drafting table.[67] Kendrix attacked it through the media. His job was to sell Liberia as a worthy investment to American business interests, a partner in democracy to the American public, and a functioning democracy to international observers. To challenge notions of Liberia's insignificance, he constructed the African nation as a model and pillar of American values and Western democracy. Contemporary discourses about U.S. responsibility and superiority circulating in the immediate postwar moment provided tropes useful to this project. After the war, U.S. officials and the American public had a greater sense of the United States in relation to a larger, global community. In this context, U.S. politics were characterized by "a newly perceived, acknowledged, and shouldered set of universal responsibilities."[68] This vein of universalism distinguished American foreign policy after World War II. John Fousek explains how postwar U.S. foreign politics assumed the universality of "American values," such as "freedom, equality, and justice under law," and had the objective to establish them globally. This particular form of globalism challenged the supremacy of the Soviet Union, the other world power that emerged after the war, and served as a justification for U.S. global leadership.[69] In 1947 President Harry S. Truman transformed this ideology into policy in an address to Congress in which he declared the United States had the duty to protect democracy throughout the world and assist "free peoples . . . to maintain their freedoms."[70] Central to this policy, dubbed the Truman Doctrine, were historicist ideas that elevated Western democracy and peoples as the apex of civilization and measured the progress and fitness for self-rule and full citizenship of other global populations in relation to their adherence to the ideas and practices essential to Western culture.[71]

Displaying awareness of the popularity and potency of this ideology, Kendrix devised a multifaceted publicity campaign that presented black Liberia as essential to the expansion and security of democracy. Using the Liberian News Service that he established, Kendrix trumpeted Liberia's status as a founding member of the United Nations and represented it as an outgrowth of Western, and specifically U.S., culture. Press items he orchestrated, for example, stressed how Liberia "borrowed nearly all of its political principles from America" and patterned its government, its constitution, and even its flag on "those of its parent, the United States of America."[72] The Liberian Centennial Commission also circulated essays that claimed that, located as it was in West Africa, Liberia furthered the "extension of English speaking people" and "enlightened thinking." Through these media materials, Kendrix pushed Liberia as essential to the economic and ideological triumph of Westernism, and specifically the United States, in the postwar global order.[73]

In 1946 the centennial commission published a brochure advertising Liberia's significance to "the world at peace" (see Figure 26). Entitled *Centennial and Victory Exposition, Monrovia Liberia, 1947–1949*, the brochure assured readers that the world would see the nation's "progress and development" by way of exhibits that fell into one of five categories: agriculture, transportation and communications, Liberian government special exhibits, industrial arts and handicrafts, and concessions. The booklet also constructed Liberia's importance as a partner in democracy by promoting its value to the democratic United States as a trade partner. "Conditions of climate and other circumstances natural to Liberia," the text reported, "provide agricultural, mineral and other resources of a type well adapted . . . to meet various demands of people outside of [Liberia's] borders." Printed on heavy stock and in color, this pricey publicity piece reflects the commission's considerable investment in the ideal of a modern(izing), progressive, and globalized Liberia. The brochure echoed Robinson's contemporary architectural and landscape plans and marketed the Victory Exposition as "a unified and comprehensive picture" of the Liberian population's belonging to the community of "other progressive peoples of the world."[74]

Beyond serving U.S. state and commercial interests and the centennial commission's objectives, the very Western, very democratic, modernizing Liberia that Kendrix publicized also interested African American political thinkers. Prominent civil rights activists and scholars viewed this Liberia as a route to advance the freedom of black Americans within the Western democracy that was the United States. Following World War II, racist ideologies about black inferiority continued to impede the freedom of black Americans, perhaps most evident in Jim Crow's healthy postwar condition, discrimination against veterans in federal policy, and hostilities toward returning black soldiers. Many African Americans believed it was necessary to counteract the ideas that underlay these discriminatory policies and behaviors with contrary evidence in order to raise their social and political status. In a letter to Walter White, a representative of a black organization in Atlanta suggested the NAACP spearhead efforts to funnel financial and political support to Liberia. Doing so, he claimed, would not only promote, and thus secure, the small republic's place in the postwar world order; it would also publicize and garner "favorable international sentiment" for the "Negro's 'problem' in America."[75] Constructed by Kendrix's public relations campaign as a "successful experiment" in black government, Liberia, the black press declared, proved "Negroes, when given the required opportunities, are capable of governing themselves." Kendrix's representation of a black republic performed as "convincing evidence" of black intelligence and ability, which served African Americans' postwar efforts to claim full citizenship.[76] The notions of black modernity that he proposed on behalf of the centennial commission aligned with propaganda about African Americans' racial progress that the State Department produced at the time to counter international criticism of U.S. antiblack racism.[77] Like Gordon Parks's Farm Security Administration and Office of War Information work, Kendrix's postwar public relations campaign ensured that African Americans not only figured within race propaganda that served state agendas but also designed, produced, and disseminated it.

The public relations campaign for Liberia's centennial entailed wrestling with multiple, and sometimes competing, definitions of blackness and black progress. To make Liberia useful to domestic political agendas, the centennial commission and influential black figures defined it away from its foreignness and Africanness. To accomplish this, they invoked Liberia's past as an American colony in complex manners that coincided with the official narrative of postwar U.S. race relations, in which U.S. democracy was portrayed as the best form of government for African Americans to realize progress and freedom.[78] Through the commission's news service, Kendrix funneled histories to the press detailing Liberia's colonization by black American freedmen, the descendants of whom (Americo-Liberians) continued to rule Liberia in its independence. These histories conveniently omitted the centrality of American slavery to Liberia's origins. For instance, an article circulated by the centennial commission reconstructed Liberia's founding in terms of pioneering and depicted the freedmen who settled Liberia as "black pilgrims," similar to the "Pilgrim Fathers who . . . anchored the 'Mayflower' off the New England Plymouth Rock."[79] This portrayal of Liberia's founders obscured their enslaved past and provided an image of (black) Americans bringing civilization to "the dark continent," which buttressed black Americans' claims about their fitness for practicing and experiencing democracy freely. The representation of the black Americans who colonized Liberia as "early American pioneers" also suggested the civilizing effects of U.S. democracy, which both reflected and furthered the universal Westernism central to postwar U.S. foreign policy.

By emphasizing Liberia and the belonging of its ruling class to the Western world, Kendrix's public relations campaign contributed to a discourse about the superiority of black Americans in relation to other black populations. Press items distributed through Kendrix's Liberian News Service referred to Liberia as a "daughter" republic and "in every sense of the word . . . the child of the United States."[80] While intended to stress obligations the United States had to its former colony, this statement infantilized Liberia and Liberians, presenting them as less developed U.S. dependents. Similarly, in an essay that circulated through the Liberian News Service, Howard University professor Rayford Logan defined Liberia as a "'foundling' of the United States." Presumably, he meant to position Liberia as a partner—albeit a junior one—in the endeavors of perpetuating and securing ideals and standards of U.S. democracy. Moreover, by emphasizing Liberia's American parentage, Logan made the West African republic and its black inhabitants less "foreign," which he leveraged to encourage U.S. investment in Liberia's future. But in his formulation of U.S.-Liberian relations, Logan rendered Liberia less civilized by defining black Americans' support of black Liberia as their taking up the duty of bringing civilization and Christianity to developing parts of the world. In a questionable rhetorical choice, he borrowed language from Rudyard Kipling's famous imperialist poem "The White Man's Burden" to advise black Americans. "By all ye will or whisper, by all ye leave or do," he warned, "your black Liberian Brothers will weigh your God and you."[81] With prose and poetry, then, Logan placed African Americans higher within a hierarchy of civilization than their Liberian counterparts—who, in turn, he placed above indigenous Africans.

Logan's words coincided with Kendrix's overall representational strategy regarding Liberia. When promoting black consumer markets, his representations of blackness transcended boundaries of race, nation, and time. He made little effort to distinguish or even define black consumers. By contrast, he distinguished African Americans from Americo-Liberians as citizens of the world. To prompt the desired American political and economic support, Kendrix presented Liberians as being in a state of need and worthy of assistance, which he achieved by presenting them as inclined to modernity but requiring American, especially African American, investment and instruction to realize that state. These representations placed the issue of black progress in the "broader sphere of 'modern civilization'" and emphasized the progress of blacks in the United States relative to that of other populations of African descent.[82] Similar to Kendrix, Logan intended to advance Liberia's cause (and worthiness). And, like Kendrix, he put forth an order of blackness that black political thinkers in the United States at that time no doubt found useful to African Americans' civil rights cause.

The slant of Logan's message, hardly anomalous among Liberian Centennial Commission publicity, is all the more interesting when placed in the context of the anticolonial politics that major black civil rights activists and organizations in the United States espoused at the time. The principles of the 1941 Atlantic Charter—which outlined the Allied powers' vision of a postwar world—gave, if only temporarily, oppressed peoples the world over reason to hope for and even demand self-determination.[83] And throughout World War II, the NAACP, among others, tied race issues and racial oppression in the United States to the circumstances of colonized people of color in India and Africa. Logan himself had bristled at what he deemed an imperial approach toward Liberia on the part of the U.S. company Firestone. Questioned about U.S. commercial interests in Liberia at a banquet promoting Liberia and its centennial (organized by Kendrix, of course), Logan responded that Liberia was nothing but "the spare tire of the Firestone Tire and Rubber Company."[84] (Logan, perhaps, best demonstrates the complex, shifting, and sometimes contradictory attitudes African Americans held regarding U.S.-Liberian relations.) The centennial commission's dominant representation of a hierarchical relationship between African Americans and Liberians suggests that the anticolonial sensibilities that World War II inspired among black Americans allowed them to "embrace" Africa, but not necessarily identify with Africans.[85]

The centennial commission's formulation of Liberia—as a U.S. outgrowth—furthered an ideal of black civilization and progress that challenged common notions about the primitiveness of black people and their unsuitability for political modernity. Again, many African Americans found conceptions of blacks' political maturity and cultural modernity helpful as essential grounds for their civil rights demands. Yet this representational strategy also undermined black civil rights efforts because it contributed to a conception of civilization that held that a nation or peoples must progress through particular stages of development before being civilized *enough* for self-determination, self-rule, or the rights of first-class citizenship. Opponents to black equality could activate the formulations of evolution and the corresponding order of blackness that the Liberian Centennial Commission proposed to argue that neither Africans nor African Americans had yet to advance to a stage of civilization or political development capable of first-class American, or global, citizenship.

Historicist ideologies of progress or development empower the ruling class to decide when subaltern groups are "ready."[86] By defining Americo-Liberians and West Africans as less developed in comparison to black Americans, the Liberian Centennial Commission lent credence to ideas of civilization that justified "the imaginary waiting room of history."[87] This conceptual space describes the limbo in which black Americans found themselves after the war. In the face of growing international scrutiny of U.S. antiblack racism and violence, President Truman made several advances on the civil rights front. These included the establishment of the President's Committee on Civil Rights to investigate the status of black civil rights and the desegregation of the federal workforce and armed forces via Executive Orders 9980 and 9981, respectively. Primarily symbolic, however, these measures made little difference in the lived experiences of African Americans, and racially motivated discrimination and violence continued apace. The federal government also produced propaganda that deemphasized America's shameful past with slavery and black Americans' second-class citizenship status and praised American democracy as the only system in which African Americans could have progressed so far and so fast (especially given their extreme handicap).[88] By extension, U.S. democracy was the only governmental and societal system in which blacks could possibly achieve freedom. This formulation undercut black demands for racial equality and "freedom now!" with the promise of racial equality and black freedom, eventually. Despite African Americans' war service and the expectations it might have justified, the "only in America" propagandist discourse buttressed the U.S. government's measured approach to black civil rights.[89]

The centennial commission's representation of Liberia and Liberians in relation to the United States and black Americans contributed to this freedom-by-degrees-and-development discourse. A media event that Kendrix organized to promote the Liberian centennial offers a prime example.

In 1947 he successfully lobbied Virginia governor William Tuck to proclaim a "Joseph Jenkins Roberts Day" to honor the Virginia-born boatman and barber who became Liberia's first president. The J. J. Roberts Day fete, which took place on March 15, 1947, was carried over the Mutual Broadcasting System radio network and covered by the *Washington Post* and *New York Times*. During this mainstream media event, Tuck gave a speech in which he honored Roberts and promoted the centenary celebration, announcing plans for the federal U.S. government's participation in the Victory Exposition.[90]

It might seem unexpected for a southern governor to celebrate a black president in the mid-1940s. The Roberts Day ceremony, however, provided Tuck an opportunity to minimize racism in the United States that was couched in a celebration of black progress and to advance the "only in America" and "not yet" concepts that stymied postwar black equality efforts. Standing at the podium, Tuck described Roberts as "an inspiration to . . . his race in overcoming handicaps" and paralleled Roberts's progress to that of blacks' in the United States. Tuck said he knew "no race which has exceeded the pace" of African Americans' "remarkable advancement." With this presentation of black progress, the governor assumed a fine-line stance common to statements U.S. government officials made in the early Cold War years, which reflected an awareness of a global audience's observance of U.S. race relations. Carried to the American public over radio airwaves and through mainstream newspapers, Tuck's words affirmed the "notable success and progress" of African Americans in the United States, as well as in the West African Republic of Liberia. The southern politician, however, then went on to imply that black freedom in the United States was nearly sufficient. "The Negro in America," he stated, "is closer to attaining the standing as a citizen he desires than is admitted by the professional troublemakers among us representing both races."[91] Here, Tuck used the images of black potential and progress (not to mention the platform) that Kendrix provided to refute domestic and international accusations concerning the second-class status of blacks in the United States. Moreover, he placed the responsibility for obtaining first-class citizenship squarely on black Americans, while at the same time negating the racism or discrimination hampering their ability to do so. With his comments, Tuck tacitly endorsed the status quo and impeded the "insistence on the 'now'" in the civil rights movement.[92] In this sense, J. J. Roberts Day was a complex event that served overlapping but also conflicting agendas, including promotion of Liberia and its centennial, celebration of black progress and American democracy, and curtailment of civil rights politics.

By far, the most prominent and sophisticated public relations and promotional event Kendrix organized for the Centennial Commission of the Republic of Liberia was the stateside celebration of Liberia's centennial, which occurred on July 26, 1947 (Figure 29). The day began with a face-to-face meeting at the White House between Tubman and Truman. A radio program on the CBS network followed, which featured the Army Air Forces band, a statement by Tubman, and an address from London by Fisk University president Charles Johnson.[93] Immediately following the radio broadcast, a ceremony took place on the west front lawn of the capitol grounds that included a "stirring address" by Associate Supreme Court Justice Robert Jackson and the unveiling of a plaque that depicted two clasped hands reaching from the United States to Liberia within a globe flanked by the two nations' flags (Figure 30). A message prepared by Truman that was read during the ceremony echoed the plaque's representation of unity: "We are certain that the friendship . . . symbolized by the clasped hands [on the plaque] will continue to grow and that the United States and Liberia will march together during the next century in the same cooperation and mutual trust which has distinguished their association during the century just passed."[94] Kendrix had arranged for all of this (Figure 31). Following the event of "thanks and pomp," the black press identified him as a "hustling publicist" and a "super Public Relations expert [and] resourceful . . . newsman" who "[made] Liberia a household word."[95]

From 1945 through 1947, Kendrix exhaustively promoted Liberia as an American interest. As Liberian Centennial Commission public relations officer, he secured both political and financial support for the centenary celebration and promoted the Victory Exposition through multiple channels, using varied tactics. On any given day, if he was not out and about pressing the flesh or speaking on behalf of the centennial, one would find him in the commission's Eleventh Street DC office writing letters to solicit funds, sponsorship, or participation from business leaders across various industries or to pressure House representatives to pass the legislation necessary to allow their respective states' participation in the Victory Exposition. By 1947, he could claim fifty-one nations were expected to participate

Figure 29. Moss Kendrix admires bronze plaque commissioned for presentation to Liberian officials, July 1947. Moorland-Spingarn Research Center.

Figure 30. Congressman William L. Dawson (*left*) and Liberian envoy Charles D. B. King at celebration of one hundredth anniversary of Liberia, Washington, DC, 1947. Moorland-Spingarn Research Center.

Figure 31. Celebration of one hundredth anniversary of Liberia, west front of capitol, Washington, DC, 1947. Moorland-Spingarn Research Center.

in the exposition, and sixteen U.S. states had bills pending for the appropriation of funds for exhibits at the exposition.[96] In addition to lobbying, Kendrix continued to generate publicity for Liberia and its centennial celebration. For example, he commissioned Duke Ellington, with whom he was solidly acquainted through his work for Negro Press Week and the Fort Benning chorus, to compose a musical score in celebration of the Liberian centennial. Securing the composition might have been enough for some, but not Kendrix. He arranged a photo op of the staged presentation of the commission to "the Duke" for what would be called the *Liberian Suite*, the resulting images of which appeared in prominent black newspapers.[97]

Ultimately, however, Liberia could not live up to the image Kendrix and the centennial commission manufactured. In the spring of 1947, the black press began reporting that the Victory Exposition was in trouble. Despite claims of its development, it became clear that Liberia's *under*development—particularly its lack of transportation and telecommunications infrastructure—was hindering plans for the centennial celebration. In April the *Atlanta World Daily* reported that, because of difficulties obtaining materials, not enough buildings could be built on the exposition grounds to support its opening.[98] Then, in June, one month before Liberia's centennial, the U.S. State Department announced it would not seek funds to finance U.S. participation in the exposition because of "certain actions taken . . . by the Liberian government itself."[99] Then, two weeks before Duke Ellington premiered the *Liberian Suite* before Liberian heads of state at Carnegie Hall on December 26, 1947, Tubman postponed the exposition indefinitely, citing setbacks caused by war shortages.[100] As 1947 ended, so, too, did the Liberian Centennial Commission, and the Victory Exposition never occurred.

This is not to say that U.S.-Liberian relations ended. Hardly. Corporate interests, which desired access to the country's natural minerals, converged under the name of the Liberia Company and used "private capital and public influence" to aid in the development of Liberia's infrastructure and ports of entry. This private, white, corporate-controlled outfit pursued a policy of "dollar diplomacy" toward Liberia, under the guise of "a worldwide American business attack on poverty," which followed the logic of Cold War, U.S. globalist foreign policy.[101] With this turn of events, Kendrix and the other African Americans who had formed the centennial commission no longer had a hand in shaping American-Liberian relations. In the end, the development and modernization of black Liberia required it to become the dependent of wealthy, white American businessmen, which undermined its function as a representation of black independence or progress.

The collaboration of RKS also ended with the cancellation of the Victory Exposition and the end of the centennial commission. (No doubt the demise of RKS also had something to do with Kendrix's suing his business partner and boss, Hilyard Robinson, in a dispute regarding his compensation as the centennial commission's public relations officer.)[102] For Kendrix, however, the road to Liberia's centennial exposition was hardly a dead end. Throughout his tenure as the public relations officer for the centennial commission, he forged business connections across various fields, such as the automobile and home manufacturing industries, which positioned him well to take advantage of the nation's reorientation to domestic production after World War II. He belonged to a small group of black entrepreneurs operating in the postwar economy who recognized ignorance of black peoples' progress and aspirations for what it was: a business opportunity. As Liberia's pitchman, he presented black markets and their purchasing power as the reward for investing in the black West African republic and its future development in the image of the United States. He marketed his private firm as a bridge that allowed American corporations to enter into black markets without having to comprehend (or even interact with) black people. As a budding black businessman operating in the immediate postwar moment, Kendrix found it possible, even logical, to pursue his private business objectives while he served on the centennial commission because Cold War concerns and geopolitics allowed him to tie black progress to U.S. national strength and security. His postwar public relations work while in the employ of Liberia draws direct links between postwar black enterprise, black citizenship and civil rights politics, and international commercial and diplomatic relations. To trace these connections reveals how U.S. capitalism intersected with black civil rights agendas and exposes African Americans' role in larger political projects. The story of the Liberian Centennial Commission also reveals how postwar economic interests affected African American conceptions of, and commitment to, other black populations.

To sell RKS and Liberia, Kendrix devised public relations campaigns that constructed blacks as adherents to principles (such as democracy and capitalism) and practices (mass consumerism, industrial development, and globalization) that U.S. officials deemed vital to U.S. economic strength and dominance in the post–World War II global order. The conceptions of blackness that he publicized proved politically expedient to immediate efforts to counter notions about black inferiority and primitiveness. Predicated as these representations were on the relative civilization of black peoples and cultures, however, they upheld frameworks of race-based inequality that stymied black self-determination and freedom in both the United States and West Africa. Geopolitical, economic, and racial dynamics of the early Cold War moment encouraged Americans on both sides of the color line to perpetuate monolithic or evolutional concepts of black people and frustrated attempts to advance complex notions of blackness. The same dynamics, however, allowed Kendrix to carve out a relatively influential space in postwar American politics and business. From that position, he promoted conceptions of black progress and modernity that were valuable to African Americans' citizenship campaigns and were the grounds on which he established a public relationship enterprise through which, as detailed in Chapter 5, he dominated as a representative of black markets throughout the early Cold War era.

Chapter 4

Black Appeal: The Profits and Politics of Representing Black Female Sexuality

What's wrong with a decent picture of a Negro girl?

—Letter to the editor, *Negro Digest*, June 1948

Historians have been kind enough to say that I invented a new journalism that made it possible for Black media to weather the storms of change. This is a flattering assessment, but I wasn't trying to make history—I was trying to make money.

—John H. Johnson, *Succeeding Against the Odds*

After the war, John H. Johnson was also fixated on black consumers. He had spent the war years on Chicago's South Side, which he experienced as "a place of special and sassy Blacks who did things they didn't do . . . anywhere else."[1] Blessed with a high lottery number, Johnson was not snared by the "Jim Crow Draft."[2] He took advantage of his reprieve from war service to launch *Negro Digest*. As "a compendium of the best and most significant articles on the Negro appearing in white as well as black publications," the magazine was unprecedented in form and immediately found an audience.[3] Within eight months of its debut in November 1942, *Negro Digest* had a circulation of over fifty thousand, unheard-of numbers for any black magazine. The publication exposed a market of African Americans thirsty for publications specifically targeted at them. Therefore, as soon as the war ended—and restrictions on paper lifted—Johnson launched *Ebony* magazine.

A black photo-magazine, *Ebony* was an entirely different undertaking from Johnson's first publication. *Negro Digest* consisted primarily of re-

Figure 32. Lena Horne on cover of *Ebony*, March 1946. Ebony Media Operations, LLC.

printed material and carried no graphics. By contrast, *Ebony* used a photojournalistic format and contained original content and multiple visual images; as a result, Johnson's second magazine carried considerably higher production costs, the fulfillment of which required advertising revenue. Before *Ebony*, no advertising-based black magazine had survived. Johnson's "positive" magazine, however, broke sales record after sales record "like a thoroughbred stallion."[4] Within a few short months, *Ebony* had become so popular that celebrities with considerable star power, such as singer-actress Lena Horne, agreed, even requested, to be featured in the magazine—or, in the case of Horne, on its cover (Figure 32). The success of Johnson's second magazine was the basis on which Johnson became the first African American to be named among *Forbes*'s list of wealthiest Americans.[5] How did he establish a successful commercial, advertising-based black magazine when no such thing existed? How did he triumph when all others had failed? The short answer: sex. More accurately, he relied on images that highlighted black women's beauty and sex appeal. Beginning with *Ebony*, the Johnson Publishing Company (JPC) used visually provocative pinup images of attractive, shapely, and minimally dressed black women as its primary method to increase readership. With this tactic, the company made black consumers visible to major advertisers as a profitable market to pursue through advertising in the media space that Johnson provided.

Using images of sexualized black womanhood as a marketing strategy, Johnson contributed to the "tried-and-true" status of "sex sells" marketing and popularized the figures of the black pinup girl and sex goddess in mainstream print culture. The "girlie" images central to JPC's marketing both assumed and promoted black women's physical attractiveness and highlighted their role as the object of heterosexual male desire, black and nonblack. By making such images popular, *Ebony* brought them to the fore as a site of heightened activity and discussion. In turn, African Americans evaluated, debated, and approached these sexualized representations as a potential route to their equality and belonging according to definitions of what it meant to be American in the United States after World War II.[6] Whatever their thoughts or feelings about such images (and likely precisely because of their thoughts and feelings), blacks consumed them in large numbers, which, in turn, allowed JPC to sell all manner of products and ideas.

In his 1957 book *Black Bourgeoisie*, black sociologist E. Franklin Frazier identified *Ebony* as a lifestyle manual that encouraged the black middle class in what he considered a pathetic "aping" of whites and a rejection of "any genuine identification with the black race."[7] The important distinction, however, is that African Americans appeared to be "acting white" when performing their middle-class-dom because dominant ideologies have made "middle class" and "white" synonymous. Armed with this clarification, some have come to the defense of *Ebony*, asserting the magazine's importance in politicizing black consumption and the creation of new black identities.[8] In the process, however, they have accepted Frazier's formulation that *Ebony*'s significance lies in the final product and failed to consider matters of production, including the business decisions that shaped it as a consumer product within a particular historical moment.

Although entirely economic in purpose, JPC's early marketing decisions bear significantly on the history of black representation, as well as civil rights history. The advertising revenue this strategy returned allowed Johnson to develop multiple magazines that injected numerous and varied definitions of blackness, all of which black consumer demand helped shape. Sexualized imagery and the profits it generated were the foundation on which Johnson created the largest, most successful, and most powerful black-owned means of communication in the postwar world. In addition to its ability to shape and popularize notions of blackness, this media empire achieved such a place within black America that it had the power to unite and organize African Americans around issues of race and racism. As discussed in this chapter, there is no better example of this than the role of JPC in publicizing the lynching of Emmett Till in 1955. Business decisions that Johnson made in relation to selling the fourteen-year-old boy's murder galvanized African Americans nationwide. These decisions included a reliance on sexualized images of black women as a marketing tool, which contributed to Till's murder's becoming a catalyst for black activism central to the civil rights movement and helped fix it in our national memory.

The sexy visuals of black women found on the covers and in the pages of *Ebony* and other Johnson publications are evidence of the coming together of black capitalism, black representational and consumerism desires, and black citizenship campaigns, which included civil rights and national belonging efforts. African Americans came out of World War II with expectations warranted by their status as citizens, as well as by their explicit performances of citizenship in relation to the war. In the expansive consumer and media culture of the postwar period, first-class citizenship included experiencing visualizations, and other articulations, of that status in the marketplace. Black "girlie" images were the means through which JPC delivered on that experience for African Americans.

Johnson came to mediamaking early. As a student at Wendell Phillips High School and then Du Sable High School on Chicago's South Side, he worked part time through the National Youth Administration (NYA).[9] As an NYA work-study student, he founded and produced a mimeographed magazine entitled *Afri-American Youth* [*sic*]; it was his first publishing experience. Johnson engaged in many journalistic activities as a high school student, including serving as the editor for the school's paper. These activities begat opportunities to demonstrate his writing and oration skills and to comment on current affairs, particularly as related to race matters, before local and national audiences. In the spring of 1936, Johnson traveled to Washington, DC, to represent Du Sable High School at a conference titled "Problems of Negro Youth." Howard University had organized the event in response to Langston Hughes's call in the National Association for the Advancement of Colored People (NAACP) publication the *Crisis* for black students to be "an antidote to the docile dignity of the meek professors and well-paid presidents," lest "American Negroes in the future . . . expect only cowards from the college."[10] (Interestingly, Hughes accused black academia's elders—the professors—of the very apathy that Moss Hyles Kendrix had, in the same moment, used the *Maroon Tiger* to lay squarely at the feet of black college students.) Johnson's participation in the conference earned him recognition in the *Chicago Defender*, the national black newspaper of record, and put him in the orbit of prominent black political thinkers, including NAACP attorney Thurgood Marshall and secretary of the National Negro Congress John P. Davis.

Johnson's academic and journalistic accomplishments caught the attention of Harry Pace, president of the Supreme Life Insurance Company, which, at the time, was the largest black-owned business in the northern United States. Pace offered Johnson a scholarship to attend college part time and simultaneously work at Supreme Life after high school. Surrounded by Depression-weary and unemployed African Americans, Johnson had managed to land a white-collar job at a successful black business, as well as a ticket to higher education.

The summer following his graduation in June 1936, Johnson began writing articles for the *Defender* on the black "Youth Front" and local politics under the byline John H. Johnson, jettisoning "Johnny" and adding the *H* to stand in for the middle name he did not have.[11] He also began work at Supreme Life as a clerk but quickly worked up to Pace's personal assistant. As Pace's assistant, Johnson assiduously tracked "black Chicago" through newspapers, magazines, and gossip for his boss, who deemed it good business to stay abreast of "what was happening in the Black World."[12]

Johnson decided that others might also be interested in such happenings, which is how *Negro Digest* came into being in November 1942.[13]

The editorial statement in the first issue of *Negro Digest* explained that Johnson's first publication was offered as an "easy-to-read . . . complete survey of current Negro life and thought . . . dedicated to . . . interracial understanding and the promotion of interracial unity."[14] In less than a year after its debut, the digest had a circulation of over fifty thousand, and it soundly changed Johnson's life.[15] In 1943 he left Supreme Life and devoted himself completely to his publishing venture, which he moved from its one-desk outfit in the Supreme Life building to "a typical Chicago storefront" that he purchased on South State Street, the first "official" headquarters of JPC. He and his new bride, Eunice (Walker), "moved on up" from their three-bedroom rental to the first floor of a three-story apartment building that Johnson purchased with a $9,000 down payment.[16] Although financially "secure" for the first time in his life, Johnson remained unsatisfied: he wanted to expand his business, which required expanding his market. He began to study the African Americans around him. When he was not tracking black America through other publications and laboring to get his digest printed, Johnson walked the streets of Chicago's black neighborhoods, paying close attention to black consumer desires and the media or cultural trends that affected those desires. Close scrutiny of this readily available focus group led to two key observations that greatly affected Johnson's next move as a black mediamaker.

First, Johnson understood that African Americans had more money than they ever had. While blacks continued to be the "last hired, first fired," this dynamic was much less devastating during the war than it had been during the Depression because of the labor the war effort required. Postwar economist Marcus Alexis reported that, during the war, employers "more widely accepted" blacks in skilled and semiskilled jobs. As African Americans' employment opportunities improved, their median income nearly tripled during the war years and they had a combined disposable income of $7 billion.[17] In a related trend, as a group, blacks became an increasingly urban population as they chased defense industry jobs to the cities; their relocation allowed advertisers to access them more easily through mediums such as radio and, of interest to Johnson, magazines.[18] As Johnson surmised, the consumer status of African Americans was shifting with their increased purchasing power.

Johnson's second observation concerned the type of publications that interested African Americans. He kept a keen eye on his competition and often polled vendors at newsstands about current purchasing trends. Based on this "crude market research," to use Johnson's description, he discovered that, among Chicago's blacks, the strongest competition for *Negro Digest* was *Life*, an oversize photo-magazine published by Time Incorporated, the sales of which were second only to those of *Reader's Digest*.[19] *Life*'s success had soundly demonstrated the market value of photojournalistic images. Johnson realized that print media had "giv[en] way to the blitzkrieg of the photograph."[20] Based on these observations, he determined that African Americans had a desire to see themselves in the mainstream photographs of the print media. They were "going places [they] had never been before and doing things [they had] never done before, and [they] wanted to see that."[21] Others shared this observation. Writing in the *Defender*, academic Samuel Ichiye Hayakawa painted a grim picture of how African Americans experienced media. Of Japanese ancestry, Hayakawa noted how, in movies, popular magazines, and billboards, "the ideas of gentlemanly dignity . . . 'graceful living,' [and] achievement and beauty and magnificence" are all "portrayed by white characters."[22] Given these circumstances, Johnson decided to bank, quite literally, on the representational desires of black Americans. In November 1945 he launched his black photo-magazine, the mission of which he summarized as "*Black* words and pictures, and a holistic presentation of the Black image" (emphasis in original).[23]

"Most white magazines deal with Negroes as second-class citizens or freaks," Johnson explained to *Time* magazine when interviewed about his new publishing enterprise.[24] He offered *Ebony* as a corrective to the images, or lack thereof, of black people and black life put forth by the white media. He and his editorial staff, he explained, believed that "Black Americans needed positive images to fulfill their potential," and subscribed to the idea that "you have to change images before you can change acts and institutions."[25] The emancipatory power of "positive" images was an idea commonly held among African Americans and members of other marginalized groups. Hayakawa, for example, asserted that the visual products of artists and other cultural producers "determine the content of our visual imagination," and the ideals rooted in that imagination, rather than events, determined the lived experiences of all Americans, of all people. Different experiences required different visuals.[26] The concern among people of color about their media representation explains the *Chicago Defender's* consistent reportage on black publishing, including, especially, the arrival, content, format, and demise of black magazines.[27]

If taken at his word, Johnson recognized that the visual representation of black America that *Ebony* made possible, which was a radical departure from the conventional stereotypical depiction, was both historically and politically significant. Change, however, was not the intended or main objective. Offering an alternative representation of blacks was subordinate, albeit essential, to his primary goal of establishing a successful magazine. Johnson rightly supposed that a magazine that provided a "holistic" image of blackness would be profitable precisely because of the psychic and political demands he wagered it would fulfill among black consumers. Having identified a market to serve, he founded *Ebony* believing, as he explained, he could "improve [himself] economically."[28] In this vein, Johnson capitalized on several dynamics specific to the post–World War II moment, including an expanding media culture increasingly organized around visual imagery; greater opportunities for African Americans to produce media and access mainstream media channels; and the increased purchasing power of African Americans. These circumstances made media images that depicted African Americans in the manners they desired smart business. Having identified an unsatisfied demand, Johnson rushed to meet it.

Publishing a black magazine was a risky venture despite public demand for new and varied black media representations. One contemporary editor explained, "Black magazines were consistent, short-lived flops."[29] *Negro Digest*, then only in its toddler stage, was the only existing commercially successful black publication one could point to. Only the *Crisis* and the Urban League's *Opportunity*, which were noncommercial, civil rights journals, had survived as regularly published black periodicals. Johnson was determined that *Ebony* would not go the way of all the other black magazines before it. To ensure its success, he studied and then put into action strategies that had worked for other successful publishers.

Historians—as well as Johnson's peers and Johnson himself—have routinely defined him as a leader and innovator in publishing because of the number of "firsts" he accomplished with his various publications. In building his publishing company, however, he followed as much as, if not more than, he led. In building his company, he used, as he told *Time* magazine, "a simple formula—putting out 'Negro Magazines' in a format that has been successful with white people."[30] This strategy had worked with *Negro Digest*, which he modeled after *Reader's Digest*, the nation's top-selling magazine. Johnson did not set out to reinvent the wheel with *Ebony* either; rather, he copied already winning formats. Ben Burns, a white newspaperman and one of Johnson's first collaborators in publishing, witnessed this formula firsthand. Burns helped Johnson design, produce, and launch *Negro Digest*, all while moonlighting from his job as national editor of the *Chicago Defender*. When it came to *Ebony*'s design, Burns surrounded himself with copies of *Life* so he could replicate page layouts, title types, and writing styles, which he did "religiously."[31] The most blatant example of *Life*'s influence was the *Ebony* logo, which mirrored precisely that of the "general market" publication, with the magazine name set in large, white capital block letters and encased in a bright-red rectangle (Figures 33 and 34). At 13¾″ × 9¾″, the magazine also matched the large format of its white prototype. Finally, *Ebony* mimicked *Life*'s photo-essay format: it contained a mix of profiles on noted African Americans, human interest stories, and essays and editorials pertaining to matters of black interest, all of which were either supplemented by or composed primarily of captioned photographs.[32]

That Johnson borrowed conventions established by publishers of white print media testifies to his careful tracking of and contributions to innovations that shaped mainstream publishing in the mid-twentieth century. More importantly, his tactics reveal that the representation and marketing strategies of the most powerful black media- and imagemaking institution of the postwar United States did not emerge purely out of black culture or a set of black sensibilities or politics, or even from methods and models defining black publishing or the black press at the time. Indeed, Burns's involvement in JPC testifies to the racial hybridity behind Johnson's "black" publications from the onset. Johnson borrowed talent and tactics from white print media because it offered successful models to emulate. He did not look to "ape" white publishers (as Frazier would have it) when formatting or marketing his magazines as much as he looked to copy methods that produced commercially successful publications. His approach allowed him to accomplish what no other black publishing outfit had: the production of multiple specialized publications of quality with circulations that rivaled those of successful white magazines. His mimicry methods also resulted in the modern black magazine publishing industry's having roots within white print media.

Figure 33. Cover of *Ebony*, September 1947. Ebony Media Operations, LLC.

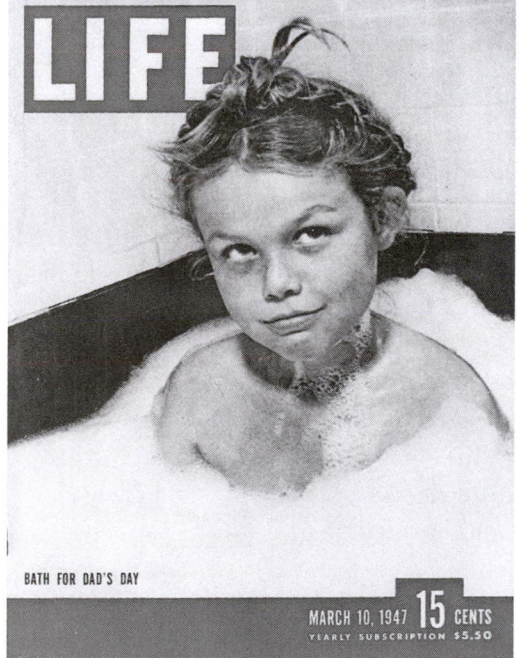

Figure 34. Cover of *Life*, March 10, 1947. © 1947 Time Inc. All rights reserved. Reprinted/translated from LIFE and published with permission of Time Inc.

Despite a tendency to follow suit, Johnson made one radical departure from convention when he launched his new magazine: he debuted it with no advertisements.[33] To launch his photo-magazine without advertising was risky. Ad revenue, not newsstand sales of the twenty-five-cent magazine, was (and continues to be) the lifeblood of commercial magazines. Historically, black publications failed because they could not secure advertising schedules from large corporations. Advertisers resisted appealing to black markets through black publications because they accepted a common belief that African Americans lacked purchasing power, they feared alienating white consumers, and they viewed black print media as an inferior, ineffective medium for reaching customers.[34] Consequently, advertisements commonly found within the black press were those of minor, local merchandisers or mail-order ads. These advertisements were generally small and of poor production quality, and they pushed products of questionable reputation and taste. For example, ads for blackface figurines, ashtrays, and bottle openers commonly appeared in black publications—an unfortunate but necessary concession of black publishers unable to secure other forms of advertising.

Johnson was keenly aware of the negative reputation that black publications held among major and white advertisers. Consequently, he reasoned that accepting low-grade advertisements that previous black publishers had secured (as a necessary evil) would adversely affect regard for his magazine, which, in turn, would impact his ability to secure major advertisers. For *Ebony*, Johnson said he wanted "the big four-color ads that were the staple of the White magazines," because they were a marker of a quality publication and because such advertising brought in more money.[35] He rejected all advertising initially to separate *Ebony* from the standard set by black magazines that had come before. He announced through the press that he would not accept advertising in *Ebony* until the magazine had reached a circulation of one hundred thousand per monthly issue. He then guaranteed that circulation of one hundred thousand to advertisers, stating that he would refund their money if the magazine did not sell at least that many copies.[36] In other words, he promised to deliver a sizeable market and alleviate the risk to advertisers and merchandisers on either side of the color line who elected to court that market. Johnson's gamble made building *Ebony*'s circulation essential to the future of his magazine and his company. The primary method for doing so quickly became the use of photographs and illustrations that highlighted black women's physical attractiveness and sexual appeal, a marketing strategy that mirrored trends visible in popular "white" print media of the time.

The mass production and circulation of sexually evocative images of women became more prevalent during World War I. Risqué pinup images and other blue material that featured shapely, minimally dressed women, commonly referred to as "cheesecake" images, first emerged in the less socially acceptable mediums of "girlie" calendars and magazines and illicit postcards traded among soldiers as morale boosters. Cheesecake images then made their way into mainstream publications, particularly those catering to American men, during the 1930s. Fueling this trend was the popular men's magazine *Esquire*, which "attempted to elevate [risqué cheesecake material] to the higher realm of urbane good taste."[37] *Life* magazine also displayed editorial faith in the effectiveness of such images for drawing, and keeping, readers when it began to routinely feature photographs and covers that celebrated, as one of the magazine's editors remarked, people's "imperious desire to see, and see again, the female form divine."[38]

When Johnson and his staff used sexy images of black women to build circulation among black consumers, then, they were not breaking new ground: they were stepping onto ground that their (white) counterparts already had proved quite solid. Still, they stepped gingerly onto this terrain with *Ebony*'s first issue. The inaugural cover featured an innocuous photograph of an interracial group of smiling, young boys and gave no indication that sexy pictures might be among the magazine's content.[39] A hint of things to come could be found in the "Entertainment" section, which featured a pinup photograph of a young, black woman (Figure 35). A one-page profile introduced readers to Sheila Guyse, a twenty-year-old African American woman who, in 1945, made her Broadway debut in *Memphis Bound*, in which she played the female lead opposite famous tap dancer Bill "Bojangles" Robinson, the mostly highly paid African American entertainer of the time.[40] The feature captured a black starlet on her way up and signaled *Ebony*'s commitment to celebrity and potential for star making. (Guyse went on to star in other Broadway shows and Hollywood films and enjoyed relative success as a nightclub performer and recording artist.) In the history of the magazine, Guyse stands as its first pinup girl. In the photo, she sits wearing a showgirl's outfit, the spaghetti straps of which emphasize her bare shoulders and modest cleavage, and the skirt of which is hiked

Figure 35. Publicity pinup photograph of Sheila Guyse appearing in first issue of *Ebony* magazine, November 1945. Ebony Media Operations, LLC.

above her knees to reveal her crossed, bare legs. The accompanying text spins Guyse, identified as a "Mississippi-born pinup," as a Cinderella girl-next-door figure whom "folks back home" hoped would receive "her glass slippers and fancy coach" in the form of a Hollywood career, lest she remain a "pinup without a position."[41] While the photograph promotes Guyse's sex appeal, contextualized by the text, it works as a sexy, but still sweet, representation of black womanhood. In this form, *Ebony*'s first pinup traded in sex appeal but bore the mark of black anxiety regarding representations of black women that strayed too close to the stereotypical Jezebel figure that dated back to slavery of the hypersexed, sexually experienced, and promiscuous black woman. The image was buried deep within *Ebony*'s debut issue, toward the back of the magazine. When *Time* magazine previewed *Ebony* a month before it became available to consumers, however, it advertised the new black magazine by highlighting the Guyse pinup as a feature to anticipate.[42]

Ebony's first pinup image also played on a visual discourse of American white womanhood popularized during the recent war that identified female beauty as both the roots and bounty of American patriotism. Sexy-sweet black pinups provided JPC a means to build profitable associations between *Ebony*, black consumers, and dominant ideals that defined American citizenship and values. During World War II, American female beauty took on heightened significance as the physical, tangible representation of the value of American women and their womanhood. U.S. politicians, military officials, and news and entertainment media all pointed to beauty as a reason why "American boys" served in the armed forces, and as a marker of American superiority. In the U.S. fight against fascism, the pinup emerged as a potent symbol of moral obligation and national pride, which exonerated it from previous condemnations as unsuitable, blue imagery.[43] Pinup images circulated openly throughout World War II in two basic forms. First, there was the "girl next door" pinup image, which typically featured a commonly attractive woman in form-revealing attire, such as a bathing suit or tight sweater, smiling over her shoulder. These pinup girls served as stand-ins for the "real" women back home and thus operated as "icons of the private interests and obligations for which soldiers were fighting" (Figure 36).[44] In addition to these relatively "sweet" representations, there were "bombshell" pinup images such as those in *Esquire*'s Varga Girls series, vibrant pinups painted by Alberto Vargas y Chavez (Figure 37). Varga Girls were

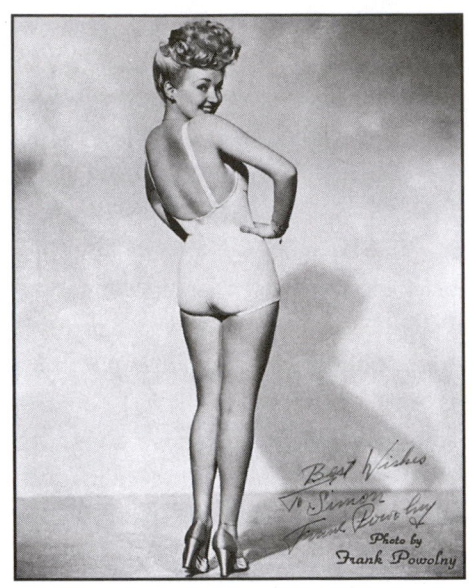

Figure 36. World War II pinup photograph of Betty Grable, 1943.
Figure 37. "Varga Girl" pinup girl, 1940. Alberto Vargas y Chavez. Getty Images.

clearly intended as appeals to heterosexual male desire; however, this imagery also provided new conceptions of female sexuality as, to quote one historian, "remarkably self-aware and aggressive."[45] This definition coincided with women's relatively empowered position within U.S. culture, which was a product of changing gender dynamics motivated by the wartime promotion of and reliance on womanpower.[46]

In contrast to cheesecake pinups, the commonness of the "girl next door" (or "apple pie" pinup images) was especially accessible for nonmodel and noncelebrity women to embody. (Many American women took up pinup poses in photographs they sent to "sweethearts" serving overseas.) The ideal, however, was drawn along lines of race. It constructed, and celebrated, the whiteness symbolized by famed pinup girl Betty Grable, especially, as representative of American womanhood and its supremacy. African American men's contributions to the war, however, positioned the pinup image to be co-opted for black political agendas that promoted black womanhood, normative black masculinity, black patriotism, and, by extension, black national belonging.

The political utility of the pinup to citizenship claims within a war context helps explain why the NAACP made limited but noteworthy use of the visual pinup discourse in the *Crisis* during World War II. In June 1942, well before the debut of *Ebony*, a nineteen-year-old Dorothy Dandridge began her cover girl career when she appeared as the *Crisis*'s first pinup cover girl (Figure 38). Previously, the NAACP magazine's cover girl images generally consisted of head-and-shoulder glamour shots trained on the black female subject's face and formulated to highlight markers of middle-class respectability, including feminine and fashionable clothes and hairstyles, tasteful makeup, and, typically, light skin.[47] By comparison, the cover photograph of Dandridge provides a full-length view of the aspiring singer-actress propped in the fork of a massive tree. She wears a form-fitting striped blouse; high-waisted, white shorts that provide an extremely fleshy perspective of her legs; and the high heels obligatory to the classic pinup. Her pose in the photograph, combined with her clothing, wide smile, and popular roll hairdo, creates the sweet-while-sexy quality essential to wartime pinups' mainstream popularity. This cover photograph, which was a marked turn away from the *Crisis*'s traditional representation strategies, helped the black civil rights journal access wartime discourses that defined U.S. citizenship through gendered dynamics of obligation in which American men

Griffin-Siminoff

Figure 38. Pinup photograph of Dorothy Dandridge appearing on cover of the *Crisis*, June 1942. Photo credit Griffin-Siminoff.

fought to protect American women who performed and appeared as objects worthy of the effort. The photo's caption articulates these associations: it explains that the "colored" enlisted men of the Seventh Regiment of the California State Guard had recently crowned Dandridge their "sweetheart" based on her "beauty, personality, and character."[48] Dandridge's turn as a pinup cast a spotlight on blacks' sharing values deemed uniquely American and their significance to national security. When she occupied the role of NAACP pinup girl, Dandridge assisted the civil rights organization's wartime agenda to assert African Americans' full citizenship based on their patriotism and contributions to democracy.[49]

After the war, the pinup quickly fell from her position of relative grace once stripped of her wartime functions. Faced with hordes of returning male soldiers, popular media supported governmental efforts to promote the nostalgic morals and gender definitions that ensured these soldiers could resume their prewar societal roles.[50] In this climate, many mainstream periodicals, including "pin-up pioneers" *Life* and *Esquire*, "deemphasized or altogether eliminated their pin-up features in the postwar era."[51] But this trend applied primarily to white pinup images. When the war ended, the *Crisis* did revert to its prewar representational practices emphasizing female respectability. However, at the precise moment major white magazines pulled from their pages the pinup representation they had helped popularize during the war, JPC began to mainstream black pinup and cheesecake imagery with its publications. Johnson's use of these images stemmed at least as much from his objectives as a black entrepreneur as from his agenda as a professional black imagemaker.

Johnson used pinup imagery in his new magazine to connect to the black readership he both imagined and constructed, African Americans who conceived of themselves in relation to the war effort. When devising *Ebony*, he envisioned black communities infused by returning black veterans who had traveled to different parts of the world and would be looking for "more glamour and more pizzazz" than *Negro Digest* provided.[52] If she had lost her place of honor within white print media, the pinup girl offered Johnson a way to appeal to the black veterans Johnson considered central to the market he sought. Moreover, by using imagery so heavily identified with World War II, Johnson drew out the associations between black Americans and their war service, unprecedented in its extent and forms. Beyond offering ideological routes to the consumers Johnson desired, this tactic also furthered an ideal of the black American that many political thinkers believed was essential leverage for blacks in their quest for first-class citizenship and social equality. In addition to presenting profiles on black entertainers and articles that heralded black achievement—all of which worked to offer "relief from the day-to-day combat with racism," present "the happier side of Negro life," and guide the postwar consumerism of blacks—early issues of *Ebony* repeatedly hailed blacks as a population that had contributed to the war effort.[53] The inaugural issue of *Ebony* included pieces that offered "inspiration for veterans" wounded in service and mapped out black expectations following the war. An editorial concerning fair employment practices, for example, rooted its argument for blacks' fair and full employment in the postwar United States based on their having "fought the enemy side by side with their white brothers in uniform."[54] Prominent media and U.S. officials pushed Americans to shift into a postwar state of mind and adopt the optimism and behaviors necessary to stimulate the mass consumption deemed essential to the nation's recovery and secure global position. Johnson, however, approached his target readership not as postwar Americans but as post–war *service* Americans. As a representation of womanhood popularized during the war, the pinup visually carried forth an ideological context that Johnson believed would attract black consumers and result in the circulation numbers he sought.

The second issue of *Ebony* brought cheesecake to the fore by placing a pinup image on, not in, the magazine. The cover of the December 1945 issue featured a pinup-style photograph of Hilda Simms (Figure 39), the star of the popular Broadway show *Anna Lucasta*, which told the story of an innocent girl driven to prostitution.[55] Simms was a light-skinned black woman with long, wavy hair—much like Guyse, the "pin-up without position" who appeared in the previous issue, and the *Crisis* cover girl Dandridge. Her appearance as JPC's first cover girl suggested that, in its representation of black womanhood, the outfit meant to honor a politics of color among African Americans in which "bright [was] right." In her cover photograph, Simms appears propped against a light pole, which alluded to *Anna Lucasta* publicity materials that featured a sketch of a wantonly dressed Anna reclining casually against a lamppost, an image that had become a visual trademark for the successful show (Figure 40).[56] Presumably, the desire to exploit *Anna Lucasta*'s popularity explains the selection of a black woman celebrated for her portrayal of a prostitute as *Ebony*'s first cover girl. The editorial staff wagered that the popularity of Simms and the recognizability of *Anna Lucasta* publicity materials outweighed the risks of evoking negative or stereotypical connotations of black womanhood by featuring the prostitute-portraying Simms and mimicking the "lady by the lamppost" image. The decision demonstrated an early faith on Johnson's behalf in using sexualized representations of black women to attract readers and helped determine the central role these images had in the rise of Johnson's imagemaking and media empire. It also increased mainstream circulation of such images through U.S. visual culture as definitions of modern blackness and black womanhood.

The explicit display of black female beauty and sexual appeal on the covers of *Ebony* quickly helped the magazine achieve the guaranteed circulation of one hundred thousand that Johnson required to turn the publication into an advertising vehicle. The issue of *Ebony* with the pinup-style Simms cover sold over fifty thousand copies. With these sales, *Ebony* bypassed its sister magazine, *Negro Digest*, to become the best-selling black magazine in the world.[57] Then, in March 1946, *Ebony* colorized black female beauty by introducing its first full-color cover—and cover girl—in an effort to make the magazine more attractive.[58] The change in the cover's finish and format put the magazine on a more level plane with *Life*, its main competition in terms of quality and visual appeal; color covers also showcased its models as being of color and highlighted the various colorings—in skin tone, eye color, and hair color—among African Americans.

The first *Ebony* color cover was the March 1946 cover featuring Lena Horne (see Figure 32). At the time, Horne was riding high as a successful black songstress and actress. Since age sixteen, when she became a Cotton Club chorus girl, Horne had drawn attention as a light-skinned, fine-featured beauty with a voice of "dramatic intensity."[59] Her career took off in 1942, when she crossed over from successful nightclub singer to bona fide star signed by Metro-Goldwyn-Mayer Studios (MGM) and became Hollywood's "Negro Cinderella."[60] During the war years, her fame and popularity steadily grew with her performances in the successful MGM musicals *Stormy Weather* and *Cabin in the Sky* and her extensive touring with the United Service Organization to perform for American troops. She had been the premier pinup girl among black GIs. Because of her ambiguous racial beauty, she also experienced crossover popularity with nonblacks, as evidenced by the numerous requests MGM received for her picture that

Figure 39. Actress Hilda Simms, cover of December 1945 issue of *Ebony* magazine. Ebony Media Operations, LLC.

Figure 40. Promotional poster for 1945 Broadway play *Anna Lucasta*. Schomburg Center for Research in Black Culture.

were "by no means confined to Negro men."[61] It is little wonder that Johnson elected Horne to represent an important milestone in his magazine's journey toward becoming a first-rate publication with wide appeal. To whet consumer appetites, Johnson announced the upcoming glossy, color cover appearance of black America's "champion pinup girl" in the *Defender*. The announcement signaled the significance of color photography within the history of black publishing, as well as the assumed market appeal of a pretty black woman.[62] On her first (of many) *Ebony* covers, Horne appeared as the Hollywood sex symbol she had become. In the head-and-shoulder, three-quarter glamour shot, she wears an off-the-shoulder, bold, floral-print blouse and stares out at the viewer with a seductive gaze enhanced by her coquettish, red-lipsticked smile. When the issue hit newsstands, *Ebony*'s circulation soared to 275,000, skyrocketing past the circulation of any black magazine in history, as well as Johnson's predetermined benchmark for accepting advertisements.[63]

Ebony's unprecedented circulation numbers made the magazine and, by extension, JPC a successful enterprise, and, as early as 1946, Johnson's two-magazine operation moved into a new and bigger headquarters.[64] In a publishing paradox, however, *Ebony*'s sales put both the magazine and publishing company in jeopardy. In fact, as Johnson put it, the success of his picture magazine "was killing [him]."[65] Despite its impressive circulation numbers, *Ebony* remained a black publication, and its impressive sales were insufficient to generate the interest among advertisers Johnson had anticipated. When Johnson began accepting advertising in the spring of 1946, only four major advertisers—Kotex, Chesterfield, Murray's Hair Pomade, and the Supreme Liberty Life Insurance Company—took advantage of the opportunity. And only two of these advertisers were not black companies selling what were considered "black" products.[66] By year's end, *Ebony* had generated only $27,000 in gross advertising revenue.[67] Without consistent advertising schedules from major, national (white) companies, Johnson could not afford the costs associated with printing and distributing *Ebony*. In particular, he struggled to cover the costs of the "slick paper" and the "million-dollar presses" required to produce the higher-quality magazine, which was higher in page count and larger in size than his digest. In addition, the postage required to deliver *Ebony* to its numerous subscribers was cripplingly expensive. The more issues of *Ebony* that Johnson produced to meet the increasing demand, the more money he lost.

Only subscription sales of *Negro Digest* were keeping JPC afloat. Johnson's first magazine could survive on its subscription base because it carried low production costs as a two-tone, smaller publication (measuring 7½" × 5") printed on coarse, matte paper. Reducing *Ebony*'s press run was not an option, however. As Johnson explained, "It was a simple matter of arithmetic": "The more *Ebony* readers, the more potential advertisers," which Johnson understood to be where significant profits would be found.[68] Unlike his predecessors, he did not endeavor to produce one successful black publication. Johnson sought to create a business and mediamaking empire that profited from satisfying African Americans' various, and neglected, demands for entertainment and information, as well as their representational desires. Resolute, Johnson pushed on with his original plan to make *Ebony* irresistible as an advertising medium. He doubled down on his strategy and announced a new circulation guarantee of four hundred thousand.[69]

A pattern developed during 1947 in which *Ebony*'s editorial staff used sexualized images of black women more and more to attract consumers and achieve the sales necessary to lure advertisers. First, in the spring of that year, cover models began appearing in two-piece outfits, which revealed their midriffs, but not their navels. This display of the female body walked a fine line of decency determined largely by contemporary Hollywood codes that policed levels of appropriate undress for the female body. These codes deemed display of a woman's belly button offensive.[70] In May 1947 *Ebony*'s editors boldly crossed the line with an article entitled "Miss Fine Brown Frame," which reported on a national black beauty contest and profiled the "darkest entrant" and winner, Evelyn Sanders.[71] The piece included several photographs as evidence of the "fine frame" that earned Sanders the title over her lighter-skinned competition. Taken by Gordon Parks, one of two professional photographers who freelanced for *Ebony*, the images showcased Sanders's almost-nude body.[72] The article's lead image, for example, pictured her entire, bikini-clad body, on which her measurements were superimposed. Absent from the picture, however, was Sanders's head, which had been cropped out. With no head, Sanders's body was the clear object of focus, in the image and in the article. In addition to Sanders's navel, the photographs exposed the entirety of her legs and a decent portion of her backside.

Risqué, these images were also risky, because they evoked racist conceptions about the accessibility of the black female body and the inherently lascivious nature of black women. Many African Americans believed such representations were injurious to black uplift, and they let Johnson know it in the form of letters to the editor.[73] Whether or not he saw them as such, Johnson did not approach such representations as shameful or debilitating to black progress. A dyed-in-the-wool capitalist, he evaluated them for their marketing utility. The May 1947 issue achieved a circulation of 352,000, the highest to date, despite—or more likely because of—the taboo "Fine Brown Frame" photographs.[74] JPC's methods demonstrated that, as part of a commercial venture—rather than an explicitly political endeavor—the risqué display of black women proved highly profitable.

By the third quarter of 1947, *Ebony* remained shy of the consumer base of four hundred thousand that Johnson had guaranteed for his photo magazine the previous fall, so the magazine continued to limp along with few advertisers. In response, *Ebony*'s creators upped the ante. They recycled the "Fine Brown Frame" representational tactic in a much more visible and declarative fashion: they put it on the cover. The July 1947 *Ebony* cover, which boasts of an inside scoop on vacation spots, pictures a full-body photograph of a busty and "deep-hipped" young black woman leaning back against a bright-white sail, wearing only a slight bikini that fully exposes her midsection—navel and all—and her thick thighs (Figure 41).[75] Uncloseted in the postwar marketplace, images such as this visually screamed "LOOK AT ME!" to the passing public and made consumers out of those seduced by the other message inherent to pinups on the covers of commercial publications: "You can have me."[76]

Desperate for advertisers, Johnson bucked convention in the summer of 1947 and went to the heads of major corporations personally to convince them of the profit of targeting African Americans through his publication. He brought the July 1947 issue of *Ebony* to those meetings to demonstrate the quality of his product and to provide the white male executives with whom he met a picture—formulated through "Black words and pictures"— of the black market he could deliver to them. That issue, he claimed, helped convince Zenith Radio Company president Eugene McDonald to buy advertising in *Ebony* and encouraged chairpersons of other major corporations to do the same.[77] This was the turning point for *Ebony* and JPC.[78] In short order, other major advertisers—including Pepsi-Cola, Colgate, Beech-Nut, Old Gold, MGM, and Capitol Records—bought ad space on a consistent basis. By the end of 1948, *Ebony*'s circulation was well on its way to half a million and the magazine was a financial and cultural success.[79]

Figure 41. *Ebony* cover, July 1947. Ebony Media Operations, LLC.

Dissemination of black cheesecake through *Ebony* moved this imagery to the fore of black media and popular culture and, by extension, postwar black representation politics. Johnson controlled the medium through which these images circulated; however, by no means did he have unilateral control over the images. His success depended on appealing to his black consumers' needs and desires, especially their wishes to see themselves and their lives reflected back to them. This meant that, in the production of media images of black people and black life, he consistently negotiated—

sometimes abiding by, sometimes upsetting, and sometimes disregarding altogether—the image politics of his consumers.

The high sales of *Ebony* demonstrated that JPC's alternative—or "holistic," to use Johnson's descriptor—portrayal of black Americans and black life clearly appealed to African Americans. No aspect of the magazine concerned them more, however, than its representation of black women's bodies. Nothing received more frequent or consistent comment within the "Letters" department during the magazine's first five years than its use of pinups, cheesecake material, and glamour shots of black women.[80] Collectively, *Ebony* consumers' letters formed a dialogue in which African Americans theorized about how these images served, or failed to serve, various black political and social agendas.

The public's critiques of JPC's depiction of sexualized black femininity across its magazines reveal that cover girls were of primary interest (and concern) to consumers (defined here as both those who purchased these magazines and those who merely viewed them). *Ebony* cover girls circulated out in the open, exposed on newsstands and coffee tables for all to see. Both Johnson and his consumers recognized that the visibility of JPC's black cover girls amplified their power. To the commercial publisher, cover girl images were an effective marketing tool that drew both male and female consumer attention and could double as promotions for current cultural trends or attractions, as in the case of the cover portraying Simms as *Anna Lucasta*. The African Americans purchasing or viewing these images invested them with multiple, and sometimes contradictory, purposes and meanings.

In one of the first letters to appear in *Ebony* concerning its representation of black women, New Yorker Holmes Morgan claimed black cover girl images could combat the ubiquitous "anti-black propaganda" inspiring inferiority complexes among blacks. The presumably black man believed pretty pictures of pretty black women could soothe psychic wounds, and he called on *Ebony* to "start the ball-a-rolling" by putting "black beauties" on its covers.[81] Notably, *Ebony*'s editors selected Morgan's statements about the potential of black media representations of black women as an initial comment on the magazine's use of cover girl images. They shaped the conversation these letters formed on the topic, as they picked the voices (letters) to be heard (printed). By positioning Morgan's letter as the first proposition in what would be an ongoing debate within the "Letters" department over "black beauties" on the magazine's covers, *Ebony*'s editors rationalized their controversial use of them.

In the "Letters" department of *Ebony*, African American consumers approached black beauty as the constructed and contested concept it is, which opened the way for the magazine to stray from the dominant ideal of black beauty. The moment was ripe for renegotiating standards of American beauty. In a climate of increased consumerism, new and expanding visual media, and Cold War discourses of us (Americans) versus them (Soviets), American women's physical attractiveness took on particular value. In the postwar United States, the media, merchandisers, and women themselves defined beauty as something that could be purchased. The notion of buying beauty coincided with state-sponsored campaigns promoting the mass consumption deemed necessary for the nation to recover and remain globally secure. Furthermore, American female beauty figured within nationalist discourses that presented it as a symbol of rewards unique to living in a capitalist democracy. In the Soviet Union, being beautiful, or striving to be beautiful, was bad, because it represented energies taken away from being a good worker, mother, and wife; by contrast, in the United States, being beautiful was considered very, very good. American women's beauty represented the superiority of a capitalist economy that provided women the motivation, the freedom, and, most important, ample consumer products to both fulfill and enjoy their "natural" feminine role, rather than be an "asexual female worker drone."[82]

The concept of what constituted American female beauty in the postwar moment was not open to all women. As was true of the classic pinup, the dominant ideal of beauty was a raced concept that assumed and simultaneously promoted beauty as the purview of white women—that is, heterosexual, middle-class, white women. In the postwar years, representations valorizing white women's beauty saturated U.S. visual culture. A contemporary black artist looked on the visual world around him and declared that the subtle but significant effect of these visuals was to give whites "a monopoly on beauty."[83] By comparison, mainstream images that celebrated or even acknowledged black female beauty were scarce and almost always segregated within the black press's coverage of black beauty contests. Then came JPC with its colorful black cover girls, which intervened sharply as representations that highlighted black women's physical attractiveness.

Black consumers enlisted JPC cover girls, especially, as assertions of black beauty that served the larger cause of disrupting racist ideologies that denied African Americans the capacity for beauty, a denial that aided ideas of black inferiority. Corporal James L. Hudson, one of Johnson's consumers, claimed that the colorful pinup images of black women functioned as "American art" and counteracted the idea furthered in white media that "Negro beauty does not even exist."[84] Esther P. Oliver of Los Angeles agreed and claimed the black cover girls performed "a great service" in "embrac[ing] something besides the Nordic type."[85] Similar to those who wrote letters calling for dark-skinned models, Hudson, Oliver, and consumers like them recognized *Ebony*'s cover as prime visual real estate for the strategic display of alternative images of American beauty that interrogated the politics of race, color, and class that precluded many African American women's ability to claim beauty.[86] By simply putting a photograph of a black woman on the cover of its magazines, JPC claimed the pictured woman as beautiful by virtue of the media space she occupied. Johnson's cover girls made the boundaries of normative beauty visible, even as they transgressed and redrew them.

Consumers of Johnson's publications typically focused on how images of black beauty performed among African Americans as reflections that encouraged black pride and discouraged the self-loathing inspired by internalized racist ideologies of blacks' inferiority. In contrast, they analyzed JPC's accentuation of black women's sexuality or sexual appeal—qualities rooted in the recognition of black women as sexual beings—primarily in relation to the circulation of these images beyond black circles.

In March 1947, two months before the "Fine Brown Frame" issue, Apollo Girl Mabel Lee appeared on the cover of *Ebony* in full stage makeup and a skimpy, see-through two-piece costume that closely resembled lingerie, making hers the most highly sexualized of *Ebony*'s cover girl representations to date (Figure 42). The public's reaction was swift and pronounced. In Mississippi, Major D. Lucas viewed the decision to put Lee on the cover "almost naked" as "absolutely prideless." Irving Cornelius Hale of the Bronx agreed, fearing the impression the image would make on people "unfamiliar with *Ebony*." Confirming these fears was Mary William, a white woman who subscribed to *Ebony* as a favor to her family's longtime black maid. Williams informed *Ebony* editors that she took the image of the scantily clad black showgirl as evidence that blacks were choosing an "irreligious,

Figure 42. Apollo Girl Mabel Lee, *Ebony* cover, March 1947. Ebony Media Operations, LLC.

immoral" path.[87] Though not expressly marketed to her, *Ebony* made it to Williams by way of the informal and unpredictable manners in which consumer products and pop culture items travel. And, upon encountering the magazine, Williams examined and judged it and the people she assumed to be its intended market, African Americans. Black consumers' reaction to the Lee cover reflected their awareness of this unregimented flow of mainstream images. Their letters revealed the understanding that a community's representations of womanhood "[signified that] community . . . to mainstream society . . . [and opened] up its values to public scrutiny."[88] Circulating in the open, the sensational photograph of Lee smuggled along injurious messages about African Americans' lack of morality and civility. The image, in other words, was not a politically expedient representation of blackness for a group trying to claim its normalcy or equality.

JPC constantly negotiated the fears and criticisms of black consumers in its reliance on sexualized representations of black women. Each time the company pushed the representational and respectability boundaries that had long determined the portrayal of black women in black print media, the public reined it back in. A brief appearance of pinups on the covers of *Negro Digest* demonstrates this push-pull relationship. In late 1946, JPC extended the practice of using cheesecake as a marketing tool to Johnson's first publication. Johnson conceived his digest as a magazine to keep African Americans "abreast of local and national events," and he considered it a "serious magazine," particularly in comparison to its younger sibling, *Ebony*. Published monthly, the small digest was text heavy. During its first four years of publication, the covers of the magazine, printed on matte paper, featured only text and doubled as the publication's table of contents. In format, the *Negro Digest* cover mirrored closely the cover of its white counterpart *Reader's Digest* and reflected its less sensational content. That is, until November 1946, when *Negro Digest* hit newsstands with a cover featuring a glossy, full-color Kodachrome image of a busty, young, extremely light-skinned woman with bright-red lips and long, wavy, shiny black hair who posed as a college coed dressed in a yellow sweater and wraparound, red-and-black tartan skirt (Figure 43). A picture had never appeared on the magazine's cover, let alone one so vibrant. In this context, that first *Negro Digest* "girlie cover" appeared electrified.[89]

Here, Johnson deviated from his habit of mimicking his white competitors: it was, after all, unthinkable that *Reader's Digest* would turn up with a similar display of a white woman on its cover. JPC's finances at the moment prompted the move, however. As previously discussed, with the "success" of *Ebony* dragging JPC further and further into debt, Johnson relied on sales of "the steady, undramatic" digest to sustain his company. He explained, "If *Negro Digest* collapsed, [he] and the whole structure were going down with it."[90] Therefore, despite the serious intent and content of the digest, Johnson opted for the representational and marketing practice that

Figure 43. Kodachrome pinup girl image, cover of *Negro Digest*, November 1946. Ebony Media Operations, LLC.

had proved successful with *Ebony*. He put "frothy" images of attractive black women on the covers of *Negro Digest*.[91]

Immediately, consumers of the digest took issue with these covers. Their predominantly negative response clearly led to the demise of the *Negro Digest* pinup-style covers. Several, especially male, consumers celebrated the covers, with one Howard University student asking the question that propelled the complex, ongoing postwar debate concerning the visual representation of black female beauty and sexuality: "What's wrong with a decent picture of a Negro girl?"[92] The majority of those reacting to them, however, believed the girlie covers were incongruous with, and even an "abuse" of, what they believed the magazine's purpose was, or should be.[93] The sexy images, readers explained, mitigated the magazine's potency as the "Magazine of Negro Comment," making it appear more pulp than substance to some readers. In November 1947, the editors announced that, "after a year of . . . connubial bliss," the magazine was "getting a divorce from the 'cheesecake girls,'" because, as the editorial explained, the campaign to gain readers by "er, ah, eh . . . sex" had "frankly not clicked" with the magazine's readership. JPC would take a new approach with *Negro Digest*, or, more accurately, an old one—there would be no more pinup images on its covers. *Negro Digest*, the editors realized, was firmly pigeonholed as a magazine for "a higher grade, brainier type of citizen . . . interested in serious, intelligent articles," a distinct market that made possible the existence of the alternative publication, *Ebony*.[94]

Black cheesecake and girlie covers eschewed traditional black respectability image politics. Concerned with profits, not politics, Johnson reasoned, "We're not the NAACP. We're a business."[95] In *Ebony*, sexualized representations mixed and competed with multiple and varied representations of blackness. In addition to cheesecake, images appeared in the magazine that asserted black women's normative sexuality, largely by portraying black women as the nucleus of middle-class homes and healthy families. An editorial in the March 1947 issue (the issue that featured Lee on the cover) drew links between black women's ability (and availability) to perform as homemakers in their *own* homes and "domestic peace." The full-page photograph (from Gordon Parks's Frederick Douglass housing project series) that accompanies the editorial (Figure 44) pictures a black woman peeling potatoes at her kitchen table while looking out a window framed

Figure 44. Mother preparing dinner, *Ebony* magazine, March 1947. Photograph by Gordon Parks, 1942. Library of Congress Prints and Photographs Division.

by frilly curtains at two small, well-dressed black children playing in the front yard.[96] In addition, ad images within the magazine presented black women in the role of middle-class homemaker, wife, and mother tending to children's wounds, delighting in various kitchen appliances, and serving beverages to their husbands and meals to their families.

Portraits of black female heterosexual domesticity promoted, as much as they rehabilitated, notions of black familyhood, which was routinely defined as dysfunctional and abnormal in the media. The "feminized worker" ideal was also present in the magazine in photographs with captions that identified the subjects as receptionists, mothers, and wives. This representation of black womanhood advanced a respectable, middle-class femininity discernable through the performance of gender-appropriate work and the adoption of visible markers of a type of beauty, poise, and charm, which became commodified after the war, due in no small part to aspirations *Ebony* was guiding its consumers to embrace.[97]

Why did domestic and respectable female worker images appear in *Ebony*? Such representations of black womanhood seem incongruent with the magazine's regular depiction of black cheesecake, which corresponded with its frank approach to black female sexuality. During its early years, discussions of black women's sexuality and sexual practices became more and more common to *Ebony*. In a 1948 article, for example, an anonymous "Midwest [black] woman" shared her attitudes about her sexual experimentation and her illicit affair with a married coworker.[98] Historians have commented on what they view as *Ebony*'s dualistic, even conflicting, construction of womanhood. They credit JPC with a deliberate effort to put forward a more progressive or more complex image of black women that challenged the status quo.[99] This assessment reflects a focus on the politics of *Ebony*. Attention to the business of *Ebony* reveals that the magazine's sometimes schizophrenic representation of black womanhood primarily reflects its function as a commercial product.

Both sets of images—the domestic-respectable ideal and the sexual object—were crucial to Johnson's mediamaking empire. "Girlie" pictures helped Johnson sell more magazines and secure more advertisers. They made the magazine (and the publishing company) possible. The homemaker-mother and feminine worker images, on the other hand, served Johnson's corresponding project of selling the black middle class to major advertisers. Throughout the postwar decade, in both *Ebony*'s editorial and advertising content, Johnson constructed, instructed, and promoted a black middle class both as an actual, small but growing population and as an ideal. Doing so served his agendas to develop a consumer ethos among his readership (which translated into more product sales) and to secure advertisers by leveraging the buying power of middle-class black markets.

Beyond Johnson's entrepreneurial objectives, *Ebony*'s role as essentially *the* mainstream black magazine serving black America affected its representation of black womanhood. In the 1940s white Americans had a myriad of magazines targeted at them that recognized their various experiences and aspirations as divided along lines of gender, class, and special interests. These included, to name but a few, *Time, Newsweek, Ladies' Home Journal, Housekeeping, Redbook, Vogue, Cosmopolitan, Fortune, Esquire, Popular Mechanic,* and *Outdoor Life.* By contrast, in the period directly following World War II, black consumers had essentially two commercial magazines directed at them, *Ebony* and *Our World,* a competitor black lifestyle magazine over which Johnson lost much sleep until it folded in 1957.[100] Not enough knowledge about black readers or trust among advertisers existed to support production of numerous, specialized black magazines. As it grew in size and influence, JPC would become a key force in the market segmentation of African Americans. In the company's early years, however, it was left to produce *Ebony* as a hybrid. The magazine contained a cross section of articles, editorials, and images so that it might appeal to the various and as yet unidentified niche markets of a huge consumership of diverse interests, tastes, and experiences. This approach contributed to prevailing notions within the advertising and marketing industries of African Americans as one big, monolithic "special" market. But *Ebony*'s hybridity also ensured that Johnson drew enough readers for his one publication to make it successful. So, whereas readers of *Ladies' Home Journal* could rest assured they would not run across a nearly naked Varga Girl, *Ebony* readers in the postwar decade got *Esquire*-like pinup and cheesecake representations alongside recipes and fashion features that counseled black women in domesticity and grooming. The mixture of these representations in the pages of *Ebony* implied that one ideal did not preclude the other, which allowed for a more complex, or more nuanced, reflection and construction of black womanhood.[101] It is also necessary, however, to understand that *Ebony*'s convoluted imaging of black womanhood after the war was the result of particular historical circumstances and strategies JPC used to reach multiple and diverse populations through a single commercial vehicle.

By 1950, *Ebony*'s circulation neared a half million, and the JPC operation moved into a showy building on Michigan Avenue south of the Loop, Chicago's prime business district.[102] The revenue and consumer data that *Ebony* generated allowed Johnson to expand his enterprise, and he launched four additional magazines during the early 1950s. These included two romance magazines, *Tan Confessions* and *Copper Romance*, which Johnson intended as black counterparts to *True Confessions*, a wildly popular magazine that targeted young (white) females and provided serious competition for *Ebony* among black consumers. To compete with the celebrity magazine *Quick*, Johnson offered up *Hue*, a small digest that dealt in black celebrity and gossip. Last, there was *Jet* magazine, also a small digest but published weekly, that summarized the "biggest Negro news" and offered "frothy coverage" of black celebrity.[103] Fifteen cents per issue (half *Ebony*'s newsstand price), *Jet* was a publication for the black working class, or the "black masses." Its large target market helped Johnson's second digest reach a circulation of three hundred thousand within six months: it became JPC's second-best-selling magazine.[104] Notably, in 1951, Johnson discontinued *Negro Digest*. The magazine had been his workhorse and plowed the publishing ground in which he planted his budding media empire. With its staid content and template, however, it became the old nag in a stable of show horses bred for the consumerist and materialist culture of the postwar United States.

The unprecedented success of his flagship magazine allowed Johnson to build a media empire that injected into postwar visual culture myriad media representations that claimed to define black America, in the form of advertisements, photographs, articles, and editorials. Johnson's enterprise also achieved real power to affect how other mainstream media institutions perceived and presented blackness. The company's influence in this manner is clearly evident in how it shaped the media representation of singer-actress Dorothy Dandridge.

Dandridge had earned a reputation during the 1930s and early 1940s as a "winsome" entertainer within black circles as a member of the singing trio the Dandridge Sisters.[105] By 1950, with a failed marriage behind her and her mentally disabled and only child a ward of the state, Dandridge hoped to reinvent herself as a solo act. She dispensed with any appearance of girlish innocence and worked the nightclub circuit, wearing "cocoonlike" gowns and singing suggestive songs.[106] She made her way into *Ebony* in this form. In April 1951, at twenty-nine years old, she appeared on the magazine's cover for the first time. In the color cover photograph, Dandridge poses as Melmendi the African princess, her character in the contemporary movie *Tarzan's Peril* (Figure 45). She wears a skimpy two-piece outfit that fully exposes her legs. Her sexualized depiction is further amplified by a tagline on the cover advertising that issue's report about "sex on the campus."[107] Her inaugural visual presentation in *Ebony* reflected a steadfast faith in the ability of sex (in the form of a sexy black woman) to sell the magazine.

JPC increasingly emphasized, displayed, and profited from Dandridge's role as a black sex object through the early 1950s. Numerous articles and photographs in the magazine signified explicitly on Dandridge's sexiness.

Figure 45. Cover of *Ebony* featuring Dorothy Dandridge, April 1951. Ebony Media Operations, LLC.

A photo-essay that detailed her nightclub act, for example, included photo-graphs of Dandridge in slinky, glamorous evening gowns, and the accom-panying text sexualized her with a description of her "torrid" singing, "lithe figure," and "bewitching" wardrobe. The same feature article dis-closed information about male suitors waiting backstage for Dandridge and reported that, during her act, cigarette girls sold the Kinsey Institute's newly published *Sexual Behavior in the Human Female*, all of which pointed to the product for sale—Dandridge's sex appeal.[108]

When he anointed Dandridge a Hollywood star in the April 1951 issue of *Ebony*, Johnson staked a claim in Dandridge's celebrity. His main com-petitor, *Our World*, and white publications like *Life*, *Look*, and *Quick* were all left to follow his lead.[109] Thereafter, *Ebony* regularly featured news items and photo-essays about Dandridge's personal life and career.[110] The maga-zine chronicled her stardom even as it manufactured it, which it had the power to do.[111]

By the mid-1950s, JPC had publicized Dandridge to broad audiences as a black sex goddess figure, which facilitated her selection to play the lead in the film adaptation of the hit Broadway play *Carmen Jones*, based on Georges Bizet's opera *Carmen*. In both the play and the film, Carmen Jones is a ciga-rette girl turned parachute maker during World War II who seduces Joe, a handsome and innocent military police officer, but then takes up with an-other man, prompting a crazed Joe to track her down and strangle her. Un-like *Tarzan's Peril*, *Carmen Jones* was a class-A movie produced by a major studio (Twentieth Century Fox) and directed by a renowned director (Otto Preminger).

When the movie hit theaters in the fall of 1954, it was the best-financed, best-produced, most publicized, and most widely received mainstream media representation of black people and black life in the history of U.S. popular culture.[112] Dandridge's sexiness was essential to the film's success. The marketing campaign mounted by Twentieth Century Fox centered on her "stimulating" performance and looks, and the press characterized the film as a "red-hot and black" and credited Dandridge with "putting the torch to Bizet's babe."[113] This publicity helped *Carmen Jones* surmount the race barrier, and, as one newspaper reported, "members of both races . . . jamm[ed] the doors and aisles" to see the "all-Sepia" film.[114] In Cinema-Scope widescreen format and DeLuxe color, the sexualized Dandridge that JPC began marketing three years prior found the largest audience of any representation of black womanhood to date, save, perhaps, Aunt Jemima. A critically acclaimed box office hit, the movie and its star received wide press, and Dandridge earned an Academy Award nomination for her portrayal of Carmen. In addition to significantly boosting Dandridge's profile as an actress, these events promoted the black sex goddess ideal popularized through *Ebony* to consumers across the color line.

Nothing symbolized or cemented the bona fide popularity of Dandridge the sex goddess more than her appearance on the cover of the November 1, 1954, issue of *Life* magazine (Figure 46). In the mid-1950s, mediamakers took their cues from *Life*, so when the editors selected Dandridge as a cover girl, they signaled her relevance to other media outlets. The cover photograph is a classic pinup representation featuring a made-up Dandridge in her *Carmen Jones* signature outfit of a black off-the-shoulder blouse and form-fitting orange pencil skirt. With her hips facing away from the viewer, she turns at the waist to deliver an over-the-shoulder look—quintessential pinup posture—and a coy smile that renders her simultaneously obtainable and just out of reach. The image thoroughly collapsed the line between Dandridge and the proudly sexual Carmen and marked the culmination of her ascendancy as a sex goddess.

On the cover of *Life*, which had close to five million subscribers and was a best-selling newsstand publication, Dandridge's depiction as Carmen Jones became the leading visual representation of black femininity and black female sexuality of its moment. It was a powerful promotion of black women's capacity for beauty, as it positioned Dandridge within a group of *Life* celebrity cover girls accepted at the time as undeniably appealing, including Audrey Hepburn, Grace Kelly, Eva Marie Saint, and Marilyn Monroe. Dandridge's *Life* cover challenged popular portrayals of black women as unattractive, asexual, and even masculine. It indicated the influence of JPC, which introduced an image of black womanhood into popular print culture that glorified and invited the celebration of black female sexuality, rather than its perversion or denigration. Moreover, Dandridge's "turn" on the cover of *Life* reflected the acknowledgment of black America by the magazine's producers. The embodiment of a black entertainment property, Dandridge, as Carmen Jones, returned the gaze of a consumer group she could safely assume included that portion of the population that had, to that point, tracked her career (and possibly lusted after her) through Johnson publications. The Dandridge/Carmen Jones *Life* cover photograph

Figure 46. *Life* magazine cover featuring Dorothy Dandridge as Carmen Jones, November 1, 1954. © 1954 Time Inc. All rights reserved.

hailed black Americans as consumer-viewers, too, which brought them into the postwar consumerist fold as cultural citizens. Dandridge's *Life* cover girl image represents a remarkable moment within the history of African Americans' recognition and visual definition in U.S. media and pop culture. The moment constitutes both a culmination and continuation of the project Johnson took up with *Ebony*, in which he first identified or made visible black consumer markets and then compelled advertisers to take those markets into consideration when selling their products.

Dandridge's *Life* cover image was not without its problems. For one, it reflected, as much as it perpetuated, the valorization of light-skinned, heterosexual black female sexuality and determined the limited grounds on which the white media would accept black women and black female beauty. Also, because the photograph depicts Dandridge in character as the "fast and loose" Jones, it also reinscribed associations between black women and hypersexuality. Yet Dandridge's *Life* cover image is a far cry from the magazine's first "black" cover photograph in 1937 (discussed in the introduction) of an unidentified shirtless black male laborer sitting atop a load of watermelons with his bare back to the camera. From her position on the cover of the most popular photo-magazine in the world, Dandridge turns to look at the viewer: she simultaneously seeks recognition and recognizes those looking at her. In her *Life* cover image, Dandridge assumes subjectivity in a manner that the faceless black male of the 1937 *Life* cover could not.

JPC's reliance on the representation of black women as objects of sexual desire helped facilitate this historic representation of black subjectivity. This process could not have worked with the representation of black men, however. At the time, the sexualized black male body continued to provoke anxieties, among whites especially, rooted in long-standing stereotypes that figured black men as oversexed animals, the primary prey of which were white women and their purity. It is no coincidence that, in the postwar decade, Johnson's publications represented black men primarily as entertainers, servants, intellectuals, and athletes. The representation of black male sexuality or sex appeal did not serve Johnson's business plan: to the contrary. Many African Americans would have vehemently opposed such representations for the danger they presented as catalysts of white fear. Within a year of *Life*'s valorizing Dandridge as a black sex goddess, the lynching of Emmett Till, a fourteen-year-old black boy from Chicago, demonstrated the horrible consequences of white fear and hatred inspired by the specter of sexualized black masculinity.

The story is well known. While visiting his southern relatives in Mississippi during the summer of 1955, Till was alleged to have made advances toward a white woman, Carolyn Bryant.[115] Upon hearing this, Bryant's husband, Roy, enlisted his half brother J. W. Milam and the two men kidnapped, tortured, and shot Till; they then dumped his body into the Tallahatchie River. Despite being weighted down by a large cotton gin that Bryant and Milam barb-wired around the dead boy, Till's body surfaced three days later on the last day of August, and the race began for control over the "facts." Depending on who did the telling, the villain at the heart of the story was redneck murderers, a vulgar boy, the northern media, outside agitators like the NAACP, or southern law enforcement.

African American activists of the period and subsequent historians commonly cite the lynching of Till as a watershed moment in civil rights history. His murder caused national outrage and stands for many as the origin point of the civil rights movement. The question is why. Lynching of black men—especially for their supposed transgressions against white womanhood—is embedded within the history of southern "justice" systems. By the mid-twentieth century, the rate of lynchings in the South had decreased markedly compared to the nadir period of the 1890s, when over 150 African Americans were lynched in a single year. The extralegal mob killing of blacks, however, remained tragically common. Records of the Tuskegee Institute (now Tuskegee University), which tracked lynchings nationwide, reveal that 3,437 African Americans lost their lives to lynching between 1880 and 1950, which includes a spike in the immediate postwar period when some white southerners adjusted—or, more accurately, failed to adjust—to the attitudes, expectations, and behaviors of African Americans returning from the war.[116] Despite consistent efforts by the NAACP to draw attention to these events, none garnered the same attention as the Till case would. Only three months before Till's murder in Money, Mississippi, whites in Belzoni, Mississippi, lynched Rev. George Lee, described as "the Delta's most militant minister," after he refused to withdraw his name from the town's voter registry.[117] While the NAACP condemned Lee's killing and the FBI did investigate, the incident barely registered beyond the local newspapers and the black press. What accounts for the difference?

For one, Till was not a man: he was a boy, a child. His age certainly contributed to the shock experienced, across race lines, in response to his murder. "It would appear," NAACP head Roy Wilkins said, "that the state of Mississippi has decided to maintain white supremacy by murdering children."[118] Two additional factors account for why the public's response to Till's lynching moved beyond the moment of initial shock and outrage to become what many consider a catalyst of the modern civil rights movement: Till's mother, Mamie Till Bradley, and JPC.

Bradley made incredible, courageous, and even generous choices upon receiving her son's body. After Till's casket was transported to the A. A. Rayner and Sons Funeral Home on Chicago's South Side, she insisted it be opened. She then allowed David Jackson, a photographer employed by JPC, to take pictures of Till, who had been so horribly tortured that his mother wondered "why they wasted a bullet because it surely wasn't necessary." In death, the body of her son, whom she called "Bobo," looked "like it came from out of space," not at all like that of a human boy.[119] Further determined to shine a light on "what they did to [her] boy," Bradley opted for an open-casket funeral, which took place the following day, September 3, 1955, and then allowed the body to lie in state for several days so members of the public could view it.[120] Thousands did just that, with mourners becoming spectators to an exhibition of racial violence that might have been unthinkable otherwise.[121] What they saw was the corpse of a boy whose embalmed, beaten, and bloated body was mercifully covered by his funeral suit. Above the neck, however, there was no mercy.

In the days surrounding Till's funeral, pictures of his relatives, the grieving throngs, shocked mourners, the funeral procession, and Till's open casket appeared in black newspapers, most notably the *Chicago Defender*. No photographs of Till's corpse were printed, however.[122] Those who were unable to attend the funeral or view Till's body as it lay in state might never have witnessed what Bradley worked to make visible if not for the images Jackson captured at the funeral home. Nearly two weeks after the boy's funeral, Jackson's photographs appeared in *Jet* magazine, at which point greater black America began to consume the images that testified to the brutality of Till's murder.[123]

Civil rights historians rarely fail to mention *Jet* magazine when discussing the Till case.[124] They point to how the magazine's publication of photographs of Till's mangled corpse made visible the horror of his death and the race hatred behind it, and how this generated black activism. Many African Americans, particularly those coming of age at the time, cite exposure to these ghastly photographs in *Jet* as the cause of the birth or maturation of their race consciousness and the reason for their involvement in the modern black freedom movement. In a letter to the editor of the *Chicago*

Defender, Fred Poindexter, a resident of Chicago who very well may have been one of the thousands to view Till's body, appealed to "all black men in America to stand up and be men, and . . . resolve not to fear death when the cause is just."[125]

Jackson's Till photographs gave birth to a generation of "radicalized" youths.[126] Charles Diggs Jr., the first black congressman for Michigan and the only congressman to attend the murder trial of Bryant and Milam, corroborated the effect of the Till images—over that of any news reports about the murder or subsequent trials—on the black consciousness. "I think the picture in *Jet* magazine showing Emmett Till's mutilation was probably the greatest media product in the last 40 or 50 years," he said, "because that stimulated a lot of interest and anger on the part of blacks."[127] Diggs identified the photographs' psychic value as visual testimony and implied their marketplace value as such. Consciously or not, his comment recognized that the political and historical significance that historians, political thinkers, and activists ascribe to the Till case in relation to African Americans' freedom struggle cannot be separated from the business of distributing details of the lynching and subsequent trial.

As Jackson's employer, JPC owned his photographs and first published them in the September 15, 1955, issue of *Jet* magazine. The photographs accompanied the magazine's reporting on Till's abduction and murder. Evidence of the horrific crime, they became a valuable commodity. The throngs of people that came to view Till's body made visible a desire among African Americans to "see"—not just contemplate—the nature of racism that took children as its prey. Many, it seemed, desired to see *in order to* contemplate such hatred. Like the open casket, Jackson's photographs of Till's corpse had the capacity to satisfy this need to see, rather than imagine. It was reasonable, then, to assume there would be a market for them. From the late nineteenth century, lynching photographs had circulated through white consumer spaces as advertisements for lynching festivities or as gruesome souvenirs for purchase.[128] The business decisions behind the reproduction of Jackson's images of Till's body and the circulation of them through commercial media reveal how the convergence of Jim Crow racism, segregated consumer markets and products, and the rise of black periodical publishing made the Till lynching photographs a visual product created, sold, and bought (primarily) by African Americans. The difference was that white Americans had bought such photographs from a position of identifying with the lynch mob, whereas African Americans who purchased the Till images did so from the position of identifying with the dead black boy.

Given the gravity of the subject matter, one might have expected JPC to use *Ebony* to report on the Till case: it was, after all, the company's journalism vehicle. *Jet*, by comparison, was a digest-tabloid mix that, in addition to news items, offered its assumed black readership celebrity news and photographs and gossip across multiple areas, including entertainment, crime, politics, and sports. (When Moss Kendrix's wife, Dorothy (Johnson), filed for divorce, due in part to the demands of his work, JPC identified this as *Jet*-worthy content. This "news" would not have found space in *Ebony*.)[129] Compared to *Ebony*, *Jet* was literally the lesser magazine, measuring less than one-fourth the size of the elder publication—small enough, as its marketing claimed, to fit in one's pocket. *Jet* was a carrying-around publication, the contents of which consumers traded as if it were their own gossip—it was a real conversation starter. Consumers of *Jet* sought sensational news, not serious journalism—which is not to say they would not take the latter, only that they expected the former. One observer recalled that *Ebony* was the magazine that African Americans kept on the coffee table; *Jet* was the magazine they kept next to the bed.[130]

Why, then, did Johnson elect to use *Jet* to sell content pertaining to Till's lynching?

The obvious explanation is that *Jet* was a weekly publication, whereas *Ebony* was a monthly. When Johnson introduced his weekly digest in 1951, he heralded its frequency and brevity of form, declaring, "In the world today everything is moving along at a faster clip. There is more news and far less time to read it."[131] Events surrounding Till's lynching moved fast, too fast for a monthly. Till's funeral occurred within six days of his abduction, Bryant and Milam were on trial for kidnapping and murder just weeks later, and after only five days, to the surprise of very few, an all-white jury acquitted both men. Only *Jet* allowed JPC to report on happenings in the Till case in a timely and profitable manner. In 1955 *Ebony*'s monthly circulation hovered around 475,000. *Jet* had a weekly circulation nearing 450,000.[132] Even at half the price of its older sibling, *Jet* generated more in sales revenue per month, making it the more lucrative vehicle for a fast-moving story of great interest to JPC's consumer base.

Publishing schedules and sales numbers alone did not determine the digest's appropriateness over that of *Ebony*. The Till story landed in *Jet* because of Johnson's decision to publish Jackson's spectacular photographs. Again, *Ebony* may seem the logical choice as a photo-magazine, and, since its founding, the magazine had included photographs spectacular and even salacious in nature. But, generally, these took the form of the pinup images discussed earlier or "freak" photographs of, for example, a black woman with four legs. *Ebony* did not trade in gross, gruesome, or grisly, all of which described the images of Till in death. Such content may have offended the white advertisers Johnson had worked so hard to secure for *Ebony*.[133] And, as Johnson explained, any threats to his flagship publication would put "the whole company . . . at risk," because *Ebony*'s advertising revenue was the foundation of the media enterprise.[134] Therefore, ironically, *Jet* was best suited for the Till content that included Jackson's lynching photographs in large part because of the weekly's lack of gravitas. The digest's propensity for scandalous, controversial, and vulgar fare made it an appropriate media context for graphic images of the mutilated body of a black boy.

The selection of *Jet* also allowed for unrestrained use of black cheese-cake—a proven marketing tool—to sell, and thus publicize, the Till case. Sexualized representations of black women were part and parcel to the publication. Whereas such images gradually increased in appearance in the pages of *Ebony*, they were ubiquitous in and on *Jet* from inception, precisely because of their proven popularity through *Ebony*. Busty women with bare shoulders, bare midriffs (navels and all), and bare legs were a staple of the magazine's covers, and every issue included a two-page pinup spread (predecessor to the "beauty of the week" pinup feature that persists to the present day in *Jet*, now a digital magazine).

In circulating pinup imagery through *Jet*, JPC merely employed the marketing tactic that had proved crucial to *Ebony*'s success and, by extension, that of the enterprise as a whole. By the summer of 1955, however, these representations of black womanhood were no longer as present in the photo-magazine. Changing circumstances had altered their utility as a marketing strategy for the magazine. Although *Ebony* remained the most successful commercial black publication, its newsstand sales had begun to fall. The country had moved from a postwar boom into a recession, which for many African Americans—particularly those in the steel and automotive industries—translated into unemployment. Therefore, Johnson could no longer rely on revenue from impulsive newsstand sales to sustain his prize magazine, or his company. Consequently, he put more emphasis on building the subscription sales of *Ebony*. Attracting home subscribers, however, required different strategies from those for driving newsstand purchases. Taking advantage of the hard economic times, Johnson developed programs in which churches and schools made money by selling *Ebony* subscriptions, which prompted a shift in the magazine's editorial content. Having enlisted schoolchildren and churchwomen to pedal *Ebony*, Johnson determined that sex and sensationalism were no longer as effective, let alone appropriate, for marketing the magazine.[135]

In addition, Johnson realized "the world was changing and people wanted *Ebony* to be more serious."[136] Events like the *Brown v. Board of Education* Supreme Court decision in May 1954, which mandated desegregation of public schools, and the backlash it inspired—including, arguably, the murder of Till—pushed African Americans' struggle for civil rights into the national spotlight. In response, JPC slowly adapted *Ebony* to reflect that struggle through editorials on the movement and features like an "Advice for Living" column written by Martin Luther King Jr.[137] Originally, Johnson conceived of *Ebony* as an escape from "the day-to-day combat of racism" for blacks.[138] By the mid-1950s, however, increasingly visible black activism and its brutal opposition required that Johnson's journalistic publication intentionally take up the civil rights struggle in its pages. Otherwise, the magazine could no longer compete in an expanding news media culture or remain relevant to the large portion of black America engaged in the "day-to-day combat" inherent to their position as second-class citizens. The shift in function for *Ebony* made sensationalist representations of black sexuality notably incongruous. The market for such material, however, remained quite bullish during the 1950s and sustained other JPC magazines, including *Copper Romance*, *Tan Confessions* (which became *Tan*), *Hue*, and *Jet*, all of which trafficked heavily in black cheesecake. Week to week, *Jet* offered up girlie covers and pinup spreads with no guile or apology, along with rumor-driven coverage of black celebrity and quick-and-dirty news.

Therefore, when the September 15, 1955, issue of *Jet* hit newsstands with a scantily clad cover girl, consumers had little reason to expect anything remarkably different in content. Nothing about the cover distinguished the issue from those that came before or after.[139] The majority of the cover was taken up by a body-length photograph of a young, light-skinned black woman, tagged as a "pretty Los Angeles City College coed," seated on a rock. In addition to a long string of pearls, the woman wears a complicated strapless and sleeveless one-piece outfit that bares the entirety of her leg closest to the camera and is cinched around her bosom in a manner to create cleavage (Figure 47). Surrounding the cover girl image were headlines for inside stories on "Negroes in college" and "the Moore-Marciano fight." The racy cover signaled to consumers that the pages within might contain coarse and even sensational content; however, it did not prepare them at all for the photo-essay contained within, entitled "Nation Horrified by Murder of Kidnapped Chicago Youth," which included Jackson's grisly photographs of Till's corpse.

In that issue, the tragedy of the Till lynching unfolds visually over four pages. The four photographs in the first two-page spread of the essay include one taken in much happier times of Emmett "Bobo" Till and his mother, who radiates maternal pride, and photographs of Till's Mississippi relatives, who were witness to events in the case. The fourth image depicts a white man (identified by the caption as Greenwood sheriff John Cochran) squatting next to a large—two hundred pounds, the reader is told—metal wheel-like mechanism. Many Mississippians would likely immediately recognize the implement as a cotton gin, but to the "outsider" its belonging in the picture is unclear. The barbed wire hanging from the gin is also troubling: Why wrap something clearly intended to rotate in wire? Only when taken together do the four images begin to cohere as documentation of a race tragedy: a happy black mother and son clearly posed for a photo taken in better times; two young black boys with wary looks on their faces and marked by their clothing as less city, more country than their cousin Emmett; a close-up of the wrinkled, distressed face of Emmett's great-uncle Mose Wright, who witnessed his nephew's kidnapping; and finally a white lawman inspecting something out of place.

When readers turned the page, Jackson's photographs of Till's corpse affronted them, at which point all the pieces fell into place. In the first, Mamie Till Bradley stands at the head of the undertaker's table on which her son has been dressed and laid out, her hands clasped around a tissue. Her boyfriend, Gene Mobley, a tall black man dressed in a suit and hat, holds her from behind. To the right of this image is a close-up, frontal photograph

Figure 47. Cover of *Jet* magazine, September 15, 1955. Ebony Media Operations, LLC.

of Emmett Till's face taken from above, which revealed to *Jet* readers what his mother beheld as she stood there unable to look away. In the portrait, Till's face looks like a mass of unmolded clay, discernable only as head and face by the snatch of curly hair on top, nostrils, and the semblance of lips where a mouth should be.[140] On the opposite page is the photo-essay's clear destination: a full-page, extremely close-up photograph of Till's face. Taken from the left side, this photograph is a study in torture (Figure 48). It reveals clearly the extremity of the beating Till took, evidenced by a missing ear, a missing eye, clownish lips, and skull fractures and skin tears—the result of being shot at least once at point-blank range—held together by heavy twine, which "served to emphasize [Till's] torture, rather than conceal it."[141] This one photograph told the story: it was, as its caption read, "mute evidence of [a] horrible slaying."[142]

The visual evidence of the "horrible slaying" was the issue's raison d'être. Why, then, make the pretty coed pinup the focus rather than advertise the explosive article contained within that concerned a topic of great interest to black Americans? Perhaps Johnson chose this route so as not to appear to be advertising or capitalizing on Till's gruesome murder, even as the publisher introduced into circulation a product—Jackson's photographs—for which he had good reason to believe there would be a strong market. He was not wrong. The initial run of the September 15, 1955, issue of *Jet* (numbering approximately four hundred thousand copies) sold out, only the second issue to do so (the first being the magazine's debut issue of a much smaller run).[143] The issue became the most popular, iconic, and historically significant of the publication's entire run.[144]

In the next issue of *Jet*, JPC republished one of Jackson's close-ups of Till's battered face. Recirculating the one image (as opposed to all three) showed deliberate restraint even as the publisher resold that for which consumers had displayed such high demand the week before. This issue also stayed true to the girlie cover formula and featured a photograph of an unknown, pretty, light-skinned black model in a sexy, off-the-shoulder dress. As in the previous week's issue, no images relevant to the Till case appeared on the cover. The cover did, however, tease the issue's Till content, an obvious attempt to alert readers to material the previous issue had revealed to be profitable regardless of any questions about its suitability. In addition to the one photograph of Till after death, the issue provided new compelling images, including photographs of the large and slightly plump fourteen-year-old Till when alive and well, Mamie Till Bradley wailing at her son's grave, the stump in the Tallahatchie River that supposedly snagged Till's body, a white pastor and pallbearer collapsed at Till's gravesite, and a headshot of Carolyn Bryant. While nowhere near as provocative as the lynching photographs, these images—combined with the one image of a boy in death—breathed new life into the drama.[145]

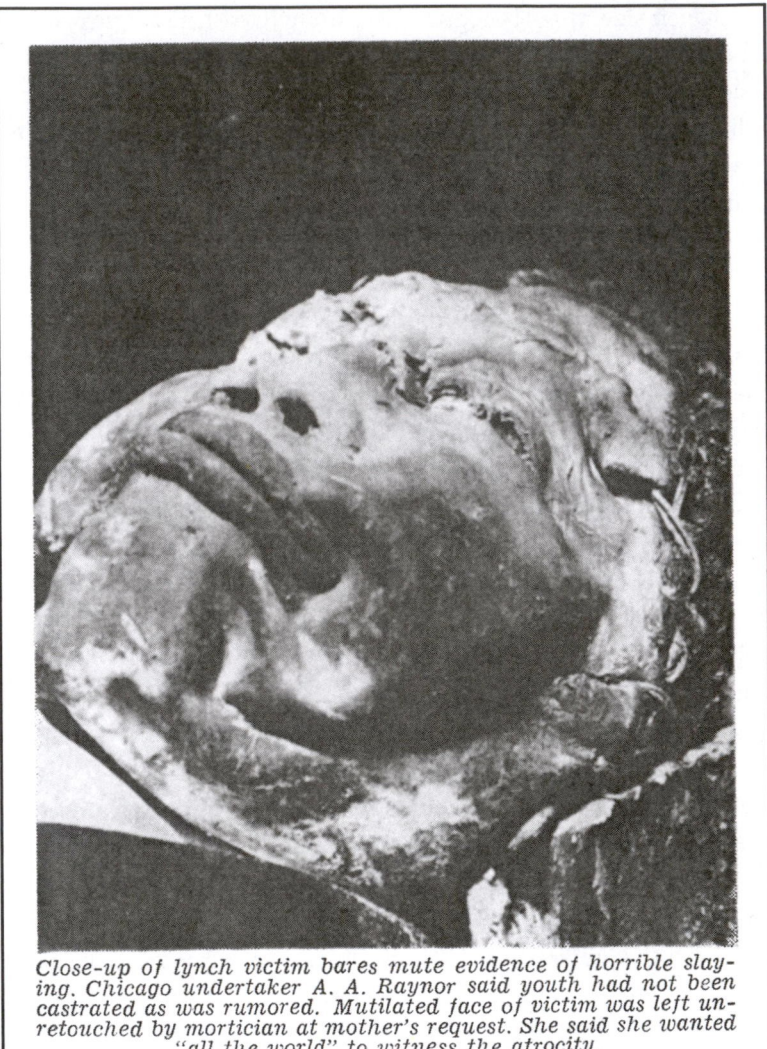

Close-up of lynch victim bares mute evidence of horrible slaying. Chicago undertaker A. A. Raynor said youth had not been castrated as was rumored. Mutilated face of victim was left unretouched by mortician at mother's request. She said she wanted "all the world" to witness the atrocity.

9

Figure 48. David Jackson's photograph of lynching victim Emmett Till, August 1955. Ebony Media Operations, LLC.

The repeated but judicious use of Jackson's photographs reflects awareness of how the documentary value and market value of these images overlapped. Years later, Johnson stated he had reservations about publishing the photos.[146] The claim confirms his sensitivity but obscures his business acuity. Johnson anticipated the photographs' marketability as powerful testimony to the lethal barbarism of white supremacy, as evidenced by the work his staff put into obtaining them. According to Simeon Booker, *Jet's* associate editor at the time, he and Jackson "staked out the funeral home," waiting for Till's body to arrive so that Jackson could "get the pictures to show how badly Till was beaten." "From midnight to morning" they waited in their car, and when the body arrived, they accompanied Bradley and the wooden box holding her dead son inside. When Bradley insisted the box be opened, they "weather[ed] the stench of [his] unembalmed body" right along with her. "When the boy's skull fell off as the mortician lifted the body from the wooden box," Booker recalled, "calmly, Dave replaced the skull" and began taking close-up pictures of Till's mangled body.[147] Jackson absolutely had Bradley's permission to take these pictures; she was, remember, determined that the "whole world to see."[148] Still, Booker's and Jackson's actions were those of paparazzi determined to scoop the competition.

The combination of sensational, salacious marketing and spectacular content underwrote JPC's continued coverage of events surrounding Till's murder throughout the fall of 1955, which kept the case before the public. Whether intentional or not, the formulation also championed the appeal of black women as equal to that of white women. Central to the Till case was the accusation that the fourteen-year-old boy had "wolf whistled" at, and possibly manhandled, Carolyn Bryant. This alleged act and the consequences it brought implied a combined sexiness and sacredness for white women above that of black women. This implication even sneaked its way into the black press. On September 17, 1955, the *Chicago Defender* announced the trial against Roy Bryant and Milam on its front page. Printed above the article was a glamorous headshot of Carolyn Bryant, which looked as if it had been pulled from the portfolio of a professional actress. In the image, soft, shaped, and full curls frame Bryant's soft but serious face, with its perfectly groomed eyebrows and dainty mouth emphasized by precisely applied lipstick, which, despite the black-and-whiteness of the photograph, one imagines to be an appropriately understated but feminizing red. Printed above Bryant's head in bold title case is the caption, "The Cause of It All."[149]

Combined, the image and text elevated Bryant's white beautifulness and beautiful whiteness to be so powerful and seductive as to be lethal. The *Jet* girlie covers that fronted the drama of race, sex, and violence that was the Till case were interventions in a narrative that aggrandized white female beauty.

Having effectively used the images of Till's corpse in two consecutive issues to document the heinousness of the boy's lynching and increase *Jet*'s circulation, Johnson retired the corpse photographs. By this point, these graphic images were not only emblazoned in the minds of African Americans across the nation; they were in the actual possession of African Americans across the nation. Furthermore, having successfully primed black interest in the Till case through their use, the photographs were no longer a required component for marketing the story. In the following weeks, it was enough to indicate Till content on the girlie covers of *Jet* with bold, prominently positioned and provocative headlines such as "Will Mississippi 'Whitewash' the Emmett Till Slaying?," "Where Is the Third Man in Till Lynching?," "The Strange Trial of the Till Kidnappers," and "Exclusive: What the Public Didn't Know About the Till Trial."[150] After the fall of 1955, the Till lynching photographs would not appear again in *Jet* until three weeks after Lyndon B. Johnson signed the hard-won Civil Rights Act in July 1964, when the magazine published a "special report" on Mississippi, the cover of which advertised "shocking pictures" and "startling stories."[151]

That John Johnson funneled the Till lynching photographs through *Jet* demonstrates his savvy about the markets for and potential of his various publications as distinct media spaces. In their grotesque, inflammatory nature, Jackson's photographs ran the risk of repelling advertisers and those *Ebony* readers who would consider such visuals gratuitous within their respectable, black lifestyle magazine. Conversely, *Jet*'s coverage of the case clearly drew new consumers to the magazine, some of whom had been strictly *Ebony* readers. This crossover between black markets was certainly profitable to the black publishing company most responsible for serving those markets, as evidenced by the September 1955 sales of *Jet*. The manner in which JPC reported on and publicized events surrounding Till's lynching attended to several business concerns, including the circulation and standing of its publications and the overall solvency of the enterprise.

JPC's motivations concerning the Till case, it should be clear, were more capitalistic than moralistic or altruistic, which is not to say they were not politically significant. The marketing practices and business objectives behind *Jet* magazine's coverage of the case account for why Till's lynching was not lost to obscurity, as were so many others in the long history of white men killing black men in the South in the name of white womanhood. In the months following Till's funeral, *Jet* addressed the Till case more than any other contemporary popular magazine, far outpacing coverage in *Ebony, Look, Life, Time*, and *Newsweek*. Moreover, the sensationalism of that coverage ensured, as civil rights activist Amzie Moore has claimed, that Till's murder was the "best advertised lynching" in U.S. history.[152]

The uneasy realization for some is that, precisely because it was the best advertised, Till's was also arguably the most consumed lynching in U.S. history, and the bulk of those consumers were African Americans. Consideration of the profitability of the Till lynching photographs for JPC reveals that representations of black torture and white hatred also had a market value to African Americans living in a state of second-class citizenship. For whatever reasons, African Americans wanted or needed to see. Bradley allowed them that opportunity. But inevitably, the casket closed and the body went to burial. In the pages of *Jet*, JPC offered the opportunity to see, and look again and again. Is it any wonder that Till's lynching holds such a prominent place in civil rights history and in the collective memory and imagination of black America?[153]

Johnson's tremendous success as a publisher lay in his early and frequent use of black cheesecake as a marketing tool. Images of black female beauty and sexuality were essential to his success as a postwar black capitalist, and to the civil rights work he performed. JPC's trade in sexy visuals of black women established a revenue base that funded the myriad of ways in which the company served black interests and political agendas. For one, the impressive circulation numbers generated by the "sex sells" tactic made black markets visible and attractive to major (white) advertisers and made African Americans comprehensible as consumers, which, as discussed in the next chapter, proved fundamental to black citizenship claims. In addition, the sales and advertising revenue that JPC's use of "girlie" pictures generated enabled the media enterprise to circulate new and alternative representations of blackness, visual and otherwise, through its multiple publications. JPC magazines also featured stories on the lives of both ordinary and extraordinary black people; reported on the accomplishments or actions of black politicians, educators, artists, designers, inventors, and criminals; opened a window into black celebrity; highlighted black entertainment and artistic forms; and provided the space for the publicizing of black thought across all manner of topics. Never before had this amount or type of popular media space been dedicated to representing black Americans according to their desire and design. In the postwar black "struggle over images" that bell hooks has claimed constitutes the crux of the black freedom struggle, JPC offered a uniquely productive site for battle.[154]

Finally, JPC's reliance on cheesecake enabled the company to publicize, comment on, and generate interest in the "day-to-day combat against racism" inherent to African Americans' status as second-class citizens. In the case of Till, Johnson's capitalism became a driving force that propelled the anguish and activism that accounts for why many African Americans associate Till's lynching with the beginning of the civil rights movement. As *Ebony* editor Ben Burns explained, "Black publishers—like other American publishing companies—were in the business to make money." The race politics of the postwar United States combined with new opportunities for African Americans in image- and mediamaking to make "the fight for racial equality [a] vehicle for financial success."[155] Unabashed and unapologetic in his capitalism—"I wasn't trying to make history—I was trying to make money"—Johnson made the market work for racial progress on his way to making money.[156]

Chapter 5

A Consuming Image: The Civil Rights Work of Marketing Black Citizenship

The Negro is first and foremost an American consumer, a "purchasing agent."

—Joseph Wootton, Interstate United Newspapers, 1951

In the fall of 1953, hundreds of thousands of African Americans went to the local newsstand or their mailbox to collect the October issue of *Ebony* magazine. Some began turning the pages on the spot; others certainly waited until they settled in the chair reserved for reading in their living rooms; and scores of black men and women alike thumbed through it while having their hair cut, pressed, or set at local barber or beauty shops. Wherever they were when they opened the magazine, they all likely registered some degree of surprise. On the inside cover, taking up the entire page, was a full-color Coca-Cola advertisement featuring Reece "Goose" Tatum, the star member of the popular exhibition basketball squad the Harlem Globetrotters (Figure 49). It was not unusual for *Ebony* readers to encounter a Coke ad when flipping through the magazine. The Coca-Cola Company had been placing advertisements in the popular black photo-magazine for close to two years. To that point, however, these ads had all been generic, "general market" ads that pictured Coca-Cola bottles or vending machines. They did not feature people, save Santa Claus when Christmas neared; they most definitely did not feature black people. Whether they understood it or not, consumers who opened their *Ebony* magazines to discover the Harlem Globetrotters' most famous player offering them an "ice-cold" Coke experienced a historic moment in marketing history.

Since Coca-Cola's founding in the late nineteenth century, on the rare occasion that African Americans appeared in company marketing, they did

Figure 49. "Negro market" Coca Cola advertisement featuring Harlem Globetrotter Reece "Goose" Tatum, 1953. The Coca-Cola Company.

so in servile roles. The Tatum advertisement marked a new day. In the ad, Tatum wears a bright, toothy smile, in keeping with his public persona as an entertainer whose popularity stemmed from his comedic antics on the court as much as from his superior athleticism. A basketball comfortably rests in the upturned palm of his very large right hand—at six feet four inches tall, the basketball superstar had an arm span of almost seven feet. On top of the ball balances a full bottle of Coke—a trick that audiences would not have been surprised to witness during a Globetrotters performance. Tatum wears the Globetrotter uniform, which consciously evokes the American flag with its blue tank-top jersey decorated with stars and its red-and-white-striped, belted boxer shorts. Set against a bright-yellow background and amplified by the glossy finish of the cover paper, Tatum's megawatt smile, muscular brown build, and patriotic uniform pop off the page, as does the classic large, round, red Coca-Cola symbol in the bottom right-hand corner. The advertisement's position in the most coveted and therefore most expensive location—the inside cover—ensured it was the magazine's first and most visible marketing, save its actual cover. Given the costs associated with an advertisement of this size, color, and placement, Tatum's Coke ad signaled the Coca-Cola Company's decision to literally invest in cultivating the so-called Negro market for its product. The advertisement belonged to the company's first campaign to place African Americans as central figures in marketing materials. Tatum's position in the advertisement invested him, as a black man, with the standing and authority inherent to representing the world's number one cola drink. "Follow the Champions," reads the large copy next to the famous athlete: "Have a Coke."

The Tatum Coke ad is the prologue to the story of how, in the 1950s, the Coca-Cola Company participated in a black-engineered public relations campaign that advanced African Americans' normality as American citizens. For two years, from 1953 to 1955, the corporation followed the celebrity spokesperson formula and produced marketing materials featuring a host of famous black athletes and entertainers. Then Coca-Cola moved beyond its celebrity "Negro market" campaign to produce advertisements that pictured African Americans as housewives and family men, homeowners, high school students, vacationgoers, and leisure lovers. These ad images forged associations between blackness and the now-iconic version of the "American dream" of a middle-class, family-centered—and exceedingly heteronormative by present-day standards—suburban lifestyle.

Moss Kendrix single-handedly engineered Coca-Cola's turn toward black consumers and its imaging of African Americans *as* consumers. After the Liberian Centennial Commission folded in 1947, he reinvented himself as a black markets specialist, or an "expert" on African American consumer desires and habits. Having done so, he became the first such specialist the Coca-Cola Company employed. As the corporation's first black pitchman, he compelled the beverage giant to target black consumers through public relations campaigns and marketing materials that circulated through the market and redefined African Americans against stereotype and according to prevalent notions of Americanness.

Similar to John H. Johnson, Kendrix fixated on African Americans as consumers after the war. He, too, deemed them essential to his postwar business ventures. He differed from the publisher slightly in his approach, however. Johnson's initial business plan relied on selling his publishing products to African Americans in numbers that eventually drew the advertising revenue he coveted—and needed. Kendrix, however, immediately went after the advertisers, to which he held out the promise of marketing directly to African Americans. The two businessmen's capitalism overlapped and converged, each reliant on the other. Sales of Johnson's publications revealed the extent to which African Americans consumed, aspired to consume, and desired to be recognized as consumers; in addition, his magazines provided advertising vehicles through which to reach these consumers. Kendrix instructed advertisers about what form that advertising should take. The Tatum Coke ad in the October 1953 issue of *Ebony* represents a moment when the enterprises of these two professional imagemakers intersected.

The story of how black marketers—or "Brown Hucksters"—promoted the "Negro market" is not new. Throughout the first half of the twentieth century, a handful of black and white Americans—primarily men— advanced blacks' consumer position. These included Claude Barnett, best known as founder of the Associated Negro Press and also founder of one of the nation's first black advertising firms, Claude A. Barnett Advertising, in the 1910s; William B. Ziff, the white owner of an advertising firm that represented black newspapers; Paul K. Edwards, a white scholar who researched and publicized African Americans' consumer habits and desires; David Sullivan, an advertising manager for the *New York Amsterdam News* who founded his own advertising firm in the 1940s; William Graham, who founded the W. B. Graham marketing agency during the war; Vince Cullers, an early *Ebony* art director who opened his own advertising firm in Chicago in the mid-1950s; and, of course, Johnson, whose publishing company profoundly altered corporate America's approach to African Americans.[1] In this sea of men, Sarah Breedlove—better known as Madam C. J. Walker, the "mother" of the black hair and skincare industry in the United States— and Ophelia DeVore—a model and publisher who helped found one of the first black modeling agencies—stand out as early women marketers. Kendrix is missing almost entirely from the history of the rise of black consumer marketing, which, as this chapter demonstrates, is nothing short of astounding given his centrality to promoting the African American market and to developments in marketing, especially advertising, that continue to shape the industry to this day.

As an entrepreneur, Kendrix holds no place in the civil rights story either. In this, he is not alone. Conventional narratives of the struggle focus on grassroots activism and highlight resistance activities. Even as the criteria have expanded for inclusion in the history of the black freedom movement, the ticket for entry remains an activist identity. Kendrix and other black marketers, including, most notably, Johnson, are unintelligible within these narrative frameworks because they were not activists or overtly connected to activist endeavors. They were dyed-in the-wool capitalists, and proudly so (which is *not* to say they had no civil rights concerns or politics). The form their capitalism took, however, is precisely the premise for their inclusion in the history of how African Americans combatted racism and pursued their civil rights.

Kendrix and Johnson each developed businesses around representing African Americans—both in acting on their behalf and in actually imaging them—as consumers. As a demographic, African Americans made the turn toward materialism with everyone else after World War II, encouraged by their markedly increased incomes and economic trends including a booming economy, mass production of material goods, an explosion in commercial marketing, and the rise of consumerist definitions of Americanness. As others have argued, these forces encouraged all Americans to engage in individualistic consumption for private gain, which reflected a reliance on the marketplace to provide economic security and deliver on the social and political promises of democracy. The consumer boycotts of the civil rights movement demonstrate that African Americans continued to embrace prewar public-minded conceptions of consumerism, in that they used their consumer role as part of their activism to secure equal access to public accommodations, a collective benefit. In the expansive consumer culture of postwar America, however, black individualistic materialism also offered a means to advance the collective goal of first-class citizenship. Through this form of consumerism, African Americans asserted their belonging as members of the American consumer class, which, in the mid-twentieth century, was a key—if not *the* key—criterion of authentic Americanness.[2]

Mainstream marketing images that presented, even highlighted, African Americans' consumer selves were vitally important to conceptions of African Americans as normal. Kendrix—along with other black marketers, including Johnson—devised marketing that visually cultivated African Americans' consumerist identity, which made them culturally intelligible as fundamentally and, more importantly, equally American. While the product of profit-driven motives, these images enabled black citizenship claims and thus performed work essential to concurrent civil rights campaigns. The case study of Kendrix's work with Coca-Cola reveals the labor and infrastructure necessary to enlisting white corporate America to recognize and, importantly, represent African Americans as typical valuable consumers. This project was protracted, arduous, complicated, and uniquely necessary; given the race politics of the time, it was also a financially sound and politically significant enterprise.

When the Liberian Centennial Commission disbanded, Kendrix was left without a job, but not without opportunity. After a decade of developing public relations skills—working on behalf of the federal government, the black press, and the Republic of Liberia—he had expertise, a sterling professional reputation, and great business connections. Looking to capitalize on these assets, in 1948, he opened his own public relations and marketing firm, the Moss H. Kendrix Organization (MHKO). The core mission of MHKO, Kendrix espoused, was to promote and target "the Negro market." His motto (which appeared on all MHKO stationery) reflected—and, of course, advertised—this single-minded, straightforward business model: "COURT THE NEGRO MARKET AND COUNT THE RESULTS!" Now a private business owner, Kendrix's pitch to potential clients was simple: "I will help you increase your share of the Negro market."[3] Although it was effective with black companies, Kendrix coveted major, white, corporate clients, especially those with marketing budgets big enough to absorb the risk of developing quality black advertising campaigns. He viewed these white companies in the same way that he encouraged them to view "the Negro market," as untapped territory with tremendous profit potential.

As an aspiring marketer, Kendrix deviated from the path of other African Americans. Most of his professional peers began—and sometimes spent their entire careers—as a, or *the*, black markets specialist for a single major advertiser or advertising agency. This was the experience of James Jackson with Esso Standard Oil Company, Herbert H. Wright with Philip Morris Company, William Graham with Pabst Brewing Company, Charles Wilson with Pepsi-Cola, and Leonard Evans Jr. and Clarence Holte with the ad agencies Arthur Meyerhoff and Company and Batten, Barton, Durstine, and Osborn, respectively.[4] Several other black marketers did establish their own firms. These private business owners included Sullivan, who, in 1943, opened the Negro Market Organization (NMO), a Fifth Avenue agency that concentrated on appeals to African American consumers and compiled data on them; and Graham, who, after an impressive stint with Pabst, opened an advertising agency in Times Square.[5] Kendrix also opted to strike out on his own, lest he be subsumed into a large white corporate structure as a lone black employee of limited influence. The owner of his own firm, he experienced autonomy and greater authority.

Kendrix's firm differed from those of other black marketers. His contemporaries (and competitors) traded in market data or dealt in the advertising aspect of marketing, with operations that contracted ad space, brokered advertising schedules, produced actual ad materials, or supplied models for use in advertisements. In contrast, MHKO elevated the public relations piece of marketing, which required that Kendrix concern himself with his clients' reputation and relationships with the public, in addition to how to advertise his clients' products and services. His business, in other words, combined imagemaking (conception and production of advertising materials) with image management (cultivation of a corporate brand). The attention to public relations reflected Kendrix's quest for white corporate clients, whereas marketers such as Graham created advertising and bought ad space for black merchandisers such as Murray's Pomade.[6] White advertisers could not assume goodwill or trust among African American consumers: these sentiments would have to be encouraged and earned. Kendrix viewed public relations as elemental for fueling brand awareness and loyalty among African Americans. His approach emphasized a two-way market exchange that involved more than a trade in money for goods.

As an independent businessman, Kendrix had the ability to serve several clients simultaneously, a business model with the potential for more profit. This prospect surely appealed to a man described by those close to him as a "pure entrepreneur." During his firm's infancy, Kendrix pitched to business interests big and small, black and nonblack. In DC, he approached cab companies and department stores with the message, "The mere knowledge that [the business] has retained the services of a Negro organization to promote the sale of its merchandise in the Negro market would be sufficient 'courting' to bring additional Negro buyers to the particular [business]."[7] At the national level, he pitched to the executives of major airlines, tobacco companies, and hotel chains. And he was dogged. When Conrad Hilton, president of Hilton Hotels, responded that he was "not in a position" to consider hotels marketed to blacks, an unfazed Kendrix followed up by asking the hotel mogul for the names of business associates or friends who *were* in the position to do so.[8] To the vice president of American Airlines he marketed not only his public relations experience but his travel experience as well. He claimed that he had flown over thirty-six thousand miles in the previous year (presumably chasing business for MHKO), which, he contended, qualified him to communicate "the advantages, conveniences, and comforts of [American Airlines]" to African Americans, who, he informed the airline executive, "are traveling widely these days, domestically and foreign."[9]

The entire time he was courting these other prospects, Kendrix steadily pursued his white whale, the Coca-Cola Company. A native son of Atlanta, Kendrix grew up in the company's figurative shadow. Incorporated in 1892 by business tycoon and future Atlanta mayor Asa Candler, Coca-Cola was headquartered in the southern city, having taken up its permanent North Street residence in 1921, adjacent to America's first housing project, Techwood Homes, and the Georgia Institute of Technology. Far removed from Kendrix's West End neighborhood socially and geographically, Coca-Cola nevertheless became a part of his world at an early age, but not, as one might assume, in the form of a consumer product.

In his youth, Kendrix took up golf.[10] More accurately, he took up caddying to contribute to his household and to get some "folding money" for himself. For a black boy in Atlanta, caddying was the rare decent paying job, due, in part, to the paternalistic relationships white golfers formed with their black caddies. Kendrix made this paternalism work in his favor. During the first half of the twentieth century, many of Atlanta's top executives were members of the Atlanta Athletic Club. The early years of the private club, which was founded in 1898, coincided with the founding of some of Atlanta's most prominent corporations, including the Georgia Electric Company, the Industrial Aid Association, and the Coca-Cola Company. In addition to a tony, ten-story downtown clubhouse, the club had a location in Atlanta's easternmost neighborhood of East Lake, which boasted a nine-hole golf course designated "the best . . . in the South."[11] Candler had been instrumental to the development of the East Lake Golf Club in the early 1900s, and Coca-Cola executives had frequented it since.[12] Kendrix entered the Coca-Cola orbit on the East Lake greens. A quick study of the game and able to carry two golf bags at once, he was the preferred caddy for the wealthy white men who golfed at East Lake. He was so popular, club members drove to his black neighborhood to pick him up.[13]

In one of the many paradoxes of Jim Crow culture, caddying allowed Kendrix to have intimate interactions with Atlanta's white elite. He formed significant relationships on the golf course, even friendships, with powerful white businessmen, especially Coca-Cola executives. According to family lore, when Kendrix's mother, Mary, suffered a severe head injury in a streetcar accident, these businessmen saw to it that she was treated at Emory University Hospital, which was quite segregated; Coca-Cola king Candler founded the hospital. Whether true or not, as Kendrix passed down this story, it indicates how he envisioned his relationship to the Coke family.[14] He spent hours shadowing Coca-Cola bigwigs at East Lake and received lessons in the politics and practices (not to mention the trappings) of private enterprise. He determined he wanted to be among those men, of that world. The trick was getting in the door.

When Kendrix first began to woo Coca-Cola, he massaged the paternalistic tradition of white patronage fostered by southern race politics and worked his former Coca-Cola connections. In the summer of 1945, while the Allied leaders gathered in Potsdam, Germany, to discuss the unconditional surrender or total destruction of Japan, he began a dialogue with Harrison Jones, chairman of the board of the Coca-Cola Company in Atlanta, about winning the war for black dollars. He proposed that the company contract him to design marketing programs geared directly to African Americans.[15] Jones expressed interest but explained, "Conditions involved in war time production of Coca-Cola rendered it inexpedient for the company to consider any additional promotion of its product."[16] A year later, Kendrix tried again. Writing to Coca-Cola vice president Felix Coste, he advised, "SPECIFIC PROMOTION OF [COCA-COLA] FROM THE NE-GRO ANGLE WOULD GREATLY INCREASE YOUR SALES VOLUMN [*sic*] [AMONG AFRICAN AMERICAN CONSUMERS]."[17] He was politely informed that "severe sugar rationing" precluded the company's taking action to target "the Negro market."[18]

In refusing to take up Kendrix on the offer of his services, Coca-Cola opted to stay the course concerning African American consumers, which meant disregarding them. Since its establishment in the 1880s, the company had done little to cultivate a share of the black consumer market. While the company certainly sold to black consumers, as a southern, white-owned, and white-operated company, it hired African Americans for only the most menial of positions and did not explicitly direct advertising to them.[19] For their part, blacks also had little use for Coca-Cola. They favored Pepsi-Cola, which came in 12-ounce bottles that sold for the same price as the 6.5-ounce bottle Coca-Cola offered. A former black Coca-Cola employee explained, "Black people was working folks, so when they [drank], they want[ed] a lot of it, so they spent their money with . . . Pepsi, and any other company that made larger drinks."[20]

Coca-Cola was hardly singular in its approach to black consumers. Before World War II, the majority of large advertisers ignored or refuted the African American consumer market. Paul K. Edwards, a Fisk University researcher who documented attitudes of and toward the "southern urban Negro" in the 1930s, determined that racist practices and ideologies were at the root of these decisions. His research showed that because national brands advertised almost exclusively in magazines, which did not have large black readerships, and they chose not to advertise in the black press, their appeals were neither directed to nor seen by African Americans.[21] Subsequent research revealed that merchandisers and advertisers ignored black markets because they believed African Americans lacked purchasing power and they feared alienating whites.[22] For executives of these corporations to target "the Negro market," they needed first to conceive of and care about African Americans as consumers. Historically, this had not been an easy sell.[23]

Kendrix and his contemporaries, such as Johnson, however, operated in a climate more amenable to the premise. African Americans' increased concentration in urban centers and their higher employment (because of the increased productivity, labor shortages, and antidiscrimination orders of the World War II years) made them more accessible and attractive to American businesses, black and white. Concurrently, and not at all coincidently, chatter among marketing and advertising specialists increased about the potential of "the Negro market." The description of blacks in the United States as a $12 billion to $15 billion market with purchasing power equivalent to that of Canada's entire population became ubiquitous within industry publications.[24] Within this conversation, the African American consumer market took on a monolithic character. Journalists and marketing executives of the postwar period interchangeably used the terms "the Negro" and "the Negro market" to describe a single entity "twice as big as . . . Belgium, Greece, or Australia" that was "on the move, seeking new opportunities."[25] Coming from white and black marketing men, these generalizations negated the diversity among African Americans, which often reflected a failure to see or grant it. Other times, however, it stemmed from a fear that its recognition might hinder collective claims or diminish the scope of the market under discussion.

Postwar discourse regarding black consumerism also exposed a lack of familiarity with or understanding about blacks as "purchasing agents," as evident in the repeated framing of black markets as uncharted, untapped, and newly discovered terrain.[26] Before World War II, little information about blacks as consumers was available, which indicated, and also perpetuated, a lack of interest in them. The bulk of what information did exist was largely the result of the research or speculation of whites, a problematic basis for formulating appeals to African Americans.[27] During the war years, however, several black institutions sponsored studies of the lifestyles that African Americans had or to which they aspired because these outfits desired "more complete and dependable facts . . . than had previously been collected and analyzed."[28] From the resulting data pools, a clearer picture of the black consumer market began to take shape. Coming out of World War II, the black population in the United States numbered over thirteen million and was better employed, better paid, and more urban than ever, with scores steadily moving out of the rural South.[29] With an aggregate income of over $10 billion and an estimated $7 billion in disposable income, African Americans spent the bulk of their money (over $2 billion) on food, followed by clothing (between $1.5 billion and $2 billion). They spent similar amounts on furnishings and toiletries ($350 million) and tobacco and vehicles ($150–$200 million).[30]

Kendrix was a serious student of African Americans and their purchasing habits—a must, given that he anchored his business plan in claims of expertise regarding black consumption. As head of MHKO, he adopted the model that public relations pioneer Edward Bernays advocated, in which the public relations counselor must do the research of a social scientist.[31] He stuffed folders with reports, clippings, and articles identifying where African Americans lived and where they moved; what they earned and how they earned it; what they ate, drank, and drove; and what they said about any of those things. Throughout his career, he collected and interpreted the most current data available about black markets, which he employed at first to lure clients to his firm and then to guide them in their approaches toward African American constituencies. In his earliest proposals, he relied most heavily on Sullivan's NMO reports.[32] Armed with Sullivan's research, Kendrix impressed on potential clients that, in the period of reconversion and recovery, African Americans held more potential as a market than ever before.[33] Not only did Sullivan provide Kendrix a professional role model and business plan to follow in opening his public relations firm, he also provided him with the data necessary to construct the black consumer market as a wise investment.

It was Kendrix's deviation from Sullivan's model, however, that explains how he succeeded when the elder professional's business failed. Sullivan built a reputation as a black markets expert by dispensing his research and knowledge concerning African American consumers through articles written for trade publications and speeches delivered before various professional organizations. As Kendrix would after him, Sullivan spoke from the position of "the insider." In his writings, he counseled his imagined audience of presumably ignorant white businesspeople and advertisers about the consequences of ignoring or, worse yet, offending black consumers. In a 1943 *Sales Management* article, he advised advertisers and merchandisers on the "don'ts" of marketing to blacks, which included not using blackface characters, mammy figures, dialect, or racial slurs in their advertising.[34] This piece provided advice about how to not repel black consumers; notably, it did not provide a formula for attracting those same consumers (beyond not insulting them). Sullivan's methods established him as an expert on "the Negro market" and "implicitly position[ed him] as a consultant."[35] Trafficking his expertise through public forums, however, did not translate into a consistent profit-making enterprise for Sullivan, because others could, and happily did, access and utilize his counsel without paying for it. Consequently, the NMO shuttered within a decade of its founding.[36] By contrast, Kendrix required payment for the do's of courting the black market. When he resumed his campaign for Coca-Cola business in the late 1940s, he again marketed himself as the conduit to African Americans. This time around, rather than simply write the corporation's executives, he supplied them with a prospectus that sold the potential of "the Negro market" and emphasized his special ability to tap that market.

An extreme do-it-yourself production, the MHKO Coca-Cola prospectus reflected the earnest striving of a fledging business (Figure 50). Pasted on the proposal's cover were two cutout graphics: the Coca-Cola's white-against-red logo and a picture of Jackie Robinson. Robinson broke baseball's color line when he took the field for the Brooklyn Dodgers in 1947 and, that same year, took the title of Rookie of the Year. His inclusion on the Coca-Cola prospectus cover signaled Kendrix's knowledge of current black interests: the combination of the ballplayer's image and the Coke logo visually forged a connection between Coca-Cola and those interests. Robinson was also quite popular across the color line, which suggested his product endorsement had potential value beyond the black market. But most importantly, besides being a national celebrity, the barrier-breaking athlete passed the Cold War test as appropriately patriotic. In July 1949 Robinson was called before the House Un-American Activities Committee (HUAC) to testify about "communist infiltration of minority groups." A committee member characterized the hearings specifically as "an opportunity to . . . combat" statements made by the world-famous singer, actor, and ex-athlete Paul Robeson.[37] Several months earlier, while attending the Paris Peace Conference, Robeson asserted, "We [colonial peoples] denounce the policy of the United States Government which is similar to that of Hitler and of Goebbels. We want peace and liberty and will combat for them along with the Soviet Union."[38] Run through the mill of the Associated Press, Robeson's words, already provocative, became downright incendiary. "It is unthinkable," Robeson was reported to have said, "that American Negroes

Figure 50. MHKO Coca-Cola prospectus with Jackie Robinson graphic missing, ca. 1948. Photograph from the Alexandria Black History Museum.

would go to war on behalf of those who have oppressed us for generations against a country [the Soviet Union] which in one generation raised our people to the full dignity of mankind."[39] Classified as a "friendly witness," during the HUAC hearings, Robinson explicitly, publicly, and under oath declared his allegiance to the United States and American democracy. Robinson called Robeson's statement "very silly" and explained that he had "too much invested . . . in the future of this country" to be led astray "because of a siren song sung in bass." Robinson did go on to advise the committee that Communists were not "stirring up Negroes. . . . Negroes were stirred up long before . . . and they'll stay stirred up . . . unless Jim Crow has disappeared." Still, compared to Robeson, who was painted as a Communist sympathizer, Robinson—a veteran—appeared the loyal American, the good citizen, and he received the committee's endorsement as such. "You have rendered a great service to your country and to your people," pronounced southern Democratic committee member Morgan Moulder. "And we are proud of you."[40]

Kendrix evoked the ideal of Robinson as a good black American. The contents of the prospectus detailed a program in which Coca-Cola would sponsor nationwide Jackie Robinson "Coke Clubs" and "Good Citizenship Corps" targeted at "Negro Youth." These public relations efforts, Kendrix explained, would buy goodwill among black parents. Moreover, targeted as they were at black youths, the programs promised to produce "future markets" of (black) Coke consumers. Through the proposal, Kendrix implied that, in addition to drawing on Robinson's immense popularity among black communities, Coca-Cola's direct hail to African Americans as "good citizens" would prove an effective strategy to motivate their Coke consumption.[41]

Kendrix's pitch suggested that he was uniquely qualified to execute "the Negro angle" by virtue of his professional expertise, and also his race. In the Coke prospectus, he devoted an entire section to his vast experience with "black projects" (Figure 51). From college through World War II, all of his public relations work had involved projects either publicizing black people or their interests or soliciting their support. Certainly, this particular résumé was the result, in part, of Kendrix's receiving positions based on previous experiences. However, dominant theories of the time about race and marketing also constructed him as "innately" equipped to reach African Americans, and he strategically engaged these ideas. Long before Gayatri Chakravorty Spivak coined the term *strategic essentialism* in the 1980s to connote a political tactic used by marginalized and minority groups, Kendrix enacted his own version as a professional tactic. In doing so, he transformed the thing that might have been his biggest liability when approaching white corporations—his race—into his biggest asset, the thing that distinguished him in a predominantly white profession.

Figure 51. Handcrafted collage marketing Moss Kendrix's publicity work, ca. 1948. Photograph from the Alexandria Black History Museum.

In the postwar period, American business leaders and ad industry experts and trade publications viewed blacks as a "special" market separate from the "general" market of white, preferably middle-class, consumers. *Tide* magazine, for example, declared that blacks were "a nation within a nation—a great 'in-group.'"[42] Rather than disrupt or challenge this as a notion, which flattened and segregated blacks as a group, Kendrix catered to it. He referred to blacks as a "Market Within a Market" who required "promotions and sales schemes . . . psychologically angled toward [them]."[43] He had to construct African Americans as a unique group, because he presented himself as uniquely qualified as a black marketer to bridge the gap that existed between "the Negro market" and white corporate America. The rationale underlying his pitch to clients relied on a circular logic in which black consumers made black market specialists necessary as professionals who could demystify this particular niche market. In turn, the necessity for black markets specialists was evidence of the distinctiveness of black markets.

By the early 1950s, Coca-Cola was more receptive to this pitch. Having largely neglected the black consumer market, the company was losing that market to its competition, most notably the Pepsi-Cola Company. Research that Kendrix supplied to Coca-Cola indicated that, in postwar New York City, Pepsi was the cola preferred by almost 50 percent of African Americans, compared to the 20 percent who preferred Coca-Cola.[44] His proposal suggested that this discrepancy resulted, in part, from Coke's failure to target black consumers directly, a mistake Pepsi was not making. In 1948 Coca-Cola's chief competitor hired four black sales representatives whose sole purpose was to increase the company's market share among African Americans. Coca-Cola's failure to exert similar energies regarding black consumers did not go unnoticed. In May of that year, *Ebony* reported on the small but growing pool of African American marketing and sales personnel and the white companies that employed them. The article took Coca-Cola to task for having "no Negro sales representatives." Conversely, the black magazine praised Pepsi-Cola for its progress on that front.[45] An unidentified Coke representative offered assurances that the company was "studying the employment of one black salesperson," undoubtedly a reference to Kendrix.

It is unclear what ultimately convinced Coca-Cola to contract Kendrix's services. It is probable that the corporation was enticed down this path by its competitor Pepsi-Cola, which had a black markets team numbering ten black salesmen by the early 1950s.[46] Also, during the same period, the company's chairman of exports James Farley entreated President Harry S. Truman to abandon civil rights legislation, which generated bad press and bad feelings among African Americans.[47] Another public relations problem, particularly in relation to black attitudes, was Coca-Cola's employment practices. In 1950 the National Fair Play Committee initiated a boycott of Coca-Cola after discovering its New York operation had "not hire[d] a single Negro salesman, distributor, clerk or stenographer."[48] Among Coca-Cola bottlers in the South, "the only jobs blacks had were pulling the Coca-Cola cartons off the trucks."[49] A southern plant manager confirmed that African Americans were "the laborers, the loaders and clean-up men, those who did the heavy-duty."[50] They were not allowed even to drive the trucks, because drivers were considered sales personnel, which was one rung too high on the company's ladder for a black employee.

Up to that point, generally speaking, African Americans did not buy Coke because there was no incentive or invitation to do so. In the 1950s, however, African Americans actively turned away from Coca-Cola and were encouraged to do so because of the company's approach to black employment and consumerism. For the first time in the company's history, its neglect or disrespect of black consumers—whether real or a matter of perception—presented a real liability, given the increasingly visible, vocal, and influential campaigns asserting African Americans' civil rights. Events such as the *Brown v. Board of Education* Supreme Court decision in 1954, which prohibited segregation of public schools; the brutal 1955 lynching of fourteen-year-old Emmett Till; and the drama of the yearlong bus boycott in Montgomery, Alabama, throughout 1956 made "the struggle" front-page news around the world and eroded the foundation on which the United States claimed its moral authority as a global leader. Kendrix identified the period as one of "extreme sensitivity of the Negro community" and warned, "Extensive boycotts against unpopular firms [were] a real factor."[51] In other words, to offend African Americans and their supporters could be very costly in the current climate. By the same token, the very dynamics underlying that climate could make efforts to court those communities with targeted, respectful, quality public relations and advertising could be very profitable. Ultimately, Coke executives accepted that their corporation was in need of a public relations specialist with the talents Kendrix claimed,

Figure 52. Moss Kendrix in his office at Moss H. Kendrix Organization. Lucille Arcola Chambers, *America's Tenth Man: A Pictorial Review of One-Tenth of a Nation* (New York: Twayne, 1957), 272.

and in April 1951—after six years of his pitching his services—Coca-Cola contracted MHKO as its black markets public relations and consulting firm (Figure 52).[52]

The structure of Kendrix's business relationship to Coca-Cola benefited both parties. At the time, the Coca-Cola Company employed zero African Americans in "white color" positions. Because Kendrix was an external consultant, his inclusion in the corporation's operations did not disrupt its racial order or organizational structure, yet his association conferred a degree of credibility when it came to the black public. For Kendrix, his contract with the cola king cemented his firm's viability and prestige (Coca-Cola would be MHKO's flagship client for the next sixteen years). Moreover, his outsider-insider position afforded him considerable influence, relatively speaking, within one of the most successful American corporations, influence essential to his ability to direct the corporation's "special markets" practices. In contrast to the mass market or "general market," which assumed a generic white public, or white niche markets such as teenagers or suburban housewives, "special markets" were racialized segments of the consuming public. In the 1950s *special markets* referred primarily to African Americans.

With his foot finally in Coke's door, Kendrix began building bridges between his "senior" client and African Americans. He determined that, to increase its share among African Americans, Coca-Cola must first generate goodwill among them. In other words, in his plan, public relations preceded advertising. If Coca-Cola did not establish inroads into black communities, no amount of advertising would bring them to the product.[53] In addition to establishing various sponsorship programs in black communities, Kendrix immediately began to cultivate direct sales channels for Coke to black businesses. Because he theorized that black markets required black marketing specialists, opening these channels required that African Americans be responsible for points of sale in black communities.

The structure of Coca-Cola made it a unique challenge to shift employment practices to accommodate African Americans in new positions. At the time, the company relied on over one thousand independent bottlers that bought syrup from the parent company to distribute much of its product. And, as Kendrix found it necessary to repeatedly clarify, "The Coca-Cola Company [was] completely without control of the political, social and other activities of the men and women who bottle Coca-Cola."[54] Kendrix pushed his client to hire African Americans as drivers at the bottling operations over which the parent company did have control.[55] Black drivers not only increased sales to black businesses—an obviously desirable return for Coca-Cola—they encouraged individual black consumers to buy Coke because the drivers circulated through black communities as symbols of Coca-Cola's commitment to fair hiring practices.

The next phase of Kendrix's plan was hiring actual black salespeople to promote Coca-Cola in different regions of the country. Many bottlers balked at the idea of hiring black salespeople. When presented with the idea, the head of the Birmingham Coca-Cola Bottling Company said, "How could we have a Negro salesman in the locker room? . . . If we put on a Negro sales-man, every white salesman we've got will quit."[56] Kendrix devised a work-around in which individual bottlers hired black men as "Negro Special Representatives" who were different and, more importantly, separate from the sales personnel. Supplied with vehicles, these men performed as islands unto themselves within the Coca-Cola operation as they called on and sold product to black schools, businesses, and institutions.[57] They performed on the local level very much like Kendrix at the national level, as freelancers contracted to cultivate and manage separate but significant black consumer markets.

Kendrix oversaw the hiring of qualified black men (an early black Coke rep shared, "Didn't nobody dream of nothing like [hiring black women]") as Coca-Cola "Negro specialists."[58] He was directly responsible for the first hiring of a black professional by a Coke bottler when he guided the Bir-mingham bottling operation to hire Jesse J. Lewis. A high school dropout and World War II vet, Lewis was in the midst of earning a business admin-istration degree when the Coke bottler hired him, an event the *Birming-ham Mirror* described as "historic." Proving Kendrix's predictions correct, in the first year Lewis worked for the Birmingham outfit, he increased sales among black customers 26 percent. Kendrix promptly employed Lewis at MHKO on a part-time basis to help him convince other bottlers to hire "Negro specialists."[59]

Surprisingly, it proved much easier to insert black marketing men into southern bottling outfits than it did in northern operations. Believing the reverse would be true, Lewis first went to New York and Chicago. "I couldn't even get my foot in the door," he remembered. By contrast, in the South, he convinced bottlers in Jackson, Memphis, Atlanta, and New Orleans to hire black marketing men. By 1954, local bottlers in Maryland, Virginia, Alabama, Mississippi, Tennessee, Louisiana, and Texas had hired black rep-resentatives. Several more years would pass, however, before northern bottlers took on black sales representatives.[60] Jim Crow culture allowed an opening for black businessmen in Coca-Cola, as long as they operated separately from the bottlers' white marketing and sales personnel and worked solely with black customers. In this race culture, it was not hard to convince whites or blacks that it made sense for black reps to handle black clients and consumers; this was in keeping with the separate-but-equal logic of segregation. The integrated politics and policies attributed to (if not realized) in the North allowed only for all-or-nothing solutions. Given that choice, northern Coca-Cola bottlers initially opted for nothing.

Kendrix was hardly in the position to effect a revolution in the hiring policies of a large white-owned and white-operated southern corporation as an external black consultant. His advent of "Negro specialists" actually helped Coca-Cola maintain segregationist and discriminatory racial orders and employment practices, even as the company profited from perceptions that it was reforming both. However, he devised the crack through which African Americans slipped into white-collar employment at Coca-Cola and could affect the company's practices toward African American consumers. Only three years after Kendrix came on as the company's *entire* black marketing force, at least ten black men were working as Coca-Cola marketing and sales representatives. Furthermore, dressed in suits, not uniforms, and appearing at business functions and in corporate spaces and pictured in newspaper photos with top-level Coca-Cola executives, these men presented an image that furthered conceptual associations between African Americans and white-collar, corporate professionalism (Figure 53).

Figure 53. First African American "special" markets representatives employed by the Coca-Cola Company, April 1954. The Coca-Cola Company.

The Coca-Cola "Negro specialist" force that Kendrix organized institutionalized the notion that only African American market representatives could comprehend, address, or develop black markets, and, relatedly, that black marketers were best suited to work with black publics. This problematic negotiation of mid-twentieth-century racism in the United States illuminates the dynamics of that racism. Kendrix's strategy also reflects a transitional moment in African Americans' relationship to consumerism and marketing. Accustomed to being ignored and even ridiculed by advertisers and merchandisers, many African Americans viewed being sold to by members of their own race as a consumer right and as a marker of their equal worth in the market, which they took as proof of their social advancement. Kendrix viewed, presented, and helped establish black markets specialists as an innovation in marketing, rather than a concession to racism; to his way of thinking, these professionals legitimated black consumers, which elevated their desires and demands among advertisers. His practice was in keeping with, but also, importantly, a force driving, postwar market segmentation.

With the public relations aspect of Kendrix's Coca-Cola African American market plan fully under way, the next step was advertising to this market. The obvious and primary reason for the Coca-Cola Company to produce advertising targeted at African Americans was to promote consumption of its products among them. The greater significance is the effect of Coca-Cola's black markets advertising on popular conceptions of African Americans and their position within U.S. society.

Just through the act of advertising directly to African Americans, Coca-Cola and other large advertisers affirmed their consumer role. Of course, African Americans were consumers; in fact, well into the twentieth century, black women were often the head purchasers for the white households that employed them, in addition to their own households. As is well documented, it was through their actions as consumers that African Americans advanced many of their civil rights claims. The efficacy of "Don't Buy Where You Can't Work" campaigns and nonviolent protest actions such as the Montgomery bus boycott of 1955–56 and the lunch counter sit-ins of the early 1960s relied on leveraging the profits African Americans could deny establishments or brands that ignored or discriminated against them. The success of such actions accounts for why the civil rights narrative pays considerable homage to how African Americans used their economic power—as consumers—

to secure equal access to public accommodations or sites of consumerism. There is a difference, however, between partaking in the consumer actions of buying—or boycotting, as it were—and being perceived as a consumer, and the distinction mattered.

By the 1950s, consumerism carried heightened political, as well as economic, significance as a civic duty. Certainly, an ethos of material consumerism was not new within the United States. The nation did not suddenly transform into a consumer capitalist society after World War II. Thorstein Veblen coined the now famous phrase "conspicuous consumption" in the late nineteenth century to describe, and lament, what he deemed ostentatious and wasteful consumption compelled by the rise of corporate capitalism and its attendant robber baron class.[61] What distinguished the consumer culture of postwar America was its elevation of materialism as "good," even necessary for the "greater good." All major institutions touted individualistic consumerism because "[the nation's] economic recovery . . . depended on a dynamic mass consumption economy."[62] Moreover, in the context of the burgeoning Cold War against the Soviet Union, mass consumption signaled, and also secured, one's commitment to capitalism. Consumerism "stood at the core of how Americans regarded their society" and their place in it.[63] Representatives of the state, business leaders, news and pop media, and commercial marketing all instructed Americans to buy. They should buy big and they should buy lots; ideally, they should purchase new homes in new developments, new appliances and furniture to fill those homes, and new cars to park in the driveways of those homes. "Improved living standards for the rest of the nation," declared *Life* magazine, required that an American family "buy more for itself."[64] Self-interested consumerism had become a widely endorsed, valued, and intelligible act of American citizenship.[65] To be denied a consumer identity was a real problem.

It is clear that, up to that point in U.S. history, major advertisers, generally speaking, did not see African Americans as consumers, judging by how they depicted blacks in advertising, if at all. Well into the 1940s, the bulk of print media marketing materials, billboards, and consumer goods packaging did not assume African Americans were consumers or represent them as such. A content analysis of advertisements in magazines published in 1946 with circulations over 250,000—including *Time, Newsweek, Housekeeping, Vogue, Esquire,* and *Fortune*—revealed that in over 75 percent of instances, African Americans appeared as maids, waiters, personal servants, slaves, or field hands, or as the Aunt Jemima or Uncle Tom type.[66] Put another way, over 75 percent of the time, these advertisements portrayed blacks not just as nonconsumers but as anticonsumers.

A series of advertisements for Aunt Jemima pancake mix from the 1940s is emblematic of how mainstream marketing formulated African Americans. Long and rectangular in form, these ads typically took up the whole length of a magazine page. In the bottom half of these advertisements, Aunt Jemima appears from the shoulders up. She is a typified mammy-like character wearing a head kerchief, smiling, and testifying about her "Happyifyin'... Pancakes." The upper half features illustrated cartoon scenes of white families in various mealtime scenarios.[67] These ad images displace Aunt Jemima from the white family while at the same time signifying her centrality to the production of their meal. Combining these images with the Aunt Jemima figure's testimony (in the ads' copy) about "[her] secret recipe," the ads further construct her as the producer, rather than the consumer, of pancake mix. She labors, the family consumes (literally, by eating the pancakes). The content and formulations of the Aunt Jemima ads were hardly unique. Up to and through World War II, African Americans' representational function in the discursive and visual landscape of mainstream marketing was to set off and highlight the consumer identity of white Americans through the lack of their own such identity. These marketplace images reduced blacks to as much of an object as the products featured. They formed a visual archive that negated African Americans' consumer selves and thus undermined their claims of Americanness.[68]

The Coca-Cola Company almost never featured blacks in advertisements during the first half of the twentieth century, unless they appeared as persons serving the corporation's general market. In the postwar period, the beverage company's print ads glorified a white, suburban middle-classdom. A 1953 Coke advertisement clearly illustrates this design. Full page in size, the color advertisement (Figure 54), which appeared in popular magazines such as *Ladies' Home Journal*, contains a rectangular illustration that runs lengthwise and fills the left side of the page. Set against a white background, the picture features a white man and woman, presumably a (married) couple in an outdoor setting. The image is closely cropped such that the two people fill the frame almost entirely; however, visual clues indicate the setting to be a cookout. The husband figure holds in his right hand a meat fork, which is resting on or in a steak cooking on a built-in grill, the corner of which is visible. To the left of the grill is a table covered with a mauve-orange cloth. The portion of table that is in frame shows one full place setting of a yellow plate, enamel- or plastic-handled cutlery, and a folded cloth napkin that matches the tablecloth. Viewers are left to assume similar settings around the table. A large bowl holding a colorful salad clearly meant for sharing is set in what appears to be the center of the table. The woman pictured is frozen in the motion of placing two open green-glass bottles of Coca-Cola on the table. Her wavy, dark hair is nicely set, and she wears a cheerful shade of red lipstick. Her slim figure is accented by her pale-yellow halter-top dress, the torso of which has a sweetheart neckline and fits neatly. Her nails are painted light pink, and the only piece of jewelry she wears is a simple, yellow gold wedding ring. The man is dressed casually in a robin's-egg-blue, grid-patterned button-up shirt, the top button of which is open, and khakis. His blond, wavy hair is full and neatly combed and parted on the side. He smiles admiringly at the wife figure. Behind the couple, grass, bushes, and a large leafy tree are visible, as is one green-shutter-framed window to what appears to be a white house with a stone foundation. The image implies the two are in their backyard, a reading affirmed by the ad copy to the right of the picture, which implies they are hosting. "What better way to show esteem for your guests," the text reads. "Serving delicious ice-cold Coca-Cola is hospitality at its best . . . thoughtfulness your guests will remember." Above the copy is a graphic of one large full but uncapped bottle of Coca-Cola. Below is a six-pack of bottled Cokes in a bright-red cardboard carrier with the iconic, cursive Coca-Cola logo printed in white along the longer side of the rectangular case and the shorter moniker "Coke" printed, also in white, on the short side.

This advertisement pictures nine bottles of Coke in total. This repetitive branding, combined with other aspects of the ad—the couple's fashionable dress, grooming, and smiles; the table setting; the built-in grill; the manicured yard and well-kept house; and the lessons in hosting—produces a visual formulation in which lifestyle of affluence, comfort, health, leisure, pleasure, and community is accessible by consuming Coke products. This suburban lifestyle was synonymous with the "American dream" in the 1950s United States, and those people who achieved this life were profoundly American. Therefore, it mattered that Coca-Cola advertisements repeatedly figured that life as a middle-class, white experience defined by homeownership and the enthusiastic consumption of goods, services, and experiences

Figure 54. "General market" Coca-Cola advertisement, 1953. The Coca-Cola Company.

by small, nuclear consumption units (families). Coke ads' celebration of this exclusionary ideal further cast out African Americans as consumers.

Many factors ensured African Americans' denial of the middle-class, suburban lifestyle. These included discriminatory loan practices of the Federal Housing Authority, denial of GI benefits to black veterans, redlining policies, un- and underemployment, and white flight to the suburbs and the accompanying decay of the urban centers where many African Americans found themselves marooned. Their separation from whites took on new meaning. After World War II, African Americans increasingly defined the promise of American citizenship in terms of access to "the dream," rather than (or, at least, in addition to) the traditionally expressed markers of political and personal freedom within a democracy—the rights to vote, marry at will, move about unhindered, assume equal protection under the law, and so on. In 1953, after two years of being turned away on the basis of race, Major League Baseball player Jackie Robinson and his wife, Rachel, succeeded in buying a house in a Connecticut suburb. They desired suburban living for their children, and they could certainly afford it. Of becoming a suburban homeowner, Rachel Robinson said, "I don't know that I ever have felt closer to being a real American . . . closer to having lifted from my shoulders the nagging doubts and insecurities that are the heritage of the American Negro."[69]

Rachel Robinson did not discuss the purchase of their home in a white neighborhood in relation to integration (which is not to say she did not think of it in these terms). Her comment reveals how, after the war, African Americans defined what it meant to be American in terms of *what* they could consume, not just *where* they could consume. Notably, when her husband testified before HUAC in 1949, the professional ballplayer discussed his national loyalty in vaguely economic terms: "I've got too much invested for my wife and child and myself," he said. Jackie Robinson reiterated this sentiment when he played himself in the 1950 film *The Jackie Robinson Story*, which concludes with a dramatic reenactment of the HUAC hearings. "I know that democracy works [and] I . . . have too much invested . . . to throw it away."[70] The Robinsons were among the many African Americans who measured freedom, in part, by their ability to buy in—most literally— to the "American dream." Advertisements such as Coca-Cola's visually underwrote their exclusion from that dream and, by extension, from Americanness.

After the war, black marketers increasingly encouraged major corporations to devise marketing campaigns that hailed African Americans directly. Industry experts of the time, both black and white, commented regularly on the need to target black consumers through specialized advertising. One black market authority insisted that African Americans "[have] an almost childlike desire for recognition."[71] In less patronizing terms, *Tide* summarized, "The Negro rightfully wants to be advertised to [and] to know that their business is earnestly desired."[72] As Coca-Cola's principal "Negro market" specialist, Kendrix insisted the corporation invest in marketing that reflected African Americans' belonging within the consumerist culture of the postwar United States. Similar to Johnson, he did not set out to reform the black public image, or even the marketing industry. He believed marketing of this sort was essential to attract black buyers to the brand.

In 1953, with Kendrix's prompting, Coca-Cola finally produced its first advertisements targeted specifically at African Americans. By contrast, the Pepsi-Cola Company had begun producing "black ads" shortly after the war. In 1947 the Coke competitor launched the innovative, and highly successful, "Leaders in Their Fields" campaign, which consisted of advertisements that featured notable African Americans, including diplomat Ralph Bunche and photographer Gordon Parks.[73] These ads ran in *Ebony* and black weeklies, and had generated significant excitement and goodwill among these publications' predominantly black reader base.[74]

Kendrix's fingerprints are all over Coca-Cola's first black markets campaign. Contracted with the express purpose of increasing the corporation's market share among African Americans, he possessed considerable influence over the formulation of the company's black ads. Moreover, because Coca-Cola had no special-markets division, his operations fell under Coke's director of advertising, Edward Delony (E. D.) Sledge. At the time, Sledge had one of the largest advertising budgets in the world, which allowed Coca-Cola greater leeway and power to shift marketing representations of black America.[75]

The Coca-Cola Company's first African American market advertising campaign consisted of print ads, billboards, and point-of-purchase displays featuring famous black athletes and entertainers. Kendrix drew from the numerous connections he cultivated through his previous public relations work to negotiate deals with black celebrities to appear in this campaign. These celebrities included Willie Mays. Kendrix contacted the recently called-up New York Giant and suggested that appearing in Coke point-of-sale displays and advertisements would be "a good type of publicity" for him.[76] He approached numerous other famous African Americans in the same manner. His efforts resulted in advertisements such as the

Globetrotter Reece "Goose" Tatum full-page ad that appeared in the October 1953 issue of *Ebony* as the magazine's first Coke ad featuring an African American (Figure 49). Within a year, eleven African Americans who were popular in the worlds of sports and entertainment appeared in Coca-Cola black marketing materials.[77] The campaign had the desired effect and boosted sales among African Americans.

Coke's first black ads caught the attention of Pepsi, an indication they were of some significance. In 1954 Harvey Russell, one of Pepsi's special-markets representatives, advised company higher-ups that Coca-Cola was running weekly advertisements that "carr[y] the picture of a well-known Negro character."[78] Interestingly, by that time, Pepsi had turned away from advertisements featuring African Americans after being an industry leader in making direct hails to black consumers. Thus, at the same time *Ebony* readers encountered Coke ads with Tatum and the like, the magazine carried Pepsi advertisements that featured wispy-thin, glamorous white women (Figure 55) with taglines such as "Refreshing—Not Filling."[79] These ads, an obvious attempt to tap women consumers' objectives or anxieties concerning their weight, missed the market with African Americans.

The black celebrity Coke ads were a significant development in the ad world, but they were not radical. They provided a "safe" entry point into marketing to African Americans, because the black figures at their center—such as Tatum, Cleveland Indian baseball infielder Larry Doby, and musicians Graham Jackson, Lionel Hampton, and Larry Steele—were renowned for entertaining audiences.[80] The role of entertainer was one through which black people had historically met various needs of whites. Notably, in the Tatum Coca-Cola advertisement, Tatum is not pictured consuming the product: in fact, he does not even touch the bottle of Coke. Instead, he balances it on the ball, which he holds out and away from his body, very much as if he is offering the Coke to viewers on the serving tray that is the ball. Not only did black ads such as this run less risk of offending whites' sensibilities, they might have actually appealed to members of the general market.

Coca-Cola heralded its black celebrity campaign. Its trade publication the *Refresher* pointed to the campaign as proof that it was "a participant in the Negro market."[81] Kendrix and his associate Jesse Lewis, however, viewed this campaign as the compromise it was. Even as Coca-Cola's first "Negro market" appeals courted African American consumers, they failed

Figure 55. Pepsi advertisement, circa 1955. PepsiCo.

to present African Americans as consumers. To the contrary, the black celebrity ads implicitly maintained the stereotypical black server ideal. Moreover, they did not further conceptions of black normality, focused as they were on African Americans who had considerable talent, fame, and wealth. These figures were hardly representative of "average" African Americans, or Americans for that matter.

Kendrix and Lewis argued for a new approach. "We wanted people to see an ad that looked like black people normally look," Lewis explained. "Everybody don't play football, everybody don't play basketball, and everybody don't sing." For this reason, Coca-Cola's first two special-markets reps lobbied for black ad images like those "[that] they put in *Ladies' Home Journal*."[82] In doing so, they echoed the desires of the African Americans they targeted. The Coke ads featuring black athletes and musicians were a first step, perhaps the necessary first step. Soon, however, they proved insufficient to inspire or maintain brand loyalty among black consumers. A contemporary industry expert explained that blacks were "tired of seeing the same old faces" whose experiences did not reflect their own.[83] They wanted the ads white Americans got.

Developments across consumer culture and marketing encouraged Coca-Cola's turn toward advertising that appealed to and also represented African Americans as consumers. An increasing number of major corporations began to produce advertisements that depicted African Americans as "everyday" Americans, including the Schlitz Brewing Company, the American Tobacco Company, and Pet Milk. Coca-Cola needed to follow suit if the company hoped to remain competitive in black markets.

The existence of the Johnson Publishing Company (JPC) helped Kendrix persuade his flagship client to follow the trend. Johnson had spent the latter half of the 1940s engaged in the same project as Kendrix, promoting African Americans as valuable, enthusiastic consumers to corporate America. This project unfolded on the pages of *Ebony*. Through its existence, editorial content, and advertising, the magazine implied, displayed, and encouraged black consumerism. Johnson's enterprise relied on advertising revenue; therefore, it was essential to convince major advertisers—primarily white advertisers—to see African Americans as consumers and desire them as customers for their goods and services. To that end, Johnson commissioned studies, compiled data, and produced propaganda that furthered a

certain picture of the black consumer market, which he conflated with the
JPC market. Using research available to him through JPC's membership
in the Audit Bureau of Circulations and collected through surveys he financed, Johnson reported that, by 1950, approximately half of *Ebony* readers lived in cities and, of that population, 28 percent earned more than
$4,000 annually, 36 percent owned homes, 41 percent owned new cars, and
22 percent owned television sets.[84] He even provided information about
how many *Ebony* readers had dogs: one out of five.

Johnson encouraged perceptions of African Americans, and, especially,
Ebony readers, as urbane consumers who either had or desired a middle-
class lifestyle defined by materialism and social mobility—the most profitable of consumers to the advertisers whose business he sought. Johnson
framed his research to highlight how many blacks *did* have college educa-
tions, *did* have higher incomes, and *did* own certain markers of middle-class
life; but that same research revealed that a majority of African Americans,
including *Ebony* readers, were not college educated, did not have higher incomes, and did not own homes, cars, or televisions. The image that JPC
put forth of a sizeable, conformist, black middle-class belied the working-
class, even working-poor, experience shared by a predominance of African
Americans in the mid-twentieth century. The overwhelming popularity of
Ebony, however, implied that those who could not afford the lifestyle of consumption that the magazine encouraged "express[ed] a positive orientation"
toward that life.[85] This notion of black aspiration made African American consumers more attractive as a market. *Ebony* provided advertisers a
vehicle for reaching those consumers.

Johnson's flagship magazine also provided a model of the middle-class
lifestyle to which African Americans might aspire and guidance in that lifestyle. Black women were primarily the target audience for such lessons. In
1946, for example, *Ebony* introduced "Date with a Dish," a monthly feature
in which *Ebony* food editor Freda DeKnight detailed celebrities' favorite
dishes and other creative, healthy, tasty, and glamorous recipes for feeding
the family or entertaining.[86] Similarly, in 1948, the magazine debuted its
"Fashion Fair" section to help black women "keep up with the newest styles,"
which included "budget-wise" casuals, swimsuits "too fabulous for words,"
and mink coats "especially appropriate for cocktails."[87] These sections were
valuable to African American women seeking instruction in performances

of postwar middle-class womanhood. They were also profitable for JPC as features that invited sponsorship by large advertisers such as Hunt's Tomato Sauce, Alaga Syrup, Borden's Evaporated Milk, and Felso Laundry Detergent.

African Americans' aspirations to or performances of middle-class-ness should not be assumed as their engagement in a "politics of respectability." Traditionally espoused by black leadership, the politics of respectability assumed that African Americans' public embrace and enactment of manners and mores valued by the dominant class (whites) was essential to their advancement as a race.[88] This formulation between "respectable" behavior and racial uplift was more suited to pre–World War II civil rights politics, when class hinged as much on social status and reputation as on income. After the war, Americans increasingly conceived of middle-class-dom in terms of one's consumerism and accumulation of stuff, even more so than wealth, and commitment to a particular type of nuclear familyhood. In the new consumer culture of the postwar period, materialism certainly provided the means for African Americans to assert their equality.[89] An *Ebony* editorial of the time explained that the ability to purchase particular items—a Cadillac in this instance—was "a solid and substantial symbol . . . that [blacks are] as good as any white man."[90] Recognition that blacks were equal was essential to their political quest for equal citizenship rights. Recognition that they were normal was essential to their quest for Americanness.

Prominent black political thinkers commonly identified African Americans' normalization as necessary to their social advancement. When National Association for the Advancement of Colored People executive secretary Walter White called for "normal" representations of African Americans during World War II, he sought media images that portrayed blacks against stereotype and normatively, which he cited as essential to their acceptance as integral members of American society.[91] Integrationist civil rights leaders insisted that African Americans must behave as "good Americans," as defined by the dominant class, to surmount challenges to their citizenship.[92] This political strategy reflected, or at least coincided with, the theories promoted by sociologists of the era. In *An American Dilemma*, Gunnar Myrdal reported that prevailing notions of blacks as peculiar and even pathological barred them from full citizenship. He concluded, "Recognition of increased cultural similarity is not unimportant in the general attitude of whites toward Negroes." If African Americans sought integration into mainstream society, he theorized they must "acquire the traits held in esteem by dominant white Americans."[93] Frazier explained that African Americans would experience "gains of civilization" to be had "from participation in the white world" by adopting the sexual behaviors and family patterns of that world.[94] These theories of racial uplift were in keeping with the "politics of respectability," which identified exceptional normativity as a prerequisite to African Americans' obtaining equal recognition and rights as citizens.

By the 1950s, however, conceptions of normal shifted. Advances in social science technologies resulted in the unprecedented surveying of Americans about everything from their preferences in laundry detergent to their sex lives. This development prompted the cultural redefinition of *normal* to mean "common." The data that pollsters and academics collected pooled into constructs of the "average American," by which Americans evaluated themselves individually and as a national group of people, a body politic united by their commonness.[95] Moreover, in the Cold War context, an "American type"—conceived of, at the time, as individuals who strove for and benefited from the material comforts and opportunities for upward mobility—was a useful discursive tool for arguing the inferiority of its opposite—non-Americans or, more specifically, the "communist type." Large factions of government, academia, and pop culture celebrated a culture of conformity and consensus. The elevation of the "average American" suggested that, instead of a politics of respectability, a politics of normality might be a more effective route to full citizenship. For African Americans and other marginalized groups, being typical—rather than individualistic or exceptional—provided a way to be culturally visible (as ideal Americans) and strategically invisible (as controversial, disturbing, or different figures) in all the right ways.

The challenge of a politics of normality was that normal was a raced concept that assumed middle-class whiteness. In lieu of actually being white, African Americans employed consumerism as an alternative route to normality. Joseph Wootton, the director of the radio division for Interstate United Newspapers, a trade group of black newspapers, took this route when, in 1951, he claimed, "The Negro is first and foremost an American consumer, a 'purchasing agent.'"[96] Wootton highlighted the behavior (consumption) that theoretically had the potential to erase, or at least make inconsequential, racial difference.

Through their respective outfits, MHKO and JPC, Kendrix and Johnson strongly encouraged African Americans to embrace a consumer ethos. After all, their businesses depended on it. As successful entrepreneurs, however, they also viewed consumerism as a form of politics—perhaps the most important form—in a capitalist society. "He who starts lastest, runs fastest, can be firstest," Kendrix asserted.[97] Not everyone agreed. Martin Luther King Jr., for one, rebuked African Americans for their increased conspicuous consumption. In an advice column entitled "Advice for Living," the renowned civil rights leader asserted, "Well has it been said . . . that Negroes too often buy what they want and beg for what they need." "Negroes" must "practice systematic savings," he preached, if they were to acquire the purchasing power he posited as necessary for a better standard of living.[98] Ironically, as leader of arguably the most successful consumer boycott in U.S. history, he failed to acknowledge that purchasing power requires demonstration of that power. Equally ironic, King's column appeared monthly in *Ebony* magazine. He used the most consumerist, commercial black publication in the world so that he could widely "spread the gospel" of antimaterialism. His column reflects how civil rights activism intersected with, even relied on, consumer trends and market dynamics.

For African Americans who subscribed to a politics of normality, mass consumption provided an alternative to protest and legislative battles in the quest for full citizenship, because, in the postwar United States, nothing was considered, or constructed as, more normal or American than buying stuff. Therefore, as opposed to merely satisfying personal wants, black materialism could be consciously public minded.[99] Historically, however, the fact that African Americans bought goods and services had failed to solidify recognition of them as consumers. They needed to be clearly, even primarily, intelligible as people who fully engaged in or aspired to a materialistic lifestyle that helped keep the engine of capitalism purring like a kitten. Coca-Cola helped make them so.

During World War II, the government deemed Coca-Cola so important to "the building and the maintenance of morale among military personnel" that it was exempted from sugar rationing in its sales to military or outlets servicing soldiers. Furthering its status as a product representing all that America stood for, Coca-Cola president Robert Woodruff declared that, no matter the cost to his company, "every man in uniform gets a bottle of Coca-Cola for five cents, wherever he is."[100] As a result, Coke came out of the war as iconically American, with Kendrix himself defining it, in one of his characteristically convoluted analogies, as "American as education and as free as enterprise."[101] A brand of such popularity and so esteemed worldwide, Coca-Cola had the cultural capital and the advertising budget to affect popular definitions of blackness.

Eventually, Sledge signed off on moving ahead with African American market advertising designed to mirror that intended for white consumers. Kendrix and Lewis oversaw the production of Coca-Cola's first marketing campaign to feature black noncelebrities. They studied the general-market ads of Coca-Cola and other national brands. The white suburban housewife-homemaker, as a figure of respectability and feminized heterosexuality, was a ubiquitous representation in popular entertainment media— embodied by figures like June Cleaver in *Leave It to Beaver* and Donna Stone in *The Donna Reed Show*—and crossed over into advertising. The black counterpart to this ideal was the "Brownskin," "a heterosexual and feminine creature who was visibly African American and virtuously middle-class."[102] Demand for representations of middle-class black Americanness in advertising, along with the rise of popular black magazines, helped give rise to and professionalize the industry of black modeling. National brands looking for African Americans to portray the Brownskin turned to modeling and advertising agencies, such as the black agency Brandford Modeling or D'Arcy Advertising, to find the appropriate talent to feature in their marketing materials.[103] Kendrix and Lewis, however, took another route. Rather than hire professionals to portray middle-class black Americanness, they sought actual middle-class black Americans to appear in Coke's first noncelebrity black market ads.

Kendrix and Lewis steered clear of models because they did not want "any glamour people," claimed Lewis. They sought authenticity, "the average person you would see every day."[104] They also may have sought the better deal. In the early years of black advertising, it was not unusual for corporations, especially black corporations, to feature "real" people, because the expense of professional models was one that many black advertisers could not afford and was a pill that was hard to swallow for white corporations unaccustomed to targeting black consumers.[105] Whatever the reason, rather than rely on modeling agencies, Kendrix went back to his old stomping grounds—the historically black colleges and universities of Atlanta. There, he scouted the student bodies for African Americans to appear in phase two of Coca-Cola's targeted advertisements. He and Lewis selected a handful of young black men and women from Clark College (now Clark Atlanta University) and Morehouse College. Their most significant "find" was Clark student Mary Cowser (now Mary Alexander), whom Kendrix auditioned in the presence of her housemother. According to Lewis, Cowser—whom Coca-Cola recognizes as the first noncelebrity African American to appear in the company's advertising—was the perfect choice.[106] "Of the potential models they identified," he explained, she was "the least sexy . . . just plain Jane. [She had] nothing other than the fact that she was a typical average American."[107] With Cowser, they may have avoided the "glamour" they feared in "real" models, but it appears they did seek models with a certain degree of appeal, accomplishment, and reputability. After all, in addition to being a secretarial science major and member of numerous clubs, Cowser had been named Miss Clark—designated by the school yearbook as the "most coveted beauty title"—in 1955. She had been a runner-up for the same title the previous year.[108] Just how plain could she have been?

Having procured the right "talent," Kendrix and Lewis moved to production. In some cases, Lewis, who learned photography while serving in the war, personally photographed the models. Otherwise, Kendrix chaperoned the female models on shoots with professional photographers, owing to concerns about how they might be treated as young and inexperienced black females. These events culminated in the introduction of Coca-Cola's first round of noncelebrity black market ads into the marketplace in 1955. These materials pictured the black amateur models in various social tableaux that signified African Americans' belonging to the middle-class American experience central to contemporary definitions of "the American way of life" and American exceptionalism.[109] Among them were portraits of black women shopping, teaching, and typing; black men wielding golf clubs or relaxing in a "favorite chair" after work; a dungaree-wearing black boy playing leapfrog or bicycling; young women gossiping, playing tennis, and dressed for prom; and young couples flirting, picnicking, and studying. In this set of marketplace images, the black subjects appear in modern settings and fashionable clothing, and all are holding, reaching for, transporting, or drinking Coca-Cola. In other words, the ads represented them as consumers of the product.

A favored tableau in Coke's first black, noncelebrity marketing campaign was the representation of black consumerism centered in family. One ad belonging to that campaign pictures a well-dressed and presumably married couple and their equally well-groomed and handsome son sipping from bottles of Coke while eating sandwiches and watching television in a modern living room (Figure 56). The "family" central to that first series featured Mary Cowser as "Mom"; John Oneal, also a Clark student, who, small framed and young looking, portrayed "the son"; and Napoleon Johnson, a tall, fine-featured Morehouse student who portrayed "Dad."[110] From 1955 to 1957, this same "family" appeared repeatedly in the marketing materials for the "Family Favorite" Coke campaign.[111]

In keeping with the general-market advertisements of numerous national brands of the time, Coca-Cola's noncelebrity black ads targeted women as the primary shoppers. Mary Cowser's "Mom" character appeared in multiple advertisements and other marketing materials as the key figure responsible for keeping the home and facilitating family moments such as sharing a meal, enjoying a family outing, doing homework, or having a barbeque. She is not always the most prominent person in frame, but the physical relation of Cowser's "Mom" to food in many of the "Family Favorite" advertisements makes her intelligible as the hailed shopper, as the person responsible for providing the Coke products held by her "son" or "husband." In addition, the ads primarily spoke to (black) women with ad copy that referenced the prescribed duties of the homemaker. They instructed women to "make certain you have enough Coke for everyone," keep Coke in "the coolest part of your refrigerator," and "serve delicious Coca-Cola at mealtime. It's your family's favorite refreshment."[112] Through visual images and copy, these marketing pieces assigned African American women the homemaker role previously denied to them in pop culture or media representations. Black women's occupation of the valorized housewife-homemaker role in these ads helped formulate the black "husbands," "boyfriends," and "sons" featured as representations of normative manhood. These new representations pictured African Americans in keeping with contemporaneous definitions of the typical and normative American family. The noncelebrity "Negro market" marketing images circulated in

Figure 56. "Family Favorite" Coca-Cola advertisement, 1956. The Coca-Cola Company.

black spaces, such as black businesses, in the form of point-of-purchase placards, and in black periodicals in the form of advertisements. But they also appeared in open spaces visible to all. Cowser's brother was shocked, for example, when he saw a Coca-Cola billboard featuring his sister while driving through Mississippi. Others reported seeing Cowser's Coke ad when riding the subways in New York.[113]

The image of black familyhood depicted in the Coca-Cola black market ads mirrored the image that Kendrix modeled as part of his own performance of professional black manhood (Figures 57 and 58). A 1953 *Sepia* magazine article about Kendrix included a picture of him, dressed in a light-colored suit accented by a dark tie, walking hand in hand with his wife, Dorothy, and two sons during a working vacation in Atlantic City. Dorothy is wearing a sleeveless belted dress that accentuates her slim figure, and, although dressed more casually than their father, Moss Jr. and Alex are still impeccably groomed. All four of them are smiling as they stroll along the bustling boardwalk.[114] Everything about the image—the clothing, the location as a site of shopping and leisure, the family composition as nuclear and appropriately heteronormative, the appearance of pleasure—mirrors the middle-class consumerist lifestyle promoted through Coca-Cola marketing of the time. The only thing distinguishing this image from those constructed by Coke's noncelebrity black ads is that no Coca-Cola products are in the picture. Anyone who knew Kendrix at the time would find this remarkable, since, whenever possible and appropriate, he made it a point to hold a bottle of Coke when being photographed.

The presentation of familyhood the Kendrixes offered was similar to the "Family Favorite" Coke ads in that it belied the challenges African Americans faced to both realizing and representing middle-class-dom. The entrepreneurialism that afforded Kendrix and his family a middle-class socioeconomic experience actually fractured his family. Keeping MHKO competitive and representing Coca-Cola required the better part of Kendrix's energies—at least he believed it did. He described public relations as "the total sum of one's personal relations."[115] Consequently, he was not inclined to delegate the handling of his clients to others, even if his small firm had allowed him the workforce to do so. On average, he worked twelve to eighteen hours a day and spent over two hundred days away from home in a calendar year. He reportedly rivaled airline pilots in flight time.[116] The demands of running his own firm and being one of the most successful black

Figure 57. "Family Favorite" Coca-Cola ad, 1956. The Coca-Cola Company.
Figure 58. Moss Kendrix and his family, ca. 1953. Photograph from the Alexandria Black History Museum.

marketers of the time prevented Kendrix from occupying the position of family man, the normative gender role for American men after World War II. Asked to comment on her husband's busy schedule for a media profile, Dorothy Kendrix said, "My husband is—by appointment." One can imagine a forced smile accompanying the pause in her statement. Kendrix's response to his wife's comment revealed another challenge inherent to a middle-class materialist lifestyle: "keeping up with the Joneses." "The type of bread that she likes," he said, "doesn't grow in Washington."[117] Although somewhat jumbled, his statement suggests Dorothy was a devotee to the consumerist ethos, and perhaps her desire for material things, as much as his work ethic, his aspirations, or his clients' needs, kept him from being the ideal family man.[118] Nevertheless, the media products he compelled and the image he put forth in public reveal the black ideal he wished to publicly promote.

The noncelebrity black Coke ads were a radical departure in the traditional marketplace representation of blackness. They were not, however, a radical departure in terms of Coca-Cola's representation of consumers. In fact, they mirrored the company's general-market advertisements exactly (Figures 59 and 60). Rather than visualize African Americans in culturally specific or integrated contexts, Coca-Cola's noncelebrity black advertisements featured black men and women performing the same activities while wearing the same clothing and even striking the same poses as whites in the company's other ads. The conformity of Coca-Cola's black ads to those targeted at the dominant class constituted an important shift in the popular depiction of blackness. They were "empowering and uplifting images representative of the goals and aspirations of the black population."[119] In the positive-versus-negative framework typically applied to black media images, the noncelebrity black Coke ads were "good," as representations that "reclaim[ed] and rehabilitat[ed]" the definition of blackness.[120]

These advertisements absolutely signaled progress within the mainstream representation of blackness; however, they were not wholly progressive. The Coke black market advertisements visually reinforced racial segregation, as there were never any whites in the picture. They circulated through the marketplace at precisely the historical moment when the National Association for the Advancement of Colored People dismantled the "separate-but-equal" doctrine through the *Brown v. Board of Education* case and African Americans in Montgomery, Alabama, refused their segregated status in public (consumer) spaces by boycotting the city busses

Figure 59. Coca-Cola general market ad featuring white girl, 1955. The Coca-Cola Company.

Figure 60. Cola-Cola "Negro market" ad featuring Mary (Cowser) Alexander, 1955. The Coca-Cola Company.

en masse for an entire year. Throughout the nation, journalists, courts, and activists were attacking racial segregation as an affront to democracy and freedom. Internationally, U.S. allies and foes also criticized the practice—in its de jure and de facto forms—and questioned, or rejected, American exceptionalism. Coca-Cola's noncelebrity black ads, however, reinforced African Americans' "nation-within-a-nation" status; they visually maintained blacks' essential difference on the basis of race and their separateness from other Americans, which historically had served as grounds for their discrimination.

In their separate-but-identical presentation of African Americans, the black ad images Coke generated under Kendrix's advisement actually employed an integrationist politics of representation, in which a marginalized group in the United States appears to adopt white mores, manners, and style to contest a racialized regime of representation that positions them as inferior to whites.[121] Taken on their own, the black Coke ads pictured African Americans doing things, wearing things, and styling themselves in ways that many blacks in America did, or aspired to do, which had nothing to do with a desire to appear or be white. As replicas of Coke's general market, however, the noncelebrity black market ads encased blacks in molds carved out for imagined white Coca-Cola consumers, which undermined the ads' ability to elevate the featured black figures to an equal plane as the company's privileged market. Reactions to the *Brown* decision, however, made it painfully, even violently, clear that much of white America was not ready to accept integration; it follows that visuals of racial integration might also have been unpopular.

The formulation of Coca-Cola's first black market advertisements also reflected the objectives, theories, and image politics of many African Americans at the time. Kendrix, for one, was devoted to the special-markets concept, which honored his theories about race, or, more specifically, about being black. He believed that the uniqueness of African Americans (as consumers) lay in their heightened race consciousness. For white Americans, popular culture and official policies rendered their race so normative as to make it invisible and thus not central to their sense of themselves. By comparison, Kendrix theorized, blacks' sense of themselves as raced individuals and their awareness of how the dominant class perceived them figured greatly into their everyday behaviors, including their consumption practices.[122]

He never granted, however, the formulation in which blacks' "specialness" translated into their inferiority or their being abnormal. To the contrary, he and other black marketers claimed African Americans were not just good consumers but in fact better consumers—better than whites, that is. They emphasized the extreme quality consciousness that African Americans displayed. They detailed the tendency among blacks to spend money on the highest-quality goods, despite bad times, in comparison to their white counterparts. This tendency, *Tide* magazine concluded, was a "complex" born out of an "almost unnatural attempt to gain recognition."[123] Kendrix did not dwell on the psychology behind this consumer behavior, but he repeatedly presented clients with data that testified to blacks' higher brand loyalty, demand for higher-quality goods, and desire for recognition—again constituting African Americans as consummate consumers and the most lucrative for advertisers to pursue.

Finally, it is clear that many African Americans, including Kendrix, did view "positive" marketplace representations of blackness as essential to their advancement in a capitalist society. Black Coke marketing of the mid-1950s responded to the desire among African Americans for ad images that not only pictured them as "normal" American citizens but actually privileged them. To bring whites into the frame of these ads would have only diminished the black figures depicted, given the visual politics and codes of the time.

The black market advertising Coca-Cola produced under Kendrix's direction in the mid-1950s shaped how corporations represented African Americans. The Pepsi-Cola Company, for one, quickly followed suit. When it abandoned its black marketing, Pepsi handed Coca-Cola an increased share of the black consumer market: it was time to reverse its reversed course. Pepsi's initial noncelebrity black ads mirrored the corporation's recent ad campaign featuring slim, white women. They pictured elegantly dressed African American women with chiseled features and thin frames in upscale settings, like cocktail parties, and often alone. Contrary to the "plain Janes" that Kendrix and Lewis sought for the Coca-Cola ads, the black women at the center of Pepsi's ads were professional models. Sexy, striking, and glamorous, these women were the exception, not the norm. Representations as exceptional did little good for people seeking national belonging on the basis of their normality, which may explain why Pepsi's black glamour ads did not perform as well among

African Americans as the Coke ads. Quickly, Pepsi adopted Coke's representational formula, giving the black women in their advertisements sweethearts or families and showing them doing "ordinary" activities, such as picnicking and barbequing. Pet Milk followed suit and organized its special-markets campaigns around portrayals of black middle-class familyhood and, like Coca-Cola, also used "real" people rather than models. With much guidance from Kendrix, the Coca-Cola Company had set the standard for representing African Americans.

In 1957 Coca-Cola's "Family Favorite" series earned the company top honors for "distinguished service in Negro market merchandising" in a nationwide contest that judged leading brands' visual addresses to African Americans. Coca-Cola's campaign beat out those of twenty other leading brands, including Alaga Syrup, Pet Milk, Carnation Milk, Camel, Lucky Strike, Budweiser, and Clairol.[124] The contest itself reveals a widespread turn toward black consumers within corporate America, with several major corporations routinely representing African Americans as enthusiastic consumers central to healthy and happy, nuclear families and modern, middle-class households. In a culture that celebrated an "American dream" organized around mass consumption, these marketplace images normalized African Americans—albeit of a particular type. Despite the Coca-Cola Company's initial hesitancy, its imaging of blackness became a respected model to follow.

With Coca-Cola's cooperation, Kendrix furthered African Americans' normality and, by extension, national belonging. He did not allow, however, that their belonging made them indistinct within the broader American consumer market. Rather, in contrast to his approach when doing public relations for the New Deal or Liberia, he was careful to construct African Americans as a unique subset among black peoples and Americans. Shortly after Kendrix contracted with Coca-Cola, he took measures to protect blacks' status as a "special" consumer group, which, of course, secured his place in the marketing profession as a "black markets" specialist. In 1953 he founded the National Association of Market Developers (NAMD), an organization for African American marketing and sales professionals engaged in developing "the Negro market," which, at the time, translated into a professional organization of black men. He relied on a handful of fellow black marketers to expand the organization, including Howard Naylor Fitzhugh, a Harvard-educated Howard University marketing professor;

Wendell P. Alston, employed by Esso Standard Oil; and Raymond Scruggs, employed by the American Telephone and Telegraph Company (now AT&T).[125]

Kendrix conceived of NAMD as a professional network through which black market developers could exchange information and experiences to improve the services and products they provided their respective clients. Equally important, the association would grow their place within specialized marketing and public relations, particularly by nurturing the next generation. Kendrix believed that the job of marketing to African Americans held "promise of heretofore unheard-of advancement" for "enterprising [black] youths." NAMD provided a vehicle to both reach and cultivate "this virgin source."[126] The association fostered, legitimized, and secured a place in marketing for African American professionals based on their role as special-markets experts.

Kendrix's firm, MHKO, was also a training ground for future black special-markets practitioners. Most notably, Kendrix nurtured the marketing career of Fitzhugh, who gained national recognition for his role as Pepsi-Cola's vice president of special markets, a position he assumed in 1965. That position made Fitzhugh one of the most respected black voices in marketing, as evidenced by the unofficial title he assumed within the industry as "the dean of black businessmen."[127] Before Pepsi, however, in addition to teaching at Howard, he worked as a part-time associate at MHKO during the mid-1950s, having been recruited by Kendrix. A decade later, when Pepsi executives went looking for a special-markets vice president, it is little wonder they selected Fitzhugh. Not only was he a respected black marketing scholar, he had received his professional training as a representative for their main competitor, Coca-Cola. Post-1965 news items concerning Fitzhugh omit his association with Kendrix, presumably because Fitzhugh believed he had to appear "a Pepsi man," something his former employer, a devout "Coca-Cola man," no doubt understood. This gap in Fitzhugh's professional biography is significant, however, because he is widely credited with contributing to, if not developing, the concept and initial campaigns of "target marketing"—marketing specialized to address a particular market segment. In 1967, at a meeting of the Sales Executive Club, Fitzhugh advised his professional peers, "In marketing . . . the issue is consumer wants and buying habits; in public relations, the issue is human dignity."[128] As these were principles fundamental to Kendrix's business, it seems apparent that Fitzhugh developed his special-markets approach under his guidance.

The strategies Kendrix developed to build bridges between white corporations and black consumers compelled changes in marketing that defined the industry for the remainder of the twentieth century—including the rise of "ethnic," "urban," and "multicultural" marketing. The history of how the advertisers and marketers carved up the consumer market after World War II is largely a narrative of white enterprise in which African Americans figure primarily as people on the receiving end of the business decisions that changed American consumer culture.[129] The marketing strategies that Kendrix employed place him squarely among those making those decisions. He, along with other Brown Hucksters—including his associates Lewis and Fitzhugh—and Johnson, contributed greatly to the notion of specialized markets. In fact, they insisted on it, because it better served their black businesses and, they believed, black consumers in that particular historical moment.

Kendrix and the small cadre of black marketers to which he belonged defined African Americans as a "special" market to cultivate the black consumer identity on which their enterprises depended and to secure their position as marketing professionals. Their methods contributed to the market segmentation and the melding of consumerism and politics that characterized the latter half of the twentieth century. The special-market strategy, however, also upheld boundaries predicated on race, class, sexuality, and nationality. These boundaries shifted and multiplied as advertisers identified, or constructed, more and more niche markets. They remained consistent, however, as markers of difference with power to undermine the equality claims of African Americans, as well as other marginalized groups. That the business of redefining African Americans as American generated flawed returns demonstrates the consequences of pursuing racial progress through capitalism, an institution that relies on the reproduction of inequity. The question is how African Americans pursuing equality and civil rights in the postwar United States might have done otherwise.

After a decade of noncommercial public relations work, Kendrix built a business after World War II by leveraging African Americans' postwar purchasing power and aspirations and positioning himself as a conduit to that particular consumer market. For nearly two decades, he was the chief special-markets representative for the Coca-Cola Company, even becoming a board member in the early 1960s—a position unthinkable for an African American when he began pursuing the corporation's business in 1945.[130] Through MHKO and NAMD, and with the collaboration of his corporate clients, he established the premise that African Americans required appeals uniquely targeted at them by individuals uniquely qualified to understand them. Kendrix's professional accomplishments and contributions as a marketer clearly warrant his inclusion in post–World War II business histories. His proximity to corporate America, however, has thwarted his inclusion—and that of many capitalists—in the civil rights story.

As Coke's "black ambassador," Kendrix developed or promoted theories and practices that set industry standards for marketing that recognized, respected, and conformed to African Americans' representational desires. The efficacy of these methods harnessed major advertisers to a national marketing campaign for black citizenship unprecedented in quality, size, or reach. African American marketers such as Kendrix, Lewis, and Johnson constructed African Americans as a good and profitable consumer market on their way to building profitable marketing and media enterprises. The ad images that resulted from their respective enterprises figured blacks as devotees of the mass consumption foundational to the mid-twentieth-century "American dream." In a period when all major cultural institutions lauded consensus, conformity, and consumption, these visuals of blackness figured African Americans as normal, or typical, consumerist Americans—a troublingly stubborn precondition to their experiencing the full rights inherent to their Americanness.

The Coca-Cola advertisements that Kendrix engineered, and that Johnson helped circulate, were problematic. They conformed to the corporation's general-market marketing formulas, which glorified a particular lifestyle—a particular way of being American—that was definitively middle class and heteronormative, such that it was unavailable or undesirable to many. To secure blacks' recognition according to hegemonic ideologies of who constituted consumers, Kendrix and other marketers enacted an image politics that reproduced the hierarchies undergirding those ideologies.[131] Yet, in their moment, these advertisements were also a logical, if flawed, strategy for addressing antiblack racism. As mainstream black media representations, they redefined African Americans' social identity and position by depicting them as (sought-after) consumers of a uniquely American product (Figure 61). Picturing blacks consuming rather than serving Coke, this marketing forged visual and conceptual associations between blackness and Americanness, with African Americans imbibing their American identity from green glass bottles.

Figure 61. Coca-Cola "Negro market" lithograph, circa 1955. The Coca-Cola Company.

Conclusion

What Is a Civil Rights Image?

We like our history neat. . . . Complexity, with all its
nuances and shaded realities, is a messy business.

—Gary Younge

During the "classic" civil rights years, Moss Hyles Kendrix was criss-crossing the nation to glad-hand, pitch to, and make deals with businessmen in executive boardrooms and on golf courses. On Chicago's South Side, John H. Johnson was buying up property and launching one magazine after another in his successful quest to build the largest black media empire in history. In their entrepreneurial form, these men hardly fit the conventional image of civil rights actors. Even activist-artist Gordon Parks strains the confines of that image when one considers that he spent this period helping to launch a magazine to compete with *Ebony* and traveling to and from Europe on assignment as a fashion photographer for *Life* and *Vogue* magazines. Recognizing these professionals' entrepreneurialism as civil rights work requires reconsidering what the black campaign for civil rights entailed—and why.

The mid-twentieth-century civil rights struggle was, at its core, a complex series of image campaigns. Many of these campaigns had no explicit connection to political, legislative, or protest actions but rather were strategies inspired or influenced by key forces shaping postwar America—namely, consumer capitalism and the increased sophistication and popularity of visual media. After World War II, representing black citizenship was good civil rights politics for African Americans. It was also good business. The antiblack racism that continued to hold sway in American politics, policy, and culture created demand for mainstream visuals that depicted African Americans in keeping with prevailing definitions of citizenship and Americanness. Black capitalists stepped up to meet this demand with images that asserted black patriotism, beauty, normality, and, especially, consumerism. These new media representations, which placed African Americans center frame and redefined them in the larger picture of postwar American society, propped up or created channels for African Americans' claims of equality and entitlement as U.S. citizens. This profit-based image work did not parallel the development of the modern civil rights movement; it constituted an important force of the movement.

The marketplace visuals of blackness that black imagemakers, mediamakers, and marketers generated after World War II competed with images of black protest that appeared in mainstream media with greater frequency as civil rights activism coalesced into a national movement. In the wake of the 1954 *Brown v. Board of Education* decision and the grisly lynching in Mississippi of young Emmett Till in 1955, white and national media increasingly joined the black press to cover African Americans' nonviolent direct action and the backlash it inspired. Photographers from national newspapers and news services and network news camera crews trained their lenses on the sites of conflict, understanding that dramatic confrontations made for visuals that moved newspapers and attracted larger viewing audiences. We readily accept the resulting media images as belonging to the black freedom struggle. To grant marketing images of blackness that belonging requires recognizing how market dynamics inherent to consumer capitalism, black entrepreneurialism, and black consumer demands shaped African Americans' postwar civil rights politics.

In their efforts to build businesses, to make money, and to succeed as capitalists in the world's most capitalist of societies, mediamakers and marketers such as Kendrix and Johnson advanced a visual politics of black citizenship. They cultivated media and marketplace images that claimed characteristics, contributions, and commitments for African Americans that were essential to perceptions of their Americanness. Because the black media images they produced moved through the market, they were subject to market dynamics, which accounted for some images gaining more traction than others. The sexualized images that Johnson produced found a secure place in pop culture because they proved to be a successful marketing tool for his commercial products; challenged white beauty standards and asserted the femininity, sexiness, and attractiveness of black women; corresponded to trends in print media that mainstreamed risqué representations of the female body; satisfied consumer viewing demands; and enabled circulation of other black media images and topics of black interest. The images of black consumerism that Kendrix and other black marketers engineered became standard because they served advertisers' objectives, reflected black representational desires, and corresponded with African Americans' consumerist aspirations and shifting definitions of national belonging and freedom within the postwar culture of mass consumption. These new black media images came to rival, even surpass, representations of "respectable" blackness traditionally advocated by black political leaders as a tool of social advancement.

Moreover, the ideals of black America popularized through postwar black capitalism informed civil rights activism and perceptions of that activism. Economic boycotts were a central protest strategy within the movement, yet historians consistently fail to consider how African Americans identified as consumers other than in their desire for equal access. The assumption has been that the purpose of protest actions such as the Montgomery bus boycott and lunch counter sit-ins lay in African Americans' wielding their economic power to "forc[e] open the doors of public accommodations."[1] Certainly this is accurate; but the objectives of equal access, desegregation, and integration are only part of the story. To draw attention to their consumer selves was also a sound representational tactic for claiming normality and belonging in the postwar consumer-oriented culture that exalted the purchasing agent. We must also consider that African Americans brought their consumer selves into their activism because it was central to how they conceived of themselves within society. After all, like all Americans, they had been strongly encouraged to do so—in large part by black capitalists who stood to profit from the development of black consumer subjectivities. Media and image products that black marketers like Kendrix and Johnson produced both popularized the consumerist ideal among African Americans and instructed them in how to embody it.

The business of representing black citizenship also demonstrated the value of visual media and public relations strategies to civil rights campaigns. In particular, this black enterprise contributed to African Americans' increased understanding of themselves as media subjects—that is, as agents represented through media, rather than objects portrayed in media—and how to exploit that position. These forces are clearly evident in the organized civil rights protest of the postwar decades. The "classic" civil rights movement is a series of media events in which African Americans enacted politically expedient ideals of Americanness informed by media products generated by black entrepreneurs who received training in public relations and propaganda during the New Deal era and World War II.

Beginning in the mid-1950s, the period commonly cited as the point of origin for the modern civil rights movement, black activists employed representational strategies that reflected or, at the very least, were reinforced by conceptions of blackness popularized by black capitalist imagemakers. Much has been made of how civil rights figures—like the *Brown v. Board* child plaintiffs, Mamie Till Bradley, Rosa Parks, Martin Luther King Jr. and Coretta Scott King, the Little Rock Nine, and college students who staged lunch counter sit-ins—performed as paragons of nondisturbing, black middle-class-dom, even as they disturbed the status quo with their protest.[2] Their image tactics are typically assumed to be the product of respectability politics rooted in the uplift traditions of the black elite or the stoicism of Gandhian passive resistance.[3] This overriding interpretation precludes other significant cultural resources that informed African Americans in their civil rights actions. Descriptions of nonviolent direct-action campaigns, for example, often describe black protesters as taking care to wear their "Sunday best." Given the socioeconomic status of the majority of African Americans in the mid-twentieth century, particularly in the southern locales of numerous notable civil rights protests, it stands to reason that their best clothing would also be the clothing they wore to church—assuming they went to church. The "Sunday best" designation, however, privileges formulations of civil rights activism as the work of spiritual folk motivated primarily by a deep religiosity. Certainly many African Americans who participated in the marches, sit-ins, and boycotts associated with the civil rights movement fashioned themselves in keeping with notions of civility and morality. It is equally true, however, that hundreds of thousands of African Americans in the postwar United States read black and white lifestyle magazines and consumed the products of Coca-Cola, Pepsi-Cola, Pet Milk, Beech-Nut, and Colgate—all advertisers who developed marketing directed to black consumers in the mid-1950s. These encounters with the market also affected how they chose to make their citizenship claims.

Whether activists, capitalists, politicians, celebrities, or "everyday" people, African Americans were no less affected by or participants in major currents that propelled postwar capitalism in the United States, including mass production, mass consumption, market segmentation, expanding media and marketing technologies, anticommunism, American exceptionalism, and the solidification of Americanness with a middle-class, consumerist, heteronormative lifestyle. The media images that postwar black capitalists generated popularized definitions of blackness—and Americanness—that penetrated all aspects of black life and informed, influenced, troubled, and enabled African Americans in their quests for citizenship rights and national belonging. Therefore, when we consider how Rosa Parks, the "mother of the civil rights movement," handily dressed the part of a middle-class American woman despite her decidedly working-class existence, we might remember that, as a tailor, she was able to make her own clothing, but it was her observations and encounters as a consumer that enabled her to fashion herself in keeping with current style trends and notions of normality. In other words, we would do well to remember that, after World War II, in addition to the bible on the nightstand, many African Americans had *Ebony* on the coffee table and Coke in the fridge.[4]

Notes

Preface

1. Rosa Parks, *Rosa Parks: My Story*, with Jim Haskins (New York: Scholastic, 1992), 157.
2. "The South: A Great Ride," *Time*, December 31, 1956, 10.
3. Parks uses the term "symbol shot" in Douglas Brinkley, *Rosa Parks* (New York: Penguin Putnam, 2000), 171.
4. While I was finishing this book, a thread erupted on my Facebook feed in which scholars discussed the role and responsibility of black historical subjects. The thread stemmed from Beryl Satter's review of Christina Hanhardt's and Nathan Connolly's studies of the political economy of property. See Beryl Satter, "Property Is Bad: Recent Trends in American Studies," *American Quarterly* 68, no. 2 (June 2016): 471–85; Christina Hanhardt, *Safe Space: Gay Neighborhood History and the Politics of Violence* (Durham, NC: Duke University Press, 2013); and Nathan Connolly, *A World More Concrete: Real Estate and the Remaking of Jim Crow South Florida* (Chicago: University of Chicago Press, 2014). In reference to Connolly's work, Satter objected to what she read as a concentration on African Americans' complicity (as landlords and property owners) in real estate practices that adversely affected African Americans, rather than on the white supremacist apparatus undergirding segregation and the poor living conditions many blacks endured. She accuses both Connolly and Hanhardt of "imply[ing] that minority groups should somehow abstain from participation in the financial and legal structures of the societies in which they live" (472). One contributor to the thread offered a response to the review that sums up my view: "It's an analytic, not a value judgment."
5. Walter Johnson, "On Agency," *Journal of Social History* 37, no. 1 (Fall 2003): 115–18.

Introduction

Epigraph: bell hooks, "In Our Glory: Photography and Black Life," in *Picturing Us: African American Identity in Photography*, ed. Deborah Willis (New York: New Press, 1994), 46.

1. Loudon Wainwright, *The Great American Magazine: An Inside History of "Life"* (New York: Ballantine Books, 1988), 81–82; "Pictorial to Sleep," *Time*, March 8, 1937.

2.   Walter White, *A Man Called White: The Autobiography of Walter White* (1948; repr., Athens: University of Georgia Press, 1995), 201. See also "Remarks by Walter White," Writers Congress, October 1, 1943, Los Angeles, CA, NAACP Papers, Part 18, Series B, Reel 17, University of Michigan Library, Ann Arbor.

3.   "Fifty Million Watermelons Go to Market," *Life*, August 9, 1937, 52.

4.   "Move Anew to Portray Negro Sensibly in Pix," *Variety*, November 27, 1946, 1.

5.   See Sundiata Keita Cha-Jua and Clarence Lang, "The 'Long Civil Rights Movement' as Vampire: Temporal and Spatial Fallacies in Recent Black Freedom Studies," *Journal of African American History* 92, no. 1 (Winter 2007): 274.

6.   While I insist that black image professionals performed "work" that was important in the civil rights movement, it is necessary to clarify that I do not imagine them as "workers." As constructed by labor historians beginning in the 1960s, the concept of "worker" evokes the figure of a radical, oppositional, anticapitalist member of the laboring class. See E. P. Thompson, *The Making of the English Working Class* (New York: Vintage Books, 1966); George Rawick, *From Sundown to Sunup: The Making of the Black Community* (New York: Praeger Books, 1973); Herbert Gutman, *The Black Family in Slavery and Freedom, 1750–1925* (New York: Pantheon Books, 1976); Lawrence Levine, *Black Culture and Black Consciousness: Afro-American Folk Thought from Slavery to Freedom* (Cambridge: Oxford University Press, 1977); and Nancy Cott, *A Heritage of Her Own: Toward a New Social History of American Women* (New York: Touchstone/Simon and Schuster, 1979). The figures central to this study were capitalists, and their concerns were those of the capitalist. They desired profits, the accumulation of which requires activity beyond the labor of the working class, including but not limited to purchasing and selling capital (property, paper, presses, etc.); hiring, managing, and firing employees; and forging business relationships. While not the blue-collar or physical labor we associate with "workers," these activities constitute essential work within the supply chain of capitalism.

7.   Examples include Sven Beckert and Seth Rockman, eds., *Slavery's Capitalism: A New History of American Economic Development* (Philadelphia: University of Pennsylvania Press, 2016); Calvin Schermerhorn, *The Business of Slavery and the Rise of American Capitalism, 1815–1860* (New Haven, CT: Yale University Press, 2015); Edward Baptist, *The Half Has Never Been Told: Slavery and the Making of American Capitalism* (New York: Basic Books, 2014); Sven Beckert, *Empire of Cotton: A Global History* (New York: Alfred A. Knopf, 2014); Walter Johnson, *River of Dark Dreams: Slavery and Empire in the Cotton Kingdom* (Cambridge, MA: Belknap Press of Harvard University Press, 2013); and Bonnie Martin, "Slavery's Invisible Engine: Mortgaging Human Property," *Journal of Southern History* 76, no. 4 (November 2010): 817–66.

8.   Quincy Mills, *Cutting Along the Color Line: Black Barbers and Barber Shops in America* (Philadelphia: University of Pennsylvania Press, 2013). See also Tiffany Gill, *Beauty Shop Politics: African American Women's Activism in the Beauty Industry* (Champaign: University of Illinois Press, 2010); and Doug-

las Bristol Jr., *Knights of the Razor: Black Barbers in Slavery and Freedom* (Baltimore: Johns Hopkins University Press, 2009).

9. Adam Green, *Selling the Race: Culture, Community, and Black Chicago, 1940–1955* (Chicago: University of Chicago Press, 2006); Davarian Baldwin, *Chicago's New Negroes: Modernity, the Great Migration, and Black Urban Life* (Chapel Hill: University of North Carolina Press, 2007).

10. Kendrix has remained somewhat out of reach for historians in part because records pertaining to his professional activities languished for years in a forgotten storage unit, discovered years after his death. Kendrix does figure in Jason Chambers's *Madison Avenue and the Color Line: African Americans in the Advertising Industry* (Philadelphia: University of Pennsylvania Press, 2007), which chronicles African Americans' contributions to the advertising industry. He is a fleeting character within this study, however, despite being a driving force behind the developments that Chambers charts.

11. See K. S. Miller, "U.S. Public Relations History: Knowledge and Limitations," in *Communication Yearbook 23*, ed. Michael E. Roloff (Thousand Oaks, CA: Sage, 2000). Miller explains, "The best research on public relations has adopted a business history frame, focusing on corporate PR" (381).

12. See, for example, Linda Childers Hon, "'To Redeem the Soul of America': Public Relations and the Civil Rights Movement," *Journal of Public Relations Research* 9, no. 3 (1997): 163–212; Kimberly Williams Moore, "Toward an Inclusive Trajectory of Public Relations History: The Contributions of W.E.B. Du Bois to Nonprofit Public Relations Before the *Crisis* and Beyond" (presentation, 85th annual meeting of the Association for Education in Journalism and Mass Communication, Miami, FL, August 2002); Dulcie M. Straughan, "'Lift Every Voice and Sing': The Public Relations Efforts of the NAACP, 1960–1965," *Public Relations Review* 30, no. 1 (March 2004): 49–60; Vanessa Murphree, *The Selling of Civil Rights: The Student Nonviolent Coordinating Committee and the Use of Public Relations* (New York: Routledge, 2006); Vanessa D. Murphree, "'Black Power': Public Relations and Social Change in the 1960s," *American Journalism* 21, no. 3 (2003): 13–32; and Burnis Morris, *Carter G. Woodson: History, the Black Press, and Public Relations* (Jackson: University of Mississippi Press, 2017).

13. Wendy Kozol, "Marginalized Bodies and the Politics of Visibility," *American Quarterly* 57, no. 1 (March 2005): 241–42.

14. Ariella Azoulay's examination of the power of photography to bring people, including stateless people such as Palestinians in Israel, into a citizenry is seminal within this scholarship. Ariella Azoulay, *The Civil Contract of Photography* (Brooklyn: Zone Books, 2008). Other examples include Elena Tajima Creef, *Imaging Japanese America: The Visual Construction of Citizenship, Nation, and the Body* (New York: New York University Press, 2004); Sharon Sliwinski, *Human Rights in Camera* (Chicago: University of Chicago Press, 2011); Thy Phu, *Picturing Model Citizens: Civility in Asian American Visual Culture* (Philadelphia: Temple University Press, 2012); Ariella Azoulay, *Civil Imagination: A Political Ontology of Photography* (Brooklyn: Verso Books, 2012); and Robert Hariman and John Louis Lucaites, *The Public Image: Photography and Civic Spectatorship* (Chicago: University of Chicago Press, 2016).

15. Here I rely on a summary of the varied meanings of citizenship that Linda Bosniak presents in *The Citizen and the Alien: Dilemmas of Contemporary Membership* (Princeton, NJ: Princeton University Press, 2006), 18–20.

16. Shawn Michelle Smith, *Photography on the Color Line: W. E. B. Du Bois, Race, and Visual Culture* (Durham, NC: Duke University Press, 2004).

17. Henry Louis Gates Jr., "The Trope of a New Negro and the Reconstruction of the Image of the Black," *Representations* 24 (Autumn 1988): 131–36.

18. hooks, "In Our Glory," 48.

19. Sara Blair, *Harlem Crossroads: Black Writers and the Photograph in the Twentieth Century* (Princeton, NJ: Princeton University Press, 2007), 5.

20. Benedict Anderson, *Imagined Communities: Reflections on the Origin and Spread of Nationalism* (London: Verso Books, 2016), chap. 3.

21. Anderson, 25.

22. Ardis Cameron, introduction to *Looking for America: The Visual Production of Nation and People*, ed. Ardis Cameron (Hoboken, NJ: Wiley-Blackwell, 2005), 2. See also Jessica Evans, "Feeble Monsters: Making Up Disabled People," in *Visual Culture: The Reader*, ed. Jessica Evans and Stuart Hall (Thousand Oaks, CA: Sage, 1999), 278; Coco Fusco, "Racial Time, Racial Marks, Racial Metaphors," in *Only Skin Deep: Changing Visions of the American Self*, ed. Coca Fusco and Brian Wallis (New York: Harry N. Abrams, 2003) 13; Stuart Hall, "The Work of Representation," in *Representation: Cultural Representations and Signifying Practices*, ed. Stuart Hall (London: Sage, 1997); and Carola Mason Beeney, "Visually Constructing Citizenship: Photography, Race and Immigration Policy in America" (BA thesis, Vassar College, 2011), 10–16.

23. Lauren Rebecca Sklaroff also identifies the New Deal as an incubator for black cultural production, specifically that of artists. Lauren Rebecca Sklaroff, *Black Culture and the New Deal: The Quest for Civil Rights in the Roosevelt Era* (Chapel Hill: University of North Carolina Press, 2009), 5.

24. Sarah Igo, *The Averaged American: Surveys, Citizens, and the Making of a Mass Public* (Cambridge, MA: Harvard University Press, 2007); Anna Creadick, *Perfectly Average: The Pursuit of Normality in Postwar America* (Amherst: University of Massachusetts Press, 2010). Igo and Creadick historicize and explicate the concept of normal within the mid-twentieth-century period.

Chapter 1

Epigraphs: Moss Kendrix, "Looking from the Under-side Up," *Maroon Tiger*, June 1937, 24; Edward Bernays, *Propaganda* (Brooklyn: Ig Publishing, 2005), 64.

1. "Floods Aftermath," *Life*, February 15, 1937, 9.

2. Moss Hyles Kendrix Jr., interview by author, September 9, 2009.

3. Kendrix as described in "Moss Kendrix: 'Mr. Public Relations,'" *Sepia*, March 1953, 41; "Man of the Month Publicist International," *Eyes*, June 1947, 7; and James R. Howard III, "What the Public Thinks, Counts," *Negro History Bulletin*, April 1956, 159.

4. "Moss Kendrix."

5. "Moss Kendrix."

6. "Close Ranks," *Crisis*, July 1918, 111.

7. "For Action on Race Riot Peril," *New York Times*, October 5, 1919, 112.

8. W. E. B. Du Bois, "Returning Soldiers," in *W. E. B. Du Bois: Writings* (New York: Library of America, 1987), 1179–80; originally printed in *Crisis*, May 1919, 13.

9. These include Harvard Sitkoff, *A New Deal for Blacks—The Emergence of Civil Rights as a National Issue: The Depression Decade* (Cambridge: Oxford University Press, 1978); John Kirby, *Black Americans in the Roosevelt Era: Liberalism and Race* (Knoxville: University of Tennessee Press, 1980); Patricia Sullivan, *Days of Hope: Race and Democracy in the New Deal Era* (Chapel Hill: University of North Carolina Press, 1996); Margaret Rung, *Servants of the State: Managing Diversity and Democracy in the Federal Workforce, 1933–1953* (Athens: University of Georgia Press, 2002); and Mary Poole, *The Segregated Origins of Social Security: African Americans and the Welfare State* (Chapel Hill: University of North Carolina Press, 2006). A notable exception is Lauren Rebecca Sklaroff's study of black cultural production in the New Deal. Lauren Rebecca Sklaroff, *Black Culture and the New Deal: The Quest for Civil Rights in the Roosevelt Era* (Chapel Hill: University of North Carolina Press, 2009). This work brings black artists, musicians, entertainers, and intellectuals into view and argues that New Deal fine arts and media programs provided outlets for "cultural self determination" (6).

10. "Stock Prices Slump $14,000,000,000 in Nation-Wide Stampede to Unload," *New York Times*, October 29, 1929, 1.

11. There is some debate as to the actual unemployment rate in 1933; while the Bureau of Labor Statistics cites it as 24.9 percent; other sources determine it to be closer to 20 percent. See Bureau of Labor Statistics, *Historical Statistics of the United States, Colonial Times to 1970*, pt. 1 (Washington, DC: U.S. Government Printing Office, 1975), Series D 85–86, Unemployment: 1890–1970, 135; Robert Coen, "Labor Force and Unemployment in the 1920's and 1930's: A Re-examination Based on Postwar Experience," *Review of Economics and Statistics* 55, no. 1 (February 1973): 46–55; Robert VanGiezen and Albert Schwenk, "Compensation from Before World War I Through the Great Depression," *Compensation and Working Conditions* 6, no. 3 (Fall 2001): 17–23; and David Kennedy, *Freedom from Fear: The American People in Depression and War, 1929–1945* (New York: Oxford University Press, 1999), 162–63.

12. William E. Leuchtenberg, *Franklin D. Roosevelt and the New Deal* (New York: Harper and Row, 1963), 28.

13. Walter Duranty, "Soviet Again Denies Using Forced Labor," *New York Times*, February 22, 1931, 11.

14. Leuchtenberg, *Franklin D. Roosevelt*, 28.

15. Franklin Delano Roosevelt, Nomination Acceptance Address, Democratic Convention, Chicago, Illinois, July 2, 1932; Jean Edward Smith, *FDR* (New York: Random House, 2007), 268–69.

16. Robert S. McElvaine, *The Great Depression: America, 1929–1941* (New York: Times Books, 1993), 187; Bureau of Labor Statistics, *Historical Statistics*, 135.

17. Marian Thompson Wright, "Negro Youth and the Federal Emergency Programs: CCC and NYA," *Journal of Negro Education* 9, no. 3 (July 1940): 405.

18.   Publishing magnate John H. Johnson recalls his humiliation at receiving government aid during the Depression in John H. Johnson, *Succeeding Against the Odds: The Inspiring Autobiography of One of America's Wealthiest Entrepreneurs*, with Lerone Bennett Jr. (New York: Warner Books, 1989), 75.

19.   Langston Hughes, "Ballad of Roosevelt," in *The Collected Poems of Langston Hughes*, ed. Arnold Rampersad (New York: Vintage Books, 1995), 178.

20.   Langston Hughes, "A Dream Deferred," in *The Collected Poems of Langston Hughes*, ed. Arnold Rampersad (New York: Vintage Books, 1995), 426. Regarding black expectations of the New Deal, see "The New Deal Begins," *Pittsburgh Courier*, March 4, 1933, 10.

21.   There is debate as to whether lawmakers excluded agricultural and domestic workers to discriminate against African Americans intentionally. See Larry DeWitt, "The Decision to Exclude Agricultural and Domestic Workers from the 1935 Social Security Act," *Social Security Bulletin* 70, no. 4 (2010): 49–68, https://www.ssa.gov/policy/docs/ssb/v70n4/v70n4p49.html. Regardless of intent, the legislation effectively denied many African Americans relief.

22.   Social Security Act of 1935, Pub. L. No. 74-271, § 210, 49 Stat. 620, 625 (1935).

23.   Poole, *Segregated Origins*, 15–17.

24.   Richard Wormser, *The Rise and Fall of Jim Crow* (New York: St. Martin's, 2003), 138.

25.   Richard Wright, *Black Boy*, Perennial Classics (New York: HarperCollins, 1998), 288.

26.   Poole, *Segregated Origins*, 15–16.

27.   Domestic workers in the North might make ten dollars per week, if the job did not go to one of the many poor white women seeking work. Poole, *Segregated Origins*, 15–16. See also Rebecca Sharpless, *Cooking in Other Women's Kitchens: Domestic Workers in the South, 1865–1960* (Chapel Hill: University of North Carolina Press, 2010), esp. 176–77; and Susan Tucker, *Telling Memories Among Southern Women: Domestic Workers and Their Employers in the Segregated South* (Baton Rouge: Louisiana State University Press, 2002).

28.   Karen Ferguson, *Black Politics in New Deal Atlanta* (Chapel Hill: University of North Carolina Press, 2002), 122.

29.   Police Chief Herbert Jenkins quoted in Georgina Hickey, *Hope and Danger in the New South City: Working-Class Women and Urban Development in Atlanta, 1890–1940* (Athens: University of Georgia Press, 2010), 209.

30.   Ferguson, *Black Politics*, 21–22.

31.   Bettye Jeane Jackson Lee, interview by author, August 3, 1914. Lee is the granddaughter of John Russell Hamilton.

32.   Beaver Slide resident Clara Render as quoted in Hickey, *Hope and Danger*, 209.

33.   Lee interview.

34.   Regarding the number of lynchings by state in the early twentieth century, see "Lynchings, Whites & Negroes, 1882–1968," Tuskegee University Archives, Digital Collections, accessed March 13, 2018, http://archive.tuskegee .edu/archive/bitstream/handle/123456789/511/Lyching%201882%201968 .pdf?sequence=1&isAllowed=y; *Lynchings by States and Counties in the United States, 1900–1931*, cleartype county outline map of the United States (New York: American Map Company, [1931?]), http://www.loc.gov/resource

/g3701e.ct002012/; and Robert A. Gibson, "The Negro Holocaust: Lynching and Race Riots in the United States, 1880–1950," Yale–New Haven Teachers Institute, accessed February 13, 2015, http://www.yale.edu/ynhti/curriculum /units/1979/2/79.02.04.x.html#b.

35.   "Lynching of Women Arouses Georgians," *New York Times*, January 17, 1915, 7; "Mob Law," *New York Times*, January 18, 1915, 8; "The Monticello Lynchings," *New York Times*, January 19, 1915, 8; "Southern Chivalry Rebuked by Lynching," *Indianapolis Freeman*, January 23, 1915; "Judge Park Raps Lynching," *Indianapolis Freeman*, February 27, 1915; John Dittmer, *Black Georgia in the Progressive Era, 1900–1920* (Urbana: University of Illinois Press, 1980), 139.

36.   1910 Census Place: Atlanta Ward 7, Fulton, Georgia, Roll T624_192, p. 2A, Enumeration District 0096; 1940 Census Place: Atlanta, Fulton, Georgia, Roll T627_730, p. 8A, Enumeration District 160-146, Atlanta City Directory 1921, 563, microfilm, Special Collections, Atlanta-Fulton Public Library Central Library, Atlanta, GA.

37.   Andrew Wiese, *Places of Their Own: African American Suburbanization in the Twentieth Century* (Chicago: University of Chicago Press, 2004), 176; Ferguson, *Black Politics*, 29; *Northwest Atlanta Redevelopment Plan and Perry/ Bolton Tax Allocation District*, report, November 2002, 13, https://www .investatlanta.com/assets/perry_bolton_tad_redevelopment_plan _V1DBxgL.pdf.

38.   Parcel Record 14 011600090714, Fulton County Property Records, Fulton County Board of Assessors, accessed February 18, 2015, http://qpublic9 .qpublic.net/ga_display_dw.php?county=ga_fulton&KEY =14+011600090714; Washington Park H.D. Supplementary Listing Record, National Register of Historic Places Continuation Sheet, NRIS Reference Number 00000071, February 28, 2000, https://npgallery.nps.gov/GetAsset /89dcde4b-759a-47c1-b99c-c7427a8c0b49.

39.   Lee interview.

40.   In her study of black professional women in the early twentieth century, Stephanie J. Shaw introduces the concept of "socially responsible individualism" as the combination of the seemingly contradictory impulses of individualism and social responsibility. Stephanie J. Shaw, *What a Woman Ought to Be and Do: Black Professional Women Workers During the Jim Crow Era* (Chicago: University of Chicago Press, 1996), 2–6.

41.   "John R. Hamilton Honored as St. Paul's 'Father of Year,'" *Atlanta Daily World*, June 25, 1948, 3.

42.   Lee interview.

43.   "Seven Get Honors from AU Lab High," *Atlanta Daily World*, June 2, 1934, 1.

44.   Standalone photograph, *Maroon Tiger*, Commencement Issue, 1936, 17.

45.   Ferguson, *Black Politics*, 96.

46.   Gilbert Cam, "United States Government Activity in Low-Cost Housing, 1932–38," *Journal of Political Economy* 47, no. 3 (June 1939): 366.

47.   Kit Sutherland, *Techwood Homes (Public Housing): HABS No. GA-2257* (Atlanta: KitWrites, 1995), 2, http://lcweb2.loc.gov/master/pnp/habshaer/ga /ga0600/ga0662/data/ga0662data.pdf.

48. Harvey Newman, "The Atlanta Housing Authority's Olympic Legacy Program: Public Housing Projects to Mixed Income Communities," *Research Atlanta, Inc.*, April 2002, 6; Alonzo Moron, "Public Housing from a Community Point of View," *Social Forces* 19, no. 1 (October 1940): 73.

49. Frank Ruechel, "New Deal Public Housing, Urban Poverty, and Jim Crow: Techwood and University Homes in Atlanta," *Georgia Historical Quarterly* 81, no. 4 (Winter 1997): 927.

50. Thomas Jefferson Flanagan, "Roosevelt Day," *Atlanta Daily World*, December 1, 1935. See also Ferguson, *Black Politics*, 192.

51. Moron, "Public Housing," 72–78. See also W. E. B. Du Bois et al., "A Study of the Atlanta University Federal Housing Area," report, May 1934, John Hope Papers, Robert W. Woodruff Library, Atlanta University Center, Atlanta, GA. Du Bois's report provides a detailed accounting and inventory of the housing and occupants of Beaver Slide.

52. "The Atlanta Housing Project," *Crisis*, June 1934, 175–76; Ferguson, *Black Politics*, 214.

53. Regarding the physical changes brought about by the slum clearance project, see Ruechel, "New Deal Public Housing," 924, 934; and Ferguson, *Black Politics*, 214–15.

54. Frank Ruechel offers a sustained detailing of this phenomenon. Ruechel, "New Deal Public Housing," 931–36.

55. Palmer Johnson and Oswald Harvey, *The National Youth Administration*, Staff Study Number 13, prepared for the Advisory Committee on Education (Washington, DC: Government Printing Office, 1938; repr., New York: Arno, 1974), 7. Citations refer to reprint edition.

56. Walter G. Daniel and Carroll L. Miller, "The Participation of the Negro in the National Youth Administration Program," *Journal of Negro Education* 7, no. 3 (July 1938): 362, table 1, "The Relative Participation of Negro Youth in Selected Phases of the National Youth Administration Program."

57. Robinson quoted in Florence Fleming Corley, "The National Youth Administration in Georgia: A New Deal for Young Blacks and Women," *Georgia Historical Quarterly* 77, no. 4 (Winter 1993): 740.

58. Corley, 736–38.

59. Senior profile, *Maroon Tiger*, Commencement Issue, 1938. During his tenure at Morehouse, Kendrix held the following positions: assistant advertising manager, associate editor, and editor in chief of the *Maroon Tiger*; cofounder of and national director of publicity for the Delta Phi Delta Journalistic Society; editor of *Delphid*; director of Bigger and Better Newspaper Week; member of the executive committee and chairman of the Morehouse Open Forum; vice president of the Chi Delta Sigma Debating Society; assistant editor in chief of the *"M" Book*; cabinet member of the YMCA; chairman of and volunteer for the Intercollegiate Student Peace Service; member of the Atlanta Intercollegiate Council; member of the Maroon and White Day Committee; member of the golf team; member of the *"M" Club*; and member of Alpha Phi Alpha. See senior profile, *Maroon Tiger*, June 1939, 8.

60. "The Press Agents' War," *New York Times*, September 9, 1914, 8; Eric Goldman, "Public Relations and the Progressive Surge: 1898–1917," *Public Relations Review* 4, no. 3 (Autumn 1978): 60.
61. Walter Lippmann, *Public Opinion*, reissue ed. (New York: Free Press, 1997), 158.
62. Larry Tye, *The Father of Spin: Edward L. Bernays and the Birth of Public Relations* (New York: Henry Holt, 2002), 95.
63. Bernays quoted in Tye, 92.
64. Keynes paraphrased in Stuart Ewen, *PR! A Social History of Spin* (New York: Basic Books, 1996), 238.
65. Keynes quoted in Ewen, 240.
66. Ewen, 262.
67. Stephen Duncombe, "FDR's Democratic Propaganda," *Nation*, April 7, 2008, http://www.thenation.com/article/fdrs-democratic-propaganda. Regarding FDR's fireside chats, see also Betty Winfield, *FDR and the News Media* (Urbana: University of Illinois Press, 1990), 104; Ewen, *PR!*, chap. 13; Douglas Craig, *Fireside Politics: Radio and Political Culture in the United States, 1920–1940* (Baltimore: Johns Hopkins University Press, 2005), 154–57; and Lawrence Levine and Cornelia Levine, *The Fireside Conversations: America Responds to FDR During the Great Depression* (Berkeley: University of California Press, 2010), intro.
68. "Text of President Roosevelt's Atlanta Address on National Recovery," *New York Times*, November 30, 1935, 4.
69. Walter Friedman, *Birth of a Salesman: The Transformation of Selling in America* (Cambridge, MA: Harvard University Press, 2004), 247. I directly paraphrase Friedman here.
70. Kevin Kruse, *One Nation Under God: How Corporate America Invented Christian America* (New York: Basic Books, 2015), 3–4. Kruse explains that the Depression-era efforts of NAM struck observers as self-promotion and industrialists continued to draw criticism. Business lobbies like NAM gained traction during the 1940s when, he argues, their public relations efforts forged connections between business, free enterprise, and Christianity. See also John St. Burton, *Press Professionalization and Propaganda: The Rise of Journalistic Double-Mindedness, 1917–1941* (Amherst: Cambria, 2010), chap. 5; and Robert Griffith, "The Selling of America: The Advertising Council and American Politics, 1942–1960," *Business History Review* 57, no. 3 (Autumn 1983): 388–412.
71. "The Crown Prince of Public Relations," *Sepia*, May 1964.
72. See the magazine staff as listed in the *Maroon Tiger* in March 1937, October 1927, and June 1937.
73. Moss Kendrix, "War Marches On—America What Now?," *Maroon Tiger*, October 1937, 4.
74. Kendrix, "Looking," 24.
75. Moss Kendrix, "The Educational Career of the American Negro," *Maroon Tiger*, March 1937, 4.
76. "Wanted: A Thinking Negro Youth," *Maroon Tiger*, January–February 1938, 4.
77. See "Delta Phi Delta," *Maroon Tiger*, January–February 1938, 12.

78. "Delta Phi Delta Intercollegiate Journalistic Society," prepared profile, ca. 1937, 1–2, Moss H. Kendrix Organization Papers, Alexandria Black History Museum, Alexandria, VA (hereafter cited as MHKOP).

79. "Frat Sets Feb. 27–March 5 as 'Newspaper Week,'" *Chicago Defender,* February 25, 1939, 2. In his recent study of black public relations, Burnis Morris erroneously credits the Negro Newspaper Publishers Association (NNPA) with the founding of National Negro Newspapers Week. Burnis Morris, *Carter G. Woodson: History, the Black Press, and Public Relations* (Jackson: University of Mississippi Press, 2017), 29. (Morris does recognize Kendrix as the director of Negro Press Week but identifies him as Moss Hyles Hendrix [rather than Kendrix] throughout the text.) The NNPA, which *Chicago Defender* publisher John H. Sengstacke founded in 1940 as the black counterpart to the American Newspaper Publishers Association, was a direct outgrowth of the exposure and networks Kendrix generated during his tenure as director of National Negro Newspaper Week. In 1942, members of the NNPA voted to take over sponsorship of National Negro Newspaper Week (which had outgrown the Delta Phi Delta Intercollegiate Journalistic Society) but retain Kendrix as its director. See "Publishers to Absorb Associated Negro Press," *Chicago Defender,* June 13, 1942, 1. The NNPA—now the National Newspaper Publishers Association—continues to sponsor the annual observance, which is now called Black Press Week. See National Newspaper Publishers Association website, https://nnpa.org, accessed January 19, 2018.

80. Robert Weems Jr., *Business in Black and White: American Presidents and Black Entrepreneurs in the Twentieth Century* (New York: New York University Press, 2009), 51.

81. See Kendrix, "Educational Career," 3; Kendrix, "Looking"; Kendrix, "War Marches On," 4; "Welcome Freshmen," *Maroon Tiger,* October 1937, 4.

82. P. Bernard Young, "The Negro Press—Past, Present, Future," *Spelman Messenger,* May 1938, n.p.

83. Regarding Bernays's conception of the "public relations counselor," see Tye, *Father of Spin,* 96.

84. Tye, 96.

85. Kendrix Jr. interview.

86. According to an internal memo citing Dorothy (Johnson) Kendrix's petition for divorce, she and Moss Kendrix married on January 26, 1940. See "Mr. and Mrs.," September 19, 1960, prepared news item in Johnson Publishing Company Clippings Files Collection, Robert W. Woodruff Library, Atlanta University Center. Other profiles, however, mark the year of their marriage as 1939. See Howard, "What the Public Thinks," 160; and G. James Fleming and Christian E. Burckel, eds., *Who's Who in Colored America,* 7th ed. (Yonkers-on-Hudson, NY: Christian E. Burckel, 1950).

87. "Conference of Negro State Administrative Assistants and Members of State Advisory Committees," Georgia NYA Negro Division report, Washington, DC, February 11–13, 1937, 8, in *New Deal Agencies and Black America,* ed. John B. Kirby (Frederick, MD: University Publications of America, 1984), microfilm, reel 1.

88. "Conference of Negro State," 8.

89. Kirby, *Black Americans*, 91.
90. "Final Report: The National Youth Administration, Division of Negro Affairs," circa 1943, in Kirby, *New Deal Agencies*, microfilm, reel 3.
91. Michael Holmes, "The New Deal and Georgia's Black Youth," *Journal of Southern History* 38, no. 3 (August 1972): 452–53.
92. See "Monthly Narrative Report Covering the Activities of the Division of Negro Affairs National Youth Administration of Georgia," September 1939, 4–5, and "Monthly Narrative Report Covering the Activities of the Division of Negro Affairs National Youth Administration of Georgia," October 1939, 7–9, in Kirby, *New Deal Agencies*, microfilm, reel 6; and National Youth Administration of Georgia, Division of Negro Affairs, "News Releases," partial report, n.d., in Kirby, *New Deal Agencies*, microfilm, reel 1. These reports detail how Kendrix's division promoted the NYA and publicized its programs.
93. "Monthly Narrative Report," September 1939, 5.
94. "News Releases." It is unclear whether this column actually ran in the newspaper.
95. "Moss Kendrix in Citizenship Talk," *Atlanta Daily World*, November 29, 1939, 2; "To Pine Bluff," *Atlanta Daily World*, July 21, 1940; "Talks to Ministers," *Atlanta Daily World*, October 22, 1940, 6.
96. Moss Hyles Kendrix, "Forums in Georgia," *Crisis*, November 1940, 356.
97. "State Meeting on the Program of the National Youth Administration and the Negro in Georgia," program, October 21, 1939, Atlanta, GA, in Kirby, *New Deal Agencies*, microfilm, reel 6.
98. Eleanor Roosevelt quoted in Corley, "National Youth Administration," 730. NYA director Williams voiced similar concerns: see Aubrey Williams, "The Work of the National Youth Administration," *Living* 1, no. 4 (November 1939): 65.
99. Marian Thompson Wright, "Negro Youth," 404.
100. Rebecca Stiles Taylor, "Activities of Women's National Organizations," *Chicago Defender*, November 4, 1939, 18.
101. "Moss Kendrix in Citizenship Talk," 2.
102. "Moss Kendrix in Citizenship Talk," 2.
103. B. Joyce Ross, "Mary McLeod Bethune and the National Youth Administration: A Case Study of Power Relationships in the Black Cabinet of Franklin D. Roosevelt," *Journal of Negro History* 60, no. 1 (January 1975): 2.
104. Albert Anderson, "Sadder but Wiser 'Cabinet,'" *Atlanta Daily World*, December 4, 1939, 1.
105. Regarding the NAACP antilynching campaign, see Megan Ming Francis, *Civil Rights and the Making of the Modern State* (New York: Cambridge University Press, 2014), chap. 4.
106. "New Deal Love Has Limits," *Chicago Defender*, July 11, 1936, 16.
107. Sklaroff, *Black Culture*, 2; John Hope Franklin and August Meier, eds., *Black Leaders of the Twentieth Century* (Champaign: University of Illinois Press, 1982), 191.
108. Jennie Dallas, "Grantville, Ga.," *Atlanta Daily World*, January 22, 1941, 3; "Monthly Narrative Report," October 1939, 7–9; Kendrix, "Forums in Georgia," 356–57.

109. See Tye, *Father of Spin*, 55.
110. Kendrix, "Forums in Georgia," 356.
111. Kendrix, 357.
112. Kendrix, 356.
113. Franklin D. Roosevelt, "Inaugural Address," March 4, 1933, American Presidency Project, http://www.presidency.ucsb.edu/ws/?pid=14473.
114. Franklin D. Roosevelt: "Inaugural Address," January 20, 1937, American Presidency Project, http://www.presidency.ucsb.edu/ws/?pid=15349.
115. Moss Hyles Kendrix, "Fail to Provide Defense Training for Ga. Workers," *Chicago Defender*, May 2, 1942, 13.
116. "Final Report: The National Youth Administration."
117. "Radio Address Delivered by President Roosevelt from Washington," December 29, 1940, in *Peace and War: United States Foreign Policy, 1931–1941*, Department of State Publication 1983 (Washington, DC: U.S. Government Printing Office, 1943), 598–607.
118. Moss Hyles Kendrix, "The National Youth Administration Goes to War," circa post-1941, MHKOC. I have dated this according to events mentioned within the essay, including Executive Order 8802, which Roosevelt signed on June 25, 1941, and recognizing that the NYA was phased out in 1943.
119. "Observance of Press Week in Air Program," *Chicago Defender*, March 7, 1942, 9.
120. A. Philip Randolph quoted in Langston Hughes, *Fight for Freedom and Other Writings*, ed. Christopher De Santis (Columbia: University of Missouri Press, 2001), 94.
121. A. Philip Randolph, "Call to Negro America to March on Washington for Jobs and Equal Participation in National Defense," *Black Worker* 14 (May 1941), n.p.
122. Exec. Order No. 8802, 3 C.F.R. 957 (June 25, 1941).
123. James G. Thompson, "Should I Sacrifice to Live 'Half-American'?," *Pittsburgh Courier*, January 31, 1942, 3.
124. "The Courier's Double 'V' for a Double Victory Campaign Gets Country-Wide Support," *Pittsburgh Courier*, February 14, 1942, 1. In my research, I came across one other examination of Kendrix's work in relation to the Double Victory campaign; see Laura Hymson, "The Company That Taught the World to Sing: Coca-Cola, Globalization, and the Cultural Politics of Branding in the Twentieth Century" (PhD diss., University of Michigan, 2011), 168–70.

Chapter 2

Epigraphs: Gordon Parks quoted in Andy Grundberg, "Gordon Parks, a Master of the Camera, Dies at 93," *New York Times*, March 8, 2006, http://www.nytimes.com/2006/03/08/arts/design/gordon-parks-a-master-of-the-camera-dies-at-93.html; Richard Wright, *12 Million Black Voices* (New York: Thunder Mouth, 1988), xix; Edward Bernays, *Propaganda* (Brooklyn: Ig, 2005), 37.
1. Cornelius Troup, *Distinguished Negro Georgians* (Dallas: Royal, 1962), 98.

2. G. M. deLambert, director of Northern Pacific Railway Personnel Depart-
    ment, to Gordon Parks, August 17, 1964.,Gordon Parks Papers, Wichita State
    University Special Collections and University Archives, Wichita State Uni-
    versity, Wichita, KS. This letter verifies that Parks was employed as a "Din-
    ing Car Waiter, out of St. Paul, Minnesota, June 20, 1936 and was employed
    in this capacity until October 3, 1938."

3. DeLambert to Parks.

4. "Reporter with a Camera," *Ebony*, July 1946, 26.

5. Gordon Parks, *A Hungry Heart: A Memoir* (New York: Washington Square,
    2005), 43.

6. Henry Luce, "The American Century," *Life*, February 17, 1941, 63.

7. OWI report as quoted in Lauren Rebecca Sklaroff, "Constructing G.I. Joe
    Louis: Cultural Solutions to the 'Negro Problem' During World War II," *Jour-
    nal of American History* 89, no. 3 (December 2002): 959.

8. African Americans' role as objects of propaganda has been the topic of care-
    ful study. Mary Dudziak has examined how "the federal government engaged
    in a sustained effort to tell a particular story about race and American de-
    mocracy: a story of progress, a story of triumph of good over evil, a story of
    U.S. moral superiority." Because Dudziak centers her narrative on U.S. poli-
    cymakers, blacks figure primarily (and understandably) as persons featured
    in or commenting on representations of U.S. race relations. See Mary Dud-
    ziak, *Cold War Civil Rights: Race and the Image of American Democracy*
    (Princeton, NJ: Princeton University Press, 1994), 13. Penny Von Eschen's
    study of jazz musicians in a Cold War context offers examples of African
    Americans operating as black state propagandists by functioning as ambas-
    sadors, representations, and promoters of American democracy. See Penny
    Von Eschen, *Satchmo Blows Up the World: Jazz Ambassadors Play the Cold
    War* (Cambridge, MA: Harvard University Press, 2005).

9. Gordon Parks, *Voices in the Mirror: An Autobiography* (New York: Double-
    day, 1990), 65; Parks, *Hungry Heart*, 43.

10. John Tagg, "Melancholy Realism: Walker Evans Resistance to Meaning," *Nar-
    rative* 11, no. 1 (January 2003): 3.

11. Walter Benjamin, "A Short History of Photography," *Screen* 13, no. 1 (Spring
    1972): 25. "A Short History of Photography" was originally published in *Die
    Literarische Welt*, September 18, September 25, and October 2, 1931.

12. John Dos Passos quoted in Jacqueline Goldsby, "The High and Low Tech of
    It: The Meaning of Lynching and the Death of Emmett Till," *Yale Journal of
    Criticism* 9, no. 2 (Fall 1996): 255.

13. Regarding the number of photographs, see "Farm Security Administration/
    Office of War Information Black-and-White Negatives," Library of Congress,
    accessed August 15, 2016, http://www.loc.gov/pictures/collection/fsa/; and
    "Farm Security Administration/Office of War Information Color Photo-
    graphs," Library of Congress, accessed August 15, 2016, http://www.loc.gov
    /pictures/collection/fsac/about.html.

14. See Anne Whiston Spirn, *Daring to Look: Dorothea Lange's Photographs and
    Reports from the Field* (Chicago: University of Chicago Press, 2009).

15. See Wendy Kozol, *Life's America: Family and Nation in Postwar Photojournalism* (Philadelphia: Temple University Press, 1994), 8–12. See also Sara Blair, *Harlem Crossroads: Black Writers and the Photograph in the Twentieth Century* (Princeton, NJ: Princeton University Press, 2007), 6–7.

16. *Life* prospectus as quoted in Loudon Wainwright, *Life: The Great American Magazine* (New York: Ballantine Books, 1986), 36. Luce was right: Americans did clamor "to see, and to be shown," in the midst of their depression. Within four months, *Life*'s paid circulation hit the one million mark. By spring 1938, circulation was two million, with a pass-along readership of approximately eight readers to one copy. Wainwright, *Great American Magazine*, 90, 110. The success of *Life* inspired a host of imitators, including *Look, Photo-History, Foto, Pic, Picture, Picture Crimes, See,* and *Click*. See "Click," *Time*, January 10, 1938, http://content.time.com/time/magazine/article/0,9171,758844,00.html. The very titles of these magazines signaled the increased cultural significance and ubiquity of documentary images, and the magazines themselves ensured it.

17. Parks, *Hungry Heart*, 43.

18. Gordon Parks, interview by Richard Doud, December 30, 1964, Archives of American Art, Smithsonian Institute, http://www.aaa.si.edu/collections/interviews/oral-history-interview-gordon-parks-11480.

19. Excerpt of letter from Roy Stryker to Arthur Rothstein, August 26, 1939, Roy Stryker Papers, Special Collections and Archives, University of Louisville, Louisville, KY.

20. Roy Stryker to Marion Post Wolcott, shooting script, FSA, 1941, Roy Striker Papers.

21. Shooting scripts, Roy Striker Papers. ca. 1937–42.

22. Parks, *Voices in the Mirror*, 65.

23. Arthur Rothstein, *Words and Pictures* (New York: American Photographic, 1979), 8.

24. Maren Stange, "Gordon Parks: A World of Possibility," in *Bare Witness: Photographs by Gordon Parks* (Stanford, CA: Skira, 2006), 12.

25. Adam Green and Davarian Baldwin effectively challenge the idea that African Americans primarily struggled in or were corrupted by city life, a concept codified with the 1945 publication of *Black Metropolis*. See Adam Green, *Selling the Race: Culture, Community, and Black Chicago, 1940–1955* (Chicago: University of Chicago Press, 2006); Davarian Baldwin, *Chicago's New Negroes: Modernity, the Great Migration, and Black Urban Life* (Chapel Hill: University of North Carolina Press, 2007); and St. Clair Drake and Horace Cayton, *Black Metropolis: A Study of Negro Life in a Northern City* (New York: Harcourt, Brace, 1945).

26. See Erskine Caldwell and Margaret Bourke-White, *You Have Seen Their Faces* (New York: Modern Age Books, 1937); and Parks, *Voices in the Mirror*, 65.

27. Caldwell and Bourke-White, front matter. See also William Stott, *Documentary Expression and Thirties America* (Chicago: University of Chicago Press, 1986), 220–21; and Joel Woller, "First-Person Plural: The Voice of the Masses in Farm Security Administration Documentary," *Journal of Narrative Theory* 29, no. 3 (Fall 1999): 343–44.

28.   Allen Maxwell, review of *You Have Seen Their Faces*, by Erskine Caldwell and Margaret Bourke-White, *Southwest Review* 23, no. 2 (January 1938): 238.

29.   Caldwell and Bourke-White, *You Have Seen*, front matter, 1.

30.   Frank Hankins, review of *You Have Seen Their Faces*, by Erskine Caldwell and Margaret Bourke-White, *American Sociological Review* 5, no. 5 (October 1940): 839.

31.   See Dan Shiffman, "Richard Wright's *12 Million Black Voices* and World War II-Era Civic Nationalism," *African American Review* 41, no. 3 (Fall 2007): 447.

32.   Parks, *Voices in the Mirror*, 75.

33.   Parks, 74.

34.   Gordon Parks, *A Choice of Weapons* (New York: Berkley Medallion Books, 1967), 171.

35.   Regarding the Rosenwald fellowship, see Stange, "Gordon Parks," 13; and Jonathan Ross Nolting, "The Julius Rosenwald Fellowship Program for African American Visual Artists, 1929–1948" (PhD diss., University of Cincinnati, 2012).

36.   Parks, *Choice of Weapons*, 176–77; Stange, "Gordon Parks," 12.

37.   Parks, *Choice of Weapons*, 175, 177; Parks, *Hungry Heart*, 60–61.

38.   Parks, *Choice of Weapons*, 178–79; Parks, *Voices in the Mirror*, 79.

39.   Stange, "Gordon Parks," 13; Franklin D. Roosevelt, "Excerpts from the Press Conference," December 28, 1943, American Presidency Project, http://www.presidency.ucsb.edu/ws/?pid=16358.

40.   FSA photographer Marion Post Wolcott referred to the landscape photographs that she was often commissioned to produce as "FSA cheesecake." Wolcott as quoted in Jean Haskell Speer, *The Appalachian Photographs of Earl Palmer* (Lexington: University of Kentucky Press, 1990), xliv.

41.   Barbara Orbach and Nicholas Natanson, "The Mirror Image: Black Washington in World War II-Era Federal Photography," *Washington History* 4, no. 1 (Spring–Summer 1992): 7.

42.   Bernays, *Propaganda*, 37.

43.   George Creel claimed that Committee on Public Information agents avoided the word *propaganda* because of its negative connotation. George Creel, *How We Advertised America* (New York: Harper and Brothers, 1920), 4–5.

44.   Nicholas Natanson, "From Sophie's Alley to the White House," in "Federal Records and African American History," special issue, *Prologue* 29, no. 2 (Summer 1997), http://www.archives.gov/publications/prologue/1997/summer/pioneering-photographers.html.

45.   Stryker quoted in Stange, "Gordon Parks," 13.

46.   Charles Curtis Munz, "The New Negro," *Nation*, December 13, 1941, 620. A contemporary reviewer, Munz classified FSA photographs as excellent.

47.   Jay Prosser, *Light in the Dark Room: Photography and Loss* (Minneapolis: University of Minnesota, 2004), 93.

48.   Prosser, 93–94.

49.   "Gordon Parks' Photographs," *U.S. Camera*, December 1943, 16–19, reprinted in "Photos by Parks," *Negro Digest*, January 1944, 41.

50.   *U.S. Camera* quoted in "Reporter with a Camera," 25.

51.   Lawrence Cramer, executive secretary of the Fair Employment Practices Committee, as quoted in Orbach and Natanson, "Mirror Image," 5–6. Orbach and Natanson point out that it is unclear how much exposure FSA/OWI photography featuring black subjects actually received (21–25). What evidence exists suggests these photographs did not find their way into the domestic white or black press or the international press often. That this is true does not negate, however, war officials' initial contention concerning the importance of black photography. Moreover, the form that federal black photographic propaganda took, whether or not it was distributed, provides evidence of the guidelines that shaped the images under construction.

52.   Walter White, "Report of the Secretary for the Board Meeting of February 1942: Posters, Murals, etc., Re: Defense and Stamps," in *In Search of Democracy: The NAACP Writings of James Weldon Johnson, Walter White, and Roy Wilkins (1920–1977)*, ed. Sondra Wilson (New York: Oxford University Press, 1999), 183.

53.   Gordon Parks, *Half Past Autumn: A Retrospective* (New York: Little Brown, 1998).

54.   Caldwell and Bourke-White, *You Have Seen Their Faces*, photo insert.

55.   Parks was not the only black photographer to work for a New Deal agency. Robert McNeill photographed black life in Virginia for a text produced by the Federal Writers' Project entitled *The Negro in Chicago*. See Natanson, "From Sophie's Alley."

56.   The concept for *12 Million Black Voices* was originally Rosskam's; he approached Viking Press about the prospect of a photo-text concerning black America before meeting Wright. See Nicholas Natanson, *The Black Image in the New Deal: The Politics of FSA Photography* (Knoxville: University of Tennessee Press, 1992), 244. For the project, Rosskam drew on a 1941 government photographic survey of living conditions for African Americans in Chicago, which was commissioned in part because Wright's *Native Son* brought federal attention to this issue. See James Goodwin, "The Depression Era in Black and White: Four American Photo-Texts," *Criticism* 40, no. 2 (Spring 1998): 282.

57.   Natanson, *Black Image*, 249; Goodwin, "Depression Era," 281.

58.   Edwin Rosskam quoted in Natanson, *Black Image*, 244.

59.   Joseph H. Jenkins Jr., "Saucy Doubts and Fears," *Phylon* (1940–56) 1, no. 2 (2nd qtr., 1940): 195.

60.   Dorothy Canfield Fisher as quoted in Peter Monro Jack, "A Tragic Novel of Negro Life in America," *New York Times Book Review*, March 3, 1940, 20. Fisher wrote the original preface to *Native Son*. See Richard Wright, *Native Son* (New York: Harper and Brothers, 1940).

61.   Sales as reported in Richard Wright, *Black Boy*, Perennial Classics (New York: HarperCollins, 1998), 394.

62.   Charles Poore, "Books of the Times," *New York Times*, March 1, 1940, 25.

63.   Blair, *Harlem Crossroads*, 74.

64.   W. E. B. Du Bois ascribed African Americans with the gift of "second-sight," the ability to see themselves as others (whites) see them in addition to, but often likely in substitution of, how they see themselves. This second sight brings with it an ability to comprehend the white world in a way whites will

never be capable of understanding the world as blacks experience it. W. E. B. Du Bois, *The Souls of Black Folk* (Cambridge: Oxford University Press, 2007), 8.

65. Blair, *Harlem Crossroads*, 74. In chapter 2 of her text, Blair offers a sustained examination of Wright's relationship to, interest in, and use of photography, which was very useful to me.

66. Ralph Ingersoll, *PM* founding editor, quoted in Blair, *Harlem Crossroads*, 65.

67. Wright, *12 Million Black Voices*, xix.

68. Wright, xix.

69. Wright, 10.

70. Natanson, *Black Image*, 247. See also Stott, *Documentary Expression*, 235. For a review of criticism leveled at *12 Million Black Voices*, see Woller, "First-Person Plural," 346–47.

71. *PM*'s David Lindsay quoted in Natanson, *Black Image*, 255.

72. Shiffman, "Richard Wright's," 444.

73. Shiffman, 444.

74. Wright, *12 Million Black Voices*, 146.

75. Blair, *Harlem Crossroads*, 75.

76. Edwin Seaver, "Readers and Writers," transcript of radio broadcast, December 23, 1941, in *Conversations with Richard Wright*, ed. Keneth Kinnamon and Michel Fabre (Jackson: University of Mississippi Press, 1993), 43.

77. Richard Wright, "How 'Bigger' Was Born," in *Native Son*, Perennial Classics (New York: HarperCollins, 1998), 431–62; Shiffman, "Richard Wright's," 448.

78. Wright, *12 Million Black Voices*, 106–8.

79. Gunnar Myrdal, *An American Dilemma: The Negro Problem and Modern Democracy* (New York: Harper and Brothers, 1944), 75.

80. Ralph Ellison to Richard Wright, quoted in Shiffman, "Richard Wright's," 448.

81. Charles Munz, "The New Negro," *Nation*, December 13, 1941, 620.

82. Stott, *Documentary Expression*, 235.

83. Wright quoted in Parks, *Voices in the Mirror*, 147.

84. Parks, 85.

85. For Parks's comments regarding *12 Million Black Voices*, see Parks, *Choice of Weapons*, 190, 199; Parks, *Voices in the Mirror*, 110, 180, 182; and Parks, *Hungry Heart*, 66, 155.

86. Parks, *Hungry Heart*, 66; Wright, *12 Million Black Voices*, 147.

87. Natanson, *Black Image*, 247; Parks, *Voices in the Mirror*, 180.

88. Parks, *Hungry Heart*, 71, 109.

89. Parks, *Voices in the Mirror*, 145.

90. Parks, 85.

91. Parks originally captioned this photograph "Washington, D.C. Government charwoman."

92. Parks, *Hungry Heart*, 65.

93. National archivist Nicholas Natanson identifies *American Gothic* as a classic example of Parks's "self-styled attempts to use the camera as a weapon" during his FSA/OWI tenure. Similarly, cultural historian Maurice Berger identifies Parks's photographs as "forceful agents of change." See Natanson, "From Sophie's Alley"; and Maurice Berger, "Introduction: Online Exhibition,"

website for *For All the World to See*, exhibit, 2010, University of Maryland, Baltimore County, https://fatwts.umbc.edu/online-exhibition.

94.   Parks quoted in Grundberg, "Master of the Camera."

95.   Parks, *Voices in the Mirror*, 85; Parks interview, 5. Parks claimed that several politicians branded *American Gothic* "an indictment of America" and wanted it destroyed. See Parks, *Hungry Heart*, 66.

96.   Parks, *Hungry Heart*, 66.

97.   William Jones, *Killed*, accessed September 30, 2016, https://www.williame jones.com/portfolio/killed. See also William Jones, *Killed: Rejected Images of the Farm Security Administration* (New York: PPP Editions, 2010).

98.   In reference to *American Gothic*, Parks has said, "So it was published. I sneaked it out and published it in an old paper that used to be in Brooklyn. It was published in Brooklyn . . . a Marshall Field paper." Parks interview, 5. The paper he refers to must be *PM*, which was published by Ralph Ingersoll and financed by Marshall Field III. Several historians have accepted Parks's claim. For example, Colleen McDannell relies on the Doud interview and concludes that Parks got *American Gothic* to "the progressive New York news-paper *PM*." See Colleen McDannell, *Picturing Faith: Photography and the Great Depression* (New Haven, CT: Yale University Press, 2004), 257. How-ever, there is no evidence that the image actually appeared in the newspaper. I must thank my student-researcher Samantha Marrus for the time she spent going through six years of *PM* on microfilm (Parks produced the image in 1942 and *PM* folded in 1948) looking for the Parks photograph. Several years later, the image appeared in *Ebony* as the accompanying picture to an edito-rial about the unwanted good intentions of white "do-gooders." See "Do Do-Gooders Do Good?," *Ebony*, March 1948, 46–47.

99.   Natanson, *Black Image*, 245.

100.   Wright, *12 Million Black Voices*, 143.

101.   Blair, *Harlem Crossroads*, 75.

102.   OWI administrators' report as quoted in Sklaroff, "Constructing G.I. Joe Louis," 963.

103.   Sklaroff, 963.

104.   Notably, Wright had associated openly with Communists for years. He had expressed opposition to the war in an essay entitled "Not My People's War," which appeared in the Marxist publication *New Masses*. In the essay, he de-clared the black plight in the United States both an "embarrassment to the efforts of the war leaders" and the reason many African Americans did not support the war. See Richard Wright, "Not My People's War," in *Communism in America: A History in Documents*, ed. Albert Fried (New York: Columbia University Press, 1997), 317. Not until he published *Black Voices*, however, did he become suspect. In 1942 the War Department received a letter that suggested the picture of black life and black attitudes that Wright presented in his photo-text was subversive. See [redacted] to Henry Stimson, Octo-ber 13, 1942, in Federal Bureau of Investigation, *Richard Nathaniel Wright, Part 1 of 1*, BUFILE No. 100-157464, accessed October 20, 2018, https://vault .fbi.gov/Richard%20Nathaniel%20Wright/Richard%20Nathaniel%20

Wright%20Part%201%20of%202 (hereafter cited as Richard Wright, BUFILE No. 100-157464).

105. [Redacted] to Henry Stimson.

106. Wright, *12 Million Black Voices*, 143.

107. J. Edgar Hoover to SAC [special agent in charge], New York, December 9, 1942, in Richard Wright, BUFILE No. 100-157464; Blair, *Harlem Crossroads*, 93.

108. Parks, *Choice of Weapons*, 193. When he moved from the FSA to the OWI, Parks became a federally employed propagandist. As an intern for the FSA, Parks received a stipend of approximately $200 per month from the Rosenwald Foundation. Once with the OWI, he was put on the government payroll. See Parks, *Choice of Weapons*, 178.

109. This tendency is most evident in historians' and cultural studies theorists' discussions of black uses of visuality. In *Harlem Crossroads*, Sara Blair identifies Richard Wright as useful to her project of exploring how African Americans "wrench[ed] images from instrumental contexts for their own uses." In her discussions of black self-representation, literary theorist and activist bell hooks frames black uses of visuality and photography, especially, as almost inherently oppositional, arguing that the black images African Americans produced challenged the "white supremacist gaze" and resisted blacks' domestic colonization. Historian Shawn Michelle Smith details how, at the 1900 Paris Exposition, W. E. B. Du Bois marshaled photographs of Georgia's middle-class blacks as a "counterarchive" of "competing visual evidence" that "challenges a long legacy of racist taxonomy" and the images and theories elevated through scientific racism. Smith is careful to acknowledge how Du Bois's reliance on classed ideas of black masculine restraint and chaste black femininity to challenge racist notions elevates a particular type of blackness and reproduces a restrictive gender hierarchy. African Americanist Leigh Raiford places photography as a "liberatory tool of black self-representation" in the hands of black activists like Ida B. Wells and activist organizations such as the National Association for the Advancement of Colored People, the Student Nonviolent Coordinating Committee, and the Black Panther Party. See Blair, *Harlem Crossroads*, xix; bell hooks, "In Our Glory: Photography and Black Life," in *Picturing Us: African American Identity in Photography*, ed. Deborah Willis (New York: New Press, 1994), 49, 50; Shawn Michelle Smith, *Photography on the Color Line: W. E. B. Du Bois, Race, and Visual Culture* (Durham, NC: Duke University Press, 2004), 2; and Leigh Raiford, *Imprisoned in a Luminous Glare: Photography and the African American Freedom Struggle* (Chapel Hill: University of North Carolina Press, 2011), 15.

110. Orbach and Natanson, "Mirror Image," 15.

111. Parks interview, 6. Parks referred to himself during this period as "green as a pea" (5).

112. Parks interview, 6.

113. Parks, *Choice of Weapons*, 188.

114. Alden Stevens quoted in Orbach and Natanson, "Mirror Image," 5.

115. See Gordon Parks's "Anacostia, D.C. Frederick Douglass Housing project" photographs, Prints and Photographs Online Catalog, Library of Congress,

accessed October 23, 2018, http://www.loc.gov/pictures/search/?q=Anacostia
%2C%20D.C.%20Frederick%20Douglass%20Housing%20project.

116.   Other FSA photographers noted for producing photographs regarding black
subject matter include Marjory Collins, John Vachon, and Marion Post Wolcott. See Beverly W. Brannan, "Marjory Collins (1912–1985): Biographical
Essay," Prints and Photographs Division, Library of Congress, last revised
April 2009, http://www.loc.gov/rr/print/coll/womphotoj/collinsessay.html.
Nicholas Natanson details that even before Parks joined the photographic
unit of the FSA/OWI, its black file was "thriving": it formed 10 percent of the
FSA's photographs and was "unrivaled" among federal government collec-
tions. Natanson, *Black Image*, 68.

117.   Locales FSA/OWI photographers frequented as described in James Guimond,
American Photography and the American Dream (Chapel Hill: University of
North Carolina, 1991), 139.

118.   Parks, *Choice of Weapons*, 189.

119.   Prosser, *Light in the Dark Room*, 94; Natanson, *Black Image*, 183, 185.

120.   Founded by Mary McLeod Bethune in 1904, Bethune-Cookman College
(now Bethune-Cookman University) had been Daytona Educational and Industrial Training School until 1941, when it became a four-year college.

121.   John Vachon quoted in Guimond, *American Photography*, 139.

122.   T. J. Maloney, ed., *The U.S.A. at War* (New York: Duell, Sloan and Pearce,
1943).

123.   Parks actually took photographs of two African American female welders
who worked at the New Britain Landers, Frary and Clark plant. They are not,
however, as conventionally attractive as the NYA female welding student; I
wonder if she was not substituted to represent the black female welders who
actually worked at the same plant as the white male welder featured in
The U.S.A. at War because she was more photogenic. See Gordon Parks, *New
Britain, Connecticut. Women Welders at the Landers, Frary, and Clark Plant*,
June 1943, Prints and Photographs Online Catalog, Library of Congress,
http://www.loc.gov/pictures/item/2017859313/.

124.   Walter White as quoted in Thomas Cripps, "Walter's Thing: The NAACP Hollywood Bureau of 1946—A Cautionary Tale," *Journal of Popular Film and
Television* 33, no. 2 (July 2005): 119.

125.   White, "Report of the Secretary," 183.

126.   "Reporter with a Camera," 28.

127.   Parks, *Voices in the Mirror*, 146.

128.   Prosser, *Light in the Dark Room*, 94.

129.   Cripps, "Walter's Thing," 119.

130.   SAC [special agent in charge], New York City, to J. Edgar Hoover, director,
FBI, office memorandum, February 26, 1945, and FBI report, May 28, 1943,
5, in Richard Wright, BUFILE No. 100-157464. According to these sources,
Wright's rejection for service appears to have occurred in late 1942 or 1943.

131.   Steven Plattner, *Roy Stryker: U.S.A., 1943–1950: The Standard Oil (New Jersey) Photography Project* (Austin: University of Texas Press, 1983), 11.

132.   Abigail Foerstner, "The Man Who Inspired a Photographic Portrait of America," *Chicago Tribune*, January 25, 1985, http://articles.chicagotribune.com

/1985-01-25/entertainment/8501050719_1_standard-oil-roy-stryker-photo
graphy-project.

133.   Plattner, *Roy Stryker*, 11.

134.   "Reporter with a Camera," 25, 29.

135.   Parks quoted in Barbara Whitaker, "Landmarks: Gordon Parks Lived Here.
Don't Touch, Town Asks," *New York Times*, March 4, 2007, http://query
.nytimes.com/gst/fullpage.html?res=9F0DE5DE1631F937A35750C0A9619
C8B63; "Reporter with a Camera," 29.

136.   "Reporter with a Camera," 27.

137.   Parks freelanced for *Ebony* on occasion, but the magazine's editors also acquired his photographs through Black Star photo service, a New York photo
agency founded in 1935, which established itself by collaborating with Henry
Luce to introduce and produce *Life*.

138.   "The 15 Outstanding Events in Negro History," *Ebony*, February 1950, 46.

139.   Mary Dudziak provides a detailed reading of this booklet in *Cold War Civil
Rights*. Interestingly, however, she implies that the first photograph in the
booklet is a picture of an integrated classroom in New York, which actually
appears on page 16 of the pamphlet. Dudziak, *Cold War Civil Rights*, 49.

140.   Dudziak, 49–54.

141.   "Reporter with a Camera," 27.

142.   "Harlem Gang Leader," *Life*, November 1, 1948, 97; reader as quoted in Stange,
"Gordon Parks," 20.

143.   "Reporter with a Camera," 27.

144.   Stange, "Gordon Parks," 20.

145.   John Loengard as quoted in Stange, "Gordon Parks," 18.

146.   "Harlem Gang Leader," 97.

147.   Stryker as quoted in Stuart Ewen, *PR! A Social History of Spin* (New York:
Basic Books, 1996), 278.

148.   Parks, *Hungry Heart*, 72.

Chapter 3

An early version of this chapter has appeared in print elsewhere: Brenna W.
Greer, "Selling Liberia: Moss H. Kendrix, the Liberian Centennial Commis-
sion, and the Post-World War II Trade in Black Progress," *Enterprise and
Society* 14, no. 2 (June 2013): 303–26.

Epigraphs: Rayford Logan, "Liberia in the Family of Nations," *Phylon* 7, no. 1
(1st qtr., 1946): 11; Moss H. Kendrix to Fred Cooper, general sales manager, Kaiser Frazer Corporation, October 1, 1946, Moss H. Kendrix Organization Papers, Alexandria Black History Museum, Alexandria, VA (hereafter
cited as MHKOP).

1.   Jason Taylor and Richard Vedder, "Stimulus by Spending Cuts: Lessons from
1946," *Cato Policy Report* 32, no. 3 (May/June 2010): 1, 6–8, https://object.cato
.org/sites/cato.org/files/serials/files/policy-report/2012/2/cpr32n3-1.pdf; Jack
Stokes Ballard, *The Shock of Peace: Military and Economic Demobilization
After World War II* (Washington, DC: University Press of America, 1983).

2.   *Business Week*, September 1, 1945, 9.

3. Fred Frailey, "The Way We Were," *Kiplinger's Personal Finance* 51, no. 1 (January 1997): 130.

4. Taylor and Vedder, "Stimulus by Spending Cuts," 6.

5. "Man of the Month, Publicist International," *Eyes*, June 1947.

6. Hilyard Robinson, ed., *Centennial and Victory Exposition, Monrovia, Liberia, 1947–1949*, brochure (Liberian Centennial Commission, 1946), n.p., Hilyard Robinson Papers, Moorland-Spingarn Research Center, Howard University, Washington, DC (hereafter cited as HRP).

7. Hilyard Robinson, "An African Republic Approaches Its Centennial," *Crisis*, July 1946, 204.

8. A. Christopher to Moss Kendrix, April 19, 1945, MHKOP.

9. "For the *Atlanta Daily World*, Thursday, April 25," press release, April 25, 1945, MHKOP.

10. Moss Hyles Kendrix Jr., interview by author, September 9, 2009.

11. This figure of $10 million appears in press releases prepared by Kendrix and in a radio script Kendrix authored for an April 27, 1945, radio broadcast on Atlanta's CBS outlet, WGST. See "For the *Atlanta Daily World*." This claim may be evidence of Kendrix's use of sensationalism, because other reports credit the tour with selling approximately $2–$5 million worth of bonds. See "War Irony," *Pittsburgh Courier*, December 23, 1944, 18. I found no corroborating claim to support Kendrix's assertion that the Fort Benning Reception Center Chorus tour generated $10 million in war bond sales.

12. "The Courier's Double 'V' for Double Victory Campaign Gets Country-Wide Support," *Pittsburgh Courier*, February 14, 1942, 1.

13. "Moss H. Kendrix: Native Son," National Business League flyer, 1963, MHKOP.

14. The government of Liberia presented to the U.S. government six public works projects in hopes of securing U.S. financing for one or more of them. They included "a) to move its Capital to a new location in the interior at a cost of several millions of dollars; b) to install a sewage and water supply; c) to construct a hydroelectric plant for power; d) to construct a railroad for the development of the interior; e) to hold a Centennial celebration in 1947 which will require substantial new construction and financing; f) to construct a stadium at a cost of $300,000." "Memorandum by the Acting Secretary of State to the Vice President of Liberia (Simpson), July 4, 1945," *Foreign Relations* 8 (1945): 594.

15. Lawrence Marinelli, "Liberia's Open-Door Policy," *Journal of Modern African Studies* 2, no. 1 (March 1964): 91.

16. I. K. Sundiata, *Black Scandal: America and the Liberian Labor Crisis, 1929–1936* (Philadelphia: Institute for the Study of Human Issues, 1980), 35.

17. "Uncle Shad's Jubilee," *Time*, January 17, 1969.

18. "Plan for the Celebration of the Centennial of the Republic of Liberia," n.d., 1, HRP.

19. M. B. Salami to G. W. Gibson, chairman, executive committee, Centennial Celebration, May 11, 1944, HRP.

20. W. S. Murdoch, "Memorandum on Preliminary Budgeting-Centennial Celebration," circa May 1944, HRP.

21. "Plan for the Celebration," n.d., 1.

22. Robinson, *Centennial and Victory Exposition.*

23. Murdoch, "Memorandum."

24. "Plan for the Celebration of the Centennial of the Republic of Liberia," September 12, 1944, HRP.

25. Abayomi Karnga to member of the Executive Committee for the Celebration of the Centenary of the Republic of Liberia, May 15, 1944, HRP.

26. "Plans for Liberia Centennial in 1947 Announced by Tubman," *Atlanta Daily World*, May 5, 1946, 1.

27. "Plan for the Celebration," n.d., 2.

28. Kevin Gaines, *American Africans in Ghana: Black Expatriates and the Civil Rights Era* (Chapel Hill: University of North Carolina Press, 2006), 77–78.

29. G. W. Gibson to Hilyard R. Robinson, May 3, 1945, HRP.

30. Johnson's travels to Liberia as a member of the League of Nations commission became the basis for the book *Bitter Canaan*, a narrative of Liberian history, politics, and culture. Written and revised throughout the 1930s and 1940s, *Bitter Canaan* was published in 1987, after Johnson's death. Charles Johnson, *Bitter Canaan: The Story of the Negro Republic* (New Brunswick, NJ: Transaction, 1987).

31. "The Challenge of Liberia," *Baltimore Afro-American*, December 31, 1946.

32. "Memorandum by Acting Secretary of State [Dean Acheson] to President Roosevelt, April 4, 1945," *Foreign Relations* 8 (1945): 587.

33. "Transmittal of the Charter of the United Nations to the Senate: Message of the President, July 2, 1945," *Department of State Bulletin* 13, no. 315 (July 8, 1945), 46.

34. J. H. Mower, "The Republic of Liberia," *Journal of Negro History* 32, no. 3 (July 1947): 300.

35. "Acting Secretary of State [Dean Acheson] to President Roosevelt," 587.

36. Earl Parker Hansen [Earl Parker Hanson], "The United States Invades Liberia," *Negro Digest*, June 1947, 77 (condensed from *Harper's*, February 1947).

37. Mrs. Arthur Nelons to Walter White, February 1, 1945, NAACP Papers, Part 14: Africa-Liberia 1941–1949, Hatcher Library, University of Michigan, Ann Arbor (hereafter cited as NAACP-14).

38. Brenda Gayle Plummer and Penny Von Eschen have thoroughly demonstrated that a healthy strain of internationalism ran through black politics during the 1930s and through World War II. See Brenda Gayle Plummer, *Rising Wind: Black Americans and U.S. Foreign Affairs, 1935–1960* (Chapel Hill: University of North Carolina Press, 1996); and Penny Von Eschen, *Race Against Empire: Black Americans and Anticolonialism, 1937–1957* (Ithaca, NY: Cornell University Press, 1997).

39. Walter White to Committee on Administration, memorandum, April 26, 1947, NAACP-14.

40. Moss Kendrix to Mary McLeod Bethune, May 6, 1947, Mary McLeod Bethune Papers, Part 3, Hatcher Library, University of Michigan, Ann Arbor.

41. Walter White to Committee on Administration. See also Roy Wilkins to Leslie Perry, October 26, 1945, NAACP-14.

42. Lauren Rebecca Sklaroff, *Black Culture and the New Deal: The Quest for Civil Rights in the Roosevelt Era* (Chapel Hill: University of North Carolina Press, 2009), 10.

43. Regarding the name of organization, see "The Negro Market for Kaiser-Frazer Corporation Products," prospectus prepared by Robinson-Kendrix-Simmons, ca. 1946, Washington, DC, MHKOP. I have yet to identify the Simmons of Robinson-Kendrix-Simmons.

44. Robert Weems Jr., *Business in Black and White: American Presidents and Black Entrepreneurs in the Twentieth Century* (New York: New York University Press, 2009), 39.

45. Weems, 40.

46. Weems, 41–42.

47. Weems, 43.

48. Weems, 43–44.

49. Weems, 45–47.

50. Lancaster report *Post-war Planning and the Negro in Business* as quoted in Weems, 47.

51. Weems, 48.

52. In MHKOP, see Moss H. Kendrix to William Hobbs, July 16, 1945; Moss H. Kendrix to George Apple Jr., October 4, 1946; Roy S. Jones to Moss Kendrix, October 14, 1945; Moss H. Kendrix to O. B. Motter, September 11, 1946; and Moss Kendrix to Howard Ailes, November 12, 1946.

53. See George Apple Jr. to Moss H. Kendrix, May 2, 1946, MHKOP. This letter, a response to a pitch Kendrix made as representative of RKS to Precision-Built Homes Corporation, bears the same recipient address as the Liberian Centennial Commission office.

54. In MHKOP, see Moss H. Kendrix to William Hobbs, March 11, 1946; Moss H. Kendrix to Roy S. Jones, March 19, 1946; and Moss H. Kendrix to Felix Coste, March 20, 1946.

55. Hansen [Hanson], "United States Invades Liberia," 78. See also Earl Parker Hanson, "An Economic Survey of the Western Province of Liberia," *Geographical Review* 37, no. 1 (January 1947): 53–69.

56. James Flink, *The Automobile Age* (Cambridge, MA: MIT Press, 1990), 275.

57. Fred Vinson as quoted in Robert Hathaway, "The Economics of Partnership," in *World War II: Crucible of the Contemporary World*, ed. Loyd Lee (New York: Taylor and Francis, 1991), 314.

58. Flink, *Automobile Age*, 277.

59. Moss H. Kendrix to Fred Cooper, general sales manager, Kaiser Frazer Corporation, October 1, 1946, MHKOP.

60. J. H. Mower, "The Republic of Liberia," *Journal of Negro History* 32, no. 3 (July 1947): 300.

61. Sundiata, *Black Scandal*, 83.

62. Johnson, *Bitter Canaan*, 5.

63. Hansen [Hanson], "United States Invades Liberia," 78.

64. "The First 100 Years," *Time*, August 4, 1947.

65. Hilyard Robinson, "Drawings of Proposed Government Center and Centennial, Monrovia," ca. 1945, HRP.

66. Hanson, "Economic Survey," 54.

67. Mower, "Republic of Liberia," 265.

68. Plummer, *Rising Wind*, 3.

69. John Fousek, *To Lead the Free World: American Nationalism and the Cultural Roots of the Cold War* (Chapel Hill: University of North Carolina Press, 2000), 7.

70. President Harry S. Truman, Address Before a Joint Session of Congress, March 12, 1947.

71. Fousek, *To Lead the Free World*, 7.

72. "Liberia's Centennial," *Pittsburg Courier*, December 28, 1946, 6. See also "The Challenge of Liberia" and "The Liberian Centennial," *Black Dispatch*, December 28, 1946, editorial page.

73. Robinson, "African Republic," 204.

74. Robinson, *Centennial and Victory Exposition*.

75. Robert Thompson to Walter White, June 25, 1943, NAACP-14.

76. "Liberia—A Successful Experiment," *Chicago Defender*, January 4, 1947, 14.

77. Mary Dudziak explains how U.S. state officials produced propaganda following World War II that emphasized Africans Americans' progress within (and, as the propaganda would have it, because of) American democracy. See Mary Dudziak, *Cold War Civil Rights: Race and the Image of American Democracy* (Princeton, NJ: Princeton University Press, 1994), intro., chap. 1.

78. Here, I rely heavily on Dudziak's analysis of postwar propaganda. She details at length the propagandist efforts made by the U.S. government, and especially the State Department, to counteract other nations' accusations about U.S. antiblack racism. Dudziak, intro., chaps. 2–3.

79. Robinson, "African Republic," 205.

80. "Hail Liberia," *New York Amsterdam News*, December 28, 1946, 8; "Liberia's Centennial," *Pittsburgh Courier*, December 28, 1946, 6.

81. Logan, "Liberia in the Family of Nations," 9, 11.

82. Brent Hayes Edwards, *The Practice of Diaspora: Literature, Translation, and the Rise of Black Internationalism* (Cambridge, MA: Harvard University Press, 2003), 2.

83. Plummer, *Rising Wind*, 84.

84. James L. Hicks, "Logan Calls Liberia 'Spare Tire of Firestone Rubber Co.,'" *Pittsburgh Courier*, August 3, 1946, 19.

85. Plummer, *Rising Wind*, 159.

86. Dipesh Chakrabarty makes this argument in *Provincializing Europe: Postcolonial Thought and Historical Difference* (Princeton, NJ: Princeton University Press, 2000), 6–11.

87. Chakrabarty, 8.

88. Dudziak, *Cold War Civil Rights*, chap. 2.

89. Dudziak, 13. Dudziak describes the story of race and American democracy in the mid-twentieth century as "a story of progress, a story of the triumph of good over evil, a story of U.S. moral superiority. The lesson of this story was always that American democracy was a form of government that made the achievement of social justice possible, and that democratic change, however slow and gradual, was superior to dictatorial imposition."

90.   "The Folks Back Home," *Chicago Defender*, April 5, 1947, 13.

91.   "Gov. Tuck in Tribute to J. J. Roberts Emphasizes Progress of Negro Race," *Washington Post*, March 15, 1947, 3. See also "Virginia Will Honor J. J. Roberts Friday," *New York Times*, March 9, 1947, 27; and "Roberts Fete Planned," *Washington Post*, March 9, 1947, M3.

92.   Chakrabarty, *Provincializing Europe*, 8.

93.   "The Day in Washington," *New York Times*, July 26, 1947, 2; "Nation Notes Liberia Centenary in Broadcasts, Ceremony July 26," *Atlanta Daily World*, July 25, 1947, 1; "On the Radio Today," *New York Times*, July 26, 1947, 24.

94.   "Nation Notes Liberia"; "Liberia Given Harbor on 100th Anniversary," *Atlanta Daily World*, July 29, 1947, 1; "Truman Sees Closer Link with Liberia," *Pittsburgh Courier*, August 2, 1947, 1; "Liberia Has Anniversary," *New York Times*, July 27, 1947, 31.

95.   "Folks Back Home"; Charley Cherokee, "National Grapevine," *Chicago Defender*, August 9, 1947, 13.

96.   "51 Nations Invited to Liberia's Gala Exposition," *New York Amsterdam News*, April 6, 1946, 2; "Folks Back Home"; "Liberia Won't Curtail Plans for Exposition, Robinson Says," *Atlanta Daily World*, April 4, 1947, 1.

97.   Photo standalone 2, no title, *Chicago Defender*, June 28, 1947, 2; "The Duke," *Time*, May 19, 1947, http://content.time.com/time/magazine/article/0,9171,933659,00.html; Charley Cherokee, "National Grapevine," *Chicago Defender*, December 13, 1947, 13.

98.   "Liberia Won't Curtail Plans"; "Liberia Fair Date Uncertainty Hinders Request," *Atlanta Daily World*, July 4, 1947, 5.

99.   "State Department Backs Down on Liberian Exposition Funds," *Chicago Defender*, June 28, 1947, 1.

100.   "Exposition Off," *Chicago Defender*, December 13, 1947, 1.

101.   D. Elwood Dunn, *Liberia and the United States During the Cold War: Limits of Reciprocity* (New York: Palgrave Macmillan, 2009), 39–41.

102.   Moss H. Kendrix v. Hilyard R. Robinson, Municipal Court Case No. A 24-693 (District of Columbia, January 1948); "Kendrix Files Suit for Leave Pay from Liberia Commission," *Atlanta Daily World*, March 10, 1949, 4; "Hilyard Robinson Sued by Kendrix," *Baltimore Afro-American*, March 12, 1949, C3A.

Chapter 4

Epigraphs: Letter to the editor, *Negro Digest*, June 1948; John H. Johnson, *Succeeding Against the Odds: The Inspiring Autobiography of One of America's Wealthiest Entrepreneurs*, with Lerone Bennett Jr. (New York: Warner Books, 1989), 156.

1.   Johnson, *Succeeding Against the Odds*, 57.

2.   Johnson, 110. Johnson reports that he had a high draft number ("3990 something" out of 4,000 registrants).

3.   Ben Burns, *Nitty Gritty: A White Editor in Black Journalism* (Jackson: University of Mississippi Press, 1997), 27.

4.   Burns.

5. Douglas Martin, "John H. Johnson, 87, Founder of *Ebony*, Dies," *New York Times*, August 9, 2005, https://www.nytimes.com/2005/08/09/business/media/john-h-johnson-87-founder-of-ebony-dies.html.

6. Several historians have approached the use of sexualized imagery by black mediamakers following World War II. Their studies are useful to my purposes here; they, too, focus on John H. Johnson's publications because they formed almost the entire mainstream black magazine trade in the postwar United States. Examples include Joanne Meyerowitz, "Women, Cheesecake, and Borderline Material: Responses to Girlie Pictures in the Mid-Twentieth-Century U.S.," *Journal of Women's History* 8, no. 3 (Fall 1996): 9–35; Joanne Meyerowitz, "Beyond the Feminine Mystique: A Reassessment of Postwar Mass Culture, 1946–1958," *Journal of American History* 79, no. 4 (March 1993): 1455–82; Laila Haidarali, "Polishing Brown Diamonds: African American Women, Popular Magazines, and the Advent of Modeling in Early Postwar America," *Journal of Women's History* 17, no. 1 (2005): 10–37; Maria Elena Buszek, *Pin-Up Grrrls: Feminism, Sexuality, Popular Culture* (Durham, NC: Duke University Press, 2006); and Elspeth Brown, "Black Models and the Invention of the U.S. 'Negro Market,' 1945–1960," in *Inside Marketing: Practices, Ideologies, Devices*, ed. Detlev Zwick and Julien Cayla (Cambridge: Oxford University Press, 2011). In these works, examinations of sexualized representations generally have been brief or secondary to another objective. For example, Joanne Meyerowitz discusses black readers' response to cheesecake material in *Ebony* on her way to demonstrating that "commodified sexual representation was a 'women's issue' well before the contemporary feminist movement" (9). Within her larger history of pinups in twentieth-century U.S. culture, art historian Maria Elena Buszek points to the black pinups that appeared in *Ebony* in the immediate postwar years as evidence of the magazine's "enlightened" approach to sex (250). Laila Haidarali also discusses black women's sexualized representation in magazines such as *Ebony* and *Our World* as part of her demonstration of how these magazines reinforced "postwar valuations of heterosexual marital fulfillment" (23). Haidarali's conclusion contrasts with Meyerowitz's claim that, with its varied representations of black women, *Ebony* put forth an ideal of racial advancement that had at its center women who "excelled both in the workplace and at home" (1459). Elspeth Brown offers the most sustained treatment of black women's representation in *Ebony* while illuminating the relationship between *Ebony*'s representation practices, the development of the "Negro Market," and the growth of the black modeling industry.

7. E. Franklin Frazier, *Black Bourgeoisie: The Rise of a New Middle Class* (New York: Free Press, 1957), 190. Histories of *Ebony* tend to use Frazier's seminal critique of *Ebony* as a jumping-off point. For examples, see Jason Chambers, "Presenting the Black Middle Class: John H. Johnson and *Ebony* Magazine, 1945–1974," in *Historicizing Lifestyle: Mediating Taste, Consumption and Identity from the 1900s to 1970s*, ed. David Bell and Joanne Hollows (London: Ashgate, 2006), 55; and Adam Green, *Selling the Race: Culture, Community, and Black Chicago, 1940–1955* (Chicago: University of Chicago Press,

2006), 129. See also Brown, "Black Models," 205. In their examinations of *Ebony*, Chambers and Green combine consideration of its history as a business, commercial, and cultural product, as does Brown.

8. Dave Berkman explicates how the conflation of "white" and "middle class" affects perceptions of African Americans' behavior in "Advertising in *Ebony* and *Life*: Negro Aspirations vs. Reality," *Journalism Quarterly* 40 (Winter 1963): 62. Chambers draws on Berkman's distinction in "Presenting the Black Middle Class," 55. I particularly appreciate Green's articulation of *Ebony*'s historical significance when he asserts that it is difficult to "comprehend modern black community and identity without addressing this singular enterprise." Green, *Selling the Race*, 131.

9. Du Sable High School was built in 1934 to relieve the overpopulation of Wendell Phillips High School.

10. Langston Hughes, "Cowards from the Colleges," *Crisis*, August 1934, 226–28; "Race Students Answer Attack Made by Poet," *Chicago Defender*, May 30, 1936, 6.

11. See the following articles written by John H. Johnson: "344 Delegates in Baltimore for NAACP Meet," *Chicago Defender*, July 11, 1936, 8; "Along the Youth Front," *Chicago Defender*, May 1, 1937, 16; "What the People Say: Defends Student Club," *Chicago Defender*, October 30, 1937, 16; "Dickerson Wins First Skirmish for Race at Traction Ordinance Hearing," *Chicago Defender*, January 25, 1941, 7; "New Transit Plan Would Assure Jobs," *Chicago Defender*, March 8, 1941, 8.

12. Johnson, *Succeeding Against the Odds*, 113.

13. The origin story of *Negro Digest* has been recounted many times, often by Johnson, who proudly recalls borrowing against his mother's furniture for the $500 he needed to produce the magazine's first issue. See Johnson, *Succeeding Against the Odds*, 2.

14. Opening editorial of the first issue of *Negro Digest* reprinted in Johnson, *Succeeding Against the Odds*, 122.

15. Johnson, 128, 130.

16. Johnson, 132–36.

17. Regarding rising wages, see Marcus Alexis, "Pathways to the Negro Market," *Journal of Negro Education* 28, no. 2 (Spring 1959): 114, table 1, "Median Wage and Salary Income of Non-white Persons with Salary Income 1939 and 1947–1950." The figure of $7 billion in blacks' disposable income is derived from accounting in a 1947 *Advertising Age* article quoted in Robert Weems Jr., *Desegregating the Dollar: African American Consumerism in the Twentieth Century* (New York: New York University Press, 1998), 37. See "Food, Clothing Get Most of Negroes' $10 Billion," *Advertising Age* 18 (March 24, 1947): 50.

18. Weems, *Desegregating the Dollar*, 32; Kathy Newman, "The Forgotten Fifteen Million: Black Radio, the 'Negro Market' and the Civil Rights Movement," *Radical History Review* 76 (2000): 118. Weems reports that, by 1942, there were approximately one million new black urban residents across the United States. Referencing data from the 1950 U.S. Census, Newman reports

that, between 1940 and 1950, the number of blacks living in cities rose by 46 percent, the median income of African Americans increased by a staggering 192 percent, and black employment (outside the armed forces) was over 90 percent. See also Alexis, "Pathways," 115.

19.   Johnson, *Succeeding Against the Odds*, 153.

20.   Johnson, 155.

21.   Johnson, 156.

22.   S. I. Hayakawa, "Second Thoughts: Why Art Matters," *Chicago Defender*, April 21, 1945, 13.

23.   *Ebony* prospectus as quoted in Johnson, *Succeeding Against the Odds*, 159.

24.   "The Brighter Side," *Time*, October 1, 1945, http://www.time.com/time/magazine/article/0,9171,776180,00.html.

25.   Johnson, *Succeeding Against the Odds*, 159.

26.   Hayakawa, "Second Thoughts," 13.

27.   See, for example, Cherokee Charley's "National Grapevine" column in the *Chicago Defender*: April 7, 1945, 11; April 28, 1945, 11; May 18, 1946, 13; October 19, 1946, 13.

28.   Johnson, *Succeeding Against the Odds*, 140.

29.   Burns, *Nitty Gritty*, 28.

30.   "Purpose Without Passion," *Time*, September 22, 1952, http://www.time.com/time/magazine/article/0,9171,822525,00.html.

31.   Burns, *Nitty Gritty*, 85. In their respective autobiographies, Burns and Johnson offer different explanations for the origins of *Ebony*, with each taking credit for significant aspects of its production. In addition to the creative and journalistic differences between them (to say nothing of issues of ego), Johnson's dismissal of Burns in 1954 fueled their dispute over proprietorship of the style and content of *Ebony*. The amount of detail that Burns supplies in his accounts and his considerable publishing and editing experience—compared to that of Johnson—suggest that he likely had a larger role in the creative design and content of both *Negro Digest* and *Ebony*, while Johnson clearly handled the "business" of production, distribution, and advertising. See Burns, *Nitty Gritty*, chaps. 2, 6; and Johnson, *Succeeding Against the Odds*, chaps. 14–16, 19.

32.   Johnson, *Succeeding Against the Odds*, 161. Articles about the launch of *Ebony* in *Time* and *Newsweek* both comment on how the magazine mimicked, with varied success, *Life* magazine. See "Brighter Side"; and "*Ebony* with Pictures," *Newsweek*, September 24, 1945, 86.

33.   Johnson, *Succeeding Against the Odds*, 161.

34.   Paul K. Edwards, *The Southern Urban Negro as a Consumer* (New York: Prentice-Hall, 1932), 194–96; Alexis, "Pathways," 115.

35.   Johnson, *Succeeding Against the Odds*, 161. See also Burns, *Nitty Gritty*, 119–20.

36.   Johnson, *Succeeding Against the Odds*, 161. See also Burns, *Nitty Gritty*, 119.

37.   Meyerowitz, "Women, Cheesecake," 12. Meyerowitz offers a helpful history of the circulation and acceptance of cheesecake and "borderline material" images in U.S. culture in the early to mid-twentieth century (11–13).

38. Henry Luce's editorial staff as quoted in John Tagg, "Melancholy Realism: Walker Evans's Resistance to Meaning," *Narrative* 11, no. 1 (January 2003): 6.

39. In his autobiography, Burns notes that the first cover broke the rules Johnson later set for cover images as an attempt to ensure covers that drove sales, which included no group pictures, no unknowns, and no children. Burns, *Nitty Gritty*, 86.

40. *Ebony* identifies its first pinup "girl" as Sheila Guys, rather than Sheila Guyse. See "A Star Fizzles," *Ebony*, November 1945, 38.The first issue of *Ebony* contains several such errors (indicative of a shoestring editorial staff). *Newsweek* pointed to this "lax editing" in its review of the magazine. See "*Ebony* with Pictures," 86.

41. "Star Fizzles," 38.

42. "Brighter Side"; Burns, *Nitty Gritty*, 87.

43. Robert Westbrook makes this argument in "'I Want a Girl, Just like the Girl That Married Harry James': American Women and the Problem of Political Obligation in World War II," *American Quarterly* 42, no. 4 (December 1990): 587–614.

44. Westbrook, 596; Buszek, *Pin-Up Grrrls*, 186–87.

45. Buszek, *Pin-Up Grrrls*, 186.

46. Buszek, 187.

47. For examples, see *Crisis* covers from the following issues: January 1942, April 1943, February 1944, March 1944, June 1944, and April 1945, which bear photographs of women identified as, respectively, "Miss Jacksonville," "Recreation Center Volunteer," "Youth Council Leader," "Sarah Lawrence Student," "A New York Secretary," and "Some of the Navy's New Waves."

48. "Contents," *Crisis*, June 1942, 182; "Dorothy Dandridge in 'Sweetheart' Tilt," *Chicago Defender*, February 7, 1942, 16. See also "Sweetheart of 7th Regiment Contest Closes April 16," *Chicago Defender*, March 21, 1942, 17; and "Beauty Crowned at Gigantic Military Ball," *Pittsburgh Courier*, May 2, 1942, 12.

49. Only one other cover of the *Crisis* from the period compares to this representation of Dandridge. In July 1944, Patricia Williams, a Miss Sepia America contestant, appeared in a full-body photograph standing barefoot in a bathing suit on a ladder with her arms swung wide. A tagline below the picture reads, "Tan Tidbit—Summer Style." In language and style, this was a departure from the journal's typical cover girl captions, which identified the model's occupation or title. For more regarding the role of the black pinup during war, see Megan Williams, "*The Crisis* Cover Girl: Lena Horne, the NAACP, and Representations of African American Femininity, 1941–1945," *American Periodicals: A Journal of History, Criticism, and Bibliography* 16, no. 2 (2006): 200–218.

50. For a detailed account of the pinup in U.S. postwar culture, see Buszek, *Pin-Up Grrrls*, chap. 6.

51. Buszek, 237.

52. Johnson, *Succeeding Against the Odds*, 153.

53. Johnson, 153, 160; "Backstage," *Ebony*, November 1945, 2.

54. "Inspiration for Veterans," *Ebony*, November 1945, 40–41; "Sixty Million Jobs or Else . . . This Again?," *Ebony*, November 1945, 50.

55. See Buszek, *Pin-Up Grrrls*, 252.

56. *Ebony*, December 1945.

57. Johnson, *Succeeding Against the Odds*, 162. See also Burns, *Nitty Gritty*, 88.

58. Kodachrome is the brand name for a color reversal film introduced in 1935 by Eastman Kodak.

59. Tim Gray, "Singer and Actress Lena Horne Arrived Too Soon for Hollywood," *Variety*, June 23, 2017, https://variety.com/2017/vintage/features/singer-actress-lena-horne-1202473901/.

60. James Gavin, *Stormy Weather: The Life of Lena Horne* (New York: Simon and Schuster, 2009), 209.

61. "Cover," *Ebony*, March 1946, 2.

62. "*Ebony*'s March Issue Features Four Colors," *Chicago Defender*, March 2, 1946, 20.

63. Johnson, *Succeeding Against the Odds*, 162.

64. The second JPC headquarters was a two-story red-brick building located at 5125 South Calumet Avenue. Burns, *Nitty Gritty*, 96.

65. Johnson, *Succeeding Against the Odds*, 172.

66. Johnson, 179–90.

67. Burns, *Nitty Gritty*, 120.

68. Johnson, *Succeeding Against the Odds*, 173.

69. Johnson, 183.

70. The Motion Picture Production Code of 1930 (commonly referred to as the Hays Code after Will H. Hays, president of the Motion Picture Producers and Distributors of America) censored the display of female navels in Hollywood films. The Hays Code held sway through the 1950s.

71. "Miss Fine Brown Frame," *Ebony*, May 1947, 47–50. Maria Elena Buszek also discusses the "Miss Fine Brown Frame" feature and photographs in *Pin-Up Grrrls*, 248.

72. Burns, *Nitty Gritty*, 86. The other photographer who did freelance photography for *Ebony* during its early years was Gordon Coster, a Chicago-based commercial photographer who created advertisements for Marshall Field's, taught at the Institute of Design, and did assignments for *Life* and *Fortune* magazines. See Burns, *Nitty Gritty*, 87; "Biographical Historical Note," in "Gordon Coster Photograph Collection," Smithsonian Archives of American Art, accessed May 20, 2018, https://www.aaa.si.edu/collections/surveys/chicago/chicago-history-museum/gordon-coster-photograph-collection; and biographical note to *Chicago, Impression at Night*, by Gordon Coster, 1932, The Met website, accessed May 20, 2018, https://www.metmuseum.org/art/collection/search/265421.

73. See letters from Mrs. Thomas and Mrs. T. E. Clark, *Ebony*, August 1947, 4; and letter from Dorothy Giles, *Ebony*, September 1947, 5.

74. "Backstage," *Ebony*, November 1947.

75. *Ebony*, July 1947. Editors used the phrase "deep-hipped" to describe Miss Fine Brown Frame contestant winner Evelyn Sanders, who was similarly "thick" as *Ebony*'s July cover girl. See "Miss Fine Brown Frame," 47.

76. Johnson did not rely on the display of black female sexiness alone to attract advertisers but rather combined it with other tactics. For example, concurrent with the appearance of scantily clad black women in and on *Ebony*, he secured the magazine's admission as the "first magazine in Negro journalistic history" to the Audit Bureau of Circulation, an organization that routinely checks and verifies publications' net paid circulation. The bureau audit lent credibility to Johnson's claims for his magazine's potential as a tool for reaching black consumers. See "Backstage," *Ebony*, August 1947, 8.

77. Johnson, *Succeeding Against the Odds*, 185–88.

78. See Chambers, "Presenting the Black Middle Class," 59. Chambers provides a concise history of Johnson's challenge to obtain advertisers for *Ebony*. See also Johnson's autobiography for his recollection of how he pursued advertisers through traditional and innovative approaches. Johnson, *Succeeding Against the Odds*, chaps. 21–22. Johnson deviated from the general tactic of using an advertising agency to secure ads and instead personally pitched his magazine as a marketing tool directly to the heads of companies from which he sought advertising business.

79. Advertisers as listed in "Backstage," *Ebony*, June 1948, 10; and "Backstage," *Ebony*, December 1948, 12. Circulation numbers in Johnson, *Succeeding Against the Odds*, 189.

80. I make this claim based on a survey of letters to the editor from November 1945 through 1950.

81. "Wants Black Beauties," letter from Holmes Morgan, *Ebony*, August 1946, 50.

82. Shirley Jennifer Lim makes this argument in *A Feeling of Belonging: Asian American Women's Public Culture, 1930–1960* (New York: New York University Press, 2006), 124.

83. E. Simms Campbell, "Are Black Women Beautiful?," *Negro Digest*, June 1951, 18.

84. "Cover Girls," letter from James L. Hudson, *Negro Digest*, June 1948, 97.

85. "Lewd Material," letter from Esther P. Oliver, *Negro Digest*, April 1948, 98.

86. See the following examples of *Ebony* readers requesting visions alternative to both dominant white and elite black definitions of beauty: "Wants Black Beauties," 50; "Cover Girls," letters from Clifford Brockerton, Madame Ebony Beaute (Black Beauty), Harold Jackman, and Randolph Brewster, *Ebony*, November 1946, 4.

87. "Covers," letter from Mary Williams, *Ebony*, May 1947.

88. Lim, *Feeling of Belonging*, 144.

89. The term "girlie covers" appears in "The Mail Bag," *Negro Digest*, January 1948, 97. The models appearing on *Negro Digest* covers were, largely, African American coeds and housewives local to the Chicago area, and while some were credited with having "modeling aspirations," it is unclear whether any were professional models. I make this assessment based on the cover credits in each issue from November 1946 to November 1947. It appears that most of the Kodachrome photographs were taken by Stephen Deutch, a local Chicago photographer who, as a later issue of *Ebony* described, "work[ed] for leading Chicago department stores (Marshall Field & Co.), as well as fashion magazines such as *Mademoiselle*." See "Backstage," *Ebony*, April 1948, 10. An

indication that *Negro Digest* was also going a different route with both its marketing strategies and its content was apparent in the cover teasers that read, "You can't beat the dice," and, "What color will your baby be?" See *Negro Digest*, November 1946, cover.

90. Johnson, *Succeeding Against the Odds*, 173.

91. "Editor's Notebook," *Negro Digest*, November 1947.

92. "Cover Girls," *Negro Digest*, June 1948, 97.

93. The January 1948 issue of *Negro Digest* contains multiple letters from readers decrying the "girlie covers"; these letters point to the cover girl images' potential harm to interracial understanding and relationships. See "Girlie Covers," letters from Edna B. McBride, Mrs. Edith Beckham, and D. H. W. Hunt, *Negro Digest*, January 1948, 97–98. See also "Sexy Covers," letter from Louise Huston, *Negro Digest*, July 1948, 98. Huston identified the covers as being of the "type that too many white people connect with Negroes. Sexy, in other words."

94. "Editor's Notebook," *Negro Digest*, November 1947.

95. Johnson as quoted in Burns, *Nitty Gritty*, 89. I have yet to find this quote in another source; it is unclear whether Johnson made this statement to Burns or in public. Burns also writes that, in interviews with the *Christian Science Monitor* and *Business Week*, Johnson made the following statements, respectively: "We . . . present the good things that Negroes are doing, with emphasis on what can be done, not on the handicaps," and, "We try to emphasize and play up points on which Negroes and whites can agree rather than stress points on which they disagree" (89–90).

96. "Good Bye Mammy, Hello Mom," *Ebony*, March 1947, 36–37.

97. Laila Haidarali discusses the "feminized worker" in "Polishing Brown Diamonds," 12.

98. "What I Told Kinsey About My Sex Life," *Ebony*, December 1948, 45–50.

99. Haidarali, "Polishing Brown Diamonds," 12; Buszek, *Pin-Up Grrrls*, 250; Green, *Selling the Race*, 152. Green observes, "Black women were compelled [by *Ebony*'s presentation of black womanhood] to endorse patriarchal patterns of domestic life, while encouraged to affirm sexual freedom" (152). See also Meyerowitz, "Beyond the Feminine Mystique," 1466–67.

100. Johnson, *Succeeding Against the Odds*, 190.

101. See, especially, Green, *Selling the Race*, 154–55.

102. Johnson, *Succeeding Against the Odds*, 199–200; Burns, *Nitty Gritty*, 111–12.

103. Laretta Henderson, *Ebony Jr! The Rise, Fall, and Return of a Black Children's Magazine* (Lanham, MD: Scarecrow, 2008), 52; Brian Thornton, "The Murder of Emmett Till: Myth, Memory, and National Magazine Response," *Journalism History* 36, no. 2 (Summer 2010): 98.

104. Henderson, *Ebony Jr!*, 52.

105. "Beauty Crowned at Gigantic Military Ball," *Pittsburgh Courier*, May 2, 1942, 12. For Dandridge's filmography, see "Dorothy Dandridge," Internet Movie Database, accessed May 18, 2018, http://www.imdb.com/name/nm0199268 /. Her early movie appearances included parts in a 1935 *Our Gang* short, the 1937 Marx Brothers feature *A Day at the Races*, and the 1940 race film *Four Shall Die*.

106.   "Eye & Ear Specialist," *Time*, February 4, 1952, http://www.time.com/time
         /magazine/article/0,9171,822075,00.html; "Two for the Show," *Time*, May 2,
         1955, http://content.time.com/time/magazine/article/0,9171,866287,00.html.
107.   *Ebony*, April 1951, cover, 48–52.
108.   "Dorothy Dandridge: Seductive Singer Captivates Hollywood at Mocambo
         Opening," *Ebony*, December 1953, 100–101.
109.   When *Ebony* ran a feature or cover story on Dandridge, Johnson's competi-
         tors followed suit with articles of a similar tone. For evidence of this pattern,
         see "Hollywood's New Glamour Queen," *Ebony*, April 1951, 48–50; "Shy No
         More," *Life*, November 5, 1951, 65–66, 69–70; "Don't Be Afraid of Sex Ap-
         peal," *Ebony*, May 1952, 24–31; and "Can Dandridge Outshine Lena Horne?,"
         Our World, June 1952, 28–32.
110.   See "Hollywood's New Glamour Queen"; "The World's Sexiest Negro
         Women," *Jet*, December 27, 1951, 38; "Don't Be Afraid"; "Hollywood's Best
         Negro Movie," *Ebony*, April 1953, cover; "Dorothy Dandridge," *Ebony*,
         December 1953, 101–3; "Screen Test: Dorothy Dandridge Wins *Carmen Jones*
         Title Role with Sizzling Performance," *Ebony*, September 1954, 37; "Holly-
         wood's Newest Love Team," *Jet*, September 30, 1954, cover, 60–61; "Five Most
         Beautiful Negro Women," *Ebony*, January 1955, 47; "Will Hollywood Let
         Negroes Make Love?," *Tan*, January 1955, cover; "Dorothy Dandridge's Great-
         est Triumph," *Ebony*, July 1955, 37; "Dandridge Gets Red Carpet Treatment,"
         Ebony, August 1956, 24–29; and "Island in the Sun," *Ebony*, July 1957, 32–35.
111.   Adam Green makes this argument in *Selling the Race*, 155.
112.   Donald Bogle reports that *Carmen Jones* had a budget of $750,000 in *Doro-
         thy Dandridge: A Biography* (New York: Berkley Trade, 1998), 266.
113.   "The New Pictures," *Time*, November 1, 1954; "Current & Choice," *Time*, Jan-
         uary 17, 1955, http://www.time.com/time/magazine/article/0,9171,891172,00
         .html. For examples of *Carmen Jones* publicity, see advertising spreads in *Va-
         riety*, October 20, 1954, 11–13, and November 17, 1954, 10–11.
114.   "Carmen Jones Breaks Everything but Bias in Nation's Theatres," *Chicago De-
         fender*, December 18, 1954, 6. See also "No Cover Charge," *Pittsburgh Cou-
         rier*, January 8, 1955, 20. For information regarding audiences for *Carmen
         Jones* in different markets, see "'Carmen' Big $50,000," *Variety*, November 3,
         1954, 9; "'Carmen' Fancy $38,000 Leading L.A.," *Variety*, November 10, 1954,
         8; "'Carmen' Torrid 47G, 2d," *Variety*, November 10, 1954, 9; "'Carmen' Loud
         $28,000, 2d," *Variety*, November 17, 1954, 12; "'Carmen' 41G, 3d," *Variety*,
         November 17, 1954, 13; "'Carmen' Torrid at $35,000," *Variety*, November 24,
         1954, 9.
115.   While I was revising this book, the Department of Justice reopened the Till
         case "based upon the discover of new information." The Department of Jus-
         tice did not reveal the nature of that new information; however, it is reason-
         able to assume that a contributing factor may be that the white woman at the
         center of the case, Carolyn Bryant (now Carolyn Bryant Donham), has ad-
         mitted to lying about Till's actions toward her. Her retraction-confession is
         revealed in Timothy Tyson's new book *The Blood of Emmett Till* (New York:
         Simon and Schuster, 2017). With the blessing of Donham's family, Tyson in-
         terviewed the elderly woman twice for his book and then turned over the

record of those interviews to the Federal Bureau of Investigation. See Eliot McLaughlin and Emanuella Grinberg, "Justice Department Reopens Investigation into 63-Year-Old Murder of Emmett Till," CNN, July 13, 2018, https://www.cnn.com/2018/07/12/us/emmett-till-murder-case-reopened-doj/index.html.

116.   Lynching figures supplied here are based on records kept by the Tuskegee Institute. See "Lynchings, Whites & Negroes, 1882–1968," Tuskegee University Archives, Digital Collections, accessed March 13, 2018, http://archive .tuskegee.edu/archive/bitstream/handle/123456789/511/Lyching%20 1882%201968.pdf?sequence=1&isAllowed=y; Jessie Guzman, ed., *1952 Negro Yearbook: A Review of Events Affecting Negro Life* (New York: William H. Wise, 1952), 275–80; and Mary Dudziak, *Cold War Civil Rights: Race and the Image of American Democracy* (Princeton, NJ: Princeton University Press, 1994), 18–23. There are discrepancies in lynching numbers kept by different institutions (e.g., Tuskegee Institute, the NAACP, and the *Chicago Tribune*): the Tuskegee Institute statistics are relatively conservative when compared to numbers kept by the NAACP, especially. For example, in 1914, the Tuskegee Institute recorded fifty-four lynchings when the NAACP counted seventy-four. See Edward B. Reuter, *The American Race Problem* (New York: Thomas Y. Crowell, 1927), 367. Reuter explains these discrepancies as the result of different conceptions of lynching, as well as possible "minor" recording errors.

117.   "Mississippi Gunmen Take Life of Militant Negro Minister," *Jet*, May 26, 1955, 8–11.

118.   Wilkins as quoted in "Designed to Inflame," *Jackson Daily News*, September 2, 1955.

119.   Bradley as quoted in Devery Anderson, *Emmett Till: The Murder That Shocked the World and Propelled the Civil Rights Movement* (Jackson: University Press of Mississippi, 2015), 55.

120.   Bradley as quoted in Anderson, 56. Other sources quote Bradley as saying variations on this statement: see Henry Hampton and Steve Fayer, *Voices of Freedom: An Oral History of the Civil Rights Movement from the 1950s Through the 1980s* (New York: Bantam Books, 1990), 6; Green, *Selling the Race*, 196; Ruth Feldstein, "'I Wanted the Whole World to See': Race, Gender, and Constructions of Motherhood in the Death of Emmett Till," in *Not June Cleaver: Women and Gender in Postwar America, 1945–1960*, ed. Joanne Meyerowitz (Philadelphia: Temple University Press, 1994), 271.

121.   See "Slain Youth's Body Seen by Thousands," *New York Times*, September 4, 1955, S9; "Thousands at Rites for Till," *Chicago Defender*, September 10, 1955, 1; and Carl Hirsch, "50,000 Mourn at Bier of Lynched Negro Child," *Daily Worker*, September 10, 1955, in *The Lynching of Emmett Till: A Documentary Narrative*, ed. Christopher Metress (Charlottesville: University of Virginia Press, 2002), 31. These accounts put the viewers at between ten thousand and fifty thousand. Jacqueline Goldsby summarizes these varying estimates in "The High and Low Tech of It: The Meaning of Lynching and the Death of Emmett Till," *Yale Journal of Criticism* 9, no. 2 (Fall 1996): 250. The variance in estimates can be explained partially by uncertainty as to whether these sources are referring to the entire visitation period or a portion of it.

122. See "Grieving Mother Meets Body of Lynched Son," *Chicago Defender*, September 10, 1955, 5; and "Emmett Till Funeral Saddens City, Nation," *Chicago Defender*, September 17, 1955, 4.

123. While there is debate over whether, when, and where other publications published images of Till's corpse, *Jet* was the first to publish these photographs. Other magazines were left to pick up the *Jet* photographs for reprint. Some newspapers, such as the *Afro-American*, produced illustrations from the photographs. See *Afro-American*, September 24, 1955. Martin Berger points to an unpublished photograph in the *Chicago Tribune* archive (labeled "Mourners Pass Emmett Till's Casket" and dated September 3, 1955), which provides a distant view of Till's open casket, as evidence that the white press possessed and printed pictures of Till's body. There is no indication, however, that the *Tribune* published any pictures displaying Till's body. Martin Berger, *Seeing Through Race: A Reinterpretation of Civil Rights Photography* (Berkeley: University of California Press, 2011), 131–32.

124. Examples include Green, *Selling the Race*, 196–200; Berger, *Seeing Through Race*, 128; Anderson, *Emmett Till*, 56 (Anderson explicitly draws the connection between Till's murder and civil rights activism with his subtitle, *The Murder That Shocked the World and Propelled the Civil Rights Movement*); and Thornton, "Murder of Emmett Till," 100.

125. "Fight for Rights," letter from Fred Poindexter, *Chicago Defender*, November 19, 1955, 9.

126. Berger, *Seeing Through Race*, 128. Berger and Green both detail the anguish and activism that the Till photographs generated among various notable black entertainers, activists, and artists, including Anne Moody, Eldridge Cleaver, Gwendolyn Brooks, Langston Hughes, Cassius Clay (Muhammad Ali), and Lew Alcindor (Kareem Abdul-Jabbar). Green, *Selling the Race*, 198.

127. Charles Diggs Jr. as quoted in Thornton, "Murder of Emmett Till," 100.

128. Several historians have examined the commodification of lynching photographs within white consumer spaces. See Grace Elizabeth Hale, *Making Whiteness: The Culture of Segregation in the South, 1890–1940* (New York: Vintage Books, 1999), chap. 5; Shawn Michelle Smith, *Photography on the Color Line: W. E. B. Du Bois, Race, and Visual Culture* (Durham, NC: Duke University Press, 2004), chap. 4; and Amy Louise Wood, *Lynching and Spectacle: Witnessing Racial Violence in America, 1890–1940* (Chapel Hill: University of North Carolina Press, 2011), chap. 3.

129. I did not locate an announcement of the Kendrixes' divorce in *Jet*; however, there is evidence that JPC tried to contact Moss Kendrix for comment on his wife's filing for divorce for publication in the magazine. See "Mr. and Mrs.," September 19, 1960, prepared news item, in Johnson Publishing Company Clippings Files Collection, Robert W. Woodruff Library, Atlanta University Center. Scrawled in the top right-hand corner of this press item is the following note: "Call Kendrix for comment—can you let us have recent pic of you and your family one we have was taken in 1958."

130. My father, William Charles Greer Jr., related this sentiment to me when he learned I was researching the histories of *Ebony* and *Jet* magazines.

131. "Why Jet," *Jet*, November 1, 1951, 67.

132. Circulation numbers as provided in Thornton, "Murder of Emmett Till," 98. Citing the 1957 *World Almanac*, Thornton lists the circulation figures for *Ebony* and *Jet* as 441,227 monthly and 478,666 weekly, respectively. See also "From *Negro Digest* to *Ebony*, *Jet* and *EM*," *Ebony*, November 1992, 50th anniversary issue, 54.

133. See Thornton, 101.

134. Johnson, *Succeeding Against the Odds*, 235.

135. Johnson, 235–36.

136. Johnson, 235.

137. See Clotye Murdock, "Land of the Till Murder," *Ebony*, April 1946, 91–96; and "The Till Case People One Year Later," *Ebony*, October 1956, 68–74. Martin Luther King Jr.'s "Advice for Living" column appeared in *Ebony* from September 1957 through December 1958. Valerie Saddler charts *Ebony*'s content shift between 1955 and 1965 in relation to the civil rights movement in "A Content Analysis of *Ebony*'s and *Life*'s 1955–1965 Reporting on Black Civil Rights Movement Issues" (PhD diss., Ohio University, June 1984).

138. Johnson, *Succeeding Against the Odds*, 153; "Backstage," *Ebony*, November 1945, 2.

139. See the covers of the following issues of *Jet*: September 15, September 22, September 29, October 13, 1955.

140. "Nation Horrified by Murder of Kidnapped Chicago Youth," *Jet*, September 15, 1955, 6–9.

141. Green, *Selling the Race*, 197.

142. "Nation Horrified," 9. Green draws attention to how, in its presentation of the Till photos, *Jet* followed a convention editors deployed earlier that year when reporting on Rev. George Lee's murder, such as juxtaposing pictures of the victim in life to those of him in death, picturing loved ones mourning near or over the body, and providing an open-casket view of the body. See Green, *Selling the Race*, 194–95; and "Mississippi Gunmen Take Life of Militant Negro Minister," *Jet*, May 26, 1955, 8–11.

143. Gene Roberts and Hank Klibanoff, *The Race Beat: The Press, the Civil Rights Struggle, and the Awakening of a Nation* (New York: Vintage Books, 2007), 88; Thornton, "Murder of Emmett Till," 100. Thornton refers to JPC's use of the Jackson photographs as "a brilliant stroke" financially.

144. See Hermene Hartman, "The Cry of *Jet* Magazine," HuffPost, May 29, 2014, https://www.huffingtonpost.com/hermene-hartman/the-cry-of-jet-magazine_b_5397173.html. As CEO of the Hartman Publishing Group, Hartman is one of the most prominent African American women in publishing.

145. "Will Mississippi 'Whitewash' the Emmett Till Slaying?," *Jet*, September 22, 1955, 8–12.

146. Johnson, *Succeeding Against the Odds*, 240. Johnson explains that he ultimately opted to print Jackson's photographs because he felt a duty to expose the brutality and savagery of Till's murder.

147. Simeon Booker as quoted in "Best Civil Rights Cameraman in Business Dies," *Jet*, April 21, 1966, 29.

148. Hampton and Fayer, *Voices of Freedom*, 6.

149. "The Cause of It All," photo standalone, *Chicago Defender*, September 17, 1955, 1.

150. Covers of *Jet*, September 22, September 29, October 6, October 13, 1955.

151. *Jet*, July 23, 1964, cover.

152. Amzie Moore as quoted in Berger, *Seeing Through Race*, 125.

153. In 2009 Emmett Till's relatives donated his casket—which his mother, Bradley, insisted be open so the public could see the brutality of white supremacy and racial hatred—to the Smithsonian National Museum of African American History and Culture. Till's remains were transferred to a new casket after his body was exhumed in 2005 for the purpose of an autopsy and DNA analysis, which confirmed his identity. At the museum, the original casket, which required restoration after egregious neglect, is on display as part of the *Defending Freedom, Defining Freedom* exhibit. Speaking to the historical significance of Till's lynching and its impact among African Americans especially, the museum's deputy director Kinshasha Holman Conwill identifies the casket as "one of [the museum's] most sacred objects." See Krissah Thompson, "Emmett Till's Casket a 'Sacred Object' at the African American Museum," *Washington Post*, August 19, 2016, http://www.chicagotribune .com/news/nationworld/ct-emmett-till-casket-african-american-museum -20160818-story.html.

154. bell hooks, "In Our Glory: Photography and Black Life," in *Picturing Us: African American Identity in Photography*, ed. Deborah Willis (New York: New Press, 1994), 46.

155. Burns, *Nitty Gritty*, 84.

156. Johnson, *Succeeding Against the Odds*, 156.

Chapter 5

Epigraph: Joseph Wootton, director of Interstate United Newspapers, as quoted in "Selling the Negro Market," *Tide*, July 20, 1951, 37.

1. Jason Chambers provides an encyclopedic history of the African American marketers who studied, promoted, and represented African American consumer interests in *Madison Avenue and the Color Line: African Americans in the Advertising Industry* (Philadelphia: University of Pennsylvania Press, 2007), chaps. 1–2.

2. Lizabeth Cohen lays out these postwar dynamics in *A Consumers' Republic: The Politics of Mass Consumption in Postwar America* (New York: Vintage Books, 2003), 13, chap. 4.

3. Moss Hyles Kendrix Jr., interview by author, September 9, 2009.

4. Jason Chambers, *Madison Avenue*, 61. Regarding Wilson, see Chapter 2 for a detailed account of how early black markets specialists found work with large corporations. See also Stephanie Capparell, *The Real Pepsi Challenge: The Inspirational Story of Breaking the Color Barrier in American Business* (New York: Free Press, 2007), 144–46, 154–62.

5. Jason Chambers, *Madison Avenue*, 68–80; Capparell, *Real Pepsi Challenge*, 107.

6. Capparell, 107.

7. Kendrix interview. Regarding other companies Kendrix approached, see the following documents in Moss H. Kendrix Organization Papers, Alexandria Black History Museum, Alexandria, VA (hereafter cited as MHKOP): Kendrix to Mr. J. H. Carmichael, Capital Airlines, Inc., n.d.; Kendrix to R. Averill, Capital Airlines, January 26, 1949; Kendrix to R. S. Damon, American Airlines System, February 21, 1950; Kendrix to George Baker, National Airlines, Inc., February 21, 1950; Kendrix to John M. Stoddart, National Airlines, March 11, 1950; Moss Kendrix, "Proposal Designed to Promote Department Store Sales in the Negro Market of Washington," prospectus, circa 1948. See also Moss Kendrix to Mr. W. T. Smither, R. J. Reynolds Tobacco Company, February 11, 1949, Truth Tobacco Industry Documents, https://www.industrydocumentslibrary.ucsf.edu/tobacco/docs/#id=xncj0099.

8. For Kendrix's exchange with Hilton, see C. N. Hilton to Kendrix, February 9, 1950, and Kendrix to C. N. Hilton, February 20, 1950, MHKOP.

9. Kendrix to R. S. Damon.

10. Calvin H. Sinnette, *Forbidden Fairways: African Americans and the Game of Golf* (Chelsea: Sleeping Bear, 1998), 155; Moss H. Kendrix, "Be My Guest," *Tee-Cup*, February 1959, 26. "Be My Guest" appears to have been Kendrix's column, which the editor acclaims based on Kendrix's "wealth of golf know-how." See also "The Crown Prince of Public Relations," *Sepia*, May 1964.

11. Sidney Matthew and Janice McDonald, *The East Lake Golf Club* (Charleston: Arcadia, 2015), 31.

12. Matthew and McDonald, 31.

13. Kendrix interview.

14. Kendrix interview. I have been unable to confirm the story regarding Mary Kendrix's treatment at Emory University Hospital.

15. Kendrix to William Hobbs, July 16, 1945; Roy S. Jones to Kendrix, October 10, 1945; Kendrix to William Hobbs, March 11, 1946, MHKOP.

16. Kendrix to Hobbs, March 11, 1946.

17. Kendrix to Mr. Felix Coste, March 20, 1946, MHKOP.

18. Samuel A. Alter to Kendrix, March 26, 1946, MHKOP.

19. The Coca-Cola Company supplied me with evidence that the company and its product had a presence in black communities in the early twentieth century. This includes documentation that Coke was served in black-owned soda fountains in Atlanta and Los Angeles and one Coca-Cola ad that appeared in the *Freeman*, an Indiana black newspaper, as early as 1904. See Marilyn Pryce Hoytt, "Pryce's Pharmacy: Pouring Memories and Coke for Generations," Coca-Cola Journey, February 4, 2013, http://www.coca-colacompany.com/history/pryces-pharmacy-pouring-memories-and-coke-for-generations/#TCCC; "Coke in Early African American Communities" (PDF of PowerPoint slides supplied to author by Coca-Cola archives, September 15, 2014), The advertisement that appeared in the *Freeman* is small, black and white, void of any graphics or illustration, and completely generic in its copy. While this is proof that Coca-Cola was available to blacks to purchase and is evidence of the company's advertising in a black media space, it is not evidence that Coca-Cola devised advertising that explicitly recognized or represented African Americans.

20. Jesse J. Lewis, interview by author, October 4, 2009.

21. Paul K. Edwards, *The Southern Urban Negro as a Consumer* (New York: Prentice-Hall, 1932), 194.

22. Marcus Alexis, "Pathways to the Negro Market," *Journal of Negro Education* 28, no. 2 (Spring 1959): 115.

23. For a thorough discussion of earlier attempts by African American marketing men to promote the black consumer market, see Jason Chambers, *Madison Avenue*, chap. 1; and Robert Weems Jr., *Desegregating the Dollar: African American Consumerism in the Twentieth Century* (New York: New York University Press, 1998), chaps. 1–2. Chambers and Weems outline how, by World War II, a handful of black entrepreneurs, journalists, and marketing men, including Claude Barnett, William Graham, Edward Brandford, and David Sullivan, had been steadily promoting African Americans as a market, some as early as the 1920s. These men put much energy into convincing white corporations, merchandisers, and advertisers of blacks' viability as a consumer market because their entrepreneurial endeavors depended on their choosing to target "the Negro market," which many were not inclined to do.

24. Regarding the size of the black market, see David Sullivan, "The Negro Market," *Negro Digest*, February 1943, 60; David Sullivan, "The American Negro: An 'Export' Market at Home!," *Printer's Ink* 208 (July 21, 1944): 90; "The Negro Market: An Appraisal," *Tide*, March 7, 1947; "The Negro Market: A Growing Market Opportunity," *Tide*, July 20, 1951, 7; and "Selling the Negro Market."

25. "Selling the Negro Market," 38.

26. "The Negro Market: A Growing Market Opportunity," 7; "Selling the Negro Market," 37–38.

27. See Jason Chambers, *Madison Avenue*, 35, 40. Chambers explains that Paul K. Edwards's *Southern Negro as Urban Consumer* and advertiser William B. Ziff's booklet *The Negro Market* were two of the main sources of knowledge regarding black consumers.

28. Edgar Steele, "Some Aspects of the Negro Market," *Journal of Marketing* 11, no. 4 (April 1947): 399.

29. David Sullivan estimated the black population in the United States in 1945 to be 13,190,543. See David Sullivan, Negro Market Organization report, April 40, 1945, MHKOP. Census data from 1950 estimates the black population at 14,894,000. See also Weems, *Desegregating the Dollar*, 41; "The Forgotten 15,000,000," *Sponsor* 3 (October 24, 1949): 24; "The Forgotten 15,000,000," pt. 2, *Sponsor* 3 (October 24, 1949): 30; and Alexis, "Pathways," 114. Regarding employment and income, see "14 Million Negro Customers: Business Can Learn to Its Profit That Uncle Remus Is Dead," *Negro Digest*, August 1947, 57–61, condensed from "14 Million Negro Customers," *Kiplinger*, April 1947; and Blaine Branchik and Judy Foster Davis, "Marketplace Activism: A History of the African American Elite Market Segment," *Journal of Macromarketing* 29, no. 1 (March 2009): 45.

30. See "14 Million Negro Customers," *Negro Digest*; Sullivan, Negro Market Organization report; Sullivan, "Negro Market"; David Sullivan, "How Negroes Spent Their Incomes, 1920–1943," *Sales Management* 54 (June 15, 1945): 106; and Weems, *Desegregating the Dollar*, 34. See also Sullivan, "American Negro," 90.

31.   Larry Tye, *The Father of Spin: Edward L. Bernays and the Birth of Public Relations* (New York: Henry Holt, 2002), 91.

32.   For an example of how Kendrix used Sullivan's reports, see "Suggested Sales Promotion and Advertising Scheme for Kaiser-Frazer Corporation," circa 1946; "Negro Market for Kaiser-Frazer Corporation Products," prospectus prepared by Robinson-Kendrix-Simmons, circa 1946, MHKOP.

33.   Sullivan, Negro Market Organization report; Alexis, "Pathways," 115.

34.   David Sullivan "Don't Do This—If You Want to Sell Your Products to Negroes!," *Sales Management*, March 1, 1943, 46–51. See also David Sullivan, "A Catalogue of Don'ts," *Negro Digest*, June 1943, 49–51.

35.   Jason Chambers, *Madison Avenue*, 71.

36.   Chambers, 68–74, 148–50. Chambers outlines Sullivan's professional advertising career, including his struggle to get work through the 1950s and 1960s, revealing that, in that time period, Sullivan sent out over 1,200 résumés, none of which resulted in his finding employment.

37.   Ronald Smith, "The Paul Robeson–Jackie Robinson Saga and a Political Collison," *Journal of Sport History* 6, no. 2 (Summer 1979): 5.

38.   Lansing Warren, "Paris 'Peace Congress' Assails U.S. and Atlantic Pack, Upholds Soviet," *New York Times*, April 21, 1949, 6.

39.   Robeson as quoted in Martin Duberman, *Paul Robeson* (New York: Knopf, 1988), 342. See also "Robeson Misquoted? He Says So," *Chicago Defender*, May 21, 1949, 12.

40.   Smith, "Paul Robeson–Jackie Robinson Saga," 5–6; C. P. Trussell, "Jackie Robinson Terms Stand of Robeson on Negroes False," *New York Times*, July, 19, 1949, 1, 14; Howard Bryant, *The Heritage: Black Athletes, a Divided America, and the Politics of Patriotism* (Boston: Beacon, 2018), 34–38.

41.   Moss Kendrix, "The Coca-Cola Proposal," circa 1948, 8, MHKOP. I have dated the Coca-Cola proposal using letters in which Kendrix proposed the same programs to R. J. Reynolds Tobacco Company. See Kendrix to W. T. Smither, June 8, 1948, Truth Tobacco Industry Documents, https://www.industrydocumentslibrary.ucsf.edu/tobacco/docs/#id=kncj0099.

42.   "Selling the Negro Market," 39.

43.   Kendrix, "Proposal Designed"; Kendrix, "Coca-Cola Proposal," introduction, 6.

44.   See data in "Operation Columbia," a proposal of the Moss H. Kendrix Organization, July 1957, MHKOP.

45.   "The Brown Hucksters," *Ebony*, May 1948, 28–33.

46.   Capparell, *Real Pepsi Challenge*, 199. Capparell identifies the ten members of Pepsi's national "Negro-market" sales team as Edward F. Boyd, David F. Watson, Charles E. Wilson, Richard L. Hurt, Paul F. Davis, Harvey C. Russell, William E. Payne, Jean F. Emmons, Allen L. McKellar, and William R. Simms. See also the photographs entitled *Marketing Pioneers* and *Building a Department* in Capparell, n.p.

47.   Capparell, 201–3.

48.   "Fair Play Committee Boycotts Coca-Cola," *Atlanta Daily World*, December 30, 1950, 1. For a detailed account of events leading up to the boycott, see Capparell, *Real Pepsi Challenge*, 202.

49. Kendrix interview. John Lewis confirmed Kendrix's remembrance. Lewis interview.

50. Sanders Rowland, *Papa Coke: Sixty-Five Years Selling Coca-Cola*, with Bob Terrell (Asheville, NC: Bright Mountain Books, 1986), 150. My interviews with Moss Kendrix Jr. and Jesse Lewis Sr. confirm Rowland's remembrance.

51. "Preliminary Statement: Problem Areas and Recent Trends Affecting Public Relations in the Negro Market," MHKO report, circa 1957–58, MHKOP.

52. Contract signed by Moss Kendrix and E. D. Sledge, April 3, 1951, MHKOP.

53. "Man of the Month, Publicist International," *Eyes: The Picture Magazine*, June 1947, 7.

54. Kendrix to Roy Wilkins, December 7, 1955, MHKOP.

55. Kendrix interview; Lewis interview. Kendrix's papers contain MHKO press releases with pictures of black men sporting the uniforms of Coca-Cola deliverymen, accompanied by ad copy (presumably written by Kendrix or his staff) detailing their recent promotions, hires, and successes as Coca-Cola drivers.

56. Rowland, *Papa Coke*, 180.

57. "Summary of Route Salesmen," ca. 1955, MHKOP. This document lists eight route salesmen—Curtis Walton, Willie Little, Lester Brown, Edward Pitts Jr., James Stevens, Warren Leonard, Charles E. Johnson, and Joseph Dudley.

58. Lewis interview.

59. Lewis interview; "Bob's Savoy Scene of Testimonial to New Coca-Cola Man," *Birmingham Mirror*, November 21, 1953, 8; Rowland, *Papa Coke*, 181–85. Lewis does not mention his relationship to Kendrix or MHKO in interviews or biographical pieces; however, he detailed that relationship in depth when I interviewed him. It is unclear why Lewis omits this part of his history as a black marketer; perhaps crediting Kendrix undermines the narrative he has pushed over the years of being a black marketing pioneer. Lewis opened his own advertising and marketing firm in 1954, which he has represented as the first of its kind in the country. When interviewed by the author, Lewis linked his opening this firm to business he did with Kendrix for Coca-Cola. "Jesse Lewis Looks Back on a Life Full of Success," *Tuscaloosa News*, November 3, 2013, http://www.tuscaloosanews.com/article/20131103/NEWS/131109922.

60. Lewis interview; "The Negro Market," *Refresher*, April 1954; "The Coca-Cola Company and the Bottlers Cultivate the Negro Market," *Coca-Cola Bottler*, August 1954. See also MHKO press release, October 8, 1958, MHKOP. This press release announces the hiring of black sales representatives Walter Beamon and Joseph Williams by the Coca-Cola Bottling Company of New York and the Cleveland Coca-Cola Bottling Company, respectively.

61. Thorstein Veblen, *A Theory of the Leisure Class* (1899; New York: Routledge, 2017).

62. Cohen, *Consumers' Republic*, 8–9.

63. Cohen, 11.

64. "Family Status Must Improve: It Should Buy More for Itself to Better Living of Others," *Life*, May 5, 1947, 32–33.

65. Cohen, *Consumers' Republic*, 8. Cohen explicates and names these different consumer ideals. She identifies the "citizen consumer" of the New Deal and

World War II eras as collaborating with the government "to save a capitalist America . . . but also to safeguard the rights of individual consumers and the larger 'general good,'" whereas the individualistic consumerism of the post-war "purchaser as citizen" "actually served the national interest" (8).

66.   Harold Kassarjian, "The Negro and American Advertising," *Journal of Marketing Research* 6, no. 1 (February 1969): 29–39. Kassarjian conducted a content analysis of advertisements in eleven randomly selected magazines with circulation over 250,000 for the years of 1946, 1956, and 1964, none of which were "Negro publications."

67.   For an example, see "Aunt Jemima Pancakes," advertisement in *Life*, October 21, 1946, 11.

68.   Grace Elizabeth Hale has argued that the images in these ads also implied that consumption carried with it the possibility of an elevated class position—of enhanced whiteness—signified by one's possession or control of another's labor. The ads defined control of others' labor as central to what it meant to be American. See Grace Elizabeth Hale, *Making Whiteness: The Culture of Segregation in the South, 1890–1940* (New York: Vintage Books, 1999), 161–68. In the section entitled "Bound Consumption," Hale provides a detailed analysis of African Americans' representation in late nineteenth and early twentieth-century advertising.

69.   Rachel Robinson as quoted in Jason Sokol, *All Eyes Are upon Us: Race and Politics from Boston to Brooklyn* (New York: Basic Books, 2014), 65. I thank Alexandra Gazzolo for bringing this particular example to my attention.

70.   Smith, "Paul Robeson–Jackie Robinson Saga," 6; Marc Norton, "Jackie Robinson: 'I Never Had It Made,'" Daily Kos, November 3, 2013, https://www.dailykos.com/stories/2013/11/3/1252708/-Jackie-Robinson-I-Never-Had-It-Made-Review-of-the-movie-42.

71.   William Black quoted in "Selling the Negro Market," 39.

72.   "Negro Market: An Appraisal," 16.

73.   Capparell, *Pepsi Challenge*, 113–17.

74.   Capparell, 118–19.

75.   Regarding E. D. Sledge, see Mike Cheatham, *"Your Friendly Neighbor": The Story of Georgia's Coca-Cola Bottling Families* (Macon, GA: Mercer University Press, 1999), 112; and "Coca-Cola Co.," *Ad Age*, September 15, 2003, https://adage.com/article/adage-encyclopedia/coca-cola/98398/. *Ad Age* puts Coca-Cola's advertising expenditures in 1953 at $30 million. See also *Advertising Age*, August 23, 1963.

76.   Kendrix to Willie Mays Jr., February 12, 1952, MHKOP. See also Kendrix to Dan "Deacon" Towler, February 12, 1952, MHKOP.

77.   Kendrix brokered the relationships between black talent and Coca-Cola for its first ads directed at African Americans. Correspondence between D'Arcy personnel and Kendrix indicates his significance to finding the talent for Coke's black celebrity ads. See Thad Horton to Kendrix, July 8, 1953, MHKOP.

78.   J. W. Jackson (Wilmington, North Carolina, Pepsi bottler) as quoted in Capparell, *Real Pepsi Challenge*, 248.

79.   Capparell, 249.

80. Bill Bateman and Randy Schaeffer, "Black History and the Coca-Cola Company," *Cola-Cola Collectors News*, February 1987, 9.

81. "The Negro Market," *Refresher*, April 1954, 1–2.

82. Lewis interview.

83. African American sales pioneer William Graham as quoted in "Selling the Negro Market," 39. See also Bateman and Schaeffer, "Black History," 9–11.

84. "Backstage," *Ebony*, August 1947, 8; "Backstage," *Ebony*, September 1950, n.p.

85. Paul Hirsch, "An Analysis of *Ebony*: The Magazine and Its Readers," *Journalism Quarterly* 45 (1968): 261–70, 292.

86. See, for example, the "Date with a Dish" feature in *Ebony* for April 1951, 66; September 1951, 70; February 1952, 100; and May 1952, 74.

87. "Backstage," *Ebony*, April 1948; "Fashion Fair," *Ebony*, April 1951, 82; "Fashion Fair," September 1951, 81; "Fashion Fair," February 1952, 87.

88. A concept coined by Evelyn Brooks Higginbotham, the "politics of respectability" "equated public behavior with individual self-respect and with the advancement of African Americans as a group." See Evelyn Brooks Higginbotham, *Righteous Discontent: The Women's Movement in the Black Baptist Church, 1880–1920*, rev. ed. (Cambridge, MA: Harvard University Press, 1994), 14. As Higginbotham explains, the politics of respectability was embraced and often enforced and enacted by the black elite (particularly the women of this class), whose "assimilationist leanings" resulted in this class's encouraging "blacks' conformity to the dominant society's norms of manners and mores" (187).

89. See Jason Chambers, "Presenting the Black Middle Class: John H. Johnson and *Ebony* Magazine, 1945–1974," in *Historicizing Lifestyle: Mediating Taste, Consumption, and Identity from the 1900s to 1970s*, ed. David Bell and Joanne Hollows (London: Ashgate, 2006).

90. "Why Negroes Buy Cadillacs," *Ebony*, September 1949, 34.

91. Walter White, *A Man Called White: The Autobiography of Walter White* (1948; repr., Athens: University of Georgia Press, 1995), 201.

92. Thaddeus Russell, "The Color of Discipline: Civil Rights and Black Sexuality," *American Quarterly* 60, no. 1 (March 2008): 103.

93. Gunnar Myrdal, *An American Dilemma: The Negro Problem and Modern Democracy* (New Brunswick, NJ: Transaction, 1996), 929, 966.

94. E. Franklin Frazier, *The Negro Family in the United States*, rev. and abridged ed. (1939; Chicago: University of Chicago Press, 1966), 368.

95. I rely especially on the works of Sarah Igo and Anna Creadick, as well as Julian Carter, to historically contextualize the concept and significance of "normal." See Sarah Igo, *The Averaged American: Surveys, Citizens, and the Making of a Mass Public* (Cambridge, MA: Harvard University Press, 2007); Anna Creadick, *Perfectly Average: The Pursuit of Normality in Postwar America* (Amherst: University of Massachusetts Press, 2010); and Julian Carter, *The Heart of Whiteness: Normal Sexuality and Race in America, 1880–1940* (Durham, NC: Duke University Press, 2007).

96. Joseph Wootton quoted in "Selling the Negro Market," 39. Wootton's term echoes the ideal of the "purchaser as citizen" introduced by Cohen. Cohen uses the "purchaser as citizen" concept to describe the consumer who, in buy-

ing to satisfy personal material wants (more so than personal needs), "actually served the national interest." Cohen, *Consumers' Republic*, 8.

97.   "Crown Prince of Public Relations."

98.   Martin Luther King Jr., "Advice for Living," *Ebony*, March 1958. See also Russell, "Color of Discipline," 117.

99.   Here I part ways with Cohen, who defines the consumerism of the postwar period as individualistic and private minded—while ultimately good for the republic—in contrast to the public-minded "citizen consumer" of the New Deal era. While Cohen outlines the experiences of women and African Americans before and after World War II, she often employs the generic "American" or "consumer," which fails to distinguish various marginalized groups from the dominant class, thus implying that her consumer ideals hold across race lines—even if the experiences of those ideals did not—such that materialism had the same meaning for white and black Americans. See Cohen, *Consumers' Republic*, 8–9, 113–14, 119, chap. 4.

100.   Letter from an exchange officer to a Coca-Cola bottler and Woodruff as quoted in Mark Pendergrast, *For God, Country and Coca-Cola: The Definitive History of the Great American Soft Drink and the Company That Makes It* (New York: Basic Books, 2000), 199.

101.   Regarding Coke's post–World War II iconic status, see Frederick Allen, *Secret Formula: How Brilliant Marketing and Relentless Salesmanship Made Coca-Cola the Best-Known Product in the World* (New York: HarperCollins, 1994), 258; "Moss Kendrix: 'Mr. Public Relations,'" *Sepia*, March 1953, 41.

102.   Laila Haidarali presents and explicates the figure of the "Brownskin" in "Polishing Brown Diamonds: African American Women, Popular Magazines, and the Advent of Modeling in Early Postwar America," *Journal of Women's History* 17, no. 1 (2005): 12.

103.   Similar to Haidarali, Elspeth Brown traces the growth of black modeling in relation to the rise of black market advertising and the rise of popular black magazines. See Elspeth Brown, "Black Models and the Invention of the U.S. 'Negro Market,' 1945–1960," in *Inside Marketing: Practices, Ideologies, Devices*, ed. Detlev Zwick and Julien Cayla (Cambridge: Oxford University Press, 2011), 185–211.

104.   Lewis interview.

105.   Pet Milk offers an example with its long use of actual black families and, especially, the Fultz quadruplets in its advertising. See Kimberley Mangun and Lisa M. Parcell, "The Pet Milk Company 'Happy Family' Advertising Campaign," *Journalism History* 40, no. 2 (Summer 2014): 70–84.

106.   See Phil Mooney, "Mary Alexander—Early African American Model," Coca-Cola Journey, February 21, 2008, https://www.coca-colacompany.com /stories/mary-alexander; Phil Mooney, "Mary Alexander, in Her Own Words," Coca-Cola Journey, February 25, 2009, https://www.coca-colacompany .com/stories/mary-alexander-in-her-own-words; Amy Cross, "A Humble Trailblazer: Meet Mary Alexander, the First African-American Woman to Appear in Coca-Cola Advertising," Coca Cola Journey, April 12, 2013, https://www.coca-colacompany.com/stories/a-humble-trailblazer-meet -mary-alexander-the-first-african-american-woman-to-appear-in-coca

-cola-advertising; "Mary Alexander Tells Her Story at the World of Coke," Coca Cola Journey, February 26, 2009, video, 3:44, https://www.coca -colacompany.com/videos/mary-alexander-tells-her-story-at-the-world-of -coke-ytpjhz2qbvuw8; and Harriet Daniels, "Resident Was First Black Woman in Coca-Cola Ads," *Ocala (FL) StarBanner,* September 4, 2007, http:// www.ocala.com/article/20070904/news/209040332.

107. Lewis interview.

108. *The Panther,* yearbook, 1955, 1956.

109. Roland Marchand describes the social tableaux as advertisements "in which persons are depicted in such a way as to suggest their relationships to each other or to a larger social structure." Roland Marchand, *Advertising the American Dream: Making Way for Modernity, 1920–1940* (Berkeley: University of California Press, 1985), 165–67.

110. John Oneal, "Second Transmission [Regarding Requested Information]" (email to the author, August 17, 2009). John Wesley Oneal, a Clark student recruited for the campaign, remembered that in the photo shoots in which he participated, "all scenes were depicted as a family setting."

111. Kendrix-inspired "Negro market" Coca-Cola ads, ca. 1955–58, MHKOP.

112. See Coca-Cola advertisements 6-42-N, 6-44-N, 6-46-N, 1956, MHKOP.

113. Mary Alexander recounts these "sightings" in several forums. See Coca-Cola Mary Alexander Heritage Series video; Daniels, "Resident."

114. "Moss Kendrix: 'Mr. Public Relations,'" 41.

115. "Crown Prince of Public Relations."

116. "Crown Prince of Public Relations."

117. "Moss Kendrix: 'Mr. Public Relations,'" 41.

118. Ultimately, the time and energy he spent helping Coca-Cola to redefine the public image of black consumers and the black family caused the demise of his marriage.

119. Jason Chambers makes this general assessment of ad images created or facilitated by African Americans who successfully infiltrated the advertising image. He argues that, in response to an industry with a history of producing, even relying on, stereotypical, racist representations of blackness, black imagemakers in advertising created "their own versions of the African American image." Chambers, *Madison Avenue,* 9.

120. Chambers, 14.

121. Stuart Hall describes the integrationist strategy of representation in "The Spectacle of the 'Other,'" in *Representation: Cultural Representations and Signifying Practices,* ed. Stuart Hall (London: Sage, 1997), 270.

122. I make this assessment based on the data and essays Kendrix sourced in one of his early pitches. In a proposal for Washington, DC, department stores, he referred to an article printed in the newly founded *Kiplinger* magazine that claimed that "race-consciousness is a strong factor in Negro buying." Kendrix referred to this race consciousness as an "extremely significant trait on the part of . . . the Negro market." He then held up companies that recognized African Americans as "different" and asserted that "the major basis of this difference is built around 'race-consciousness.'" Kendrix, "Proposal Designed"; "14 Million Negro Customers," *Kiplinger,* April 1947, 22.

123.   "Selling the Negro Market," 39–40.

124.   "Coca-Cola Places First in Contest Featuring Negro Market Merchandising Posters," MHKO press release, October 1, 1957, MHKOP.

125.   "The National Association of Market Developers (NAMD)," Moss H. Kendrix: A Retrospective, accessed February 26, 2016, http://prvisionaries.com/kendrix/namd.html.

126.   Lucille Arcola Chambers, *America's Tenth Man: A Pictorial Review of One-Tenth of a Nation* (New York: Twayne, 1957), 272.

127.   "Dean of Black Businessmen," *Black Enterprise*, January 1974, 23.

128.   "Tells Companies They Must Show Their Respect," *New York Amsterdam News*, July 22, 1967, 19. Regarding Fitzhugh's relationship to the development of "target marketing," see Wolfgang Saxon, "H. Naylor Fitzhugh, 82, Educator and Pioneer in Target Marketing," *New York Times*, July 29, 1992, http://www.nytimes.com/1992/07/29/nyregion/h-naylor-fitzhugh-82-educator-and-pioneer-in-target-marketing.html. Regarding advertising and public relations campaigns Fitzhugh devised, see "V-President Humphrey Lauds Pepsi Campaign," *New York Amsterdam News*, December 28, 1968, 5.

129.   Cohen details the phenomenon and effects of market segmentation. In her study, African Americans are not the actors effecting this change. Weems and Jason Chambers, in particular, brought African Americans into the history of marketing. See, respectively, *Desegregating the Dollar* and *Madison Avenue*.

130.   "Breakthroughs in Business," *Ebony*, November 1964, 64. This piece claims Kendrix became a Coca-Cola board member in 1962.

131.   Glen Coulthard skillfully expounds on this dynamic in "Subjects of Empire: Indigenous Peoples and the 'Politics of Recognition' in Canada," *Contemporary Political Theory* 6, no. 4 (2007): 437–60.

Conclusion

Epigraph: Gary Younge, "She Would Not Be Moved," *Guardian*, December 16, 2000.

1.   Lizabeth Cohen, *A Consumers' Republic: The Politics of Mass Consumption in Postwar America* (New York: Vintage Books, 2003), 166, 185.

2.   The day the Montgomery bus boycott began, December 5, 1955, Martin Luther King Jr. identified Rosa Parks at the boycott's first mass meeting as "a person nobody could call a disturbing figure." King as quoted in "MIA Mass Meeting at Holt Street Baptist Church [December 5, 1955]," in *The Papers of Martin Luther King, Jr.*, vol. 3, *Birth of a New Age*, ed. Clayborne Carson (Berkeley: University of California Press, 1997), 72. Again, this designation as nondisturbing is typically classified as a reference to respectability—and I believe King meant it as such. However, how to be nondisturbing as an African American in the United States has shifted over time; and, as argued in Chapter 5, being a nondisturbing figure in postwar America required perceptions of one's normality or typicalness, as well as—or even more so than—one's respectability, as exceptionally normative.

3.   For example, see Marisa Chappell, Jenny Hutchinson, and Brian Ward, "'Dress Modestly, Neatly . . . as If You Were Going to Church': Respectability,

Class and Gender in the Montgomery Bus Boycott and the Early Civil Rights Movement," in *Gender and the Civil Rights Movement*, ed. Peter Ling and Sharon Monteith (New Brunswick, NJ: Rutgers University Press, 2004).

4.   In the 1950s monthly circulation of *Ebony* wavered between four hundred thousand and five hundred thousand. (The Johnson Publishing Company's second-most-successful magazine, *Jet*, had weekly sales of approximately four hundred thousand). See "Backstage," *Ebony*, May 1952; John H. Johnson, *Succeeding Against the Odds: The Inspiring Autobiography of One of America's Wealthiest Entrepreneurs*, with Lerone Bennett Jr. (New York: Warner Books, 1989), 189, 207. Regarding refrigerators, in the postwar period, the working-class status of many African Americans did not preclude their owning refrigerators. The refrigerator was the number one appliance Americans bought, making it ubiquitous in American households by the mid-1950s. See H. Laurence Miller Jr., "The Demand for Refrigerators: A Statistical Study," *Review of Economics and Statistics* 42, no. 2 (May 1960): 197, table 1, "Sales of Electric Refrigerators and Related Information, 1921–57"; and Shelley Nickles, "More Is Better: Mass Consumption, Gender, and Class Identity in Postwar America," *American Quarterly* 54, no. 4 (December 2002): 588. Miller's study reports that household ownership of refrigerators rose from 52.6 percent in 1945 to 95.5 percent in 1957. Similarly, Nickles reports that refrigerator ownership increased from approximately 44 percent to 90 percent in the postwar period. See also Paul Gansky, "Refrigerator Design and Masculinity in Postwar Media, 1946–1960," *Studies in Popular Culture* 34, no. 1 (Fall 2011): 69. In 1956 *Time* magazine reported that 85.6 percent of African Americans living in Houston owned refrigerators. See "The Negro Market," *Time*, August 13, 1956, http://www.time.com/time/magazine/article /0,9171,865470,00.html. Another useful indication of refrigerator ownership rates among African Americans is the statistic that by 1950 approximately 80 percent of American farms and over 90 percent of urban households had refrigerators. See Barbara Krasner-Khait, "The Impact of Refrigeration," *History*, February/March 2000, https://www.history-magazine.com/refrig.html.

Index

Page numbers in italics refer to figures.

Acknowledgments

The downside of the time it takes to research and write a first book is the number of people who pile up in the "I wish to thank" column. The upside, of course, is the very same thing. For years, I have kept a mental list of these people and looked forward to this moment when I can put it to paper and publicly recognize the generosity, talents, and intelligence of the many who helped bring this book into being. Forgive me for the lengthy roll call to follow, but I am a historian: I believe in recording things. It pains me that I cannot include everyone who deserves mention—doing so would require another book altogether. If you believe your name belongs here, you are most certainly correct and you have my apologies and also my gratitude.

The journey to this book began with those people who put me on the path to becoming a historian. At the top of that list is my mother, Mary Catherine Hughes-Greer, who drove me all over Wisconsin as a child chasing down historical markers, who has always encouraged my sentimentalism, and who tells me all the family history she has to tell. When high school ground me down to a depressed and angry teenager with no ambition or imagination, she researched colleges until—with a strong assist from Rosemary Berke and Bob Obrohta—she found the right place for me. At Beloit College, a handful of educators took up the baton, including, most notably, Anita Andrew, who encouraged me to study history. When, years later, I summoned the courage to apply for graduate school to do just that, she helped clear the way for me. Anita passed away suddenly while this book was in its final stages of production. I had always imagined sending her a copy as evidence of how she shaped my mind and changed my life.

I found a scholarly home in the Afro-American studies program at the University of Wisconsin–Madison. In this program, I found a crew in Jerome Dotson, Dave Gilbert, Tyina Steptoe, and Zoë Van Orsdol. Compelled by the example, encouragement, and friendship they provided, I "bridged" with them into the university's history program, where the crew expanded to include Kathy Kae (who kept me in stitches and awe with her irreverent tenacity, and taught me Ojibwe along the way—*Miigwech Niijikwe!*), Ryan Quintana (who brought humor to even the darkest of moments), Heather Stur (who literally ran beside me, spurring me on as a friend and confidant), Maia Surdam (who gave our group a touch of grace with her ethics, modesty, and quiet strength), and Stephanie Westcott (who taught me how to teach, rather than entertain). The group of us moved through the U.S. history program as a posse, committed to one another's success and wellbeing. I am blessed that I continue to experience the care and brilliance of all of them.

I benefited from excellent advising and mentorship while at Madison. I would not have considered pursuing a career in academia without Nan Enstad—and I certainly would not have succeeded. Nan, you encouraged me to be rigorous in my work, but also my self-care. I strive to do the same with my own students. Susan Johnson, I could not have asked for a better model of quiet, principled genius. I am fortunate to have been the beneficiary of your generous spirit and faith. Cindy I-Fen Cheng, I admire your classiness as much as your scholarship and activism. It was you who told me I could have an academic career and a life, a family. I never let go of that, and it turns out you were right. Steve Kantrowitz, you appreciated the degree to which teaching figures in my scholarship and championed this as an asset, rather than a distraction. Tim Tyson, if you had not made me go on that demoralizing jog with you umpteen years ago to discuss my future as a historian, who knows what I would be doing now. You taught us to always remember that, as historians, we are storytellers—and the people at the center of our stories matter. Nellie McKay, I wish my awe of you had not gotten in the way of my letting you care for me. There is no proper way to thank you for the incredible sacrifices you made for all us who went through the program you helped create. I hope my achievements reflect your work.

My post-UW life brought new mentors. Chief among these are my senior colleagues in the Department of History at Wellesley College, each of whom has supported me in myriad ways and all of whom, as I have often said, would jump in front of a (student- or administration-driven) bus for me. Special mention must go to Nina Tumarkin, who has repeatedly invited my family into her home and came through for me at pivotal moments in this project. I am also grateful to Jay Cook (University of Michigan), whose scholarship, counsel, and endorsement eased my turn to the history of capitalism. Elspeth Brown (University of Toronto), having met me just once, you agreed to be my "official" mentor and quickly became my friend and savior. Not only did you read for me (a lot), you legitimized my struggles and saw me through. Lastly, I am blessed to have been guided through this journey by Robert Lockhart of the University of Pennsylvania Press. Your vision, patience, forthrightness, and skill, Bob, helped me see this project for what it could be; I pray it honors your labor and generosity.

A number of other people have contributed to my successes in and my enjoyment of my profession. These include my history colleagues Katherine Grandjean, Simon Grote, Alejandra Osorio (my walking partner), Nikhil Rao (who unwittingly unlocked a key piece of my project), and Quinn Slobodian. Above all, Ryan Quintana has been cheering me up and cheering me on since our days back at Wisconsin; I am fortunate to have one of my oldest friends working by my side. Others who have propped me up during these "early years" include the 2010–11 Erskine Peters Fellowship cohort (most especially Holly McGee), the 2014–15 Newhouse Center for Humanities Fellows cohort, Fiona Barnett, Michael Broshi, Kimberly Juanita Brown, Joshua Clark Davis, Carol Doughtery, Laura Grattan, Michael Jeffries, Karen Lange, Sara Ludovissy, Irene Mata, Maria McKenna, Jennie Pyers, Laura Reiner, Joe Swingle, Nithia Swingle, Luiza deCamargo Susan Wood, and Kimberley A. Yates. Special mention goes to Andre Porter of Boston, who provided me with a room, both my own and with a spectacular view, in which I was able to finish writing this book. Finally, Nikki Greene and Tracey Cameron: Where would I be without my Wellesley crew of two?

This project has benefited from funding and other forms of support from multiple sources, including the Andrew W. Mellon Society of Fellows in Critical Bibliography, the American Council of Learned Societies, the Woodrow Wilson National Fellowship Foundation, the Newhouse Center for Humanities, the Erskine A. Peters Fellowship, and Wellesley College. As the Knafel Assistant Professor of Social Sciences at Wellesley College, my work has benefited immeasurably from the largesse of Sidney R. Knafel. I am also in debt to many archivists and librarians—and their respective institutions—for their expertise, patience, and persistence, including Jamal Booker (the Coca-Cola Company), Audrey Davis (the Alexandria Black

History Museum), Joellen ElBashir (the Moorland-Spingarn Research Center), Kayin Shabazz (the Atlanta University Center), and Lucy Waldrop and Mary Nelson (the Wichita State University Libraries). In addition, interviews with the following people were essential to my ability to piece together this history: Mary (Cowser) Alexander, John ONeal, Jesse J. Lewis, Bettye Lee, and, Moss Hyles Kendrix Jr. Finally, I am grateful to the two anonymous readers whose insights thoroughly transformed this book.

People typically use the phrase "it takes a village" in reference to raising a child, and now that I have a child, I appreciate its veracity. A village of friends also helped me in the care and feeding of this book. Marolyn Bahr, you have known me all my life and held my life dear. Deb Sapp Lynch, you delight in my every joy and make me feel treasured. Paige Adams and Emily Diesl, you made it possible for me to be a mother and a scholar, and you have brought more love and joy to my child's life than I dared dreamed for her. Tweedle Lawrence, you cannot know what your praise means to me as a black professional woman and educator. Others who belong to my village of fictive kin are Rachel Ashby, Jacquelyn Boggess, Mary Kate Bonner, Karl Bower, Marcie Bower, Y'Vonda Davis ("my buddy, my buddy"), James Hannon, Rob Johnstone, Linda "L. D." Oakley, David Pate, Kathy "Ovenbird" Swanson, and Maggie Ward (how I miss you, woman).

One has friends, and one has sister-friends. Mine are Zoë Van Orsdol and Stephanie Westcott, who, among other things, took on the huge task of securing image permissions for this book. You two are as much my family as the one that raised me or the one I have created in my own home. Zoë, you are the most honest person I have ever known, about yourself and with others; your integrity inspires my awe, love, and unfailing trust, which, as you know more than most, is no small thing. Stephanie, I meant what I said at your wedding: your friendship saved me in a very real sense and changed the course of my life. You two, with your unsurpassed wit and intelligence (and sarcasm, of course), are a consistent life source, and I love you with my whole heart, brain, and funny bone.

My blood kin have always looked after the bigger project that is me, which allowed me to dream bigger. Mom, look what you did! Sarah Greer (Sarah-beara, chickadee), as my twin, you have been my safe space since we came into the world together. Thank you for the love and actual labor you lent to this book. Nathan Greer, as my brother, you get me and the world, and me *in* the world, like no one else—this is likely because you have been taking care of my heart and ego since you were a young boy. Do you remember when you told me that you would rather build a pyramid with your bare hands than write a dissertation? That was the kindest thing anyone could have ever said regarding the effort this work requires. Hesper Wolfe, from one warrior woman to another, here is to always getting our people to higher ground. Naima Rose Greer, your being in the world delights and motivates me, sweet girl. Dad (William Greer Jr.), you stepped up when I needed it most; I love that you will talk with me and that I make you proud. Peggy (Margaret) Sleeper, thank you for loving me as I am—and as I was. Grandma Hughes, you were a formidable woman, and I am better for your example.

During the years it has taken to produce this book, I was lucky to have my family expand with the Blanton clan. To John Blanton, Beth Balschi, Corinne "Nana" Blanton, Sarah Blanton, Eamon Roche, Cleo Roche, and Atticus Roche, you make me feel embraced and impressive, both of which are much needed and appreciated.

Finally, my husband and daughter: Matthew William Blanton and Nala Wynn Marie Greer. Matt, no one can ever fully know what we have come through: a journey that testifies to just how much I love, like, and respect you, and you me. From our first coffee "date" at Mother Fool's in Madison, I knew I had found the person with whom I could share this passion for studying, teaching, and thinking about race, gender, and history. You pulled me into a life full of family, friends, fun, and adventure (big and small). Your intelligence, ethics, and goofiness are outstripped only by your humanity. I fully appreciate how much you have stretched and endured to love and support me. Above all, you brought me to Nala, when past experiences and present worries might have kept me from her. She is your biggest gift to me besides yourself. Thank you for always, always, always believing that I have what it takes, as a historian, a teacher, a writer, and a mother. You made me believe it, too. Nala, baby girl, you brought me peace, purpose, and perspective I had never known or imagined: my life's goal is helping you find the same.

My family and friends deserve immeasurable credit for all of my successes. Yet no one has inspired me in this work more than my students, particularly the young women I have had the honor of knowing, teaching, and learning with during my seven years at Wellesley College. The HIST 252 crew of spring 2012 will always hold a special place in my heart: I can only hope to experience the magic of that class again. Many from that group continue to sustain me with news of their achievements. Yes, I am looking at you, Francis G. Leeson, Makenna Murray, Chibuzo Okoro, and Vanessa Wilkins. A handful of students with whom I worked closely have uniquely inspired and transformed me. Nora Mishanec, it is with no trace of hyperbole that I say that you are the most resolute, fearless person I have ever known. You educated me in how to push past false barriers and mine the treasures of any place or situation. When I was in college, my mother sent me a card the front of which read, "No matter where you go, there you are." I hear those words any time I think of you, Nora. Kalina "Ky" Yingnan Deng, what you have already accomplished in your life is nothing short of stunning: it is thrilling to watch your star rise. Thank you for all the knowledge you continue to share with me, which I pass to my current students. Jaqueline "Jaki" Gaylon, what a light you are. What if everyone had the appreciation for thinking that you do? I would love to live in that world. Meredith Wade, you walked into my office as a high school senior touring colleges the day before my birthday: happy, happy birthday to me. It is rare that one so ridiculously smart and gifted is also so modest and altruistic. You honored me by working with me. Sofie Werthan, you also graced me with your research, your time, and your intelligence, and I thank you for your patience with me as an adviser as I tended to this book. Emma Carter, my admiration and respect for you is boundless.

There are a number of other students who have challenged me, made me laugh, taught me, and researched for me. They include Leah Abrams, Dina Al-Zu'bi, Kit Cali, Tashay Campbell, Jordan Conway, Alexandra Gazzolo, Ananya Ghemawat, Isobel Handler, Katharine Harper, Hannah Herde, Atiya Khan, Kerri Knerr, Katherine Leung, Sabrina Leung, Juliet Liu, Sammy Marrus, Thai Matthews, Carrington O'Brion, Sandra Riano, Grace Roberts, Denesse Salto, Angelina Spilios, Cali Stenson, and Elaine Tang. Finally, the "honorary godmothers"—Lucy Anderle, Meredyth Grange, Michaela Jackson-Smith, and Jasmyne Keimig: you four gifted me a vision of working motherhood that I could envision and embrace.

Many think teaching is a selfless vocation. Nothing is further from the truth. My students keep me focused, committed, and inspired with their dreams, their intelligence, and especially their questions. They want that I should thrive, rather than survive, as a woman and as a woman of color in academia. And they have made it so.